Arbitration Law in America

Arbitration Law in America: A Critical Assessment is a source of arguments and practical suggestions for changing American arbitration law. The book argues that the eighty-year-old Federal Arbitration Act badly needs major changes. The authors, who have previously written major articles on arbitration law and policy, here set out their own views and argue among themselves about the necessary reforms of arbitration. The book contains draft legislation for use in international and domestic arbitration as well as a detailed explanation of the precise justifications for proposed legislative changes. It also contains two proposals that might be deemed radical – to ban mandatory arbitration related to the purchase of products by consumers and to prohibit mandatory arbitration of employment disputes. Each proposal is vetted fully and critiqued by one or more of the other co-authors.

Edward Brunet is the Henry J. Casey Professor of Law at Lewis & Clark Law School. He specialized in business litigation in private practice in Chicago. His major academic interest is relating principles of economics to the content and practice of law. Brunet has published in leading law journals, including the *Virginia, Michigan, Cornell, Duke,* and *Tulane Law Reviews.* He is co-author of a book on summary judgment with Professor Martin Redish of Northwestern University School of Law and co-author of a book on alternatives to trial with Professor Charles Craver of the George Washington School of Law.

Richard E. Speidel is the Beatrice Kuhn Professor of Law Emeritus at Northwestern University School of Law and is also a visiting Professor at the University of San Diego School of Law. Professor Speidel's specialties include public contract law, contracts, commercial transactions, and arbitration. He has published extensively in each of these areas. He has co-authored two leading casebooks, *Commercial Transactions: Sales and Leases of Goods* with Linda Rusch and *Studies in Contract Law* with Ian Ayers, and a critically acclaimed treatise on federal arbitration law.

Jean R. Sternlight is the Saltman Professor and Director of the Saltman Center for Conflict Resolution at the University of Nevada, Las Vegas. She is co-author of two other books: *Dispute Resolution: Beyond the Adversarial Model* (2004) and *Materials on Mediation Theory and Practice* (2001). She has written numerous articles on arbitration, which have appeared in many prestigious journals including the *Stanford Law Review,* the *University of Pennsylvania Law Review, Law and Contemporary Problems,* and the *William and Mary Law Review.*

Stephen J. Ware is Professor of Law at the University of Kansas. Following a clerkship with the U.S. Court of Appeals for the Second Circuit (Judge J. Daniel Mahoney), he joined the New York law firm of Davis Polk & Wardwell where his practice consisted of commercial and financial litigation. He is the author of the *Hornbook on Alternative Dispute Resolution* (2001) and more than a dozen articles on arbitration in both scholarly and popular journals.

Arbitration Law in America

A Critical Assessment

Edward Brunet
Lewis & Clark Law School

Richard E. Speidel
Northwestern University School of Law

Jean R. Sternlight
William S. Boyd School of Law University of Nevada, Las Vegas

Stephen J. Ware
University of Kansas

Cambridge
University Press

CAMBRIDGE UNIVERSITY PRESS
Cambridge, New York, Melbourne, Madrid, Cape Town,
Singapore, São Paulo, Delhi, Mexico City

Cambridge University Press
The Edinburgh Building, Cambridge CB2 8RU, UK

Published in the United States of America by Cambridge University Press, New York

www.cambridge.org
Information on this title: www.cambridge.org/9781107406117

First published 2006
First paperback edition 2012

A catalogue record for this publication is available from the British Library

Library of Congress Cataloguing in Publication Data

Arbitration law in America : a critical assessment / Edward Brunet . . . [et al.].
p. cm.
Includes bibliographical references and index.
ISBN-13: 978-0-521-83982-2 (hardback)
ISBN-10: 0-521-83982-3 (hardback)
1. Arbitration and award – United States. 2. Dispute resolution (Law) – United States.
3. Mediation – United States. I. Brunet, Edward J. II. Title.
KF9085.A963 2006
347.73′9 – dc22 2005021612

ISBN 978-0-521-83982-2 Hardback
ISBN 978-1-107-40611-7 Paperback

To Katherine L. Ware

To Sylvia Rebeca Lazos

To Elizabeth West Speidel

To June Starkes Brunet

Brief Table of Contents

Detailed Table of Contents

Appendices

Acknowledgments

Professor Ware thanks his co-authors and Professor Chris Drahozal for providing patient and thoughtful comments and suggestions over the years. He also thanks the University of Kansas School of Law for a research grant supporting his work on this book.

Professor Sternlight expresses her admiration for the efforts of Paul Bland and Cliff Palefsky, who have lead the fight in the courts, in Congress, and in the public eye against mandatory arbitration. She also thanks the University of Nevada Las Vegas Boyd School of Law and Michael and Sonja Saltman for the support that made possible her work on this book.

Professor Speidel would like to thank Northwestern law graduates Ms. Ashley Baynham and Ms. Veronica Li for research assistance and the students in his international arbitration course at the University of San Diego School of Law over the past six years for a never-ending supply of questions. In addition, he is grateful for the administrative support received at both the University of San Diego School of Law and Northwestern University School of Law and for the special help provided by his long-time administrative assistant at Northwestern, Ms. Shirley Scott. Finally, he would like to express his admiration and gratitude for the influential arbitration scholarship and friendship of his former colleagues, Professors Ian R. Macneil and William (Rusty) Park.

Professor Brunet wishes to thank Maja Haium of the Lewis & Clark class of 2006 and Seneca Gray, Research Librarian, Lewis & Clark Law School, for valuable research assistance. He also would like to thank the founders of the Henry J. Casey Professorship for the financial assistance that accompanies his endowed chair, the Carr Ferguson Summer Research Fund, and Lisa Frenz for the invaluable administrative assistance that she gave to this (and other) projects.

Introduction

The Federal Arbitration Act (FAA) is now eighty years old. The time is right for a complete reformulation of federal arbitration law, whether that be international or interstate. The old FAA, passed in the Roaring Twenties, is completely outmoded. This eighty-year-old statute has been consistently disregarded by the Supreme Court, which has recast arbitration in an activist set of cases that largely ignore careful legislative history and even the explicit words of the FAA. Most of the authors feel that the Supreme Court has largely failed in this attempt to refine arbitration doctrine through the use of setting forth rules in individual cases. We also regret the failure of Congress to confront the problems that age, fragmentation, and omission have caused for the implementation of federal arbitration law. We prefer a legislative solution in the form of a new and improved FAA.

This book sets forth the principal themes that a new reformed FAA should follow. We here lay out our thoughts on the main parts of an ideal federal arbitration law. This is legal writing that deals with optimal legislation and policies. Our task is not to criticize or analyze past mistakes by the courts in interpreting the old FAA. We collectively have written far too many words critical of the present state of arbitration doctrine. This, instead, is a policy-based effort that focuses on the more difficult task of rebuilding a new FAA.

We have given substantial thought to what topics within the field of arbitration should be emphasized. This book is not a comprehensive arbitration treatise, but, instead, focuses on optimal arbitration policy. Rather than try to cover every conceivable topic in this broad field, we have selected what we think are the most pressing problem areas within American arbitration. These topics include consent to arbitrate, arbitration of consumer and employment disputes, the scope of federal arbitration legislation as compared to state arbitration legislation, federal preemption of state law, the role of the courts in reviewing arbitration, and the application of federal law to international arbitration.

We need to clarify the methodology used to write this book. We are four scholars who each have already written that federal arbitration law needs to be reformed. In this book we have each selected areas and written individual chapters. Each designated author of every chapter should be considered the sole author of the chapter. Nonetheless, each of the four authors has served as an editor of each individually written chapter. As individual chapter authors, we each have benefitted from the comments and criticisms of our co-authors. These editorial comments should not be confused with co-authorship. In short, each of the first six chapters identifies a sole author and each chapter, while not jointly authored, has been edited by the other three co-authors of this work.

Chapter 7 represents an outlet for stressing our major differences. In this, our final chapter, there is no one author. Instead, we set forth our individual views in a point-counterpoint fashion.

Our collective view is that new federal arbitration legislation is needed. Our appendices constitute new proposed legislation consistent with the positions set forth in our preceding chapters. We believe a legislative solution is needed and oppose reforms achieved by the present water-torture of case-by-case reformation. Although there may be differences in our individual positions, we are unified in our belief that there is an immediate need to reform federal arbitration and to accomplish this by legislation and not by a difficult to decipher set of federal judicial decisions.

March 1, 2005

CHAPTER ONE

The Core Values of Arbitration

Edward Brunet

Arbitration appears to rest on a firm bedrock of presumed policies: efficiency, the opportunity for a fair hearing, party autonomy, privatization, arbitrator expertise, neutrality, and finality. These familiar policies, now often mere generalizations, need to be isolated and repackaged in a reformulation of American arbitration doctrine. This chapter discusses the presumed policies purportedly advanced by arbitration and seeks to identify the preferred values that form the foundation of arbitration policy. I stress that four arbitration policies – party autonomy, privatization, arbitrator neutrality, and the opportunity for a fair hearing – occupy center stage in arbitration theory. The chapter de-emphasizes arbitration values supported mostly by mythology and asserts that policies relating to expertise, efficiency, and finality are often trumped by higher order principles that support arbitration. The chapter's conclusion also reveals a previously understated additional arbitration value, that of a public dimension underlying the seemingly private arbitration process.

Section 1.1 Party Autonomy: Allocating Disputing Power and Freedom to the Disputants

Arbitration rests on a firm foundation of party autonomy. The parties own the dispute[1] and should be able to control the details of their disputing process. They may chose to litigate, mediate, or arbitrate. If the parties select arbitration, they may broadly agree to arbitrate without specifying a particular type of arbitration procedure or, alternatively, they may tailor their

[1] *See* Carrie Menkel-Meadow, *Whose Dispute Is It Anyway? A Philosophical and Democratic Defense of Settlement (In Some Cases)*, 83 Geo. L. J. 2663 (1995).

arbitration arrangement by agreeing to use particular procedures appropriate to their needs.

A contract is central to the success of party autonomy in arbitration procedure. A contract to arbitrate can set forth the essentials of the arbitration process, ranging from restrictions on discovery to the selection of a more judicialized form of arbitration, which is characterized by adopting procedures associated with conventional litigation. Parties to an arbitration agreement may contract to take a limited number of depositions or to mandate that the arbitrator apply substantive legal principles. They may also require the arbitrator to enter findings of fact or conclusions of law.

Assertions of party autonomy represent manifestations of party control of the arbitration process. The courts often state the cliché that arbitration is the creature of contract.[2] As stated in the *Mastrobouno* decision, "[p]arties are generally free to structure their arbitration agreements as they see fit."[3] Such language legitimizes the parties' implementation of pre-dispute arbitration clauses by means of contract. Professor Ware has appropriately asserted that "the entire FAA embodies a strongly contractual approach to arbitration law."[4] Under a contractual approach the parties exercise their will by covenanting for specific arbitration procedures rather than merely opting for an undefined agreement to arbitrate, which will leave much of the choice of the arbitration procedure to the arbitrator or organization selected to administer the arbitration process.

In a democratic society, party autonomy should be the fundamental value that shapes arbitration. The personal autonomy inherent in arbitration constitutes a dominant policy in all areas of a democracy.[5] The freedom to select arbitration procedure is a choice that one anticipates should exist in a state

[2] *See, e.g., Fils et Cables D'Acier de Lens v. Midland Metals Corp.*, 584 F. Supp. 240, 243 (S.D.N.Y. 1984). Professor Ware, writing in 1999, found 177 cases that used the phrase "arbitration is the creature of contract." Stephen J. Ware, *Default Rules from Mandatory Rules: Privatizing Law through Arbitration*, 83 Minn L. Rev. 703, 709 (1999) (hereafter *Default Rules*). *See also Volt Information Sciences, Inc. v. Board of Trustees of Leland Stanford Junior University*, 489 U.S. 468, 479 (1989) (stating that court's role is to "ensur[e] that private agreements to arbitrate are enforced according to their terms").

[3] *Mastrobouno v. Shearson Lehman Hutton, Inc.*, 514 U.S. 52 (1995).

[4] Ware, *Default Rules*, *supra* Note 2 at 729.

[5] *See generally* Richard C. Reuben, *Democracy and Dispute Resolution: The Problem of Arbitration*, 67 Law & Contemp. Prob. 279, 303 (2004) (hereafter cited as Reuben, *Democracy and Dispute Resolution*) (identifying connection between arbitration autonomy and personal autonomy in a democratic system of government, but concluding that present arbitration doctrine departs from democratic norms); Richard C. Reuben, *Democracy and Dispute Resolution: Systems Design and the New Workplace*, 10 Harv. Neg. L. Rev. 11, 48–50 (2005) (emphasizing the individual's loss of personal autonomy in mandatory employment arbitration under the FAA).

that values personal autonomy. Arbitration liberty is achieved by making party autonomy the highest priority in the pantheon of arbitration values.

Viewed in this light, the important value of party autonomy is directly related to the freedom essential in a democratic state. A strong version of arbitration party autonomy exemplifies the significance of freedom of contract. In a state such as ours characterized by the respect for individual liberty, courts should enforce customized agreements to arbitrate and the legislature should regulate minimally.[6] In a society governed by rules of the free market, contract norms that guide exchanges are necessarily based on autonomous action of individual economic actors.[7]

Judicial approval and enforcement of the parties' selection of arbitration procedure contributes to private ordering. The delegation to a private arbitrator of hand-forged procedures to resolve a dispute creates a form of self-governance that operates outside more direct government regulation. When courts enforce party crafted procedures, they create an incentive for parties to draft their own rules of dispute resolution rather than leave the problem of future disputes to government. In this way, law is internalized by the disputants who form their own private culture.

Self-determination, long thought of as a central tenet of mediation theory, meshes well with arbitration's self-governance value. As recently explained by Professor Lisa Bingham, party control is also a central advantage of binding arbitration.[8] Sophisticated, repeat users of arbitration possess control over the type of process they wish to use in resolving disputes, and they can exert their self-determination by customizing arbitration clauses to embrace specific desired procedures. Over time, disputants within some industries have developed successful and hand-forged systems of arbitration that illustrate the self-determination of individual members.[9]

[6] Reuben, *Democracy and Dispute Resolution*, at 308 (concluding that democratic theory suggests that courts should not require mandatory arbitration but should "implement the will of the legislature by policing agreements to arbitrate"); Ware, *Default Rules, supra* Note 2 (explaining modern arbitration as a system of privatization and non-regulation with legislation that only sets forth rules of default applicable where the parties have not created their own set of arbitration norms).

[7] *See, e.g.*, Milton Friedman, CAPITALISM AND FREEDOM 13 (1962) (lauding voluntary cooperation of individuals in economic transactions as permitting exchange without government coercion) (hereafter cited as Friedman, CAPITALISM AND FREEDOM).

[8] Lisa B. Bingham, *Control Over Dispute-System Design and Mandatory Commercial. Arbitration*, 67 LAW & CONTEMP. PROB. 221, 227 (2004) (asserting that business users of arbitration "have the power to define, through negotiation, the dispute-resolution system that culminates in arbitration," citing COMMERCIAL ARBITRATION AT ITS BEST: SUCCESSFUL STRATEGIES FOR BUSINESS USERS, Thomas J. Stipanowich & Peter H. Kaskell, eds. (2001)).

[9] *See, e.g.*, Lisa Bernstein, *Private Commercial Law in the Cotton Industry: Creating Cooperation through Rules, Norms and Institutions*, 99 MICH L. REV. 1724 (2001) (describing a

There is evidence that sophisticated, repeat users of arbitration are willing to pay higher transactions costs for a more complicated and judicialized style of arbitration. This trend is evident when one considers the role of substantive law in arbitration. Turn of the century textile arbitrations eschewed reliance on law and relied, instead, on expert intra-industry arbitrators to decide the dispute equitably, often by relying on trade-usage norms.[10] Modern commercial arbitration frequently operates outside the intra-industry context that often incorporates industry norms as the rule of decision. Today's arbitration parties face a choice: leave the selection of the rule of decision to the arbitrator's discretion or tie the arbitrator's hands by opting for a specific legal regime or procedure. Some business parties, unhappy with the possibility that the arbitrator may issue a compromise award at odds with legal formality, have inserted choice of law clauses in their arbitration agreements and implemented their choice by demanding that the arbitrator enter conclusions of law. The success of the National Arbitration Forum, an arbitration provider that advertises and mandates that its arbitrators must follow the law,[11] provides some evidence that there is considerable business demand for a judicialized type of arbitration.

The use of judicialized arbitration increases transaction costs by complicating the arbitration procedure and increasing the possibility that a court might set aside the award. Nonetheless, numerous business parties appear to be opting for such clauses and some courts appear willing to approve their use by means of a contract model rationale.[12] Reliance on the contract model contributes to party autonomy by upholding the intent of the parties in their choice of arbitration procedure. This reliance suggests that arbitration procedure, if left to the parties, is textured and full of variety.

Rigorous attention to consent is central to party autonomy. The policy of self-determination inherent in party autonomy must incorporate a broad notion of actual consent to arbitrate. Bilateral consent to arbitrate is essential

successful arbitration system created by disputants within the cotton industry that includes such innovations as a seven-member arbitration panel, a custom of unanimous opinions, and written opinions of an arbitration appeals board).

10 *See* Edward Brunet, *Replacing Folklore Arbitration with a Contract Model of Arbitration*, 74 Tul. L. Rev. 39, 43 (1999) (hereafter cited as Brunet, *Contract Model*), (citing *Turnbill v. Martin*, 2 Daly 428, 430 (N.Y.C.P. 1869), a dispute regarding the sale of flannels that was submitted to arbitration before dry goods merchants selected by the disputants).

11 *See* A.B.A.J. 20 (Feb., 2004) (advertising in ½ page that "All Arbitration is Not the Same" because the NAF has a "procedural code requiring arbitrators to follow the law in making decisions and awards").

12 *See, e.g., Gateway Technologies v. MCI Telecommunications Corp.*, 64 F.3d 993 (5th Cir. 1995) (overturning district court refusal to follow the parties' contract that provided for judicial review of legal error in the arbitration hearing).

to autonomy and to freedom.[13] If only one party wants arbitration, the other party loses party control. Surrogate substitutes for bilateral consent undervalue the essential policy of self-determination.

The policy of party autonomy casts grave doubt on mandatory consumer arbitration in which product manufacturers impose the arbitration option without the explicit agreement of unknowing consumers who purchase their products. Formalistic decisions, such as *Hill v. Gateway 2000, Inc.*,[14] which substitute failure to return a product for knowing consent to arbitrate, lack appropriate allegiance to the party autonomy value that is essential to arbitration. A consumer who is forced to arbitrate a dispute without having knowledgeably consented to arbitration loses both the freedom to use the court system and the freedom to contract in a knowing fashion. Mandatory arbitration of employment disputes outside the collective bargaining context is similarly plagued by lack of attention to the employee's consent to arbitrate.[15] The arbitration value of party autonomy, central to personal liberty, requires courts to take consent to arbitrate seriously.

I support party autonomy as the fundamental value of arbitration. Questions remain, however, as to how far courts should extend party intent in the arbitration arena. Subsequent subsections of this chapter and book will discuss the collision of party intent and arbitration finality and address the impact of an enhanced consent requirement upon mandatory arbitration.[16] Resolution of these value conflicts illustrate the limits of arbitration theory and the dangers of adopting rigid positions in this rapidly changing area.

Section 1.2 Privatization: On Secrecy, Privacy, and Self-Governance

Arbitration represents a volitional opt out of the conventional court system into a realm of private dispute resolution. When parties select arbitration, they privatize their dispute and take a form of market ownership of their

[13] *See* Friedman, Capitalism and Freedom, *supra* Note 7 at 13 (asserting that "[T]he possibility of co-ordination through voluntary co-operation rests on the elementary – yet frequently denied – proposition that both parties to an economic transaction benefit from it, *provided the transaction is bi-laterally voluntary and informed*") (emphasis in original).

[14] 105 F.3d 1147 (7th Cir.), *cert. denied*, 522 U.S. 808 (1997). The court held that the buyer of a computer assented to a form arbitration clause included in the box with the computer by using the computer.

[15] *See* Section 7.2(1), *infra* (arguing that arbitration doctrine should ban arbitration clauses that are mandatory conditions to employment outside the collective bargaining context).

[16] *See* Section 3.5, *infra* (arguing that the arbitration parties should have the power to contract for enhanced judicial review).

disputing procedure. Rather than litigate in the conventional public court system, the parties to an arbitration agreement opt for adjudication in a private forum. In this context, an arbitration clause operates as a sort of forum selection clause and can be conceived as a rejection of the public courts. As explained by Professor Drahozal, businesses select arbitration as a means to avoid jury trials and obtain a perceived "better" decision than that rendered by a jury.[17]

Private arbitration forums function in a free, competitive market. Private firms compete for the role of administering arbitrations. Private arbitrators, largely unregulated by the state, compete for the task of arbitrating disputes. Entry into the market is easy; new rival suppliers abound. Arbitrators often apply private law and eschew publically created legal rules.

Privacy and secrecy pervade the arbitration process. Hearings take place in private facilities and locations, such as hotel conference facilities, law firms, or space provided by an arbitration administrator. These hearings are effectively and intentionally shielded from the public eye. They are private because they are secret.

The desire for secrecy can be a prime determinant in selecting arbitration. Often one or more party to an arbitration agreement has an interest in avoiding a public trial with unwanted adverse publicity. It should come as no surprise that repeat users of arbitration include banks, credit card issuers, computer manufacturers, physicians, securities brokers, car dealers, and chain restaurant franchisers – each businesses with a strong desire to avoid potentially negative publicity that may accompany a public court hearing. Many of the arbitration claims involving such parties, who generally draft boilerplate arbitration arrangements, center on discrimination claims. The last thing a restaurant chain or a bank needs is a public airing of dirty linen involving allegations of discrimination. In this context, secrecy in disputing may be the primary reason that a business seeks arbitration. Professor Mentschikoff wrote years ago that the "desire for privacy" was one of the "chief motivating factors underlying commercial arbitration."[18] Assuming that there is true bilateral consent, a pre-dispute agreement to hold a private hearing should be respected.[19]

[17] *See* Christopher R. Drahozal, *A Behavioral Analysis of Private Judging*, 67 Law & Contemp. Prob. 105, 131 (2004) (noting that "[A] commonly cited reason that businesses include arbitration in their contracts with consumers is to avoid jury trials" and observing that businesses think arbitration is "a way to avoid aberrant jury verdicts, implicitly if not explicitly assuming that arbitrators make 'better' decisions than juries").

[18] Soia Mentschikoff, *Commercial Arbitration*, 61 Colum. L. Rev. 846, 849 (1961).

[19] *See* Judith Resnik, *Due Process: A Public Dimension*, 39 U. Fla. L. Rev. 405, 429 (1987) (questioning a public role in pre-lawsuit arbitration because "parties are not required to file lawsuits") (hereafter as Resnik, *A Public Dimension*).

Some arbitrations are private in a different sense, that of constituting secret disputes between members of a particular culture who seek to confine or cabin their dispute by placing it within the boundaries of a particular culture or industry. Professor Lisa Bernstein has described Manhattan arbitrations between disputing diamond merchants.[20] In this culture it was common for two diamond merchants to contract for arbitration to resolve their disputes and to select a respected fellow diamond merchant to be the arbitrator. The dispute might be even more inwardly focused by having the arbitrator choose to apply customs and usages of the diamond trade as a way to adjudicate the dispute. Under this form of privatized arbitration, the expert and known commodity arbitrator eschews law in deciding the dispute and, instead, looks to general principles that govern his or her business as a determinant or rule of decision.[21] The process of selecting a fellow merchant as an arbitrator facilitated the choice of a knowledgeable, expert arbitrator. Particular arbitration cultures have arisen over time. There has been a diverse use of intra-industry arbitration ranging from arbitration between cotton or textile merchants as evidenced by the inclusion of arbitration in the charter of the New York Cotton Exchange[22] and the governance of arbitration by the General Arbitration Council of the Textile Industry[23] to arbitration for movie and television screen credits between writers disputing the validity of another writer's contributions.[24]

The American arbitration process also lends to its private nature. Typically, arbitration in the United States ends silently with a cryptic written award that does not contain a discursive opinion. Rather than publicize the arbitration result and its reasoning, American arbitrators typically sign a one-page award that merely denotes the final result of a dispute without explanation and thereby facilitates a silent resolution of the case. Privacy is enhanced by this common technique of eschewing written, discursive

[20] *See* Lisa Bernstein, *Opting Out of the Legal System: Extralegal Contractual Relations in the Diamond Industry*, 21 J. Legal Stud. 115 (1992).

[21] *See, e.g.*, William L. Ranson, *The Organization of Courts for Better Administration of Justice*, 2 Cornell L. Q. 261, 273 (1917) (asserting that businesses require a "determination of their rights under the facts as found and the applicable rules of law, as commonly observed in the community for the conduct of similar business dealings"). This choice of industry norms operates as a type of choice of law clause. Such "privatization occurs with every enforceable contract." Ware, *Default Rules*, *supra* Note 2 at 744.

[22] William Catron Jones, *Three Centuries of Commercial Arbitration in New York: A Brief Survey*, 1956 Wash. U. L. Q. 193, 217.

[23] *See* General Arbitration Council of the Textile and Apparel Industry, A Guide to Arbitration/Mediation for the Textile and Apparel Industries 4 (1996).

[24] *See* Writers Guild of America, Screen Credits Manual (1999) (detailing arbitration procedures to resolve disputes between movie and television script writers by submitting scripts and written statements to "arbitration committee" of anonymous screen writers).

arbitrator opinions. To be sure, it is common to see American arbitrators write opinions in labor grievance arbitrations and maritime arbitrations. Yet, such published arbitration opinions are exceptions to the customary norm of silent, one page awards that merely catalog the remedial result of the arbitration. This custom, along with the private nature of the typical arbitration hearing itself, has led some to describe arbitration as lacking transparency.[25]

The process of privatization occurs as well in arbitration's lawmaking and law-application context. Professor Ware noted that when parties agree to arbitrate, they often are opting out of a system of government-created rights and obligations into an arbitration system in which privately created rights and duties are substituted.[26] Professor Ware describes this process as filling contractual gaps with the arbitrator's discretion;[27] Professor Bernstein explains this as "a horizontal system of competing default regimes."[28] Arbitrators often fill gaps by interposing their own sense of equity, but this gap filling is more party-intended and industry focused; it is, thus, consistent with the contract model of arbitration and the notion of privatization. The frequent practice of arbitrators failing to apply the law furthers the creation of new private norms that replace public substantive legal principles.[29] The absence of significant judicial review of arbitration awards reinforces the creation of private law in a privatized arbitration system.

The value of arbitration privatization is related to self-governance. It comes as no surprise that intra-industry trade groups were and are attracted to arbitration. Rather than permit intrusion upon their functioning by third parties, including government, trade groups sought to privatize their disputes. Commentators have praised the virtues of using arbitration

[25] *See, e.g.*, Reuben, *Democracy and Dispute Resolution*, *supra* Note 5 at 301(asserting that "transparency is generally not an animating value of arbitration").

[26] *See generally* Ware, *Default Rules*, *supra* Note 2.

[27] *Id.* at 744.

[28] Lisa Bernstein, *Social Norms and Default Rules Analysis*, 3 S. CAL. INTERDISC. L.J. 59, 84 (1994).

[29] *Id.* at 720–4. *See generally* Soia Mentschikoff, *Commercial Arbitration*, 61 COLUM. L. REV. 846, 861 (1961) (survey of commercial arbitrators suggests that 90% feel free to ignore substantive law if it will lead to a more just result). *Accord*: Dean Thomson, *Arbitration Theory and Practice: A Survey of AAA Construction Arbitrators*, 23 HOFSTRA L. REV. 137, 154–5 (1994) (survey finds that 28% of construction arbitrators do not always follow the law in crafting awards); Ian R. Macneil, Richard E. Speidel, Thomas J. Stipanowich, FEDERAL ARBITRATION LAW: AGREEMENTS, AWARDS, AND REMEDIES UNDER THE FEDERAL ARBITRATION ACT §2.1.2 (1994, supp) (noting "highly discretionary" application of norms by arbitrators who are not bound "by the law of any particular jurisdiction") Hereafter cited as Macneil et al., FEDERAL ARBITRATION LAW).

as a means to facilitate self-governance by internalized lawmaking.[30] The parties achieve a degree of self-governance by contracting to arbitrate before a known industry expert. Allan Rau appropriately stated that "the arbitration process is in fact all about . . . private ordering and self-determination."[31]

Relational contract theory, as pioneered by Professor Ian Macneil, helps explain some of the self-governance virtues of arbitration.[32] The intra-industry arbitrations discussed previously involve disputants who often have a long-term relationship and who have chosen arbitration as a means to help preserve that relationship. The relationship might be that of repeat contractual partners over a number of years, such as franchisor-franchisee or commercial landlord-tenant. The creation of a private system of self-governance may facilitate a healthy relationship. In contrast, arbitration's privatization virtues are minimal when two strangers contract to arbitrate. The mail order buyer of a new Gateway computer who learns he has consented to arbitration by opening the cardboard box holding the computer is a party to a one-shot "transactional" deal unlikely to be part of a long-term relationship worth preserving.[33]

The privatization value also has an obvious relationship to party autonomy. Party control or choice is essential to achieve the sort of privatized self-governance provided by numerous types of intra-industry arbitration. Party autonomy achieves privatization ends. The relationship between these two policy values is further complicated by the fact that party autonomy efforts may occur because of a desire to privatize. This is not to suggest that party autonomy and privatization are interchangeable. They are two different policies that individually support arbitration; party autonomy and privatization are unique but related.

[30] *See, e.g.*, Martin H. Malin, *Privatizing Justice: A Jurisprudential Perspective on Labor and Employment Arbitration from the Steelworkers Trilogy to Gilmer*, 44 Hast L.J. 1187, 1192–9 (1993).

[31] Alan Rau, *Integrity in Private Judging*, 38 S. Tex L. Rev. 485, 486 (1997) (emphasizing the "self-determination" and "private ordering" values of arbitration). *See also* Alan Scott Rau, *Arbitration as Contract: One More Word About First Options v. Kaplan*, Mealey's Int'l Arb. L. Rep. 21 (March, 1997) (stating that "[I] have always naively assumed that arbitration was all a matter of private ordering – that it is a form of dispute resolution sharing with the process of private settlement (which it closely resembles) the legitimacy of party autonomy").

[32] *See generally* Ian R. Macneil, The Relational Theory of Contract (2001); Ian R. Macneil, *Contracts: Adjustments of Long-Term Economic Relations Under Classical, Neoclassical and Relational Contract Law*, 72 Nw. U. L. Rev. 854 (1978).

[33] *See, e.g.*, *Hill v. Gateway 2000, Inc.*, 105 F.3d 1147 (7th Cir.), *cert. denied*, 522 U.S. 808 (1997) (finding consent to use arbitration from knowing act of opening box and using computer).

Determining the appropriate or optimal level of arbitration privacy requires trade-offs with other arbitration policies. As a forthcoming section indicates, there exists a so-called public dimension that surrounds the arbitration process. Not all aspects of arbitration merit privacy or secrecy, and arbitration policy is presently in flux regarding the extent of privacy protection that ought to be achieved by private contractual measures.

Section 1.3 Arbitrator Expertise: Substantive, Procedural, or Mythical

The value of achieving a just result from an expert arbitrator appears to be a universally accepted tenet of arbitration. The research of Professor Stipanowich appropriately stressed the historical significance of using expert arbitrators to decide commercial disputes.[34] The success of construction arbitration specifically, and intra-industry arbitration generally, rests upon a clear foundation of selecting an expert arbitrator to decide the dispute.[35]

Exactly what is meant by the term "expert arbitrator" is far from clear. In textile or diamond arbitrations, it is assumed that the selection of a fellow merchant, who is in all probability not a lawyer and therefore not likely to apply legal principles, will produce a result crafted by a true expert. In this context, expertise is achieved by the selection of a respected fellow merchant. In intra-industry arbitration one often hears the refrain that the parties choose arbitration to "get an expert knowledgeable in the field." Businesses may desire arbitration to escape potentially outmoded legal principles and to achieve a result more factually focused than a comparable decision made by a judge or jury.[36] Yet, the use of specialized arbitrator expertise may be contextual. Professor Bernstein has concluded that expert cotton

[34] *See generally* Thomas J. Stipanowich, *Rethinking American Arbitration*, 63 Ind. L.J. 425 (1988).

[35] *See, e.g.*, Lisa Bernstein, *Private Commercial Law in the Cotton Industry: Creating Cooperation Through Rules, Norms, and Institutions*, 99 Mich L. Rev. 1724, 1735 (2001) (asserting that cotton arbitrators "are chosen for their industry expertise" and that industry arbitrator expertise leads to more accurate and trusted determinations); Thomas J. Stipanowich, *Beyond Arbitration: Innovation and Evolution in the United States Construction Industry*, 31 Wake Forest L. Rev. 65 (1996) (noting improvements in arbitration and other alternatives in construction disputes).

[36] *See* Paul L. Sayre, *Development of Commercial Arbitration Law*, 37 Yale L.J. 595, 615 (1928) (noting that "[B]usinessmen want arbitration which gives them experts to pass upon the facts, which are often far more important than the questions of law involved in commercial suits" and identifying a business demand for freedom of decisions by judges and juries).

industry arbitrators rely more on formalism than on trade usage in their awards.[37]

Trust issues are implicated in the concept of arbitrator expertise. The parties trust a fellow merchant; they may particularly trust a respected fellow merchant. In this sense trust, so critical to mediation theory,[38] is also of great significance to privatized arbitration systems. Unless the parties trust the arbitrator, arbitration is less attractive and demand for it can atrophy. The mediation alternative, which possesses many of the same privacy and secrecy attributes as arbitration, is premised upon trust of the mediator. Mediation, therefore, has the potential for attracting disputes should parties find arbitration problematic.[39]

Trust is also critical to achieve party acceptance of the arbitrator's decision as final. As the next subsection will stress, arbitration results are generally considered final with no or minimal right to judicial review. In conventional litigation, the parties typically respect the trial judge, but are able to appeal any adverse ruling and obtain a second opinion on the trial court's decision by an appellate court. In the litigation context, respect for the judge does not lead to finality. The litigation function of appeal is to cure inevitable errors that may occur in the adjudicatory hearing process.[40]

In arbitration, the degree of trust and respect for the arbitrator needs to be particularly strong because the arbitrator's award is almost impossible to subsequently challenge by resort to the courts. Trust of the expert arbitrator is essential to support the concept of finality.[41] The chance of error correction

[37] Bernstein, *supra* Note 35 at 1735 (concluding that despite their knowledge of the industry cotton arbitrators "use a relatively formalistic adjudicative approach that gives little explicit weight to elements of the contracting context").

[38] *See, e.g.*, Frank E. A. Sander, *A Friendly Amendment*, Disp. Res. Mag. 11 (Fall, 1999) (stressing need for parties to trust the mediator and emphasizing that "the mediation process must inspire candor by both parties"). *See also* James J. Alfini, Sharon B. Press, Jean R. Sternlight, Mediation Theory and Practice 115 (2001) (stressing the need for the mediator to gain the trust of the disputants); Piotr Sztompka, Trust: A Sociological Theory (1999) (asserting that trust is a measure of risk "about the future contingent actions of others").

[39] It is not particularly novel to assert that mediation is an attractive rival process for many parties who may consider arbitration. *See, e.g.*, Edward Brunet & Charles B. Craver, Alternative Dispute Resolution: The Advocates Perspective 545–6 (2d ed. 2001) (asserting that the "general thinking among corporate counsel is that 'mediation is the hottest ADR tool at the moment'").

[40] *See, e.g.*, Steven Shavell, *The Appeals Process as a Means of Error Correction*, 24 J. Legal Stud. 379, 425–6 (1995) (concluding that the easy availability of appeal "induce[s] trial court judges to make fewer errors because of their fear of reversal").

[41] *See* Christopher R. Leslie, *Trust, Distrust and Antitrust*, 82 Tex L. Rev. 515, 546–7 (2004) (noting that trust allows partners to undertake cooperative ventures and that "trust makes risk taking rational").

that forms the basis of appeals in litigation is typically missing from the arbitration option.[42]

Arbitrator expertise is cultivated by the organizations that administer arbitration. For example, organizations like the American Arbitration Association attempt to assure that only qualified individuals sit as arbitrators on AAA panels. Similarly, the Dispute Resolution arm of the National Association of Securities Dealers (NASD) tries to infuse a dose of securities regulation knowledge on its list of arbitrators by mandating arbitrator attendance at sessions where current developments in the area of securities are the topic of discussion. The Ruder Report recommended that the NASD boost arbitrator expertise by increasing mandatory arbitrator training sessions.[43] Similarly, the NASD's requirement that one of three arbitrators have an existing or prior job experience in the brokerage business infuses a degree of expertise on a panel of arbitrators.

Whether the previous illustrations achieve trust and respect for a panel of arbitrators is an open question. Some question whether today's contemporary arbitrator is really an expert. The growing volume of securities arbitration has made the prospect of forming expert panels of arbitrators tenuous at best. The NASD has created panels of arbitrators that include some who need training in substantive securities law.[44] This inclusion represents an admission that high volume securities arbitration might not represent a shining example of arbitrator expertise.

Securities arbitration is not the sole area where the arbitrator may lack substantive expertise. Some arbitration organizations select arbitrators based upon procedural knowledge in administering arbitration rather than substantive knowledge in a particular industry or field. It is sometimes assumed that a mediator can arbitrate. This assumption may be unfounded, particularly if the newly appointed arbitrator knows little about the subject of the dispute. Yet, the parties may be well aware of the arbitrator's substantive shortcomings, but still be comfortable with their selection for other

[42] Appeals, of course, are possible in a judicialized model of arbitration. The parties can provide for an appellate arbitration panel to cure any errors made by arbitrators at the hearing level. *See, e.g., Chicago Typographical Union No. 16 v. Chicago Sun-Times, Inc.*, 935 F.2d 1501,1505 (7th Cir. 1991) (pointing out that the parties to an arbitration agreement are free to contract for an appellate arbitration panel to review any errors inherent in the award) (Posner, J.).

[43] *See* National Association of Securities Dealers, SECURITY ARBITRATION REFORM: REPORT OF THE ARBITRATION TASK FORCE 90–119 (1996) (hereafter cited as RUDER REPORT). The Arbitration Task Force was chaired by Professor David Ruder, former Chair of the Securities and Exchange Commission.

[44] *See* RUDER REPORT, *supra* Note 43 (urging appointment of arbitrators trained in securities law).

reasons, including neutrality. Just as some respected and trusted jurists lack substantive expertise, some successful arbitrators are generalists without any particular field of special knowledge.

The value of arbitration expertise may be explained as a function of risk mitigation. An expert arbitrator reduces the risk of an erroneous decision and, for that reason, is attractive. For some businesses that select arbitration, risk mitigation means an attempt to avoid a jury. Avoiding a jury may be the main reason some firms select arbitration; fear of a runaway, break-the-bank jury award is totally independent of any notions of arbitrator expertise. Similarly, fear of class action suits appears to animate businesses that use boilerplate agreements to arbitrate consumer claims.[45] Businesses fear class actions and the accompanying risk of a huge allegedly extorted settlement and businesses associate class actions with the litigation option. For such firms, the attraction of arbitration has little or nothing to do with arbitrator expertise and everything to do with avoiding the risk of class action expenses that accompany the threat of conventional litigation.

In conclusion, the goal of achieving the parties' trust seems important. The notion of arbitrator expertise as a clear means of achieving trust rings true. Nonetheless, there are other reasons that parties come to respect arbitrators, including neutrality or litigation risk mitigation. The net result is that arbitrator expertise is an important value but one that can be subordinated or ignored, especially if the chosen arbitrator has other positive attributes.

Section 1.4 Arbitrator Neutrality: Trust and the Relationship to Expertise

Impartial arbitrators are essential to the integrity of the arbitration process. The disputants want an arbitrator who is truly neutral and not biased to one or the other party. In this sense, arbitration mirrors conventional litigation in its foundational need for an impartial decision maker.[46]

It seems beyond debate that the notion of arbitrator neutrality is an essential value underlying arbitration. The ideal of arbitrator neutrality is

[45] *See, e.g.*, Linda J. Demaine and Deborah R. Hensler, *"Volunteering" to Arbitrate through Predispute Arbitration Clauses: The Average Consumer's Experience*, 67 Law & Contemp. Prob. 55, 65 (2004) (collecting data from businesses that use arbitration clauses in contracts with consumers and noting that 30.8% of those in sample use an arbitration clause that explicitly prohibits class actions in the arbitration proceeding).

[46] *See* Lon L. Fuller, *The Needs of American Legal Philosophy*, in Kenneth I. Winston (ed.), The Principles of Social Order: The Essays of Lon L. Fuller 281 (2001) (asserting that the adjudication process cannot achieve its purpose without an unbiased presiding neutral).

enshrined in the Federal Arbitration Act (FAA), the Uniform Arbitration Act, and the internal rules of various arbitrator provider organizations. Nonetheless, recurring claims challenging arbitrator bias create the impression that the process of guaranteeing appointment of a true unbiased neutral is more complicated than it might initially appear.

First, the relationship between arbitrator neutrality and expertise needs sorting out. Both values are essential if arbitration is to achieve its potential. The previous segment of this chapter emphasizes that arbitrators are selected because of their expertise. Arbitrator expertise often carries with it a past. The expert arbitrator has usually had prior experience in the industry. This experience can lead to potential interactions with the disputants or with others related to the disputants and, correspondingly, to claims of potential bias and the lack of neutrality. For example, in the landmark bias case of *Commonwealth Coatings Corp. v. Continental Casualty Co.*,[47] the Supreme Court found an appearance of bias because the arbitrator did not reveal that he had served as an engineering consultant on the construction project at issue and had received $12,000 in fees from one of the parties to the dispute. Of course, the past experience of the arbitrator, who was known to the disputants as an expert, contributed to his expertise. In this case the past experience of the arbitrator creates a danger that bias, or at least the appearance of bias,[48] might exist.

The lesson of *Commonwealth Coatings* is to require a healthy dose of disclosure in order to avoid the appearance of bias. Although the experience of the arbitrator is essential to the value of expertise, it is no substitute for the separate value of arbitrator neutrality. Neutrality demands disclosure and prior experiences can and often will cause the parties to strike potential arbitrators off the case. This should not been seen as a flaw in arbitration theory. Rather, neutrality represents an essential feature of arbitration that, if properly administered, can co-exist with the related and separate value of arbitrator expertise.

The process of achieving arbitrator neutrality has potential problems. The disputants have asymmetrical information about the prior experiences of a potential arbitrator. One side may have experiential reasons to prefer a particular arbitrator; opposing counsel may lack any information about the arbitrator. Arbitration organizations face high transactions costs when collecting information about arbitrators listed on their panels.

[47] 393 U.S. 145 (1968).

[48] The appearance of bias was probably more relevant in *Commonwealth Coatings* because counsel for the losing party at the arbitration "candidly admitted that if he had been told about the arbitrator's prior relationship 'I don't think I would have objected because I know Mr. Capacete (the arbitrator).'"

These organizations (and their customers, the parties) rely heavily on self-reporting by the arbitrator regarding potential facts that may require disclosure. Arbitration organizations, such as the American Arbitration Association, possess rules mandating self-disclosure of conflicts by the arbitrator.[49] Yet, these rules are only as good as the ability and willingness of a potential arbitrator to reveal facts that might cost him a job he hopes to perform.

The existence of these structural inefficiencies that inhibit arbitrator neutrality are a legitimate topic of concern, but they should not deter attempts to appoint unbiased arbitrators. Neutrality is an essential concept in arbitration. It can be reached by increasing the available quantum of information regarding potential panelists and placing continual procedural pressure on arbitrators to disclose their prior business and personal histories.

Section 1.5 The Adjudication Efficiency of Arbitration: Myth or Reality?

Arbitration is adjudicatory in nature. It involves reasoned presentations of proof to a decision-making body, a single arbitrator, or an arbitration panel.[50] Like any other form of adjudication, arbitration needs to provide an efficient means to reach fair results. As the main alternative to trial, arbitration must respond to the high real and perceived transaction costs of a conventional trial. In short, a policy that seeks reduced adjudication transaction costs seems central to arbitration.

Efficiency represents one of the perceived core tenets of arbitration. Much of arbitration's popularity rests on a reputation of delivering efficient, low transaction costs results when compared to the excesses of the litigation system. Indeed, it is difficult to think of arbitration efficiency without focusing on the alternative of a conventional trial. The mythology of trial delays and excessively lengthy, overly formal trials form an important rationale for the informal and speedy alternative of arbitration. Arbitration has responded to the undue formality and delay associated with rules of evidence by essentially barring the use of formal rules of evidence at arbitration hearings.[51]

[49] *See* American Arbitration Association: Code of Ethics for Arbitrators in Commercial Disputes, Cannon 11 (2004) (mandating that "an arbitrator should disclose any interest or relationship likely to affect impartiality or which might create an appearance of partiality"). Strong arbitration disclosure requirements are the norm in international commercial arbitration. *See* Section 6.4(4)(1)(C), *infra.*

[50] *See, e.g.*, Macneil et al., Federal Arbitration Law, *supra* Note 29 at §2.1.2 (stating that arbitration "is generally understood to be a kind of adjudicatory process in which both sides have some opportunity to present their cases").

[51] *See, e.g.*, American Arbitration Association, Commercial Arbitration Rules, Rule 31 (stating that "conformity to legal rules of evidence shall not be necessary").

Nonetheless, the need for efficiency in arbitration can be subordinated to other arbitration values. For example, two business parties may agree to arbitrate in order to avoid punitive damages and the perceived possibility of a runaway jury award.[52] They insert a prohibition on punitive damages in their arbitration clause. In this situation, the parties' desire to arbitrate is unrelated to adjudication efficiency because the need for low transaction costs had nothing to do with the selection of the arbitration option. Instead, the parties' contract to arbitrate was founded on a reciprocal desire to avoid specific remedies and to seek to custom craft their own remedial system of dispute governance.

Parties select the arbitration alternative for numerous reasons unrelated to efficiency. The recent decision by Fannie Mae to not purchase mortgages containing mandatory arbitration clauses illustrates a similar point. Consumer groups had lobbied the government-sponsored Fannie Mae to prevent allegedly unscrupulous lenders from using arbitration to force secret dispute resolution and avoid public trials.[53] In this context, the decision of mortgagors to seek arbitration was apparently to minimize and keep private any adverse publicity associated with mortgage disputes.

The case for efficiency as a paramount value underlying arbitration is tepid at best. It is evident that the important value of efficiency in arbitration is not universal and can take a back seat to other arbitration values. Moreover, there is little empirical evidence that the arbitration system guarantees a more efficient outcome than trial, and emerging evidence suggests that trials can be as efficient as arbitration. The generalization that securities arbitrators are experts has been criticized recently.[54] The system of securities arbitration administered by the NASD has backlogs leading to queues awaiting an arbitration hearing of well over one year.[55] The NASD's widely publicized delay problem has existed for close to a decade and may be

[52] *See, e.g.*, Christopher R. Drahozal, *A Behavioral Analysis of Private Judging*, 67 Law & Contemp. Prob. 105 (2004) (stating that a "reason that businesses include arbitration clauses in their contracts with consumers is to avoid jury trials").

[53] *See* 72 U.S.L.W. 2463 (2004) (noting that "Fannie Mae will not buy home mortgages with mandatory arbitration clauses").

[54] *See, e.g.*, Jennifer J. Johnson, *Wall Street Meets the Wild West: Bringing Law and Order to Securities Arbitration*, 84 N. Car. L. Rev.__(forthcoming 2005) (concluding that NASD securities arbitrations lack expert arbitrators well trained in substantive legal principles); Joel Seligman, *The Quiet Revolution: Securities Arbitration Confronts the Hard Questions*, 33 Houston L. Rev. 327, 356 (1996) (emphasizing need for arbitrator competence as well as neutrality).

[55] *See* http://www.nasd.adr.com. (reporting statistics that claims concluded in 2003 took 15.2 months to reach an arbitration hearing and that the average time from case filing to hearing for the past three years was 17 months).

regarded as chronic in nature.[56] In glaring contrast, the median time from case filing to disposition in the federal district courts in fiscal year 2003 was 9.3 months.[57]

International arbitration disputes are notorious for taking long periods of time and costing sums far greater than a conventional trial.[58] Of course, speed and low costs are not the reason that international business partners choose to arbitrate. Businesses are typically attracted to the process of international arbitration out of a fear of a foreign, "home-town" litigation process and the desire of obtaining a neutral forum with an award that is readily enforceable. An empirical study of why firms select international arbitration confirms that the two most popular reasons that attract business users are the achievement of a neutral forum and the ability to gain award enforcement.[59] The perception of low costs compared to courts and speed compared to conventional litigation ranked very low in this study of the reasons firms choose international arbitration.[60]

The point of these examples is not that arbitration has become less efficient than trial. Rather, it appears that the notion of arbitration efficiency is at most a myth and may not be one of the fundamental policies that underpins arbitration theory. It is noteworthy that former AAA President Robert Coulson, whose job is to market arbitration services, asserted that AAA does not "sell arbitration by and large on the basis of speed and economy."[61]

[56] Delay in awaiting hearings in securities arbitrations was emphasized by the blue ribbon 1996 Ruder Report. *See* RUDER REPORT, *supra* Note 43.

[57] *See* http://www.uscourts.gov/cgi-bin/cmsd2003.pl (setting forth data for the fiscal year 2003 for the U.S. District Courts. The median time to disposition was 8.7 months for years 2002 and 2001, 8.2 months for 2000, 10.3 months for 1999, and 9.2 months for 1998. *Id.*

[58] *See, e.g.*, Martin Hunter, *International Commercial Dispute Resolution: The Challenge of the Twenty-first Century*, 16 ARB. INT'L 379, 382 (2000) (asserting that the "general preference for arbitration in international transactions has nothing to do with the advantages of speed and cost saving"); Christopher R. Drahozal, *Privatizing Civil Justice: Commercial Arbitration and the Civil Justice System*, 9 KAN J. L. & PUB. POL'Y 578–583 (2000) (noting comments of practictioners "that it actually can be much more expensive to go through an international arbitration proceeding than it would be to litigate in court" and emphasizing the high cost of travel for attorneys and the high costs of arbitrators).

[59] *See* Christian Buhring-Uhle, ARBITRATION AND MEDIATION IN INTERNATIONAL BUSINESS 127, 395 (1996) (noting that 72% of those who select international arbitration are drawn by a neutral forum and 64% are attracted by the availability of award enforcement). *See* Section 6.1(1)(A) (discussing data).

[60] *Id.* (noting that 11% of respondents select international arbitration because of speed compared to courts and 4% select arbitration to save on costs compared to courts).

[61] Lyons, *Arbitration: The Slower, More Expensive Alternative?* AM. LAWYER 107 (Jan.–Feb. 1985). *Accord* Martha Neil, *Litigation Over Arbitration*, A.B.A. J. 50 (Jan. 2005) (noting that "arbitrating a matter might end up costing almost as much as litigation").

I do not mean to rule out efficiency as an arbitration value. Professor Stipanowich reviewed several empirical studies of arbitration speed and concluded that the claims of arbitration speed and efficiency were well-founded, especially in small cases.[62] There are arbitration characteristics that lead to an efficient, low-cost procedure. Limited discovery is an important general characteristic of arbitration. This feature will appeal to individuals and firms that want to avoid the potentially staggering discovery costs associated with conventional court sponsored American litigation. Discovery remains the largest single cost of litigation.[63] A 1997 Federal Judicial Center study on discovery costs concluded that a party spends approximately 50% of the total litigation cost on discovery and that the cost of discovery was 3% of the amount at stake in a particular case.[64] It is true that the internal procedural rules of arbitration providers typically provide norms that make document exchanges routine and depositions possible.[65] Yet, the norm in practice is that the commercial arbitrator will rarely exercise her discretion to permit a deposition. Accordingly, arbitration does reduce the out of pocket expense of adjudication by decreasing the cost of discovery.

A reduction in discovery costs does not necessarily increase the efficiency of arbitration. A low-cost arbitration result may come at the expense of the efficiency associated with a full and fair hearing. A complete and robust notion of efficiency goes far beyond out of pocket costs and embraces the idea of outcome accuracy.[66] An inaccurate outcome achieved at a bargain price is inefficient. One of the contemporary fears that deters some from arbitration is the possibility of inaccurate, mistaken awards that cannot be corrected in judicial review.[67] A desire for more efficient and accurate outcomes has led some parties to judicialize their arbitration clauses by requiring application of substantive rules, findings of fact and conclusions of law, and the possibility of judicial review for legal error. This development is based on a fear of arbitration inefficiency and might be related to the lack of

[62] Thomas Stipanowich, *Rethinking American Arbitration*, 63 Ind. L.J. 425, 472 (1988).

[63] *See, e.g.*, Thomas Willging, Donna Stienstra, John Shapard, & Dean Miletich, *An Empirical Study of Discovery and Disclosure Practice Under the 1993 Federal Rule Amendments*, 39 Bos. Col. L. Rev. 525, 531 (1998).

[64] *Id.*

[65] *See, e.g.*, American Arbitration Association, International Arbitration Rules, Art. 19 (2003).

[66] *See* John Rawls, A Theory of Justice 67–71, 342–50 (1971) (including efficiency as a component in a multi-part aggregation of justice). *See Mathews v. Eldridge*, 424 U.S. 319 (1976) (requiring under due process clause that an outcome be accurate); Jerry L. Mashaw, Due Process in the Administrative State 102–4 (1985) (interpreting *Mathews* as a case that sets forth a utilitarian model of due process).

[67] *See* Brunet, *Contract Model*, *supra* Note 10.

information that accompanies a procedural system with limited discovery. In economic theory, perfect information yields accurate, efficient outcomes. In arbitration, limits on discovery can mean inaccurate, inefficient awards that some may regard as unfair.[68]

The values that underpin international arbitration seem largely unrelated to efficiency. It appears that parties who sign agreements triggering international arbitration are usually businesses who select arbitration to avoid the uncertainty of litigating in a foreign venue. International arbitrations are often characterized by a judicial model with lengthy presentations of evidence and comprehensive, discursive opinions by the arbitration panel. International arbitration is characterized by comparatively high costs and expense. Speed is often traded for the perception and reality of a full and fair hearing. The notion of efficiency as a value underlying the arbitration of international disputes seems misconceived.

Section 1.6 Fairness: The Opportunity for a Fundamentally Fair Hearing

Arbitration avoids some efficient procedures that conventional litigation relies upon heavily. For example, pre-trial dispositive motions, such as motions to dismiss for failure to state a claim and for a summary judgment, are conspicuously missing in the arsenal of procedures associated with arbitration. These procedures are deemed inconsistent with the opportunity for a fundamentally fair hearing, a treasured policy that belongs in the arsenal of arbitration values.

The essence of arbitration remains the adjudicatory trial process. A dispute settled by arbitration is still decided by a trial event. Like conventional litigation, an arbitration involves reasoned presentations of proof to a neutral decision maker. Although arbitration procedures are more informal than trial, they essentially constitute an event that resembles a trial. Arbitration assumes a common law approach to litigation and eschews the civil law notion that a dispute can be decided fairly on a paper record and without routinely holding a face-to-face hearing featuring live evidence.

The nature of arbitration is to provide a real opportunity for live, face-to-face evidence presentations before a single arbitrator or a panel of arbitrators. Efficient procedures, such as a summary judgment, would go far to reduce

[68] *See, e.g.*, Jean R. Sternlight, *Rethinking the Constitutionality of the Supreme Court's Preference for Binding Arbitration: A Fresh Assessment of Jury Trial, Separation of Powers and Due Process Concerns*, 72 Tul. L. Rev. 1, 92–3 (1997) (urging a due process based right to adequate discovery in arbitration).

the transactions costs of arbitration.[69] Judge Diane Wood has explained summary judgment efficiency in graphic terms as a "put up or shut up moment in a lawsuit when a party must show what evidence it has that would convince a trier of fact to accept its version of events."[70] Yet, arbitration lacks a summary judgment process because of its commitment to the presentation of live evidence and its desire to avoid procedures that detract from providing a real hearing for the arbitration parties. Faced with a clear efficiency gain available from a summary judgment, a tried and true procedure that clearly enhances adjudication efficiency, arbitration theory demands that the goal of a live hearing take precedence.

Arbitration's focus on the value of providing a trial event has received empirical support. A RAND survey compared the litigant popularity of three ways to dispose of cases: judicial settlement conferences, court-connected arbitrations, and conventional trial.[71] Parties were requested to evaluate the popularity of each of these dispute resolution methods and also to explain a reason for their selection. The results of this study found that arbitration and trial were of relatively equal popularity but that a judicial settlement conference ranked a distant third. The reason for this result appears to be that litigants value their dignity in the form of receiving an opportunity to be heard personally and to present their side of the case to a live decision maker. A judicial settlement conference lacks the opportunity for disputants to tell their side of the story to the arbitrator. Although this study evaluated court-annexed arbitration, it appears to provide reliable support for pre-dispute arbitration as well. Both of these types of arbitration rely on parties telling their stories to the arbitrator in a face-to-face fashion. It is this opportunity that parties seek to include in the dispute resolution process in general and in arbitration, in particular.

A degree of due process protection is and should be provided by arbitrators. The inclusion of due process protocols demonstrates that arbitration administration organizations have an interest in providing fair procedures such as notice, confrontation rights, and a decision based upon an exclusive record. Labor arbitrators have long applied a variety of procedural

[69] *See, e.g.*, Edward Brunet, Martin H. Redish, & Michael A. Reiter, SUMMARY JUDGMENT: FEDERAL LAW AND PRACTICE 1–3 (2d ed. 2000) (detailing goal of summary judgment to avoid unnecessary trials and to weed out disputes in which there are really no issues of fact left for trial).

[70] *Schact v. Wisconsin Dep't of Corrections*, 175 F.3d 497, 504 (7th Cir. 1999).

[71] *See* E. Lind. R. Maccoun, P. Ebner, W. Felstiner, D. Hensler, J. Resnik, & T. Tyler, THE PERCEPTION OF JUSTICE: TORT LITIGANTS' VIEWS OF TRIAL, COURT-ANNEXED ARBITRATION AND JUDICIAL SETTLEMENT CONFERENCES (RAND, 1989). The arbitrations included in this study were non-binding court annexed arbitrations.

protections under the amorphous label of industrial due process. The explicit source of arbitration due process protections has been murky.[72] Because arbitration needs a scheme of government fiat to provide effective judicial enforcement of awards, there is a strong argument that state action exists and that the Constitution itself applies in the arbitration context.[73] Arbitration would lack legitimacy and power without the potential of government enforcement.

SECTION 1.7 FINALITY IN ARBITRATION: A CORE VALUE OR A DEFAULT RULE

Professor Speidel has written that finality "is a core ingredient" of arbitration that "supposedly gives arbitration an advantage over litigation."[74] Many American arbitration decisions ring forth with the refrain that arbitration results are essentially final. Wharton Poor wrote years ago that arbitration should enforce the parties' preference for a final decision instead of an appellate court's second guess.[75]

An analysis of Poor's statement reveals a theme of party intent that accompanies the notion of finality. According to this reasoning, arbitration results are final because that is the parties' intent. Arbitration, of course, is premised upon the idea of party control or autonomy. The typical modern, boilerplate contract to arbitrate effectuates this syllogism by stating in formalistic terms that "the parties agree that the arbitration results are final and binding with no right to judicial review."

A reader of the above paragraphs would seemingly conclude that the courts have no role whatsoever in the arbitration process. The parties have agreed to accept the results of their self-selected hero, the arbitrator, and have consented to ride off quietly into the sunset following their quiescent acceptance of the award.

However, the above paragraphs fail to reflect the reality that almost every losing party of a substantial arbitration award seeks the assistance of the

[72] *See* Edward Brunet, *Arbitration and Constitutional Rights*, 71 N. CAR. L. REV. 81 (1992).

[73] *Id.; See also* Jean R. Sternlight, *Rethinking the Constitutionality of the Supreme Court's Preference for Binding Arbitration: A Fresh Assessment of Jury Trial, Separation of Powers and Due Process Concerns*, 72 TUL. L. REV. 1 (1997) (contending that the Constitution should apply in arbitration); Richard C. Reuben, *Public Justice: Toward a State Action Theory of Antitrust*, 85 CAL. L. REV. 877 (1995) (arguing that state action in arbitration enforcement mandates full application of constitutional rights in arbitration).

[74] Richard E. Speidel, *Arbitration of Statutory Rights Under the Federal Arbitration Act: The Case for Reform*, 4 OHIO ST. J. DISP. RES 157, 191 (1989).

[75] Wharton Poor, *Arbitration Under the Federal Statute*, 36 YALE L. J. 667, 676 (1927).

courts in an attempt to set aside the award. The above half-truths also fail to reflect the historical reality of the role of the courts in the history of the passage of the FAA. Although this book is seeking a normative revision of arbitration and is not tied to history or doctrine in its focus, some attention to the rich and available texture of arbitration history will yield a position that allows a limited but important role for the courts in arbitration theory.

Rather than cut off any post-arbitration hearing resort to the courts, the drafters of the FAA allowed for the vacatur of awards. Although the grounds set forth in the Act's original Section 10 were narrow, the provision in the Act for courts to set aside arbitration awards demonstrates that there always has been some role in arbitration for the court system. The cryptic reference in the Act to setting aside awards that violated the "rights of the parties"[76] provided textual clarity to the paramount nature of legal rights over the private law that might guide arbitration hearings. The drafter of the FAA, Julius Henry Cohen, asserted that "[I]f arbitrator's awards are subject to mistakes and other human frailties, as necessarily they must be, it is obvious that review solely by a judge sitting at motion term will not suffice to safeguard the party whose rights will have been substantially violated by the arbitrators."[77] This important passage, written at the time of the adaption of the FAA,[78] demonstrates not only that Cohen's conception of arbitration included rights that were paramount to the internal rules of arbitration but also that the courts were to have a post-award role in policing legal rights.

Parties are, therefore, left with an early twentieth-century form of arbitration that eschewed a model that allowed the parties to completely opt out of the legal system. Parties to an arbitration may use courts to police arbitration excess and can try to rely upon *legal rights.* The "finality" model of arbitration is a vast overstatement because the drafters of the first federal arbitration legislation possessed a vision of arbitration that was formed through collaboration between courts and arbitrators. While courts have a "limited role,"[79] they nonetheless possess a structurally important task that forms a critical review function in the arbitration process.

The previous conclusion also has important implications for the value of arbitration privacy. If arbitration were truly a private adjudicatory system,

[76] 9 U.S.C. §10(a)(3).

[77] Julius Cohen & Kenneth Dayton, *The New Federal Arbitration Law*, 12 VA. L. REV. 265, 274 (1926).

[78] The Cohen & Dayton article, *supra* Note 77, published in volume 12 of the Virginia Law Review, was a modest revision of a "brief" submitted to Congress by Cohen in 1924 that was reprinted in full in the Joint Hearings Report that preceded the 1925 passage of the FAA. *See Joint Hearing Before the Comms. on the Judiciary*, 68th Cong. 33–41 (1924).

[79] *See* Macneil et al., FEDERAL ARBITRATION LAW, *supra* Note 29 at §2.1.3.6 (describing limited roles of court and of arbitration law itself).

it would not be possible to imagine the applicability of public legal rights or resort to courts following private awards. Arbitration, it would then seem, possesses a public dimension. The public has a continuing interest in arbitration and needs to police arbitration processes. Subsequent sections of this book will wrestle with how these public policies should be integrated into an ideal arbitration system.

Section 1.8 The Public Dimension of Arbitration: The Limits of Privatization Policy

Explaining the growth of arbitration in terms of privatization makes great sense. The desire for secrecy, the attraction of moving to a custom of using industry experts as arbitrators, and the selection of trade norms as the rules of decision each play an important part in the privatization story. I support the positioning of privatization as one of the few most important values of arbitration.

However, the virtues of privatization do not eviscerate arbitration's public aspect. There are several ways that public policies and societal values wind their ways into arbitration theory. Arbitration's public dimension[80] needs to be unpackaged to fully appreciate the scope of party autonomy and privatization.

First and foremost, the need for some sort of federal legislation on arbitration illustrates that public norms and values are applicable to arbitration. It is difficult to imagine a smoothly functioning arbitration system without some accompanying federal arbitration legislation. Arbitration was left exclusively to the states until the 1925 passage of the FAA. The uncontroversial, almost celebratory march to the passage of the FAA illustrates the patent need for some default rules relating to the arbitration process. Particularly in the enforcement of agreements to arbitrate and arbitration awards, it seems plainly necessary to have some type of smoothly functioning legislative apparatus that allows the arbitration theory to work its magic. Of course, this is a value judgment and one in which the public is generally concerned.

Second, the lengthy history of the public policy exception represents a perception that society would oppose an arbitration system in which courts would enforce awards blatantly inconsistent with public policy. At present, the public policy exception is not explicitly within the text of the FAA, but does exist in case law as part of American arbitration doctrine. We support

[80] *See* Resnik, *A Public Dimension, supra* Note 19 (coining the phrase "public dimension" and integrating "public" values into aggregate of adjudicatory due process).

a narrow and prudent use of the public policy exception and include this conception of the public policy exception in our draft arbitration legislation. Rather than have a potentially undefined and judge-made public policy doctrine, we prefer the notion of legislating the doctrine and intentionally trying to cabin its potential expansion. While there is debate about the question of whether this doctrine belongs in legislation or case law, it is apparent that the existence of this doctrine demonstrates that many public policies are relevant to arbitration and that some public policies should occasionally trump court enforcement of arbitration awards.

Third, the integration of the savings clause into Section 2 of the FAA means that the original idea of enforcement of arbitration agreements could be trumped by doctrines of state contract law such as lack of consent, unconscionability, and contracts of adhesion. The latter rules are, of course, of great interest to the public and thereby add a public nature to arbitration theory. These are questions of great weight at present as we struggle to decide to what extent the form employment contract drafted by the employer should be enforced.[81] There is an obvious public dimension to these issues that prevents full implementation of party autonomy and privatization policies.

Fourth, there is a public interest in encouraging the development of arbitration, particularly in the context of arbitration agreements between members of a trade group. Such systems of self-governance are healthy manifestations of general public approval of privatization efforts.[82] Public legislation can facilitate creation of industry self-governance through arbitration. Securities regulation and Securities and Exchange Commission oversight of customer-broker arbitration illustrate this public blessing of efforts to privatize.[83] Recent legislation mandating arbitration between crab

[81] *See, e.g., Ingle v. Circuit City*, 328 F.3d 1165 (9th Cir. 2003), *cert. denied*, 540 U.S. 1160 (2004) (upholding refusal to compel arbitration of an employment discrimination claim on the grounds of procedural and substantive unconscionability); *Hooters of America, Inc. v. Phillips*, 175 F.3d 933 (4th Cir. 1999), *cert. denied*, 528 U.S. 976 (1997) (affirming refusal to compel employment arbitration on grounds that a one-sided arbitration agreement breached the covenant of good faith and fair dealing).

[82] *See, e.g.*, Jody Freeman, *The Private Role in Public Governance*, 75 N.Y.U. L. Rev. 543–7 (2000) (describing an "international trend toward privatization, deregulation, devolution, and the contracting out of (governmental) services to private providers"); Shelia B. Kamerman & Alfred J. Kahn, Privatization and the Welfare State (1989) (tracing the trend toward global privatization).

[83] *See* 15 U.S.C. §78s(b)(2) and (c)(granting power to SEC to oversee proposed changes to arbitration rules in securities industry); *Shearson/American Express, Inc. v. McMahon*, 482 U.S. 220, 233–4 (1987) (reasoning that the regulatory power of the SEC over securities arbitration was one reason to mandate arbitration of claims brought under the Securities Exchange Act). We use this example not to praise the SEC regulation of securities arbitration but merely to explain that the public can have an interest in arbitration within this seemingly private arena.

fishermen and crab processors, two groups historically engaged in continual adversary negotiations, is similarly illustrative of the public's interest in the self-governing style of arbitration.[84]

Last, the availability of judicial review casts a public aura over the essentially private process of arbitration. The most carefully guarded, private arbitration becomes public once the losing party seeks to set aside an award. Any arbitration system that tolerates a degree of judicial review has the effect of diminishing privacy. This comment is not intended as a criticism of review; it is simply axiomatic that there will be times when a well-made plan to conduct private arbitration backfires after a disgruntled participant resorts to the very public courts.

Section 1.9 Concluding Thoughts: Repackaging Arbitration Values through Trade-offs and the Paramount Value of Party Autonomy

At a gut level, each of the seven values focused upon in this chapter deserve inclusion and emphasis in an ideal arbitration system. Each has intrinsic merit and provides a different and unique value to the theory of arbitration.

Nonetheless, the reader cannot help but determine that these seven arbitration policies differ in their overall importance to arbitration. Arbitration can be effective and can thrive in contexts where some of these individual values are omitted. And, it is apparent that some of these values are simply more important than others in formulating an optimal arbitration concept.

The position of efficiency rests on a tenuous foundation. To be sure, arbitration is attractive to some disputants because of the perception that it is less costly and more efficient than its chief alternative, conventional litigation. Yet, efficiency is often a subservient or non-existent goal for some parties seeking arbitration. The desire for application of law through mandatory arbitrator findings of fact and conclusions of law can trump efficiency, and it can create a situation where arbitration will be every bit as costly and slow as litigation. For other arbitration participants, the primary goal will be to achieve a private dispute resolution system; low cost disputing is subservient to the main goal of avoiding adverse publicity.

Finality also occupies an uneasy posture when compared to other arbitration values. Finality can mean little for parties who want arbitration to reach an accurate outcome dominated by substantive legal principles. Such

84 *See* H.R. 2673, Consolidated Appropriations Act, 2004, §801(j)(2)(delegating to the Secretary of Commerce the power to regulate disputes regarding crab prices in Bering Sea and Aleutian Islands through arbitration).

parties may be willing to accept outcome uncertainty and higher arbitration costs in order to receive a potentially delayed outcome that accurately applies law to the facts. Although finality is important, it can be trumped in some contexts.

Three values relating to arbitration – arbitrator neutrality, expertise, and the opportunity for a fair hearing – appear to occupy the high ground in arbitration theory. They each advance fairness policies and are instrumental in achieving a just outcome. They form a sort of privatized "due process of arbitration."[85] To a degree, these values have already been included in the so-called due process protocols of arbitral sponsor organizations.[86] They appear important in the typical dispute and need to be factored into the optimal arbitration system. It is difficult to imagine an arbitration party willing to give up a fair hearing or a truly neutral panel. However, there are contexts where arbitration disputants might trade an expert arbitrator for a particular procedure they highly desire. Nonetheless, these fairness values cannot be readily trumped by alternative arbitration values.

Party autonomy and privacy trump efficiency, finality, and even expertise. These two policies seem critical to arbitration and have the capacity to be paramount in policy trade-offs regarding the values that should underlie arbitration. A comparison of arbitration values places party autonomy and privacy at or near the very top of values needed by an optimal arbitration system.

We intend extended discussion of how these values should guide a reformulation of arbitration and play out in subsequent chapters. Yet, the comparative policy hierarchy set forth here is significant to our thesis. Party autonomy is critical to arbitration and little should stand in its way. The primacy and breadth of party autonomy policies have major implications. These may require that many rules of arbitration procedure are little more than default rules that can be trumped by party-crafted variations. We leave further chapters to sort out such implications.

[85] *See generally* Edward Brunet, *Arbitration and Constitutional Rights*, 71 N. Car. L. Rev. 81 (1992).

[86] These protocols are, of course, unrelated to due process doctrine and are sometimes explained as mere marketing devices designed to answer the fairness concerns of those who criticize arbitration. *See* Margaret M. Harding, *The Limits of Due Process Protocols*, 19 Ohio St. J. Disp. Res. 369 (2004) (noting that arbitration providers have formulated and implemented due process protocols in their arbitrations); Jean R. Sternlight, *As Mandatory Binding Arbitration Meets the Class Action, Will the Class Action Survive?* 42 Wm. & Mary L. Rev. 1, 27 (2000) (noting that due process protocols provide that "neutrals should be skillful and impartial and apply relevant law").

CHAPTER TWO

Common Legal Issues in American Arbitration Law

Richard E. Speidel

Section 2.1 The Relationship between Arbitration Values and Arbitration Law

The purpose of this chapter is to identify the legal issues that commonly arise in arbitration. Building on the values discussed in Chapter 1, the discussion provides essential background for the chapters that follow and the proposed revisions of the Federal Arbitration Act.

The values and policies discussed in Chapter 1 are common to all arbitration systems. Their emphasis and priority, however, may vary from system to system and context to context. Thus, the primary objective in international arbitration may be to select a neutral forum and obtain reliable enforcement of arbitration agreements and awards[1] while the primary objectives in, say, textile industry arbitration might be to obtain the quick, informal, and inexpensive resolution of factual and legal disputes that arise in continuing relationships.[2]

Intertwined with these values are the legal issues that are common to most arbitration systems. The precise issue and its solution may depend upon the priority given by applicable arbitration law to the values and objectives of arbitration. For example, the extent to which courts should enforce arbitration agreements and awards or intervene in disputes arising after the commencement of arbitration but before the award will turn on how the tension between private autonomy and government control is resolved. This, in turn, may depend on whether commercial or consumer parties

[1] *See* discussion at Section 6.1(1)(A)(1), *infra.*

[2] *See* Lisa Bernstein, *Private Commercial Law in the Cotton Industry: Creating Cooperation through Rules, Norms, and Institutions*, 99 Mich. L. Rev. 1724 (2001); *Opting Out of the Legal System: Extralegal Contractual Relations in the Diamond Industry*, 21 J. Legal Stud. 115 (1992) (discussing role of arbitration in industry-specific settings).

are involved (there may be special rules for consumer arbitration) or the nature of the claim subject to arbitration (some statutory claims may not be arbitrable). Thus, the private autonomy that produces agreements to arbitrate and final awards will, in varying degrees, be subject to requirements of procedural justice and held accountable to the public policy of the country in which enforcement of the agreement or award is sought.

In the United States this analysis is further complicated by the existence of at least four possible legal regimes within which arbitration may occur. These regimes are (1) international commercial arbitration, governed by the United Nations Convention on the Recognition and Enforcement of Foreign Arbitral Awards (the Convention), as implemented by Chapter 2 of the Federal Arbitration Act (the Convention Act),[3] (2) interstate arbitration, governed by Chapter 1 of the Federal Arbitration Act,[4] (3) intrastate arbitration, governed by state arbitration law, and (4) labor arbitration, governed in the main by Section 301 of the National Labor Relations Act.[5] Although the importance of private autonomy cannot be denied, the extent of permissible legal intervention into the arbitration system may vary within these fragmented legal regimes.

As a prelude to a critical assessment in any regime, let us look at some history and identify some common issues in American arbitration law.

Section 2.2 What is Arbitration?

The essentials of arbitration as a method of dispute resolution have emerged over the years from practice and the enactment of modern arbitration

[3] United Nations Convention on Recognition and Enforcement of Foreign Arbitral Awards (1970), 21 U.S.T. 2517, implemented in 9 U.S.C. §§201–8 (the so-called New York Convention). To further complicate matters, other treaties and arrangements govern more specialized aspects of international arbitration, e.g., (1) The Convention on Settlement of Investment Disputes between State and Nationals of Other States (1965), 17 U.S.T. 1270, 22 U.S.C. §§1650–50a (ICSID Convention); (2) The Inter-American Convention on International Commercial Arbitration (1975), 14 I.L.M 336, 9 U.S.C. §§301–7 (so-called Panama Convention); (3) The Convention Establishing the Multilateral Investment Guarantee Agency (1985), 12 I.L.M. 1607, 22 U.S.C. §§290k–290k-10 (MIGA Convention); (4) The North American Free Trade Agreement (NAFTA) (1993), 107 Stat.2057, 32 I.L.M. 289. Except for a brief discussion on the Panama Convention, *see* Section 6.1(4)(C)(3)(b), *infra*, these other sources of international arbitration law will not be treated in this book.

[4] 9 U.S.C. §§1–16. Chapter 1 of the Federal Arbitration Act, originally called the United States Arbitration Act, was enacted by Congress in 1925. *See* Chapter 4, *infra*.

[5] The subject of labor or "collective bargaining" arbitration is not treated in this book. Similarly, neither employment arbitration in general nor securities arbitration in particular is treated.

legislation and international treaties.[6] Although many extra-judicial adjudicative procedures are called arbitration,[7] "true" arbitration has the following features and implicit values.

First, there is an agreement between two or more persons to submit an existing or future dispute to third persons (arbitrators) who are chosen by the parties. The power of the arbitrators to act depends upon the scope of the agreement. This is the core value of private autonomy, for without an agreement there is no duty to arbitrate.[8]

Second, there is a dispute or controversy between the parties before the arbitration is commenced. The dispute may arise out of a contract between them, but it need not do so.

Third, the arbitrators, who should be impartial and qualified, will decide the submitted dispute on the merits and make an award under procedures where the parties have a fair opportunity in private proceedings to present their case.[9]

Fourth, the arbitrator's award on the merits is normally confidential and is intended by the parties to be final between them. The matter is decided and there are no appeals on the merits.[10]

[6] Although modern arbitration legislation, such as the New York Convention, the English Arbitration Act of 1996, the UNCITRAL Model Law on International Commercial Arbitration (1985), and the Revised Uniform Arbitration Act (2000) apply to "arbitration," none of these documents define the term. The essentials must be inferred from what the legislation requires before it applies. See Ian R. Macneil, Richard E. Speidel, & Thomas J. Stipanowich, FEDERAL ARBITRATION LAW: AGREEMENTS, AWARDS, AND REMEDIES UNDER THE FEDERAL ARBITRATION ACT §2.1 (1994, supp.) (hereafter cited as Macneil et al., FEDERAL ARBITRATION LAW). If one or more of those essentials is not present, the parties have an agreed method of dispute resolution to which applicable arbitration law may not apply.

[7] *See generally* Macneil et al., FEDERAL ARBITRATION LAW, Chapter 2.

[8] *See Harrison v. Nissan Motor Corp.*, 111 F.3d 343, 350–1 (3d Cir. 1997) (holding that where agreement to arbitrate did not commit the claimant to pursue arbitration in all circumstances it was not arbitration within the meaning of the FAA).

[9] In *AMF Inc. v. Brunswick Corp.*, 621 F. Supp. 456 (E.D.N.Y. 1985), the court concluded that a procedure requiring parties to a dispute to submit it to third parties for a decision was arbitration even though the arbitrators were to examine submitted documents "in camera and *exparte*." Even without an adversarial hearing, the third parties were empowered to make a final and binding decision in an agreed mechanism that required a minimum level of impartiality. *But see Frydman v. Cosmair, Inc.*, 1995 WL 404841 (S.D.N.Y. 1995) (agreed procedure to authorize third person to determine price of corporate shares in contract to be performed was not arbitration).

[10] Of course, the losing party may seek to vacate the award. *See* Section 2.3(2)(C), *infra*. In some adjudicatory proceedings called arbitration, the decision on the merits is not final and may be subject to de novo judicial review. The courts usually conclude that these awards are not arbitral awards to which applicable arbitration statutes apply. *See Parisi v. Netlearning Center, Inc.*, 139 F. Supp. 2d 745 (E.D. Va. 2001) (ICANN dispute resolution procedure not arbitration where parties have access to courts for review before and after award).

Arbitration agreements are found in a wide spectrum of domestic and international transactions in the United States. These include (1) commercial transactions, such as sales, leases, construction contracts, and insurance, (2) consumer transactions, such as contracts between an investor and a broker-dealer or between an individual and a bank, credit card company, or manufacturer, and (3) employment contracts, whether subject to collective bargaining agreements or not. In these arbitrations, it is predicted that disputes will be decided fairly between the parties and with less formality, expense, and delay than in courts. It is also hoped that the loser will accept the arbitrator's decision and comply with the award without the need for judicial intervention. When these predictions and hopes are met, disputes are resolved between the parties without the direct intervention of government and with the collateral public benefits of commercial peace and of reducing the dockets of over-worked courts.

Section 2.3 Development and Scope of American Arbitration Law

2.3(1) Arbitration Theory

Arbitration law, in general, provides a legislative framework within which arbitration agreements are made by the parties, arbitrators are selected, hearings are held, and awards are made. Under an idealistic international theory, arbitration is a self-contained, private consensual system of dispute resolution that is not derived from domestic law and where awards are enforced under the same conditions in any country where the losing party has assets. Under this theory, which is called "A-national" or "de-localized" arbitration, the arbitration is not influenced by the national laws or attitudes of mind of the country in which the arbitral tribunal sits.[11] But as a leading commentator observed, "it would be somewhat unusual for a state to lend its support to arbitral tribunals operating within its jurisdiction without claiming some degree of control over the conduct of those arbitral tribunals, to ensure that certain minimum standards of justice are met, particularly in procedural

[11] *See* Theodore C. Theofrastous (student author), *International Commercial Arbitration in Europe: Subsidiarity and Supremacy in Light of the De-Localization Debate*, 31 Case W. Res. J. Int'l L. 455, 456 (1999) (discussing theory). *See also* Olakunle O. Olatawura, *Delocalized Arbitration Under the English Arbitration Act of 1996: An Evolution or A Revolution*, 30 Syracuse J. Int'l L & Com. 49, 56–8 (2003); Hans Smit, *A-National Arbitration*, 63 Tul. L. Rev. 629, 629 (1989) (describing A-National arbitration as a "floating and stateless arbitration and arbitral awards" that "does not owe its existence, validity, or effectiveness to a particular national law.")

matters."[12] But exactly how much control? Under another theory, private arbitration is rarely permitted by government and agreements, procedures, and awards are closely regulated to protect interests of the state.[13]

Arbitration law in the United States and other Western democratic regimes occupies a position between the extremes, exhibiting a clear preference in both international and domestic arbitration for private autonomy in dispute resolution but permitting judicial intervention to enforce and review arbitration agreements and awards. In sum, this law is permissive, in that it is premised on the assumption that private parties are free to agree to arbitrate their disputes and abide by the results. No court or government official interferes unless petitioned by one of the parties. But when cooperation or relationships break down or disputes over the arbitration process arise, the arbitration may founder unless relief is available through the courts under applicable arbitration law. That relief, at a minimum, includes the judicial power to enforce the agreement to arbitrate and to confirm and enforce an arbitral award.

2.3(2) The Stages of American Arbitration Law

What is this law in the United States and how did it develop? In approaching this question, we have identified the typical legal questions that have been presented to the courts at three different stages of the arbitration process. Stage One involves disputes over arbitrability. What are the conditions that must be met before an alleged agreement to arbitrate will be enforced and how will that agreement be enforced? Stage Two concerns disputes arising after commencement of the arbitration but before the final award. To what extent should courts be permitted to intervene in this so-called "middle ground?" Stage Three involves disputes over the enforcement of the award. What must a party do to obtain confirmation and enforcement of an award and what defenses are available to the other party? We will also briefly identify and discuss the different sources of arbitration law, that is, the agreement

[12] Alan Redfern & Martin Hunter, Law and Practice of International Commerical Arbitration 63 (3d ed. 1999) (hereafter cited as Redfern & Hunter). *See also id.* at 89–93.

[13] Controls like this are more likely in non-democratic regimes or in geographic areas that historically have resisted foreign intervention in domestic affairs. *See* Guillermo Aguilar Alvarez & William W. Park, *The New Face of Investment Arbitration*: NAFTA Chapter 11, 28 Yale J. Int'l Law 365, 366–8 (2003) (discussing "Calvos Doctrine" in South America). *See also* Raymond Shonholtz, *A General Theory on Disputes and Conflicts*, 2003 J. Disp. Res. 402 (2003) (distinguishing theories of conflict management in democratic and non-democratic regimes). For additional discussion, *see* Section 6.1, *infra.*

of the parties and the international, interstate, or intrastate principles that might be applicable to resolve these disputes.[14]

2.3(2)(A) Stage One: Arbitrability

Stage One questions involve arbitrability in a broad sense: when will an alleged agreement to arbitrate be enforced by a court? Arbitrability questions include (1) was there any agreement to arbitrate anything, (2) was the agreement in the proper form, (3) was the dispute within the scope of the agreement to arbitrate, (4) was the agreement valid (e.g., not induced by fraud), and (5) was a dispute otherwise within the scope of the agreement capable of arbitration or was it reserved exclusively for decision by a court? Arbitrability questions are usually raised when a party to an arbitration agreement files a motion in court to compel arbitration and/or to stay pending litigation or a motion to enjoin arbitration is made by a party seeking to avoid arbitration.

A critical subsidiary question is who decides the arbitrability question, the court or the tribunal, and if the tribunal decides to what extent can that decision be reviewed by the courts?[15]

2.3(2)(B) Stage Two: The Middle Ground

The "middle ground" is the territory between the commencement of the arbitration under an enforceable agreement to arbitrate and the final award. In many cases, the issues arising in Stage Two are covered by the agreement itself, particularly if the parties have chosen an institution, such as the American Arbitration Association, to administer the arbitration and have adopted the institution's rules. These rules are terms of the contract.

A well crafted arbitration agreement will normally cover such things as: (1) the place of arbitration; (2) the qualifications, selection, and removal of arbitrators; (3) the conduct of the hearing; (4) the substantive law applicable to the merits of the dispute; and (5) the making and correction of the arbitral award. These institutional agreements are typically the product

[14] For an excellent historical study, *see* Ian R. Macneil, AMERICAN ARBITRATION LAW: REFORMATION, NATIONALIZATION, INTERNATIONALIZATION (Oxford, 1992) (hereafter cited as Macneil, AMERICAN ARBITRATION LAW).

[15] For discussion, *see* Sections 4.2(1) and 6.4.5, *infra*. For an admirable discussion of this and other questions, *see* Alan Scott Rau, *The Arbitrability Question Itself*, 10 AM. REV. OF INT'L ARB. 287 (1999).

of a consensus over time (among participants and the institutions) and seek to achieve a balance between party autonomy and the arbitrator's discretion in conducting the hearing.[16] But the role of the courts in the "middle ground" is anything but clear, particularly where one parties seeks interim relief or assistance in the production of evidence or the removal of an arbitrator.[17]

2.3(2)(C) Stage Three: Confirmation and Enforcement of the Award

Stage Three issues arise after the arbitrators have made what purports to be a final award. These issues are usually treated by applicable arbitration law.

Although a final arbitral award is binding between the parties, the winner may wish to have the award confirmed by a court. Under applicable law, the winner is usually permitted to get the award confirmed by a court and entered as a judgment against the loser. If a properly documented motion to confirm is timely and the loser does not object, confirmation is automatic: the court will confirm the award.[18]

The loser, however, may attack the award either by a motion to correct it or to have it vacated. A motion to vacate may be made in response to a motion to confirm the award or in an independent action. Typically, the grounds to vacate are limited. In general, there is no judicial review of questions of law or fact decided by the arbitrators, but the award may be vacated if, for example, the arbitrators decided an issue beyond the scope of the submission, the arbitrators appeared to be or were partial to one party, one party engaged in fraud, a party was denied an opportunity to present its case, or the original agreement to arbitrate was invalid. These, at least, are the traditional, limited grounds to vacate an award.[19] They protect the merits of the award where no procedural defects can be proven.

With these generalities in mind, let us examine the legal questions arising at each stage in more detail.

[16] *See* Thomas E. Carbonneau, *The Exercise of Freedom in the Making of Arbitration Agreements*, 36 Vand. J. Transn'l L. 1189, 1205–31 (2003) (reviewing content of "modern" arbitration agreements).

[17] Many courts have concluded that they have no power under Chapter 1 of the Federal Arbitration Act (FAA) to intervene in the middle ground. See Section 6.4(1), *infra.*

[18] *See* FAA §§9–12. This is also true under the Convention and the Convention Act. Convention Art. III–V(1); FAA §207.

[19] *See* Convention Art. V; FAA §10.

Section 2.4 Interstate Arbitration: Chapter 1 of the Federal Arbitration Act

2.4(1) History

Before 1925 there was no federal statutory law on arbitration. Many states had arbitration legislation and there was an ill-formed common law of arbitration. With the exception of the New York Arbitration Act of 1920, however, agreements to arbitrate future disputes (as opposed to existing disputes) were not enforceable by a specific performance decrees. For a variety of reasons, American courts were unwilling to order or compel parties to arbitrate a dispute that arose after the conclusion of an otherwise enforceable agreement to arbitrate. Courts, however, did enforce arbitration agreements made after a dispute arose and awards made after disputes were submitted to and decided by arbitrators.[20]

2.4(2) Stage One: Arbitrability

2.4(2)(A) Basic Provisions

This "future disputes" problem and other arbitrability issues were partially resolved when Congress enacted the United States Arbitration Act (now called the Federal Arbitration Act) in 1925.[21] The key provision was Section 2:

> A written provision in any maritime transaction or a contract evidencing a transaction involving commerce[22] to settle by arbitration a controversy

[20] *See Kulukundis Shipping Co, S.A. v. Amtorg Trading Corp.*, 126 F.2d 978, 982–5 (2d Cir. 1942) (reviewing history). The history of the "revocability principle" is reviewed and an argument for its limited return is made in Paul D. Carrington & Paul Y. Castle, *The Revocability of Contract Provisions Controlling Resolution of Future Disputes Between the Parties*, 67 Law & Contemp. Prob. 207 (2004).

[21] Act of February 12, 1925, Chapter 213, 43 Stat. 883, codified and amended as 9 U.S.C. §§1–14 (2000). See Macneil, American Arbitration Law 83–121 (analyzing legislative history and concluding, inter alia, that FAA was intended for application in federal courts only). The purposes of Congress in enacting the FAA continue to spark debate, particularly on the legitimacy of the expansive interpretations by the Supreme Court. *See* Christopher R. Drahozal, *In Defense of Southland: Reexamining the Legislative History of the Federal Arbitration Act*, 78 N. Dame L. Rev. 101 (1978) (disagreeing with Macneil). The question of federal preemption of state arbitration law is discussed by Professor Brunet in Sections 3.3 and 3.4, *infra*. Professor Ware's discussion and analysis of Chapter 1 of the FAA is found in Chapter 4, *infra*.

[22] "Maritime transaction" and "Commerce" are defined in Section 1.

> thereafter arising out of such contract or transaction, or the refusal to perform the whole or any part thereof, or an agreement in writing to submit to arbitration an existing controversy arising out of such a contract, transaction, or refusal, shall be valid, irrevocable, and enforceable, save upon such grounds as exist at law or in equity for the revocation of any contract.

Important supplemental provisions were Section 3, which authorized a court to stay pending litigation when the dispute was "referable" to arbitration, and Section 4, which authorized a court to direct the parties to proceed with arbitration under an otherwise enforceable written agreement. In short, courts now had power to enforce valid arbitration agreements to arbitrate existing and future disputes by specific performance and to stay any pending litigation until the arbitration was concluded.

2.4(2)(B) Notable Omissions

Nevertheless, there were a number of omissions from and phrases in Sections 1–4 of the FAA.[23] that required interpretation. These matters were left to the courts or, in some cases, to well drafted provisions in the contract to arbitrate.

At this point, I will simply identify the omission or interpretation question and indicate how it has been resolved, if at all.

(1) Federal Jurisdiction

The first question is whether actions involving Chapter 1 of the FAA create federal jurisdiction or must other jurisdictional grounds be established? The courts have concluded that the FAA does not create federal jurisdiction. Rather, federal jurisdiction depends upon diversity of citizenship or a claim arising under some other federal statute.[24] Moreover, even if the federal courts do not have jurisdiction, the Supreme Court has concluded that actions arising under the FAA can be brought and enforced in state courts.[25] This is in sharp contrast to Section 203 in the Convention Act that creates federal jurisdiction for actions or proceedings "falling under" the New York

[23] Other issues omitted from treatment by the FAA include (1) arbitrations with multiple parties, (2) arbitrations where some of the parties to the dispute are parties to the arbitration agreement and some are not, (3) arbitrations where some of the issues between the parties are arbitrable and some are not, (4) multiple arbitrations between the same parties involving common questions of law and fact, and (5) multiple arbitrations where a class of parties has the same claim against one party.

[24] *See* discussion at Section 4.5(2)(C), *infra.*

[25] *Southland Corp. v Keating,* 465 U.S. 1, 15–16 (1984). For differing views on this decision, *see* Note 21, *supra.*

Convention and Section 205 that permits a party to remove actions falling under the Convention from state to federal courts.[26]

(2) Scope and Preemptive Effect

A critical interpretative question involves the scope of the phrase "a transaction evidencing a transaction involving commerce" in Section 2. How broadly should this be read? What effect does the FAA, when applicable, have on intrastate arbitration law? The Supreme Court has given the "involving commerce" phrase a broad meaning. It is, in effect, coextensive with the power of Congress to regulate commerce under the Commerce Clause of the Constitution.[27] Strictly speaking, in most transactions this leaves little room for state arbitration law.

Given broad scope of Chapter 1 of the FAA, is there any room for accommodation between interstate and intrastate arbitration or is state arbitration law totally preempted when the transaction involves commerce? Under current law, state arbitration law could apply to actions subject to the FAA unless that law is inconsistent the federal statute or discriminates against the federal contract to arbitrate,[28] although the precise scope of preemption is not clear.[29] It is possible, however, for parties subject to the FAA to "opt out" by choosing state arbitration law to govern the arbitration, even though that law differs from but does not conflict with the FAA.[30]

For many, these developments in and around the FAA are problematic because, on the one hand, they do not leave enough room for the operation of intrastate arbitration law that is not in conflict with the FAA and, on the

[26] *See* Section 6.2(5), *infra.*

[27] *See Allied-Bruce Terminix Cos. v. Dobson*, 513 U.S. 265 (1995). The Court has recently reaffirmed this interpretation for FAA §2. *Citizens Bank v. Alafabco Inc.*, 539 U.S. 52 (2003).

[28] The preemption doctrine is developed in (ascending order) *Southland Corp. v. Keating*, 465 U.S. 1 (1984); *Perry v. Thomas*, 482 U.S. 483 (1987) (state arbitration law inconsistent with the FAA); *Doctor's Associates, Inc. v. Casarotto*, 517 U.S. 681 (1996) (state law singles out arbitration contract for different treatment than given other contracts). *See* David S. Schwartz, *Correcting Federalism Mistakes in Statutory Interpretation: The Supreme Court and the Federal Arbitration Act*, 67 Law & Contemp. Prob. 1, 7–16 (2004).

[29] See Christopher R. Drahozal, *Federal Arbitration Act Preemption*, 79 Ind. L. Rev. 393 (2004) (identifying uncertainties).

[30] *See Volt Information Sciences, Inc. v. Board of Trustees of the Leland Stanford Junior University*, 489 U.S. 468 (1989) (parties' agreement to choose California arbitration law was enforced even though it contained a provision permitting a court to stay arbitration pending litigation which was not found in the FAA). *See* Comment, *An Unnecessary Choice of Law: Volt, Mastrobuono, and the Federal Arbitration Act*, 115 Harv. L. Rev. 2250 (2002).

other hand, are not clear on what parts of the FAA are mandatory rules the effect of which cannot be varied by contract.[31]

(3) Employment Contracts

Section 1 provides that the FAA does not apply to "contracts of employment of seamen, railroad employees, or any other class of workers engaged in foreign or interstate commerce." What is the scope of that exclusion? Are ordinary employees engaged in "foreign or interstate commerce" excluded? What arbitration law applies if a contract of employment is excluded? The Supreme Court recently held that the exclusion is limited to transportation workers as a class and that arbitration clauses in the contracts of other employees who are not in collective bargaining agreements are subject to the FAA.[32] Thus, the source of the governing arbitration law depends upon the status of the employee. More importantly, the non-unionized employee in interstate commerce who is not a transportation worker is subject to the FAA and its unitary, that is, "one size fits all," approach to arbitration, even though the nature of the contract (standard form adhesion) and the scope of the agreement to arbitrate (statutory claims) differ from the usual negotiated commercial deal.

For many, this situation is problematic but agreement on the proper solution is difficult to reach.[33]

(4) Grounds to Refuse Enforcement

Under Section 2 of the FAA, the written arbitration agreement may be denied enforcement on such "grounds as exist at law or in equity for the revocation of any contract." Subject to the preemption problem noted previously, to what body of law should the court look for those "grounds . . . for revocation?" Chapter 1 of the FAA does not answer this question.

The consensus answer is that non-discriminatory state substantive law chosen by the parties or pointed to by applicable choice of law principles applies. This is the same answer reached in other contract disputes when

[31] *See* Professor Brunet's critique and proposed solution in Chapter 3, *infra.*

[32] *See Circuit City Stores, Inc. v. Adams*, 532 U.S. 105 (2001), which excluded "transportation workers" from the FAA and reaffirmed the line previously drawn between employees subject to collective bargaining agreements and other employment contracts in *Gilmer v. Interstate\Johnson Lane Corp.*, 500 U.S. 20 (1991).

[33] There is a discussion of employment contract arbitration in Chapter 7, *infra.* Professor Ware recommends that the "transportation workers" exclusion in Section 1 of the FAA be repealed, Section 4.3(1), *infra,* and Professor Speidel recommends that employment arbitrations involving individuals be left to domestic arbitration law even though they are international, Section 6.2(1)(B)(3), *infra.*

federal courts sit with diversity jurisdiction.[34] But federal law and policy looms over this picture. For example, Section 2 of the FAA requires that the agreement to arbitrate be in writing and other federal law determines whether a particular claim is appropriate for arbitration. Moreover, in disputes over the scope of an agreement to arbitrate, the Supreme Court has stated:

> [Q]uestions of arbitrability must be addressed with a healthy regard for the federal policy favoring arbitration. . . . The Arbitration Act establishes that, as a matter of federal law, any doubts concerning the scope of arbitrable issues should be resolved in favor of arbitration.[35]

In sum, a petition to enforce an agreement to arbitrate arising under the FAA can be enforced in a state court with jurisdiction. Regardless of where the matter is heard, however, the validity of that agreement will be determined under non-discriminatory state law. The FAA, however, requires the agreement to be in writing and federal policies favoring arbitration aid in determining the intended scope of the agreement to arbitrate. What a lovely mix.

(5) Power of Tribunal to Decide its Own Jurisdiction

Under Sections 3 and 4 of the FAA, a federal district court, if petitioned, has power to decide questions of arbitrability. If the district court's decision is appealable,[36] the appellant is usually entitled to a de novo review in the court of appeals.

Suppose, however, that the defendant in a motion to compel arbitration contends that the arbitral tribunal has power to decide the arbitrability question and that the court should deny the motion and send the issue to the arbitrators. Or, suppose that after the arbitration is commenced, one party challenges the jurisdiction of the tribunal which then decides that it has power and this decision is later attacked in a motion to vacate an award. What should the court do?

Under the FAA, the courts would seem to have authority in any case but, according to the Supreme Court, the tribunal has authority only if the there

[34] A good example is *CitiFinancial, Inc. v. Brown*, 2001 WL1530352, *rev. on other grounds*, 304 F.3d 469 (5th Cir. 2002), where a federal district court sitting in Mississippi applied Mississippi law to determine that an individual was incompetent to conclude an arbitration agreement subject to the FAA. *See* Professor Ware's discussion in Section 4.5(2), *infra.*

[35] *Moses H. Cone Memorial Hospital v. Mercury Construction Corp.*, 460 U.S. 1, 24–5 (1983).

[36] An immediate appeal is available if the court's decision is final or refuses to grant a stay or refer the case to arbitration. FAA §16.

is "clear and unmistakable" evidence that the parties have conferred that power by agreement.[37] Under this test a broad, generally worded agreement to arbitrate will not be sufficient. Specific language is required.

Assuming that the tribunal has power and actually decides its own jurisdiction, the real question is the deference to which a court should give the award. Should it be treated as an award on the merits, which is insulated from judicial review, or should it be given a do novo review or, at the least, a review for clear errors of fact or law? These are questions without clear answers at this time and deserve fuller treatment later on.[38]

(6) Separability

In a dispute over "competence," there is an uneasy form of concurrent jurisdiction between the courts and arbitral tribunals. The court, however, will probably decide direct attacks on the validity or enforceability of the arbitration agreement when petitioned even though the tribunal may also have power to do so. Suppose, however, that the tribunal has no power to determine its own jurisdiction and there is a direct attack on the validity of a contract in which a written agreement to arbitrate is contained. The claim is that the underlying contract is voidable because of fraud or duress or, in an extreme case, that the alleged contract is "void" because it never came into existence. Who decides this question?

In 1967, the Supreme Court, in the *Prima Paint* decision, interpreted Sections 3 and 4 of the FAA to support a holding that the court's power was limited to disputes over the "making and performance of the agreement to arbitrate."[39] In disputes over the making and performance of the underlying contract, however, the decision was for the tribunal not the court, provided that the parties had agreed to submit the dispute to arbitration. In interpreting the FAA, the Court was bolstered by the "clear congressional purpose that the arbitration procedure, when selected by the parties to a contract, be speedy and not subject to delay and obstruction in the courts."[40]

[37] *First Options of Chicago, Inc. v. Kaplan*, 514 U.S. 938, 944–5 (1995). *See Carbajal v. H & R Block Tax Services, Inc.*, 372 F.3d 903, 905 (7th Cir. 2002) (clause covering any dispute about "the validity or enforceability of this arbitration provision or any part thereof" was, according to the court, "evidently tailored" to come within the *First Options* requirement.).

[38] *See* Sections 4.2 and 6.4(5), *infra.*

[39] *Prima Paint Corp. v. Flood & Conklin Mfg. Co.*, 388 U.S. 395, 402–4 (1967).

[40] 388 U.S. at 404.

The practical effect of the "separability" doctrine is that in most cases, an attack on the validity or enforceability of the underlying contract will not be regarded as a direct attack on the arbitration clause and that these disputes can be decided by the arbitrators under a "broad" arbitration clause.[41] The nagging exception is where one party attacks the "very existence" of the underlying contract by claiming that it was void ab initio (as opposed to voidable) or that no contract was ever formed. Here an attack on the "very existence" of the underlying contract (as opposed to its continued validity or enforcement) may be treated as a direct attack on the arbitration clause. If so, "the court must first resolve that dispute."[42]

The debate over "competence" and "separability" involves a piece of the age old struggle between courts and arbitrators. Assuming that the tribunal does not have competence to decide its own jurisdiction, the "separability" doctrine gives the arbitrators power to decide the merits of whether the contract in which the arbitration agreement is contained is enforceable. An award on a matter within the scope of the "separability" doctrine is entitled to deferential review, that is, it cannot be reviewed on the merits, even though it determines indirectly the validity of the arbitration agreement.[43] On the other hand, if the tribunal has power through agreement of the parties to determine its own jurisdiction (the case in international arbitration), the "separability" doctrine is less important. The real question, as yet unanswered, is the scope of review by a court? Should an award on competence by a tribunal with power be given deferential review by a court or should it be reviewed de novo?[44] If a deferential review is required, there is no need for a separability doctrine: awards on both competence and the merits are insulated. If, however, an award on competence is given a de novo review the separability doctrine should be retained because in a pro-arbitration regime an award within the scope of that doctrine should receive deferential review. To put the matter more specifically, an arbitration award that the underlying contract was or was not "void" will be reviewed de novo if the court concludes that a "competence" rather than a "separability"

[41] *See Highlands Wellmont Health v. John Deere Health*, 350 F.3d 568, 574–8 (6th Cir. 2003) (applying *Prima Paint* doctrine); *Primerica Life Ins. Co. v. Brown*, 304 F.3d 469 (5th Cir. 2003) (mental capacity of party to contract is for arbitrators).

[42] *See Will-Drill Resources, Inc. v. Samson Resources Co.*, 352 F.3d 211, 218 (5th Cir. 2003).

[43] Professor Ware, assuming that the tribunal does not have power to determine its own jurisdiction, has urged the repeal of the separability doctrine in cases where the existence of the underlying contract is at issue. He argues that these questions do involve the validity of the arbitration agreement contained in the contract and should be decided by the court before the arbitration commences. *See* Section 4.2, *infra*.

[44] *See* Section 6.4(5)(A), *infra*, reviewing the international arbitration cases.

issue was involved.[45] Exactly where that line should be drawn is open for debate.

(7) Public Policy Exclusions: Is the Claim Capable of Arbitration?

Are there any disputes or claims that are not arbitrable even though the parties clearly agreed to do so? Suppose, for example, that the parties intended to arbitrate claims arising under federal statutes, such as the antitrust or securities laws, Title VII of the Civil Rights Act, or claims for punitive damages. These claims probably arise under mandatory law, in that the parties cannot vary the effect of the law by agreement. But is the resolution of these mandatory claims reserved exclusively for the courts? Should it matter if the agreement to arbitrate is made after the disputes arises?[46]

Although Chapter 1 of the FAA provides no answer, the Supreme Court has outlined an approach to the arbitrability of statutory claims. If the parties have agreed to submit their claims to arbitration (by a "broad" arbitration clause), the question is, according to the Court, "whether Congress has evinced an intention to preclude a waiver of judicial remedies for the statutory right at issue." If so, the claim is not arbitrable. If not, the claim is arbitrable and the next question is whether the claimant is able to "vindicate her statutory rights in arbitration." If so, the claim is arbitrable even though "arising under a statute designed to further important social policies." In approaching this important issue, it appears that the Court presumes that the claim can be vindicated in arbitration unless there is clear evidence to the contrary, such as excessive arbitration costs in general or a reduced ability to arbitrate the claim in particular.[47]

These are matters of federal arbitration policy which preempt state law. But unless Congress clearly removes the claim from arbitration, it is highly unlikely that the so-called capability limitation will apply in interstate (and for that matter, international) arbitration.

(8) Mandatory v. Permissive Rules

If private parties agree to a dispute resolution procedure for a transaction in commerce that is not arbitration, the FAA would not apply. Some other

[45] Professor Rau has exposed the complexity and, for some, the absurdity, of these doctrines. *See* Rau, *supra* Note 15. *See also* Richard C. Reuben, *First Options, Consent to Arbitration, and the Demise of Separability; Restoring Access to Justice for Contracts with Arbitration Provisions,* 56 S.M.U.L. Rev. 819 (2003).

[46] Professor Ware argues that in any event post-dispute agreements to arbitrate claims should be enforced. *See* Section 4.4(2)(C), *infra.*

[47] *See Green Tree Financial Corp.-Alabama v. Randolph,* 531 U.S. 79, 80 (2000) (summarizing and applying test).

law would govern. We have seen, however, that if the FAA does apply, the parties may by agreement choose state arbitration law to apply, at least to the extent that the FAA does not impose mandatory rules the effect of which cannot be varied by agreement.[48] The limitation here apparently depends upon whether the chosen state arbitration law conflicts with the FAA by providing less protection than would be afforded the contract to arbitrate under federal law.[49]

Assuming the FAA does apply, a disputed question concerns the power of the parties to vary the effect of the statute by agreement. No test is provided by the statute itself, although the powers of the courts are clearly stated throughout. This issue has come to the surface over agreements purporting to expand the scope of judicial review of arbitration awards under Section 10 of the FAA to include errors of fact and law.[50] The dispute calls into question the nature of the FAA, now eighty years old: is it a regulatory statute that vests unvariable power in the courts or is it simply a variable framework that facilitates arbitration? At least for issues concerning the enforcement of arbitration agreements and awards, the "regulatory" label seems to be sticking.[51]

In sum, there are literally hundreds of federal cases interpreting Sections 1–4 of the FAA with the predictable disagreements among and between

[48] *See* Section 2.3(2)(A), *supra*. This is an issue that recurs throughout this book.

[49] *See* Section 3.4, *infra*. *See also Roadway Package Sys., Inc. v. Kayser*, 257 F.3d 287 (3d Cir.), *cert. denied*, 534 U.S. 1020 (2001) (agreement adopting state law standards for vacatur permitted under FAA). Suppose, for example, that the parties chose the arbitration law of a state that does not enforce agreements to arbitrate future disputes or excludes all statutory claims from arbitration. Without such an agreement, these state law conflicts would be preempted by the FAA. But can parties subject to the FAA select an arbitration law that provides more protection from or is more hostile to arbitration than under the FAA? The answer turns on the extent to which private parties can by agreement vary the effect of the FAA.

[50] The leading case limiting party autonomy is *Kyocera Corp. v. Prudential-Bache*, 341 F.3d 987 (9th Cir. 2003), *cert. dismissed*, 540 U.S. 1098 (2004). The case is criticized in Sections 3.5 and 4.4(4), *infra*.

[51] *See* Victoria L.C. Holstein, *Co-opting the Federal Judiciary: Contractual Expansion of Judicial Review of Arbitral Awards*, 1 J. Am. Arb. 127 (2002) (arguing against power to vary). Professor Rau disagrees. *See* Alan Scott Rau, *"Arbitrability" and Judicial Review: A Brief Rejoinder*, 1 J. Am. Arb. 159 (2002).

See Section 1 of the English Arbitration Act (1996), which states that the "parties should be free to agree how their disputes are resolved, subject to only such safeguards as are necessary in the public interest" [1(b)] and limits the intervention by courts to cases "provided by this Part." [1(c)] Schedule 1 of the Act, however, provides "mandatory" provisions that cannot be varied by agreement. This schedule identifies the core policies of the Act and includes the judicial powers regarding the enforcement of the award. For a discussion of this issue in international arbitration, *see* Sections 6.1(4)(B) and 6.2(2), *infra*.

the circuits. Thus, a somewhat confusing common law of federal arbitration has evolved within the framework of Sections 1–4 of the FAA. It is not enough to look just at the statute: the implementing case law must also be examined.[52] And that case law has developed a unitary pro-arbitration model under the FAA that is applied to every context, commercial or consumer, in the same basic way. Whether that unitary model is appropriate for interstate arbitration in the twenty-first century is the partial concern of this book.

2.4(3) Stage Two: The Middle Ground

Chapter 1 of the FAA says little about issues in the middle ground. For example, Section 5 empowers the court to appoint the arbitrators if the parties are unable to do so[53] and Section 7 gives a court limited power to compel the attendance of witnesses and subpoena documentary evidence if requested by the arbitrators.[54] Otherwise, Chapter 1 says nothing about other issues in Stage 2 or whether a court can intervene to grant interim relief to a party pending arbitration[55] or to redress deviations from agreed procedures prior to the award.[56] Given this gap and the uncertainties that go with it, courts are reluctant to intervene. With the possible exception of motions for interim relief, the usual conclusion is that relief for the alleged defects or improprieties can be obtained only in an attack on the award.

[52] *See* Guido Calebresi, A Common Law in the Age of Statutes (1982).

[53] In cases where an agreed method of appointment is not followed or where there was "no method provided" the court acts as an appointing authority. The number of arbitrators is determined by the agreement, if any, but in the absence of an agreement "the arbitration shall be by a single arbitrator." FAA §5.

[54] FAA §7. *See Hay Group, Inc. v. E.B.S. Acquisition Corp.*, 360 F.3d 404 (3d Cir. 2004) (arbitrators cannot subpoena documents held by non-party without summoning the non-party to appear as a witness). Section 6 of the FAA provides that applications for relief under Chapter 1 "shall be made and heard in the manner provided by law for the making and hearing of motions. . . . " Professor Ware argues that FAA §7 should be repealed on the ground that subpoena power cannot be delegated by the parties to the arbitrators. Section 4.4(1), *infra.*

[55] In many cases the answer is yes. *See, e.g., Application of Deiulemar Compagnia Di Navigazoine S.p.A. v. Allegra M/V*, 198 F.3d 473 (4th Cir. 1999), *cert. denied*, 529 U.S. 1109 (2000) (order preserving evidence pending arbitration hearing); *China Nat. Metal Prod. Import/Export v. Apez Digital, Inc.*, 141 F. Supp.2d 1013, 1022–8 (C.D. Cal. 2001), order set aside, 155 F.2d 1174 (C.D. Cal 2001) (writ of attachment in aid of arbitration proper if issued before tribunal is constituted).

[56] *See Paramedics Electro Medicina, LTDA v. G.E. Medical Systems Info. Tech., Inc.*, 369 F.3d 645 (2d Cir. 2004) (anti-suit injunction); *Certain Underwiters at Lloyd's v. Argonaut Ins.*, 264 F. Supp.2d 926, 936 (N.D. Cal. 2003) (discussing cases). An exception is in admiralty. *See* FAA §8.

2.4(4) Stage Three: Confirmation and Enforcement of the Award

Sections 9–13 of Chapter 1 of the FAA deal with the confirmation and enforcement of the arbitral award. On balance, they are designed to maximize the chances that an award will be confirmed by the court and a judgment entered thereon and minimize the chances that the award will be vacated or modified or corrected in a substantial way.

For example, under Section 9 a court must grant an order confirming the award if a motion to confirm is made "within one year after any award is made" to a court with jurisdiction and venue, "unless the award is vacated, modified, or corrected" under Sections 10 or 11.[57]

The statutory grounds in Section 10 for vacating the award are sharply limited. For example, an award may be vacated if it was "procured by corruption, fraud, or undue means" or where there "was evident partiality or corruption in the arbitrators."[58] In addition, an award may be vacated where there was "misconduct" or other "misbehavior" by the arbitrators that prejudiced the "rights of any party" or where the arbitrators "exceeded their powers, or so imperfectly executed them that mutual, final, and definite award upon the subject matter submitted was not made.[59] If an award is vacated before the time required by the agreement for it to be made has expired, "the court may, in its discretion, direct a rehearing by the arbitrators."[60]

Despite the voluminous litigation under Section 10, there are relatively few cases where an award was actually vacated. There is considerable authority for the proposition that arbitral awards cannot be reviewed for errors of law or fact, unless the court finds that the award was in "manifest disregard of the law" or was inconsistent with some clear public policy.[61]

[57] The judicial interpretations of Section 9 are interesting. For example, the Supreme Court, in *Cortez Byrd Chips, Inc. v. Bill Harbert Construction Co.*, 529 U.S. 193, 197–8 (2000), held that in the absence of a contrary agreement the venue for confirmation was not limited to the district within which the award was made: the motion to confirm "may" be made there but it was not required. On the other hand, the court in *Photopaint Technologies, LLC v. Smartlens Corp.*, 335 F.3d 152, 157–8 (2d Cir. 2003), held that a motion to confirm must be made within a year of the award even though the statutory language is permissive. A troublesome condition in Section 9 is that the parties must agree "that a judgment of the court shall be entered upon the award . . . and shall specify the court." The efforts of courts to avoid this restriction are treated in Macneil et al., Federal Arbitration Law §38.2.2.

[58] FAA §10(a)(1), (2).

[59] FAA §10(a)(3), (4).

[60] FAA §10(a)(5).

[61] *See, e.g., Wedbush Morgan Securities v. Robert W. Baird & Co.*, 320 F. Supp.2d 123, 126–7 (S.D.N.Y. 2004) (distinguishing review for errors of law or fact from cases where the arbitrator "appreciated and ignored a clearly governing legal principle"). *See also Baxter*

Section 11 states the limited grounds where an arbitral award may be modified or corrected. If the grounds are met, the court is authorized to "modify and correct the award," so as to effect the intent thereof and promote justice between the parties."[62]

Section 12 states the time within which a motion to vacate or modify must be filed[63] and related procedural matters. Section 13 states what documents are required to obtain confirmation or a modification of an award and the effect of a judgment.

Chapter 1 concludes with Section 15, stating that the "Act of State Doctrine" does not apply to the enforcement of arbitral agreements and awards[64] and Section 16, which states when appeals may and may not be taken from various orders of the court.[65]

In sum, Chapter 1 of the Federal Arbitration Act is now eighty years old. Does it need revision? If so, how extensive should that revision be? Professor Ware explores these questions in Chapter 4 and recommends some needed revisions. His co-authors, on the other hand, prefer more revisions along somewhat different lines.[66] And we are not alone. As Judge Diane P. Wood put it, if "arbitration is to play a significant role in the enforcement of public law the arbitration itself must become more publicly accountable" through a "careful expansion of the grounds on which the ultimate award can be reviewed by the courts."[67] These differences will be explored in Chapter 7.

Section 2.5 International Arbitration

2.5(1) History: The New York Convention

Prior to 1970, international arbitration in the United States was subject to the Federal Arbitration Act of 1925. Section 2 of the FAA covered arbitration

Intern., Inc. v. Abbott Laboratories, 315 F.3d 829, 831 (7th Cir.), *cert. denied*, 540 U.S. 963 (2003) ("a mistake of law is not a ground on which to set aside an award").

[62] The grounds include cases where there is "evident material miscalculation" of figures and "evident material mistake in the description of any person, thing, or property referred to in the award" [(a)], awards on matters not submitted to the arbitrators that affect the merits of the decision on matters submitted [(b)], and an "award that is imperfect in form not affecting the merits of the controversy." [(c)] *See Hyle v. Doctor's Associates, Inc.*, 198 F.3d 368 (2d Cir. 1999) (district court erred in making correction under FAA §11, case remanded to arbitrators who retained limited jurisdiction to correct).

[63] The motion must be filed "within three months after the award is filed or delivered."

[64] *See* Section 6.2(6)(B), *infra.*

[65] *See* Section 6.3(6), *infra.*

[66] *See* Professor Sternlight's proposals for consumer arbitration in Chapter 5 and Professor Brunet's proposals for employment arbitration in Chapter 7.

[67] Diane P. Wood, *The Brave New World of Arbitration*, 31 Cap. U. L. Rev. 383, 411 (2003).

clauses in "maritime transactions" and contracts "evidencing a transaction involving commerce." Section 1 defined commerce to include "commerce among the states or with foreign nations" and between any state or territory of the United States and a "foreign nation." Because Chapter 1 of the FAA came first we will treat it first, with the obvious caveat that what came next, the New York Convention, has the preemptive effect given a treaty under Article VI of the Constitution.

On September 30, 1970, Congress ratified and the president thereafter signed the United Nations Convention on the Recognition and Enforcement of Foreign Arbitral Awards (The New York Convention), which became effective in the United States on December 29, 1970[68] and has since been ratified by 134 countries.[69] On the same date, Chapter 2 to the FAA, enacted by Congress to implement the Convention, also became effective.[70] Section 201 of the Convention Act states that the Convention "shall be enforced in United States courts in accordance with this chapter." Thus, the Convention as enforced through Chapter 2 (The Convention Act) has the preemptive effect of a treaty under Article VI of the Constitution of the United States for transactions within its scope and displaces Chapter 1 of the FAA (dealing with interstate arbitration) to the extent Chapter 1 is in conflict with Chapter 2.[71] Chapter 1, however, supplements Chapter 2 to the extent there is no conflict. Thus, modern international commercial arbitration in the United States is framed by a forty-seven-year-old Treaty (1958), a thirty-five-year-old

[68] Convention on the Recognition and Enforcement of Foreign Arbitral Awards, June 10, 1958, 21 U.S.T. 2517. For a concise discussion of the background, *see* Macneil, American Arbitration Law 159–66. More elaborate treatment is found in Albert Jan Van Den Berg, The New York Arbitration Convention of 1958: Towards a Uniform Judicial Interpretation (1981); (hereafter cited as Van Den Berg, New York Convention); Leonard V. Quigley, *Accession by the United States to the United Nations Convention on the Recognition and Enforcement of Foreign Arbitral Awards*, 70 Yale L. J. 1049 (1961); Paolo Contini, *International Commercial Arbitration: The U. N. Convention on the Recognition and Enforcement of Foreign Arbitral Awards*, 8 Am. J. Comp. L. 283 (1959).

[69] *See* http://www.uncitral.org/english/status/status-e.htm (last visited on 10/22/04).

[70] 9 U.S.C. §§201–8. The Convention Act became effective on December 29, 1970, the date when the Convention became effective in the United States. *See* 9 U.S.C. §201. For a comprehensive assessment of the Convention and the Convention Act, see Susan L. Karamanian, *The Road to the Tribunal and Beyond: International Commercial Arbitration and United States Courts*, 34 G.W. Int'l L. Rev. 17, 29–43 (2002) (hereafter cited as Karamanian, *Road to the Tribunal*).

[71] FAA §208, which states that Chapter 1 of the FAA applies to proceedings under Chapter 2 "to the extent that chapter is not in conflict with this chapter."

implementing act, and is supplemented (Chapter 1 of the FAA) by an eighty-year-old statute.[72]

2.5(2) Stage One: Arbitrability

2.5(2)(A) Basic Provisions

The Convention deals specifically with questions of arbitrability arising in transactions within its scope[73] in Article II, as implemented in Section 206 of the Convention Act. Article II provides, in part:

1. Each Contracting State shall recognize an agreement in writing[74] under which the parties undertake to submit to arbitration all or any differences which have arisen or which may arise between them in respect to a defined legal relationship, whether contractual or not, concerning a subject matter capable of settlement by arbitration. . . .
3. The court of a Contracting State, when seized of an action in a matter in respect of which the parties have made an agreement within the meaning of this article, shall, at the request of one of the parties, refer the parties to arbitration, unless it finds that the said agreement is null and void, inoperative or incapable of being performed.

Section 206 of the Convention Act provides:

> A court having jurisdiction . . . may direct that arbitration be held in accordance with the agreement at any place therein provided for, whether that place is within or without the United States. Such court may also appoint arbitrators in accordance with the provisions of the agreement.

[72] *See* Section 6.1(4)(C), where the theme that international arbitration law in the United States is old, incomplete, and fragmented is further developed.

[73] The scope of the Convention is extracted from Articles I and II(1) of the Convention, Section 202 of the Convention Act, and the reservations of required reciprocity in commercial disputes made by the United States when the treaty was ratified. In essence, the Convention applies to arbitration agreements "if (1) there is an agreement in writing to arbitrate the dispute, (2) the agreement provides for arbitration in the territory of a Convention signatory, (3) the agreement arises out of a commercial legal relationship, and (4) a party to the agreement is not an American citizen." *Francisco v. Stolt Achievement MT*, 293 F.3d 270, 273 (5th Cir.), *cert. denied*, 537 U.S. 1030 (2002). The Convention also applies to an arbitration agreement between two American corporations where the place of arbitration is in the United States if an award, when made, would be a non-domestic award within the meaning of Section 202 of the Convention Act.

[74] What the phrase "agreement in writing" shall include is stated in Article II(2).

2.5(2)(B) Issues and Omissions

(1) Federal Jurisdiction and Venue

The Convention as implemented differs from Chapter 1 of the FAA in that Section 203 of the Convention Act provides that an "action or proceeding falling under the Convention shall be deemed to arise under the laws and treaties of the United States." Federal courts have "original jurisdiction over such an action or proceeding, regardless of the amount in controversy." In addition, there is a provision on venue[75] and a provision authorizing the removal of cases covered by the Convention from state to federal courts.[76]

(2) Enforcing the Agreement to Arbitrate

Article II(1) of the Convention is similar to FAA 2 in that it requires an agreement "in writing," but unlike the FAA Article II(2) also requires most written agreements to be signed. The exact scope of this signature requirement is not clear[77] and there is no specific validation of writings or signatures made through electronic contracting.

Article II(1) validates a written agreement to arbitrate "all or any differences which have arisen or which may arise between them" and Article II(3) authorizes a court to "refer" the parties to arbitration[78] "unless it finds that the said agreement is null and void, inoperative or incapable of being performed." Neither the Convention nor the Convention Act define arbitration agreement or provide any guidance to interpreting the "unless" phrase. Unless otherwise agreed, these questions will presumably be answered under the law of the forum.

(3) Competence and Separability

The Convention as implemented does not clarify the recurring questions of competence of the tribunal to determine its own jurisdiction or the extent to which the arbitration clause in a written contract is separate from the underlying contract. The issues are invariably covered in the international contract to arbitrate. As previously noted, in the absence of an agreement on competence and severability, the judicial interpretations under Chapter 1 of the FAA would seem to apply. Even with an agreement, the extent to

[75] FAA §204.

[76] FAA §205. Sections 203, 204, and 205 are discussed in Section 6.2(5), *infra.*

[77] *See* Section 6.3(2), *infra.*

[78] Section 206 of the Convention Act states that a court may "direct" the parties to arbitrate. *See generally* Section 6.3(2), *infra.*

which a court can review an arbitral award on these issues is still an open question.[79]

(4) Capability

The Convention as implemented differs from Chapter 1 of the FAA in that Article II(1) states that a difference between the parties must concern a "subject matter capable of settlement by arbitration."[80] This involves claims or disputes determined by legislation or judicial decisions to be capable of resolution only by courts. Put differently, public policy however expressed reserves disputes of this sort to the judicial rather than the arbitral process. The parties have no power to submit them to arbitration. The "Capability" defense, which is determined under the law of the forum, will be denied under United States law unless the legislative body creating the right or claim has clearly stated that the matter is for judicial resolution only.[81]

(5) Stay of Pending Litigation

An omission from the Convention as implemented is the explicit grant of power to a court to stay litigation pending arbitration. Arguably, this power is implied but, in any event, Section 3 of Chapter 1 of the FAA, which authorizes a stay, fills this gap because it is not "in conflict" with the Convention or the Convention Act.[82]

(6) Mandatory Rules

Neither the Convention nor the Convention Act state which rules of arbitrability are mandatory and which permit their effect to be varied by agreement. The assumption seems to be that Articles I and II of the Convention, a treaty, create mandatory rules on arbitrability. Thus, the parties could not agree that a writing was unnecessary or that an arbitration agreement should be enforced even though the dispute was not capable of arbitration or the agreement was otherwise "null and void." On the other hand, the parties have power to agree on which disputes between them shall be submitted to arbitration and to agree on the rules of procedure to govern the arbitration in the so-called "middle ground."[83]

[79] *See* Sections 2.4(2)(B)(5), (6), *supra.*

[80] Article II(1).

[81] *See* Section 6.3(2)(B), *infra.*

[82] *See* Section 6.3(5), *infra.*

[83] The proper scope of permissible variation under the Convention and the Convention Act is discussed in Section 6.2(2), *infra.* The issue arises at both the agreement and the award stages.

2.5(3) Stage Two: The Middle Ground

The Convention and the Convention Act have even less to say than Chapter 1 of the FAA about issues in the middle ground. The Convention itself is silent on these issues. Section 206 of the Convention Act states only that a court with jurisdiction may "direct that arbitration be held in accordance with the agreement" and "may also appoint arbitrators in accordance with the provisions of the agreement."[84] Given this legislative void and the importance of the issues not covered, the parties are expected to rely upon and incorporate an appropriate set of international arbitration rules, whether they are prepared for ad hoc arbitrations[85] or by institutions selected by the parties to administer the arbitration. Typically, these rules cover the full course of the arbitration proceedings, from commencing the arbitration, to selecting the arbitrators, to conducting the hearing, to making the award.[86]

This legislative void in Stage 2 has been filled by modern arbitration legislation, such as the UNCITRAL Model Law on International Arbitration,[87] or the English Arbitration Act of 1996.[88] These statutes provide, inter alia, default rules for Stage 2, most of which apply in the absence of contrary agreement. At least forty-four countries have enacted statutes based on the Model Law and at least five states in the United States have enacted the Model Law as state law.[89] Despite recurring

[84] FAA §207.

[85] In an ad hoc arbitration the parties create their own rules of procedure for and administer the arbitration. An exemplary set of ad hoc rules for international arbitration is the UNCITRAL Arbitration Rules, which can be found at the United Nations website, http://www.un.or.at/Uncitral. In an institutional arbitration, the parties have selected an organization, such as the International Chamber of Commerce, to administer the arbitration and have agreed to adopt the international arbitration rules of that organization. *See* Gerald Aksen, *Ad Hoc Versus Institutional Arbitration*, 2 ICC ICARB Bull. 8–14 (1991).

[86] *See* Roger S. Haydock, *International Commercial Disputes: Drafting International Arbitration Clauses*, 21 Wm. Mitchell L. Rev. 941 (1996) (reviewing rules and proposing appropriate variations).

[87] The Model Law was approved by UNCITRAL in 1985 and can be found at the United Nations website, http://www.un.or.at/Uncitral. An UNCITRAL Working Group is preparing or studying revisions of parts of the Model Law. For a brief summary, *see* UN Document, A/CN.9/WGII//WP.130 (12 July 2004) (provisional agenda for meeting of Working Group in Vienna in September, 2004).

[88] For indispensable background and analysis, see Bruce Harris, Rowan Planterose & Jonathan Tecks, The Arbitration Act of 1996: A Commentary (2d ed. 2000).

[89] Countries enacting legislation based the UNCITRAL Model Law on International Commercial Arbitration may be found at http://www.uncitral.org/english/status/status-e.htm. They include, of note, Australia, Canada, Hong Kong (China), Egypt, Germany, India, Japan, Korea, Russian Federation, and Great Britain. States in the United States that have enacted the Model Law include California, Connecticut, Illinois, Oregon, and Texas. Other states that have enacted international arbitration laws include Georgia, Hawaii, and

proposals,[90] however, Congress has taken no action to enact the Model Law or any other modern legislation on international arbitration. Thus, there are no legislative default rules to provide guidance in the absence of agreement and these matters are left to the courts.

2.5(4) Stage Three: Recognition and Enforcement of the Award

Articles III–VII(1) of the Convention and Section 207 of the Convention Act deal with the recognition and enforcement of an international arbitral award. They apply to an international award (or non-domestic award), whether made in a "foreign" country or the country where recognition and enforcement is sought.[91] A brief overview is appropriate at this point.

Article III imposes a duty on contracting states to "recognize arbitral awards as binding and enforce them" in accordance with local rules of procedure and the conditions laid down in subsequent articles. Article III also prohibits discrimination, in the form of "substantially more onerous conditions or higher fees, against arbitral awards to which this Convention applies."

Article IV states what documents must be submitted to obtain recognition and enforcement. These include either an authenticated original or a duly certified copy of the "original award" and the "original agreement" to arbitrate. Failure to comply with the requirements of Article IV could result in a dismissal for lack of subject matter jurisdiction.[92]

Article V states the limited grounds for the refusal by a court to recognize and enforce an international award. This Article, which is the heart of

Maryland. The utility of these state international arbitration laws has been doubted. See Sebastien Besson, *The Utility of State Laws Regulating International Commercial Arbitration and Their Compatibility with the FAA*, 11 Am. Rev. Int'l Arb. 211 (2000).

[90] *See, e.g.*, Daniel M. Kolkey, *It's Time to Adopt the UNCITRAL Model Law on International Commercial Arbitration*, 8 Transnat'l Law & Contemp. Probs. 3 (1998). For more focused proposals, see William W. Park, *The Specificity of International Arbitration: The Case for FAA Reform*, 36 Vand. J. of Transnat'l L. 1241 (2003).

[91] Article I(1) provides that the Convention shall apply to "awards not considered as domestic awards in the State where their recognition and enforcement are sought." Section 202 of the Convention Act amplifies by stating that an agreement or award arising out of "a relationship which is entirely between citizens of the United States shall be deemed not to fall under the Convention unless that relationship" involves significant contacts with one or more foreign states. For judicial interpretations of this language, *see* Section 6.2(1)(A), *infra*.

[92] *See Czarina, L.L.C. v. W.F. Poe Syndicate*, 358 F.3d 1286, 1292 (11th Cir. 2004). The court concluded that the "original agreement" required by Article IV must satisfy the requirement of Article II(1) that the agreement be in writing. *See* Section 6.5(2)(A), *infra*.

the matter, is implemented by Section 207 of the Convention Act, which provides:

> Within three years after an arbitral award falling under the Convention is made, any party to an arbitration may apply to any court having jurisdiction under this chapter . . . for an order confirming the award as against any other party to the arbitration. The court shall confirm the award unless it finds one of the grounds for refusal or deferral of recognition or enforcement of the award specified in the said Convention.

In general, Article V is discretionary (recognition and enforcement "may" be refused) and the defenses may be raised only if a timely motion for recognition an enforcement is first made. Defenses stated in Article V(1) must be raised and proved by the opposing party but defenses stated in Article V(2) may also be raised sua sponte by the court.

These defenses will be explored in some detail later in this book.[93] Suffice it to say for now, the defenses in Article V(1) go to such things as the validity of the agreement to arbitrate, imperfections in the conduct of the arbitral hearing, the scope of the agreement to arbitrate, and compliance with agreed procedures. As under Section 10 of the FAA, recognition and enforcement cannot be denied because of errors of fact or law in the award. The defenses in Article V(2) go to whether, under the law of the country under which recognition and enforcement is sought, the "subject matter of the difference is not capable of settlement by arbitration" or the "recognition and enforcement of that award would be contrary to . . . public policy."

Article V(1)(e) provides a defense that has created some difficulties in the United States and other countries. Recognition and enforcement may be denied if:

> The award has not yet become binding on the parties, or has been set aside or suspended by a competent authority of the country in which, or under the law of which, that award was made.[94]

Article VII(1) then states that the Convention shall not "deprive any interested party of any right he may have to avail himself of an arbitral award in the manner and to the extent allowed by the law or the treaties of the country

[93] *See* 6.5(2)(B), *infra*.

[94] Article VI grants the court in a country where recognition and enforcement is sought discretion to adjourn a confirmation proceeding and demand security if a motion to vacate or suspend the award has been made in the country where the award was made. *See Europcar Italia, SPA v. Maiellano Tours, Inc.*, 156 F.3d 310 (2d Cir. 1998) (describing factors to be considered in exercising discretion).

where such award is ought to be relied upon. In a controversial case,[95] the court employed Article VII(1)[96] to grant recognition and enforcement of an award which had been set aside in the country where it was made. Although other cases have eschewed the use of Article VII(1),[97] the risk that a court will do an end run around the Article V(1)(e) defense remains.

A final problem to note arises when an international award is made in the United States. Can the losing party move to vacate the award before a motion for recognition and enforcement is made and, if so, what arbitration law applies? Relying in part on Article V(1)(e), the courts have permitted a motion to vacate under Section 10 of the FAA, including the defense of manifest disregard of law.[98] In this area of concurrent jurisdiction between Article V of the Convention and Section 10 of the FAA, somewhat different defenses are available to enforcement of the international award. This problem would be avoided if Section 34 of the Model Law were enacted in the United States. This section permits a motion to set aside an award even though no motion to confirm has been made, but the grounds for set aside are the same as those stated in Article V of the Convention.[99]

In sum, there are many legal issues common to both interstate and international arbitration law in the United States, many of which flow from the failure of either the Convention or Chapter 1 of the FAA to provide guidance in the middle ground. The question is what legislative changes, if any, should be made in and around the Convention. Should Congress leave matters as they are or enact some or all of the Model Law or the English Arbitration Act of 1996? In the view of this author, the answer is clear: Federal law dealing with international commercial arbitration is outdated, fragmented, and incomplete. Substantial revisions are required.[100]

[95] *Chromalloy Aeoroservices v. The Arab Republic of Egypt*, 939 F. Supp. 907 (D. D.C. 1996)

[96] Article VII(1) provides, in part, that the Convention shall not "deprive any interested party of any right he may have to avail himself of an arbitral award in the manner and to the extent allowed by the law or the treaties of the country where such award is sought to be relied upon." Read literally, if an international award cannot be vacated under the domestic law of the country where recognition and enforcement is sought, it must be enforced even though it has been set aside under the law of the country where made.

[97] *See, e.g., Baker Marine (Nig.) Ltd.v. Chevron (Nig.) Ltd*, 191 F.3d 194 (2d Cir. 1999) (parties choose Nigerian arbitration law, award set aside under that law in Nigeria where made). *See* Section 6.5(B)(3), *infra.*

[98] A leading example is *Yusuf Ahmed Alghanim & Sons v. Toys "R" Us, Inc.*, 126 F.3d 15 (2d Cir.), *cert. denied,* 522 U.S. 1111 (1998). *See also Jacada v. International Marketing Strategies*, 255 F. Supp.2d 744 (W. D. Mich. 2003) (reviewing authorities).

[99] This solution is proposed in Section 6.5(3), *infra.*

[100] These revisions are proposed and discussed in Chapter 6, *infra,* and stated in a Revised Chapter 2 of the FAA. *See* Appendix B, *infra.*

Section 2.6 Intrastate (State) Arbitration Law

Although this book does not deal specifically with state arbitration law, its presence cannot be ignored. Every state has enacted a comprehensive arbitration law. Recently, the National Conference of Commissioners on Uniform State Laws approved a Revised Uniform Arbitration Act (RUAA) and this statute has been enacted by several states. This modern statute is more comprehensive than Chapter 1 of the FAA and should be considered in any effort to revise and approve federal arbitration law. Without endorsing the RUAA (at least in this chapter) here, with some history, is a brief overview of its coverage.

2.6(1) History

Before 1920, there was arbitration under state arbitration statutes but none of those statutes authorized courts to specifically enforce agreements to arbitrate future disputes.[101] The New York statute in 1920 was the first "modern" arbitration law in that it corrected the "future disputes" defect found in state legislation and the common law.[102] Thereafter, the National Conference of Commissioners on Uniform State Law developed a "model" arbitration law, the Uniform Arbitration Act (1955), which many states enacted. In 2000, the National Conference approved revisions to the Uniform Arbitration Act. The revised UAA is more comprehensive than the FAA – more in the style of the Model Law or the English Arbitration Act.[103] With a view to the future (and without any endorsement of the RUAA), we here provide a brief overview of the statute within the "three stages" framework.

According to the Reporter, the drafting was undertaken against the background of three "first principles:"[104]

[101] *See* Macneil, American Arbitration Law at 15–33. *See also* Wesley Sturges, Commercial Arbitration and Awards (1930).

[102] *See* Macneil, American Arbitration Law at 34–7.

[103] The Prefatory Note to the RUAA lists fourteen issues that the original UAA did not cover. The goal of the RUAA was to examine "all of these issues and provide state legislatures with a more up-to-date statute to resolve disputes through arbitration." The Drafting Committee did utilize "provisions of the UNCITRAL Model Law, the New York Convention, and the 1996 English Arbitration Act as sources of statutory language for the RUAA. *See* Timothy J. Heinz, *The Revised Uniform Arbitration Act: Modernizing, Revising, and Clarifying Arbitration Law*, 2001 J. Disp. Res. 1, 8–39 (2001) (discussing new provisions) (hereinafter cited as Heinz, *Revised Uniform Arbitration Act*). For a strong criticism of the RUAA, *see* Thomas E. Carbonneau, The Law and Practice of Arbitration 126–32 (2004) (criticizes drafting style, language, and "misguided doctrinal content").

[104] *See* Prefatory Note.

(1) Arbitration is a "consensual process in which autonomy of the parties who enter into arbitration should be given primary consideration, so long as their agreements conform to notions of fundamental fairness." In most cases, the RUAA "provides a default mechanism if the parties do not have a specific agreement on a particular issue."
(2) The "underlying reason many parties choose arbitration is the relative speed, lower cost, and greater efficiency of the process."
(3) In most cases, "parties intend the decisions of arbitrators to be final with minimal court involvement unless there is clear unfairness or a denial of justice."

We will briefly examine the nature and scope of its coverage as a prime example of intrastate arbitration law.

2.6(2) Stage One: Arbitrability

2.6(2)(A) Mandatory Rules

After sections on "definitions," notice," and "scope," Section 4 states what provisions of the RUAA can and cannot be waived or the effect varied by agreement of the parties. The general principle is that the parties have power to waive or vary unless specifically stated otherwise. There are two "otherwise" categories, those that cannot be waived or varied before a controversy subject to arbitration arises and those that cannot be waived or varied under any circumstances. For example, before the controversy arises the method for applying for judicial relief under Section 5(c) cannot be varied but after the controversy arises it may. On the other hand, Section 7 on motions to compel or stay arbitration can never be waived or varied.

2.6(2)(B) Arbitrability

The treatment of arbitrability issues at Stage One is covered in Sections 6 and 7.

Section 6(a) provides that an "agreement contained in a record[105] to submit to arbitration any existing or subsequent controversy arising between the parties to the agreement is "valid, enforceable, and irrevocable except

[105] The word "record" means "information that is inscribed on a tangible medium or that is stored in an electronic or other medium and is retrievable in perceivable form." RUAA 1(6). *See* Section 30 on "electronic signatures."

upon a ground that exists at law or in equity for revocation of a contract." This language tracks the language of Section 2 of the FAA and its effect cannot be varied by agreement before the controversy arises.[106] Parties to a valid agreement to arbitrate under Section 6(a) who refuse to arbitrate may be ordered to arbitrate under Section 7(a).

Section 6(b) provides that the "court shall decide whether an agreement to arbitrate exists or a controversy is subject to an agreement to arbitrate." This follows the American rule on "competence." But the parties may vary the effect of this principle by agreement, that is, they could agree that the tribunal has authority to decide its own jurisdiction.[107]

Section 6(c) gives the tribunal authority to decide "whether a condition precedent to arbitrability has been fulfilled and whether a contract containing a valid agreement to arbitrate is enforceable." Thus, the principle of "separability" of the arbitration clause from the contract is recognized, subject to contrary agreement. Assuming that the arbitration agreement is "valid," the tribunal apparently has power to decide all issues on whether the "contract containing a valid agreement to arbitrate is enforceable."

Section 7 states when the court has power to "compel or stay arbitration." When the appropriate motions are filed, the court must decide whether there is an "enforceable agreement to arbitrate." Depending on that decision, the court shall either "order the parties to arbitrate" or not.[108] Subsections (f) and (g) give the court power to stay judicial proceedings that involve a claim subject to arbitration, either until a decision on whether an enforceable agreement to arbitrate exists or thereafter. Decisions at this stage are not appealable unless they either deny a motion to compel arbitration or grant a motion to stay arbitration.[109]

Another issue likely to arise in Stage One is a motion for provisional or interim relief. This issue is not covered under Chapter 1 of the FAA or the Convention Act. Section 8(a) authorizes the court to grant appropriate relief before an arbitrator is appointed "to protect the effectiveness of the arbitration proceeding to the same extent and under the same conditions

[106] Section 4(b).

[107] Section 4(a) creates broad power to vary the effect of the act and this power is not limited by the specific exceptions stated in Section 4(b).

[108] Section 7(a) authorizes orders to arbitrate. Section 7(b) operates upon an allegation that arbitration has initiated without an enforceable agreement to arbitrate. Without an enforceable agreement, the court cannot order arbitration, but the subsection does not explicitly state that the court can enjoin the arbitration.

[109] Section 28(a)(1) & (2).

as if the controversy were the subject of a civil action." Section 8(b) gives appointed arbitrators broad power to issue similar orders and limits access to the court unless "the matter is urgent and the arbitrator is not able to act timely or the arbitrator cannot provide an adequate remedy."[110]

2.6(3) Stage Two: The Middle Ground

The Revised Uniform Arbitration Act covers many issues in the middle ground that under federal law must be covered in the contract to arbitrate or not at all. Most of these provisions can be waived or the effect varied by the parties.

For example, Section 9 states when an arbitration is initiated and Sections 11–14 deal with the arbitrators – their appointment, disclosure duties, impartiality, and the immunity of the arbitrators and organizations acting in that capacity.[111] The role of the court in this area is limited. When all else fails, the court is authorized to appoint the arbitrator[112] but problems in the disclosure process or with any agreed challenge procedures are rectified by a motion to vacate the award under Section 23(a)(2).[113] Put differently, the court if petitioned is not given authority to remove an arbitrator or hear appeals from an agreed challenge procedure before the award is made.

Section 15 establishes ground rules for conducting the hearing, They are permissive rather than mandatory and can be waived or varied by agreement. Thus, the "arbitrator may conduct an arbitration in such manner as the arbitrator considers appropriate for a fair and expeditious disposition of the proceeding."[114] Similarly, the arbitrator may make a summary disposition of issues presented or order a hearing. If a hearing is ordered, a party "has a right to be heard, to present evidence material to the controversy, and to cross-examine witnesses appearing at the hearing."[115] But this "right" can be waived or varied by agreement.

In support of the duty to conduct the hearing, the arbitrator is given broad power to issue subpoenas, take depositions, and conduct discovery under Section 17, including power to issue a "protective order to prevent the

[110] *See* Heinz, *The Revised Uniform Arbitration Act* at 39–42.
[111] Section 14(a), which cannot be waived or varied by agreement.
[112] Section 11(a).
[113] Section 12(c–f).
[114] Section 15(a).
[115] Section 15(d). A party to the arbitration proceeding "may be represented by a lawyer." Section 16.

disclosure of privileged information, confidential information, trade secrets, and other information protected from disclosure to the extent a court could if the controversy were the subject of a civil action. . . . "[116] The court is given power to enforce subpoenas and discovery related orders in Section 17(f–g) and to enforce other pre-award rulings by the arbitrator.[117]

Assuming that the hearing is closed, Section 19 states the form, time, and notice of the award but says nothing about choice of law to govern the merits or whether reasons for the decision must be given. Section 21(c), however, gives the arbitrator power to "order such remedies as the arbitrator considers just and appropriate under the circumstances" whether or not that remedy would be granted by a court. These remedies may also include "reasonable attorney's fees and other reasonable expenses of arbitration" if authorized in a civil suit involving the same claim or "by the agreement of the parties to the arbitration"[118] and the arbitrator's expenses and fees, which must be paid "as provided in the award."[119] Punitive damages are given a restrictive treatment: they can be awarded only if the award is "authorized by law in a civil action involving the same claim"[120] and if awarded the arbitrator "shall specify in the award the basis in fact justifying and the basis in law authorizing the award and state separately the amount of the punitive damages or other exemplary relief."[121]

Depending on the timing of the motion, either the arbitrator or the court has limited power to change an award. The arbitrator may modify or correct an award where there was an "evident miscalculation or an evident mistake" in the description of something referred to in the award, where the award was "imperfect in a matter of form not affecting the merits of the decision on the claims submitted," where the arbitrator did not make "a final and definite award upon a claim submitted by the parties to the arbitration proceeding," or to "clarify" the award.[122] The court may also modify or correct for an evident miscalculation or mistake in description and where the award was "imperfect in form," but also where the arbitrator has "made an award on a claim not submitted to the arbitrator and the award may be corrected without affecting the merits of the decision on the claim stated."[123]

[116] Section 17(e). *See* Heinz, *The Revised Uniform Arbitration Act* at 45–51.
[117] Section 18.
[118] Section 21(b).
[119] Section 21(d).
[120] Section 21(a).
[121] Section 21(e).
[122] Section 20(a), Section 24(a)(1) or (3).
[123] Section 24(a)(2).

2.6(4) Stage Three: Enforcing the Award

Assume that a final award has been made and there are no motions for modification and enforcement. Without more the award would be res judicata between the parties. How does the winner enforce the award under the RUAA? Section 22 permits that party to move for a judicial order confirming the award and states that the court "shall issue a confirming order unless the award is modified or corrected . . . or is vacated pursuant to Section 23."[124] If the order to confirm is granted, the court "shall enter a judgment in conformity therewith."[125]

Section 23 states the grounds and the procedures for vacating an award. There are six grounds listed.[126]

The first is where the award was procured "by corruption, fraud, or other undue means."

The second involves misconduct by the arbitrators, including "evident partiality" by an arbitrator "appointed as a neutral," corruption, or "misconduct . . . prejudicing the rights of a party to the arbitration proceeding."

The third involves conduct by the arbitrator during the course of the hearing which substantially prejudices "the rights of a party to the arbitration proceeding." This includes the refusal to postpone a hearing or consider evidence material to the controversy or the conduct of the hearing "contrary to Section 15."

The fourth is where the arbitrator "exceeded the arbitrator's powers."

The fifth is where there was "no agreement to arbitrate" unless the ground was waived by a failure timely to object.

The sixth is where the arbitration was conducted without the notice required by Section 9 "so as to prejudice substantially the rights of a party to the arbitration proceeding."

If an award is vacated, Section 23(c) gives the court power to order a rehearing except where the ground was that there was "no agreement to arbitrate." If the grounds were those stated in the first two categories (misconduct by the arbitrators), the "rehearing must be before a new arbitrator." On all other grounds, the "rehearing may be before the arbitrator who made the award or the arbitrator's successor."

[124] Section 27 provides the proper venue for this and other actions.

[125] Section 25(a). The court may also allow reasonable costs of the proceedings and, where permitted, add reasonable attorney's fees and other reasonable expenses of litigation. This section also applies where the award has been vacated or modified or corrected.

[126] The times within which a motion to vacate must be filed are stated in Section 23(b).

The Revised Uniform Arbitration Law is an interesting model for possible revision of Chapter 1 of the FAA. Under the shadow of FAA preemption, however, several important issues were not resolved. One of those issues is the extent to which arbitration law should permit the parties by agreement to expand or contract the grounds for vacating or correcting an award under Sections 23 and 24. Despite some cases to the contrary, Sections 23 and 24 cannot be waived or varied by agreement. Another issue is whether, in some cases, review of the merits of the award should be permitted, either directly or indirectly through such devices as "manifest disregard of the law" or public policy. Finally, the Revision presents a unitary model of arbitration law intended to fit every non-preempted setting where arbitration occurs. There are doubts whether such a model is appropriate, particularly in the relationships between consumers and stronger parties, such as employers, banks, credit card companies, and sellers of big ticket items.[127]

Section 2.7 A Note in Transition

We have now identified and evaluated the claimed "values" of private arbitration and, by examining the regimes of interstate, international, and intrastate law, identified some of the common legal issues that are covered and not covered by treaty and legislation. In the balance of the book, we will treat the special problems of arbitration in a federal system of government (Chapter 3), interstate arbitration under Chapter 1 of the Federal Arbitration Act (Chapter 4), consumer arbitration (Chapter 5), and international commercial arbitration (Chapter 6). In Chapter 7 we will expose and discuss the differences among us as we critically assess American arbitration law.

In all that follows, the reader should keep the values explored in Chapter 1 and the legal issues identified in Chapter 2 in mind.

[127] The Reporter explains these omissions. *See* Heinz, *The Revised Uniform Arbitration Act* at 3–8, 26–35.

CHAPTER THREE

The Appropriate Role of State Law in the Federal Arbitration System: Choice and Preemption

Edward Brunet

Section 3.1 Introduction and Overview

At present the role of state law in our American arbitration system is murky at best and bizarre at worst. Arbitration is a species of contract law and contract law is largely left to the states. Principles of federalism, enshrined in contract theory, could be expected to lead to a situation in which state arbitration law was applied routinely and expansively. We are supposedly in the midst of a federalism revival at the Supreme Court.[1] Yet, the present status, that of supremacy of federal arbitration law and of rare judicial application of state arbitration legislation or state common law rules, is far from hospitable toward state arbitration law. Surprisingly, the word federalism appears rarely in arbitration opinions and arbitration decisions seldom show sensitivity toward subtle points of state arbitration theory. It is strange that the recently amended RUAA is a comprehensive, modern system of arbitration that may have minimal applicability.[2] The RUAA seems to only apply to a narrow band of purely intrastate transactions under the broad holding of the leading *Allied-Bruce Terminix v. Dobson* decision.[3]

As long as a contract to arbitrate affects interstate commerce, the *Terminix* doctrine requires application of the Federal Arbitration Act (FAA). This

[1] *See, e.g.*, Richard H. Fallon, *The "Conservative" Paths of the Rehnquist Court's Federalism Decisions*, 69 U. Chi. L. Rev. 429 (2002)(referring to a "federalism revolution" and a "pro-federalism majority" of the Supreme Court).

[2] The Revised Uniform Arbitration Act (hereafter RUAA). The RUAA is summarized at Section 2.6, *supra* (noting expressly that "the revised UAA is more comprehensive than the FAA").

[3] *Allied-Bruce Terminix Companies, Inc. v. Dobson*, 513 U.S. 265 (1995) (extending the reach of federal arbitration law deep into the states to any transaction involving commerce and rejecting a more narrow test that would require the parties to contemplate interstate commerce at the time of contracting).

leaves the everyday application of the state arbitration acts to those rare instances when transactions have no impact or connection with interstate commerce. In a phrase, state arbitration legislation applies to transactions that are purely intrastate in nature.

Yet, despite the federalized nature of arbitration set forth by the *Terminix* decision, state arbitration law is sometimes applied in what I term a backdoor manner. For example, parties often select state law in choice of law clauses in contracts that also call for arbitration. Choice of law clauses, like arbitration clauses, abound. Parties universally theorize that choice of law clauses add value to the contracting process by providing the sort of predictability and corresponding cost savings desired by the parties.[4] Because party intent or autonomy is a fundamental value in arbitration, a judge should require courts to apply state arbitration law when the parties contract to have the arbitrator apply local law. The Supreme Court used this reasoning in *Volt Information Sciences, Inc. v. Board of Trustees of Leland Stanford Junior University*[5] and mandated that a court honor the parties' direction to apply California law. The Supreme Court's broad holding included California procedural law as well as California substantive law. In essence, the idea of party autonomy trumps a contrary value urging broad applicability of federal arbitration law. The essence of *Volt* means that, despite the narrow applicability of state arbitration law under the pro-federal "involving commerce" concept, there remains a major role for state arbitration legislation to play if it is selected by the parties. Under *Volt's* reasoning, the FAA constitutes a set of simple default rules that apply to those arbitrations where the parties have not selected an alternative governing mechanism.

State law applies in a second backdoor manner. In addition to state arbitration law's application due to choice of law, state law also plays a fundamental role in a scheme of federalism built into the present FAA. The savings clause of Section 2 of the FAA permits a party opposing enforcement of arbitration to attack an agreement to arbitrate on various grounds.[6] Although the FAA is silent as to whether state or federal law should apply, it appears that the typical arbitration decision bootstraps a huge amount of state law into the savings clause. A party opposing arbitration may select various

[4] *See generally* David Cavers, The Choice of Law Process (1965).

[5] 489 U.S. 468 (1989) (emphasizing the parties agreed to apply California law and interpreting such agreement to include California arbitration procedures, including a mandate that a court stay the arbitration where it involves a third party not bound by the agreement to arbitrate and where there is a possibility of conflicting rulings on common issues).

[6] 9 U.S.C. §2 (mandating enforcement of arbitration "save on grounds as exist at law or in equity for the revocation of any contract"). *See* Professor Ware's discussion of FAA §§1, 2 at Section 4.5, *infra*.

state contract law grounds – adhesion, unconscionability, lack of mutuality, breach of implied covenant of fair dealing – that might result in a court's decision not to enforce an agreement to arbitrate.[7]

We are left, then, with the situation in which state arbitration law and state contract doctrine can play a major role in the mechanics of the present FAA. In effect, state law comes in through the backdoor of federal arbitration but manages to occupy a significant place in everyday workings of arbitration. At the same time, the present set of arbitration preemption cases makes it plain that the Supreme Court will not apply state law that is more regulatory than the FAA.[8] In the words of Professor Timothy Heinsz, "[I]n the past two decades, the United States Supreme Court has developed a strong pro-arbitration stance under the FAA concerning the enforceability of arbitration clauses that override contrary state law."[9] This does not mean that state arbitration doctrine is ignored, however. State principles will apply as long as the application of state law is not inconsistent with federal law.[10]

These problems of current arbitration doctrine need further policy analysis to arrive at an optimal level of normative state arbitration law to be used in a reformulation of federal arbitration law. The fundamental question asked by this chapter is what, if any, is the appropriate role for state arbitration law in the overall scheme of a federalized system of arbitration. Although I will discuss leading cases and current doctrine, the chapter's focus will be on the normative in an effort to sort out the appropriate role of state arbitration law. Subsequent parts of this chapter will seek to sort out the issues sketched here preliminarily and will focus on articulating an efficient and fair role for state arbitration law and federal preemption analysis.

A brief roadmap of this chapter will aid the reader. I first address the boundaries that separate federal from state arbitration law in order to determine the appropriate scope of state and federal law. I then turn to preemption and urge the return to a more conventional preemption formula and the rejection of the present approach that readily preempts state arbitration

[7] *See, e.g., Hooters of America v. Phillips*, 173 F.3d 933 (4th Cir. 1999) (applying state law regarding covenant of good faith and fair dealing to void a one-sided agreement to arbitrate in an interpretation of the FAA).

[8] *See, e.g., Doctor's Associates, Inc. v. Casarotto*, 517 U.S. 681 (1996) (holding that the Federal Arbitration Act preempts Montana law because Montana singles out arbitration for distinct treatment by improperly specifying that an arbitration clause be printed at page one of a contract and also be in all capital letters and underlined).

[9] Timothy J. Heinsz, *The Revised Uniform Arbitration Act: Modernizing, Revising and Clarifying Arbitration Law*, 2001 J. Disp. Res. 1, 3 (hereafter cited as Heinsz, *The Revised UAAA*).

[10] *Id.* at 4 (noting that state arbitration law applies where it is "are not inimical to the FAA's pro-arbitration position").

laws that appear to be incompatible with federal law. The chapter then covers choice of law and the question of whether the parties can contract for the application of state arbitration rules despite the wide girth of federal law. I then cover the breadth of the parties' power to fashion their own rules of arbitration and distinguish arbitration default rules from more mandatory norms of arbitration. Finally, I discuss the subject of whether state or federal law should be used in interpreting a legislative savings clause that can be used to attack arbitrability.

Section 3.2 The Ideal Scope of Federal Arbitration Law: The Commerce Issue

The present line between federal and state arbitration regulation rests upon the fuzzy distinction between interstate and intrastate commerce. The current demarcation between interstate and intrastate arbitration was drawn by the Supreme Court in *Allied-Bruce Terminix Companies, Inc. v. Dobson*: federal law applies and state law is displaced as long as a contract affects interstate commerce.[11] Under this interpretation, the broad reach of federal law is co-extensive with the commerce clause.[12] In essence, *Terminix* adopted a "commerce in-fact" test that triggers application of the FAA whenever interstate commerce is implicated.[13]

This solution is attractive for a number of reasons and supplies a template for revision of the FAA. First, an affecting commerce approach is consistent with other distinctions between interstate and intrastate commerce and avoids the costs of forging a new answer to a recurring problem in a federal system.[14] A federal arbitration law that displaces state arbitration doctrine

[11] 513 U.S. 265 (1995). *See also* Section 2.4(2)(B)(2), *supra* (interpreting the scope of the FAA to be "co-extensive with the power of Congress to regulate commerce"). The phrase "affecting commerce" should be included in revised Chapter 1 of the FAA and replace the more obscure and potentially misleading "involving commerce."

[12] *See Terminix*, 513 U.S. at 269 (noting that the FAA extends to the limit of Congress' commerce power).

[13] *See* Note, *An Unnecessary Choice of Law: Volt, Mastrobuono, and Federal Arbitration Act Preemption*, 115 Harv. L. Rev. 2250, 2251 (2002) (explaining *Terminix* as extending federal law "to the limits of Congress's power under the Commerce Clause"); Comment, *The United States Supreme Court's Expansive Approach to the Federal Arbitration Act: A Look at the Past, Present and Future of Section 2*, 29 U. Rich. L. Rev. 1499, 1553 (1995) (interpreting *Terminix* as "adopting the 'commerce-in-fact' test and laying to rest the 'contemplation of the parties' test").

[14] *See, e.g.*, Note, *Allied-Bruce Terminix Companies v. Dobson: The Implementation of the Purposes of the Federal Arbitration Act or an Unjustified Intrusion Into State Sovereignty?*, 47 Mercer L. Rev. 645, 654 (1996) (asserting that "basing the test on the Commerce Clause allows parties to rely on established Commerce Clause jurisprudence").

whenever commerce is "affected" should come as no surprise and be readily understood. The affecting commerce reach smacks of the constitutional limits articulated by the leading case of *Wickard v. Filburn*[15] and extended to other areas of federal regulation such as antitrust.[16] Affecting commerce is a familiar solution that can be efficiently applied by both the courts and the regulated. Repeat arbitration users (and their attorneys) will prefer the bright-line of a simple and straightforward standard used to differentiate local and federal commerce.

Second, the affecting commerce concept is appealing because of its intentionally broad scope. An expansive federal law of arbitration should achieve a more predictable application of arbitration norms. The users of arbitration are generally businesses.[17] A business seeking to embark on a national course of action relating to arbitration affecting commerce would need to research just one set of laws rather than painstakingly include each of the fifty states in its research. The lower transaction costs associated with this simplified research would presumably be passed on to consumers.

The recent revision of the RUAA[18] has a mixed effect. Because this is a uniform legislative package, the costs of researching potentially applicable state laws following the RUAA may not seem as great. If the RUAA is widely adopted by the states, then much of possibly unique state arbitration law becomes identical or similar and, correspondingly, less expensive to research. Yet, uniform laws are not necessarily the same after time; they are recommended laws that can be varied legislatively or by case law. Thus, it is uncertain if the presence of a broadly available state law such as the RUAA would avoid the inefficiencies associated with researching and dealing with potentially conflicting state laws. A multi-state business would still need to research state laws despite the presence of the RUAA and would probably be more attracted to a new, modern federal counterpart than to working with individual state adoptions of the RUAA.

We should not understate the impact upon state arbitration law and federalism policies of adopting an affecting commerce test and embracing the conventional solution of Justice Breyer in the *Terminix* decision. Much,

[15] 317 U.S. 111, 125 (1942) (asserting that Congress may regulate state law where there is a "substantial economic effect on interstate commerce").

[16] *See Mandeville Island Farms, Inc. v. American Crystal Sugar Co.*, 334 U.S. 219, 234 (1948) (rejecting location of conduct and stressing that the "vital question becomes whether the effect[upon commerce] is sufficiently substantial").

[17] *See* Julius Cohen and Kenneth Dayton, *The New Federal Arbitration Law*, 12 VA. L. REV. 265 (1926) (describing that the demand for the 1925 federal arbitration legislation came exclusively from merchant business groups).

[18] *See* Note 9, *supra.*

indeed, most of state arbitration law is made inapplicable by this simple proposal. In the words of Professor Strickland, this is an "expansive application of the FAA [that] sweeps away huge bodies of state arbitration law."[19] Although the federalism costs to state sovereignty are substantial, they are outweighed and thereby trumped by the benefits to parties able to plan their actions more efficiently.

Federal lawmakers should make the federalism choice whether to trigger federal law by passing a national law relating to arbitration. Although it is tempting to grant the individual states the power to legislate more broadly, state legislatures or members of the National Commissioner for Uniform State Laws should not be the arbiters of whether there is a need for a national, uniform standard of arbitration. Use of the affecting commerce approach keeps this critical decisional power in the appropriate hands.

Section 3.3 Normalizing the Analysis of Arbitration Preemption

In order to define the proper and optimal scope of state arbitration law, it is essential to normalize the strange and misguided set of Supreme Court holdings regarding federal preemption of state arbitration decisions. In a nutshell, the Court has been overly heavy-handed in striking down state applications of local law on preemption grounds and, in so doing, has applied an unusually aggressive variety of preemption doctrine that has no place in proper constitutional analysis. In particular, this section will criticize the preemption holdings in *Southland Corp. v. Keating*[20] and *Doctors Associates, Inc. v. Casarotto*.[21] Although the basic focus of this book will be to set forth a new version of federal arbitration law, a goal necessarily focused on legislative changes, this segment of our reformulation of arbitration recommends changes in the constitutional preemption analysis used by the Supreme Court. Some change in arbitration preemption is of critical significance because, under the existing case law, state arbitration law is relegated to obscurity.

[19] Henry C. Strickland, *The Federal Arbitration Act's Interstate Commerce Requirement: What's Left for State Arbitration Law?* 21 Hofstra L. Rev. 385, 454 (1992).

[20] 465 U.S. 1 (1984) (holding California legislation interpreted to require a court to consider claims brought under state franchise act to be preempted by substantive federal arbitration law). *See also Perry v. Thomas*, 482 U.S. 483 (1987) (holding California legislation that allowed employees to litigate wage claims to be preempted by federal law).

[21] 517 U.S. 681 (1996) (holding Montana legislation that required arbitration clause to be located at page one of a contract and in all capital letters and underlined to be preempted by federal law).

The prevailing preemption approach set forth by the *Casarotto* decision is the root of the problem. In *Casarotto*, the Supreme Court held that the FAA preempted a Montana law that required arbitration clauses to be underlined in all capital letters and located at page one of a contract. The Court reasoned that Montana had improperly legislated by "singling out arbitration provisions for suspect status."[22] The "singling out" test is a hyper-demanding preemption approach that has no place in the normal arsenal of preemption inquiries. Indeed, it appears that Montana was only attempting to guarantee the contract signer's consent to arbitrate by placing the important arbitration subject front and center in underscored fashion where it would be hard for the non-drafting party to miss.

The flaw in the singling out test is that it is patently clear that the Montana legislation sought to achieve a policy goal the FAA also seeks, namely that the parties have consented to arbitrate. The basic thrust of the original FAA was to force the courts to hold parties to their prior agreements to arbitrate.[23] Consent is the glue that forms the basis of arbitration and, along with court enforcement of agreements to arbitrate, forms the fundamental intent of the existing federal law. Because both levels of regulatory authority, state and federal, sought the same goal, consent to arbitrate, the *Casarotto* decision failed to present the type of issue that calls for preemption analysis. The need to advance consent as a touchstone of arbitration is vital to both the FAA and Montana law. State law should not have been preempted because it is wholly consistent with the FAA. In the words of Professor Sternlight, states should be able to "regulate arbitration so long as the regulations are consistent with the purposes" of federal law.[24] Because Montana's legislation was designed to advance consent, a basic premise of federal arbitration law, it should not have been preempted in the unfortunate and heavy-handed *Casarotto* opinion.

Professor Ware recently noted that Montana's notice legislation was more exacting than the lower-level contract law standard of consent set forth in the existing FAA.[25] Under this line of reasoning, it is possible to argue that

[22] *Id.* at 682 (1996).

[23] *See, e.g.*, Ian. R. Macneil, AMERICAN ARBITRATION LAW: REFORMATION, NATIONALIZATION, INTERNATIONALIZATION (1992) (hereafter cited as Macneil, AMERICAN ARBITRATION LAW).

[24] Jean R. Sternlight, *Panacea or Corporate Tool?: Debunking the Supreme Court's Preference for Binding Arbitration*, 74 WASH. U. L. Q. 637, 706 (1996) (arguing that the states should be permitted to regulate arbitration to "ensure that persons enter arbitration agreements knowingly").

[25] Stephen J. Ware, *Arbitration Clauses, Jury-Waiver Clauses, and Other Contractual Waivers of Constitutional Rights*, 67 LAW & CONTEMP. PROB. 167, 170–5 (2004) (asserting that "[A]rbitration-law standards of consent are contract-law standards of consent" and noting that critics of existing federal arbitration consent argue for a "more exacting" standard).

the Montana legislation at issue in *Casarotto* was inconsistent with the FAA and, therefore, preempted. Although I acknowledge the value of this distinction, the fact remains that both Montana and the FAA similarly mandate consent to arbitrate before a court can enforce an award. Simply because the standards of consent are more demanding under state law does not mean state law is preempted; the appropriate test for preemption does not look for differences between state and federal law. Federalism concerns should not permit the Supremacy Clause to condemn mere differences between state and federal arbitration law. Because application of the Montana statute created no substantial obstacle to arbitration – compliance would have been readily accomplished by revising the boilerplate Subway franchise contract – there is still no reason to think that *Casarotto* reached the correct result.

The decision in *Volt* represents a contrasting and more appropriate type of arbitration preemption analysis. *Volt* upheld the parties' choice of local law authorizing state courts to stay arbitration pending resolution of related litigation that may reach a preclusive ruling on common issues. In the *Volt* decision, the Supreme Court held that state arbitration law is preempted only where it "stands as an obstacle to the accomplishments and execution of the full purposes and objectives of Congress."[26] The majority opinion of Chief Justice Rehnquist viewed it within the parties' power to select a state arbitration procedure that was consistent with the FAA, noting "[T]here is no federal policy favoring arbitration under a certain set of procedural rules" and characterizing the choice of California law as designed "to make applicable state rules governing the conduct of arbitration – rules which are manifestly designed to encourage resort to the arbitral process."[27]

The obstacle test constitutes a much more normal variety of preemption inquiry because it focuses mainly on the purposes behind the seemingly conflicting laws involved and gives special attention to the exact goals behind the federal law at issue. This is the sort of preemption approach that the Supreme Court regularly uses but, for some reason, eschewed in the unfortunate *Casarotto* decision. The "obstacle test" was originated in *Hines v. Davidowitz* where the Court asked if application of state law "stands as

[26] *Volt, supra* Note 5, 489 U.S. at 477. For discussion of the limits of party choice of arbitration law, *see* Section 3.4, *infra*. Although I consider the important *Volt* decision as significant both to preemption law and party autonomy, these two facets of the opinion are not intertwined. The obstacle test, a garden variety, common preemption approach, should have been used even if there was no party choice of law presented.

[27] 489 U.S. at 476. The dissent of Justice Brennan viewed the parties' choice of local law to be one to select substantive law, which failed to incorporate a choice of California arbitration procedure due to the broad applicability of federal arbitration law. *Id.* at 488–92.

an obstacle to the accomplishment and execution of the full purposes and objectives of Congress."[28]

Ordinary, conventional preemption analysis is strikingly different than the unusual singling out test used by the *Casarotto* decision. The structure typically used in preemption cases necessarily focuses upon conflict – whether conflict exists between federal and inconsistent state law. According to Professor Tribe, preemption requires "actual conflict" between federal and state law such that "the federal and state enactments are directly and facially contradictory."[29] To be sure, the state and federal laws "need not be contradictory on their face" to activate preemption; state legislation can be preempted when there exists an actual conflict "with the precise objectives that underlie" federal law.[30] Careful attention to the goals behind federal law is a critical factor in any proper preemption examination and demonstrates appropriate sensitivity toward federalism policies. The presence of an actual conflict necessitates focus on the policy objectives presented. The pursuit of federal purpose is no less important when examining state laws that allegedly supplement federal law. There, "the Court has come to uphold state regulations that supplement federal efforts so long as compliance with the letter or effectuation of the purpose of the federal enactment is not likely to be significantly impeded by state law."[31] Under this approach, state law is not preempted unless "compliance with both federal and state law is a physical impossibility."[32]

Application of these most conventional tenets of preemption analysis to the *Casarotto* case would have led to a different result. Because the purpose and effect of the Montana legislation was to improve the quality of consent, there is no apparent inconsistency with federal law. The FAA was built around a policy goal of enforcing legitimate contracts to arbitrate and, therefore, relies heavily on the need for mutual consent. No conflict, literal or actual, exists between federal and state law. Moreover, the Montana law, designed to assure consent to arbitrate, fails to conflict with the similar objective of the FAA. The *Casarotto* decision's failure to use *Volt's* more

[28] 312 U.S. 52, 67 (1941).

[29] Laurence H. Tribe, AMERICAN CONSTITUTIONAL LAW 1179 (3d ed. 2000), citing *Savage v. Jones* 225 U.S. 501, 533 (1912) (asserting that state law is preempted where federal law "is in *actual conflict* with the law of the State") (emphasis added).

[30] *Id.* at 1181. Because the critical focus in such cases is conflict between federal and state law, this species of preemption has been isolated and appropriately dubbed "conflict preemption." *See, e.g.*, Kathleen Sullivan & Gerald Gunther, CONSTITUTIONAL LAW 329 (15th ed. 2004).

[31] *Id.* at 1195–6.

[32] *Florida Lime & Avocado Growers, Inc. v. Paul*, 373 U.S. 132, 142–3 (1963).

typical "obstacle" approach to preemption doomed it to an erroneous result. Far from "singling out" arbitration for different treatment, Montana sought only to supplement the quantity of information needed to achieve consent, the *sine qua non* of federal arbitration doctrine. Placing the arbitration clause on page one of a contract and requiring it to be printed in a noticeably large format aids the goals of the FAA by assuring true bilateral intent to arbitrate.[33] Complying with both the FAA and the relevant Montana legislation was not an impossibility. Most importantly, *Casarotto* contained not one word about the basic purposes behind the FAA. This omission is striking in a preemption holding and may help to explain how Montana's efforts to supplement the FAA's need for consent went so far awry.

Abandonment of the *Casarotto* "singling out" approach and replacing it with the more conventional "obstacle" preemption formula would lead to more constitutionally appropriate results and conclusions tempered with more attention to federalism. State arbitration law can serve as a source of useful experimentation in improving the overall status of arbitration doctrine.[34] In an ideal revised FAA, principles of federalism should be weighed carefully when a court confronts any preemption issue. Deference to state contract law must include a substantial dose of deference toward state arbitration regulation, provided that state arbitration principles do not frustrate the main goals of federal arbitration law.

Application of the obstacle test would have potentially changed the result of *Southland v. Keating* as well as *Casarotto*. In *Southland Corp v. Keating*, the Court found application of California's franchise law, which required franchise disputes to be litigated, to "undercut the enforceability of arbitration agreements."[35] The Supreme Court majority's rationale, which stressed the need to apply a broad federal arbitration law in state courts and eschewed a traditional preemption test, relied on broad pronouncements.[36] The correct inquiry should have been whether application of the FAA was intended by Congress and whether application of federal law would have harmed

[33] *See* Katherine Van Wezel Stone, *Rustic Justice: Community and Coercion Under the Federal Arbitration Act*, 77 N. Car. L. Rev. 931, 962 (1999) (asserting that "courts have applied attenuated notions of consent, compelling arbitration when consent is thin, if not outright fictitious").

[34] *See* David S. Schwartz, *Correcting Federalism Mistakes in Statutory Interpretation: The Supreme Court and the Federal Arbitration Act*, 67 Law & Contmep. Prob. 5, 15 (2004) (contending that "preemption of state [arbitration] law stifles state 'experimentation,' not only by nullifying laws on the books, but also by discouraging proposals to change the law").

[35] 465 U.S. 1, 16 (1984).

[36] *Id.* (concluding summarily that "California Franchise Investment Law violates the Supremacy Clause").

federalism interests. The *Southland* majority opinion avoided the federalism issue, causing Justice Stevens to note the laws at issue were "in a field traditionally occupied by State law"[37] and Justice O'Connor to correctly point out that the majority had run roughshod over state policy interests.[38] Because the states have historically regulated franchising, it is by no means certain that a strong state concern to keep franchise disputes in the courts should have been summarily rejected.[39]

Application of the obstacle test would yield results that sometimes vary those reached by a more aggressive singling out approach. Consider hypothetical state legislation that banned the enforceability of pre-dispute arbitration clauses. This legislation smacks of an unadulterated attack on arbitration and stands as an obstacle to the idea of arbitration. This legislation would be preempted under the conventional obstacle test. Consider also California's legislation mandating a degree of arbitrator disclosure in excess of that required by federal arbitration law[40] This legislation goes beyond the more passive federal disclosure standards by expanding disclosure requirements in consumer arbitration. Because the new law singles out arbitration for special treatment not afforded to other transactions, it would probably be preempted under the singling out test. Yet, it is questionable whether such enhanced disclosure stands as an obstacle to arbitration. Consumer groups strongly supported improved disclosure and may be less tempted to attack arbitration awards successfully where there is full information about the past experiences of the arbitrator. In other words, a more rigorous disclosure requirement advances the case for enforceability and seems consistent with the federal law. Various state arbitration laws that enhance notice to the non-drafting party about arbitration (e.g., big print or red ink arbitration clauses)[41] appear similar to the problem presented by *Casarotto* and would

[37] *Id.* at 18.

[38] Justice O'Connor's dissent noted that the federal courts should allow the states an opportunity to develop "their own methods for enforcing the new federal rights" and stressed the state courts' competence at enforcing federal rights. *Id.* at 32–3.

[39] It is also interesting to reconsider *Perry v. Thomas*, 482 U.S. 483 (1987), using the obstacle test and balancing federal and state interests with care. The regulation of wage and hour laws is the subject of cooperative federalism with both the states and federal government sharing the regulatory load. It is unclear whether forcing such wage disputes to be litigated in a California court would necessarily harm the arbitration enforcement purpose of the FAA.

[40] *See* Cal. Civ. Proc. Code §1281.5 (West Supp. 2002).

[41] *See, e.g.*, Cal Civ. Proc. Code §1298 (West 2004) (mandating that arbitration clauses in real estate conveyances be printed in at least eight point bold type); N.Y. Pub. Health Law §4406-a (McKinney 2001) (requiring that HMO contracts that contain an arbitration clause be printed in at least twelve point boldface above the signature line).

probably not be preempted because they improve the consent essential to arbitration.

A revised federal arbitration law should contain succinct directives concerning the relationship of federal and state arbitration law. It is clear, as it was in 1925, that there is no and should be no federal intent to preempt the field of arbitration regulation. The revised federal act must clarify that states may regulate arbitration, provided state rules do not stand as an obstacle to enforcing consensual agreements to arbitrate. Such a clear textual statutory command should facilitate more federalism-sensitive preemption decisions and help to avoid affronts to federalism such as Justice Ginsburg's unfortunate *Casarotto* opinion.

Use of the obstacle approach permits states to supplement the FAA in legislation designed to fill gaps in federal arbitration law. For example, the RUAA legislation on the "middle ground" of arbitration does not stand as an obstacle to the FAA but, instead, represents an admirable effort to supplement it.[42] It would be nonsensical to argue such helpful legislation is preempted by federal law. The obstacle test allows local experimentation, provided state law does not frustrate the basic goals of federal arbitration law.

Section 3.4 The Backdoor Choice of Arbitration Law: Application of State Law by Choice-of-Law

Without some reference to state law in a contract, there is likely to be no role for state arbitration law. The broad, expansive reading of federal law articulated in *Terminix* limits the normal application of state law to transactions purely local in nature. However, where the parties select local law in a contract, it may be possible for state arbitration law to apply in a backdoor manner.

The popularity of choice-of-law clauses[43] is unquestioned. These clauses help to achieve simplicity in an overly complex legal and business world by restricting the number of potentially applicable laws and thereby reducing the transaction costs of negotiating and contracting. Even boilerplate form contracts with little or no specificity commonly become very focused and particular by including choice-of-law clauses. Today choice-of-law clauses

[42] *See* Section 2.6(3), *supra* (summarizing RUAA legislation dealing with arbitrators and hearing procedure).

[43] By choice-of-law clause I mean a contractual selection of a particular state or nation's law to govern the agreement, whether that is the law governing the merits of the dispute or the law governing the arbitration. I also include the parties' choice of the norms of an arbitration provider such as the American Arbitration Association or the National Arbitration Forum.

are commonplace. Courts should habitually enforce choice-of-law bargains in order to advance the desires and autonomy of the contractual parties.[44]

Both the Uniform Commercial Code and the Restatement (Second) of Conflict of Laws specifically endorse party autonomy and the corresponding enforcement of the parties' choice-of-law selection. Section 187 of the Restatement (Second) calls for courts to apply the law selected by the parties, assuming the issue is one capable of being decided by an express contractual agreement.[45] Section 1–105 of the Uniform Commercial Code allows the contractual parties to stipulate the law to be applied if it bears a "reasonable relation" to a transaction.[46] Revised UCC §1–301 enhances party autonomy in business-to-business transactions by allowing the parties to select a choice of law without regard to whether the transaction bears a reasonable relationship to the state or country designated.[47] Although these provisions are not without exception, they provide a bedrock of substantial nature to advance policies of party autonomy.

Choice-of law clauses are the key to backdoor application of state arbitration legislation. Because courts routinely uphold choice-of-law designations, a choice of a state's law should embrace all of its laws, including state arbitration law. In this way state arbitration law becomes much more significant than the exceedingly narrow stature given to it in the *Terminix* decision.

On balance, there is little reason to become upset due to the backdoor selection of state arbitration legislation. First, the quality of state arbitration legislation is salutary. The recently passed RUAA reflects years of hard work to produce a contemporary, comprehensive arbitration statute containing useful regulation of remedies, discovery, pre-hearing procedure, arbitrator disclosure, waiver, and arbitrability.[48] Parties may be motivated to select a

[44] *See, e.g.*, Larry Kramer, *Rethinking Choice of Law*, 90 Colum. L. Rev. 277, 329–30 (1990) (setting forth autonomy reasons for upholding party choice of law generally and even where their choice might invalidate their contract).

[45] Restatement (Second) of Conflict of Laws §187(1) (1971).

[46] U.C.C. §1–105. Comment 1 explains that the parties will select the law of a state where a significant portion of the making or the performance of the contract takes place.

[47] *See* U.C.C. §1–301(c). This increase of party autonomy in commercial transactions fails to occur where "one of the parties to the transaction is a consumer." U.C.C. §1–301(e) (requiring a transaction to be connected to a state or country where one party is a consumer). Section 1–301 in the current Official Text of the Uniform Commercial Code is quite controversial. At this writing it has not been adopted by any state.

[48] For a detailed summary of the RUAA, *See* Section 2.6, *supra* (noting that the Preface to the RUAA lists fourteen subjects not covered by the original UAA). I refer to the RUAA for several reasons. It represents the most modern and up-to-date arbitration legislation in the United States and appears an improvement over the prior model law. In addition, eight states, Hawaii, New Jersey, New Mexico, Nevada, North Carolina, North Dakota, Oregon, and Utah, have already passed versions of the RUAA since its approval in 1999 and bills to adopt the RUAA are under consideration in seven other jurisdictions. *See* Michael D.

state version of the RUAA because it is an attractive bundle of arbitration default rules.

Second, as a normative principle courts should uphold the choice of the contracting parties, particularly in the arbitration area. Self-governance, a fundamental value supporting arbitration,[49] is advanced by upholding the parties' selection of law. This policy would suffer if courts were to begin questioning or challenging party choice-of-law. Just as party autonomy is a fundamental value underlying contract policies, routine court enforcement of choice of law clauses is a necessary part of a party's right to bargain freely and efficiently. The contractual parties own any disputes arising out of their bargain.[50]

Third, predictability is advanced by careful adherence to the parties' choice-of-law. Professor Reese's observation that "in contracts . . . there is but one basic policy: namely, protection of the expectations of the parties"[51] makes great sense. Parties rely on the anticipation that courts will uphold their contractual choice-of-law selection and need judicial enforcement of such clauses in order to achieve intended and predictable results.[52]

Reexamination of the potentially inconsistent decisions in *Volt* and *Mastrobuono v. Shearson Lehman Hutton, Inc.*[53] helps to inform the optimal level of state choice of law. In the *Volt* case, the Supreme Court interpreted the

Diamant & Elizabeth M. Zoller, *Strategies for Mediation, Arbitration and Other Forms of Alternative Dispute Resolution*, in ALI-ABA, Litigating Trademark, Domain Name, and Unfair Competition Cases 142–3 (2004). This growing number of state adoptions in a fairly short period indicates that the RUAA has achieved market acceptance and therefore merits some treatment in this chapter. *See generally* Heinsz, The Revised UAA, *supra* Note 9.

[49] *See* Section 1.1, *supra*. Arbitration represents the parties' delegation to a private decision maker of a hand-forged mode of disputing. *See* Stephen J. Ware, *Default Rules From Mandatory Rules: Privatizing Law Through Arbitration*, 83 MINN. L. REV. 703 (1999) (setting forth a view of existing arbitration legislation as a set of default rules that may be varied by contract); Lisa Bernstein, *Opting Out of the Legal System: Extralegal Contractual Relations in the Diamond Industry*, 32 J. LEGAL STUD. 115 (1992) (describing contracts between diamond merchants to appoint a third diamond merchant to decide a dispute); William Catron Jones, *Three Centuries of Commercial Arbitration in New York: A Brief Survey*, 1956 WASH. U. L. Q. 193, 217 (noting that the charter of the New York Cotton Exchange called for arbitration of disputes among member firms).

[50] See Carrie Menkel-Meadow, *Whose Dispute Is It Anyway? A Philosophical Defense of Settlement (In Some Cases)*, 83 GEO. L. J. 2663 (1995).

[51] Willis Reese, *Choice of Law in Torts and Contracts and Directions for the Future*, 16 COLUM. J. TRANS'L L. 21 (1977).

[52] Eugene F. Scoles et al., CONFLICT OF LAWS 857 (2d ed. 2000) (noting that "predictability is served, and party expectations are protected, by giving effect to the parties' own choice of the applicable law").

[53] 514 U.S. 52 (1995) (interpreting choice of law clause to allow arbitration panel to award punitive damages despite parties' choice of New York law which would ban panel authority to award punitive damages).

parties' choice of local law[54] to mean a choice of California state arbitration law as well as state substantive norms. The *Volt* reconciliation of state choice of law is significant because by the time of the 1989 decision in the case the Court had already made it clear in *Southland v. Keating*[55] that the FAA was a substantive statute. *Southland*, a significant decision that effectively federalized arbitration law, represented a ringing endorsement of broad applicability of federal arbitration law, even in the face of an ambiguous legislative history that gave little support for the expansive interpretation awarded by Justice Burger's *Southland* opinion.[56] In other words, the *Volt* decision could have easily ignored California arbitration procedure on the simple *Southland* theory that substantive federal law trumped state arbitration procedure. *Volt's* upholding of the parties' selection of state arbitration procedure is all the more significant in this context.

The path taken by the *Volt* decision was faithful to a full and optimal level of party autonomy. If the court had held that federal substantive arbitration law trumped state arbitration procedure, it would have blatantly disregarded the choice made by the parties and devalued the governing arbitration principle of party self-determination. *Volt* also advanced federalism policies by requiring that lower courts apply state law rather than look to a more uniform set of federal arbitration rules.[57] This result left open the possibility of varied and nonuniform application of grounds used to attack arbitrability.[58]

I admit that the choice of law interpretation made by the Court in its *Mastrobuono* decision appears inconsistent with the party autonomy rationale of *Volt*. In *Mastrobuono*, the Court interpreted the parties' selection of New York law in a way that acknowledged the parties' selection of state

[54] In fact, the standard form agreement of the American Institute of Architects signed in *Volt* did not expressly refer to California law but, instead, called for application of the law of the place where the project was located.

[55] *Supra* Note 35 (requiring that state courts apply Federal Arbitration Act and interpreting FAA to be substantive in nature).

[56] *Compare* Christopher R. Drahozal, *In Defense of Southland: Reexamining the Legislative History of the Federal Arbitration Act*, 78 Notre Dame L. Rev. 101 (2002) (challenging the conventional view that *Southland* misinterpreted the FAA's legislative history and concluding that the FAA has a ambiguous legislative history) with Ian R. Macneil, American Arbitration Law, *supra* Note 23 at 111–14, 117–19, 139 (1992) (characterizing *Southland* majority's interpretation of legislative history as "History be Damned!").

[57] *See* Ian R. Macneil et al., I Federal Arbitration Law: Agreements, Awards, and Remedies under the Federal Arbitration Act §14.7.1, at 14:43 (1994, supp) (concluding that *Volt* allowed the "repatriation to state law of many arbitration agreements otherwise governed by the FAA").

[58] *Id.* (noting that *Volt* permitted "state courts wide discretion to interpret the effect of choice of law clauses on the law to govern arbitration [and] opened wide the possibility of significantly differing state rules respecting interpretation of similar choice of law clauses").

substantive law but ignored state arbitration procedure. The *Mastrobuono* decision hinted that the parties reference to New York law "might include only New York substantive rights and obligations, and not the States's allocation of power between alternative tribunals."[59] Lower court decisions have interpreted *Mastrobuono* to mandate application of the FAA unless a party choice of state law is clear.[60] These cases effectively limit the application of the *Volt* decision by mandating a choice of law clause that explicitly refers to state arbitration law rather than the far more common generic choice of a particular state's law. Under this analysis a naked reference in a contract containing an arbitration clause to "the law of New York" would incorporate New York substantive laws and the FAA; the FAA is considered part of the state law chosen.[61] Such a broad reading of the *Mastrobuono* decision cautions counsel who desire a particular state's arbitration law to be specific in their choice of law reference and avoid using generic choice of law clauses.

This broad reading of the decision in *Mastrobuono* and narrow reading of the party autonomy trade-off reached in *Volt* ignores the overriding importance of self-determination in arbitration theory. When a contract calls for the application of state law, the contract must be construed as desiring all state law and not just a part of it. Any other result displays a weak vision of federalism principles inherent in party selection and represents a mistaken construction of the contract by rewriting the custom-forged wishes of the contracting parties. Such a result is also inconsistent with the fundamental premise of the FAA, to interpret arbitration agreements in the same manner as other contracts.[62] Contracts are interpreted as a single, integrated unit and are typically read to make sense as a whole.

Of course, the *Mastrobuono* decision supports the idea that the parties may opt out of federal arbitration law and, instead, choose to govern their future disputes using the rules of arbitration organizations such as the American Arbitration Association. At one level *Mastrobuono* merely interpreted the parties' agreement to uphold a choice of the norms of the

[59] *Supra* Note 53, 514 U.S. at 60.

[60] *See, e.g.*, *Roadway Package Sys., Inc. v. Kayser*, 257 F.3d 287, 288–9 (3d Cir.), *cert. denied*, 534 U.S. 1020 (2001) (general choice of law clause not effective to displace the FAA); *Wolsey Ltd. v. Foodmaker, Inc.*, 144 F.3d 1205, 1213 (9th Cir. 1998) (interpreting *Mastrobuono* to read that "general choice of law clauses do not incorporate state rules that govern the allocation of authority between courts and arbitrators").

[61] At the international arbitration level, a reference in an international contractual transaction containing an arbitration clause to "the law of the New York" would include New York substantive law and the New York Convention, which are part of New York law.

[62] *See* Note, *An Unnecessary Choice*, *supra* Note 13 at 2266 (suggesting that FAA basic purpose is to "treat arbitration agreements the same as any other contract").

National Association of Securities Dealers, thereby endorsing the parties' autonomy to bootstrap non-federal arbitration procedure. Although one can legitimately disagree about whether the interpretation in *Mastrobuono* was correct, there is no doubt the Supreme Court allowed parties broad latitude to select the rules that will govern any future dispute. The contract model of arbitration dominates the landscape and appropriately advances policies of freedom and party autonomy.

Section 3.5 The Power of the Parties to Vary Federal Law by Agreement

The overriding principle that parties possess self-governance authority to legislate the rules that may govern their future disputes is a major theme of this book. The existence of a robust power to write custom-forged rules (e.g., the creation of an appellate arbitration panel or the parties covenanting to ban any discovery) or to bootstrap the rules of an alternative arbitration system (e.g., apply AAA rules or state arbitration law) enriches the arbitration system and advances significant democratic tenets of freedom and party autonomy. Arbitration should profit by a degree of institutional competition between the providers of arbitration who desire the degree of legitimacy created when parties select the rules of a particular arbitration provider to govern the dispute.

The case for increased customization of arbitration agreements was recently set forth by Professor Tom Carbonneau.[63] Customized agreements to arbitrate, while potentially costly to negotiate and draft, can deliver more control to the parties than the risks associated with a boilerplate arbitration clause. Customized agreements can retain legal rights and achieve the desired level of procedural formality sought by the disputants. In Carbonneau's terms, "[C]ustomization allows parties to anticipate risks, to protect and secure their rights, and to exercise greater control over the arbitral process, the arbitrators, and the arbitral procedure."[64]

Assuming the validity of the previous paragraphs, what is the precise impact of federal arbitration law? Is legislation that can be readily varied and substituted for with the stroke of a pen worth the candle?[65]

[63] *See* Thomas E. Carbonneau, *The Exercise of Contract Freedom in the Making of Arbitration Agreements*, 36 Vand. J. Translat'l L. 1189 (2003) (cataloging various terms that the parties may want to add in a fully negotiated and comprehensive arbitration agreement).

[64] *Id.* at 1231.

[65] *See* Section 2.4(2)(B)(8), *supra* (asking whether the FAA "vests unvariable power in the courts or is it simply a variable framework that facilitates arbitration?").

The answer to the previous rhetorical questions is resoundingly affirmative. We regard arbitration legislation as close to entirely permissive. Under this interpretation parties are generally free to change the terms of arbitration by agreement. Party-crafted solutions trump the legal norms governing arbitration in all but isolated circumstances. As depicted elsewhere by Professor Ware, there are two types of arbitration rules: (a) those that are mandatory and fixed and incapable of variance by the parties to a contract and (b) those that constitute default rules and apply only if the parties to an agreement have not legislated to the contrary in their contract.[66]

We suspect that the default style rules grossly outnumber the rules that cannot be varied. In a world increasingly characterized by deregulation and freedom, the emergence of an arbitration system that recognizes a healthy dose of default rules appears very sensible.

The current debate about whether courts should enforce party agreements for heightened judicial review of arbitration awards illustrates the dichotomy between default rules and mandatory rules. At present there is a split in federal circuits on this question. Several circuits appear willing to uphold the agreement of arbitration parties to elevate the degree of judicial review beyond the minimal requirements of §10(a)(1)–(4) of the FAA.[67] These decisions regard the FAA section on judicial review as a default rule capable of variance by the parties. In contrast, several circuits have resolved this question by disregarding the agreement of the parties, reasoning that the terms of the FAA regarding judicial review cannot be changed by contract.[68]

The former position, characterizing judicial review as a default arbitration norm, reaches the correct result. The policy values set out in Chapter 1 strongly support allowing the parties to contractually regulate the award review process. Arbitration belongs to the disputants who should be able to control arbitration procedure. The contract model of arbitration insists that contracting parties are free to shape the of nature of their arbitration

[66] *See* Section 4.4(2)(B), *infra*, where this distinction is developed.

[67] *See, e.g., Harris v. Parker Coll. of Chiropractic*, 286 F.3d 790, 794 (5th Cir. 2002) (enforcing the parties' agreement for expanded review); *Roadway Package Sys., Inc. v. Kayser*, 257 F.3d 287, 292 (3d Cir.), *cert. denied*, 534 U.S. 1020 (2001) (holding that FAA supports enhanced review contracted for by the parties).

[68] *See, e.g., Kyocera Corp. v. Prudential-Bache Trade Services*, 341 F.3d 987 (9th Cir. 2003), *cert. dismissed*, 540 U.S. 1098 (2004) (*en banc*) (holding parties have no power to by agreement to expand scope of review under FAA §10); *Bowen v. Amoco Pipeline Co.*, 254 F.3d 925, 935–7 (10th Cir. 2001) (concluding that expanded review beyond the terms explicitly set out by the FAA violates federal arbitration policy); *UHC Mgmt. Co. v. Computer Sciences. Corp.*, 148 F.3d 992, 998 (8th Cir. 1998) (explaining in *dicta* that expanded review prevented under the FAA).

arrangement. Refusing to enforce the parties' agreement to increase judicial review flies in the face of the original intent of the FAA – to uphold and enforce the parties' arbitration bargain.

Party self-autonomy values are advanced by decisions willing to enforce contractually enhanced review. Related self-governance values are frustrated by imposing a mandatory, monolithic model of review upon unwilling parties. Refusing to honor the parties' agreement on review undermines party control over the arbitration process and usurps the very notion of arbitral power – party authority to write a contract that establishes a mode of disputing.[69] Such a refusal smacks of the heavy-handed state telling business parties that there is only a single flavor of arbitration that must apply to all disputes.

Critics of enhanced judicial review argue that enforcement of bargains beyond the FAA minimum will greatly increase the workload of the court system. This argument is both unfounded and irrelevant. Although it is true that some repeat player arbitration parties are increasingly concerned with awards that do not adhere to the law, it is unlikely that most arbitration parties will want to pay the increased costs, including delay and opportunity costs, associated with contracting for enhanced review. Arbitration finality is an attractive value that many parties will want to retain. Allowing enhanced review, while attractive to isolated arbitration participants, is unlikely to clog the judiciary. The vast percentage of arbitration users use a boilerplate, abbreviated arbitration clause that bears no resemblance to a contract for enhanced review. For these reasons, a revised federal arbitration law should

[69] *See* Section 2.4(2)(B)(8), *supra*. The weight of academic commentary on this dispute appears to support court enforcement of enhanced review. *See, e.g.*, Sarah R. Cole, *Managerial Litigants? The Overlooked Problem of Party Autonomy in Dispute Resolution*, 51 HASTINGS L. J. 1199 (2000) (reasoning that party autonomy policies require courts to enforce contracts for enhanced review); Edward Brunet, *Replacing Folklore Arbitration with a Contract Model of Arbitration*, 74 TUL. L. REV. 39(1999) (contending that policies underlying arbitration should cause courts to enforce bargains for enhanced judicial review); Alan Rau, *Contracting Out of the Arbitration Act*, 8 AM. REV. INT'L ARB. 225 (1997) (arguing that §10 of the FAA is a default mechanism that can be varied by contract), Stephen J. Ware, *"Opt-In" for Judicial Review of Errors of Law Under the Revised Uniform Arbitration Act*, 8 AM. REV. INT'L ARB. 263 (1997) (reasoning that courts should enforce agreements for enhanced review in order to increase the confidence of parties that awards will correctly follow legal principles). For contrary reasoning, *See* Amy J. Schmitz, *Ending a Mud Bowl: Defining Arbitration's Finality Through Functional Analysis*, 37 GA. L. REV. 123 (2002) (asserting that "functional" arbitration requires minimal review set forth by the FAA); Hans Smit, *Contractual Modification of the Scope of Judicial Review of Arbitral Awards*, 8 AM. REV. INT'L ARB. 147 (1997) (contending that expanded review is incompatible with the nature of the arbitration mechanism).

follow the path taken by England and grant the parties express powers to seek enhanced review.[70]

Some critics of enhanced review argue that only courts should be able to expand the workload of a federal judge. This line of reasoning views contracts mandating enhanced judicial review as beyond the express powers of the federal courts. Judge Posner questions enhanced review because "federal jurisdiction cannot be created by contract."[71]

This reasoning ignores the express subject matter jurisdiction powers conferred on federal courts by Congress. Federal courts receive their power to hear any case involving arbitration through legislative act[72] and not by contract. Moreover, the FAA has always permitted judicial review of arbitrators' acts beyond the powers set out in the parties' agreement.[73] The established review of conduct beyond the parameters articulated by the parties signals that the original drafters of the FAA intended broad powers for the arbitration disputants, including the ability to have a court assess whether arbitrators have acted beyond the scope of their authority.[74] Section 10(a)(4) of the FAA invites the arbitral parties to place limits on the powers of arbitrators and fails to circumscribe the breadth of such limitations.

Preemption serves as a check to limit the scope of arbitration party autonomy. For example, it would not be possible for the parties to choose a state law that bars enforceability of pre-dispute arbitration agreements. Such state legislation stands as an obstacle to arbitration and, accordingly, would be preempted under the test previously set out in this chapter.[75] Short of

[70] *See* William W. Park, *The Interaction of Courts and Arbitrators in England: The 1996 Act as a Model for the United States*, 1 Int'l Arb. L. Rev. 54, 58 (1998) (explaining party autonomy in the 1996 English Arbitration Act, legislation that confers power on the parties to opt to have their awards reviewed for errors of law).

[71] *Chicago Typographical Union No. 16 v. Chicago Sun-Times, Inc.*, 935 F.2d 1501, 1505 (7th Cir. 1991).

[72] *See, e.g.*, 28 U.S.C. §§1331, 1332 (conferring federal question and diversity subject matter jurisdiction). Chapter 1 of the FAA itself has been interpreted to not trigger federal jurisdiction under §1331. *See, e.g., Moses H. Cone Memorial Hosp.v. Mercury Constr. Corp.*, 460 U.S. 1, 25 (1983). Actions arising under the New York Convention, however, create subject matter jurisdiction. 9 U.S.C. §203.

[73] 9 U.S.C. §10(a)(4) (permitting a court to vacate an award "where the arbitrators exceeded their powers").

[74] *See, e.g., Metropolitan Waste Control Comm'n v. City of Minnetonka*, 242 N.W. 2d 830, 830–3 (Minn. 1976) (providing enhanced review by contract and noting that expanded review was to determine if the arbitrators exceeded their powers).

[75] *See* Section 3.3, *supra* (arguing that a typical "obstacle" style preemption test be used to test the validity of state law and that the "singling-out" approach used in *Casarotto* be discarded).

preemption, parties should be free to vary the norms set out in a revised FAA and go beyond what I see as a set of federal default arbitration rules. Expansive party agreements are likely to be the exception because of the expense associated with both drafting and policing such tailor-made arbitration norms. In this conception of arbitration that honors party autonomy, federal law is largely limited to situations where the parties use a simple and boilerplate arbitration clause; federal law amounts to a set of norms that can be varied by agreement.

Section 3.6 Reevaluating the Incorporation of State Law through a Savings Clause

A second backdoor exists that permits wide application of state law in everyday arbitrations governed by the FAA. Under the so-called savings clause of section two of the FAA, a party to an arbitration clause may challenge enforcement of arbitration on various legal grounds.[76] Recent decisions illustrate that contemporary courts are more than willing to strike down arbitration agreements for reasons of unconscionability, adhesive terms, lack of mutuality, and breach of the covenant of good faith and fair dealing.[77] These decisions, which appear consistent with the FAA under the savings clause, bootstrap state law and eschew the application of federal law when applying the savings clause. Although the FAA is silent as to whether the "grounds" for non-application of the FAA are state or federal, a series of decisions apply state contract law to non-enforcement issues with little or no discussion of the significant federalism issues involved.[78] Even the Supreme Court failed to provide an express rationale for interpreting the savings clause to require application of state law substantive principles when it correctly observed in *Perry v. Thomas* that "state law, whether of legislative or judicial origin, is applicable . . . to govern the validity, revocability, and enforceablity of contracts generally."[79]

[76] 9 U.S.C. §2 (requiring courts to enforce arbitration agreements "save on grounds as exist in law or in equity for the revocation of any contract.").

[77] *See, e.g., Ingle v. Circuit City*, 328 F.3d 1165 (9th Cir. 2003), *cert. denied*, 540 U.S. 1160 (2004) (affirming trial court refusal to compel arbitration of an employment discrimination claim on grounds of substantive and procedural unconscionability under state law).

[78] *See, e.g., Rosenberg v. Merrill Lynch, Pierce, Fenner & Smith, Inc.*, 170 F.3d 1, 19 (1st Cir. 1999) (concluding summarily that state contract law is to govern the existence of an arbitration agreement).

[79] 482 U.S. 483, 492 n.9 (1987).

Assuming that a reformed FAA would include a savings clause,[80] there remains the separate question of whether grounds used to challenge signed arbitration clauses should be federal or state in nature. It would, of course, be constitutional for Congress to specify particular grounds for attacking arbitration agreements in the text of a revised FAA and thereby intentionally federalize a substantial portion of arbitration law. The clear "commerce-in-fact" impact of most arbitration clauses triggers federal authority to legislate. But passing constitutional muster is easy. The harder question is which arbitration values would be gained or lost by federalizing the backdoor application of state law, which presently allows courts to use state contract rules when deciding savings clause issues.

The uniformity value is central to resolution of this question. It could be argued that federalizing the savings clause doctrine would permit judges to apply one uniform set of federal norms each time a party attacks an agreement to arbitrate. This solution is arguably efficient. Rather than look to various potential state laws, a judge would simply look to one uniform group of federal decisions each time an attack on arbitration emerged. This solution also possesses the virtue of simplicity because federal law governs the FAA.

Upon reflection however, the gains associated with federalizing the savings clause doctrine may be ephemeral. Generally, no choice of law question exists as to which of two or more systems of state contract law govern a savings clause attack. Instead, the typical contract to arbitrate will identify the law of a single state, often the state of contracting. The difficulty of researching an identified state contract law is unlikely to be great. Assuming the FAA applies in state court actions,[81] state judges will be familiar with state contract rules and comfortable interpreting them as part of an FAA savings clause construction. Federal judges face similar routine interpretations of state contract law in federal diversity actions and are unlikely to find application of state law overly demanding.

[80] This is a realistic assumption. It is hard to imagine that contract law principles should not apply to agreements to arbitrate. Any party to an arbitration agreement should be free to argue that the agreement process is flawed.

[81] *See Southland v. Keating*, 465 U.S. 1 (1984) (interpreting the FAA to apply universally in the United States courts and also in the state courts). Of course, our normative approach to arbitration law leaves open the question of whether a revised FAA should apply in state court actions. Because most litigation is state in nature, a choice to depart from the *Southland* rule and to let state courts apply their own arbitration law as a default mechanism would necessarily mean that the revised FAA would have less applicability than the present version of this law. Professor Ware discusses this issue and proposes a solution in Section 4.5, *infra*.

Moreover, the task of creating new federal law on questions like contracts of adhesion and unconscionability would itself be costly and potentially inefficient. Even the Uniform Commercial Code, a document drafted to provide ready answers to rough questions, leaves issues such as the definition of unconscionablility to the courts.[82] Accordingly, a revised FAA could leave such questions to the expensive and complicated process of case law development. But busy federal judges might well ponder why they must make new federal law when potentially familiar and settled law is there for the asking, often in their own states.

The appropriate analogy would look to the process of whether to create federal common law. In *United States v. Kimbell Foods, Inc.*[83] the Supreme Court articulated a utilitarian approach to decide whether to federalize a question. Relying somewhat on a test announced decades previously in *United States v. Yazell*,[84] the Court observed that one single federal rule should be forged where a federal program was necessarily uniform in nature. Under this approach uniformity became the focus of the analysis. In contrast, where there is a lack of necessity for a nationally uniform law, *Kimbell Foods* called for incorporation of state law as the rule of decision.[85] As wisely stated by Justice Marshall, "a court should endeavor to fill the interstices of federal remedial schemes with uniform federal rules only when the scheme in question evidences a distinct need for a nationwide legal standard."[86]

Application of the *Kimbell Foods* yardstick to the savings clause issue counsels courts to incorporate state law. The need for uniformity in savings clause doctrine is minimal, particularly in view of the costs of creating new federal solutions. A strong tradition of using state contract law universally in federal diversity actions exists. Moreover, apart from government contract law, almost all contract law is state law. There is a decades old custom to look to state contract law for solutions. It is inefficient for courts to make complicated laws when state law doctrine already exists and is there for the taking. State law, not federal, needs to remain as the appropriate rule of decision in interpretations of savings clause issues.

[82] *See, e.g.*, UCC 2-302 (providing an unconscionability doctrine but not including a definition); Arthur Leff, *Unconscionability and the Code – The Emperor's New Clause*, 115 U. Pa. L. Rev. 485 (1967) (criticizing the ambiguity and lack of content of unconscionability).

[83] 440 U.S. 715 (1979).

[84] 382 U.S. 301 (1947).

[85] 440 U.S. at 728 (noting that "when there is little need for a nationally uniform body of law, state law may be incorporated as the appropriate rule of decision").

[86] *Kamen v. Kemper Financial Services, Inc.*, 500 U.S. 90, 98 (1991) (declining to fashion a federal common law rule in federal derivative actions).

Section 3.7 Conclusion: The Need for Legislative Action

Several conclusions can be drawn from the previous discussion. Courts should use a normal preemption analysis that focuses on the intent behind federal arbitration law. The strange "singling out" test should be abandoned. State arbitration law should remain applicable where the parties knowingly select its application. Courts need to enforce choice of law clauses evidencing party intent to apply state law based on the arbitration value of party self-autonomy. State law should also explicitly govern when parties attack an agreement to arbitrate. Rather than make new federal law to govern traditional contract doctrines such as unconscionability and contracts of adhesion, the ideal federal arbitration law should continue to bootstrap the application of state law by specifying that valuable and familiar tenets of state contract principles apply in constructions of the revised FAA. Last, where the parties have not made a choice of law, federal arbitration law should apply to all transactions where there is an effect on interstate commerce. The broad sweep of a revised federal arbitration law is a healthy and efficient development that simplifies arbitration, and is desirable.

Many of these recommended changes could be accomplished by simple additions to federal arbitration legislation. In particular, the FAA should be amended to provide that state law should not be preempted for merely treating arbitration agreements differently than other contracts. In other words, the singling-out test should be put to death legislatively. State arbitration law should be free to legislate rules that single out arbitration, provided they do not conflict with the policies advanced by the FAA's mission to enforce contracts to arbitrate. In order to prevent use of the wayward "singling out" formula, federal arbitration law should boldly proclaim that states may legislate in the arbitration arena, provided that state law does not present an obstacle to the objectives of federal arbitration law. This language would clearly signal that states can regulate intrastate arbitration and eliminate any possibility of so-called field preemption.

Congress has this legislative power and should exercise it. There is no question that the prevailing inquiry in matters of preemption is and should be to probe federal legislative intent.[87] Many states have notice legislation like that preempted in *Cassarotto* that seeks to warn the potential contract party

[87] *See, e.g., Pacific Gas & Elec. Co. v. State Energy Resources Conservation & Development Comm'n*, 461 U.S. 190 (1983) (asserting that legislative intent a prime determinant in preemption cases).

of the impact of signing a contract containing an arbitration clause. Such statutes are largely compatible with the FAA because they aim to produce informed consent of the parties, consent that is a requisite to achieve the federal goal of enforceable agreements to arbitrate. State notice arbitration legislation is compatible with this federal purpose and, for that reason, should not be preempted.

CHAPTER FOUR

Interstate Arbitration: Chapter 1 of the Federal Arbitration Act

Stephen J. Ware

Section 4.1 Introduction: The Contractual Approach to Arbitration Law

This chapter consists of proposals to reform the Federal Arbitration Act (FAA). These proposed reforms address only domestic (United States) arbitration law, which is covered by Chapter 1 of the FAA.[1] These reforms do not address the law governing international arbitration, which is covered by Chapters 2 and 3 of the FAA,[2] as well as by various treaties including the Convention on the Recognition and Enforcement of Foreign Arbitral Awards.[3]

These proposed reforms rest on what I call the contractual approach to arbitration law. This approach consists of at least three principles. Stated colloquially, these principles are that: (1) you should not be sent to arbitration unless you have agreed to be there, (2) if you have agreed to arbitration then your agreement should be enforced, and (3) your arbitrator's powers are only those that you and the other party to the agreement gave the arbitrator. Stated more precisely, these three principles of the contractual approach to arbitration law are:

> **First Principle:** a court should not send a dispute to arbitration unless the parties have formed an enforceable contract requiring arbitration of that dispute.
>
> **Second Principle:** arbitration agreements should be enforced "save upon such grounds as exist at law or in equity for the revocation of any contract."[4]
>
> **Third Principle:** because an arbitrator's power derives from the parties' contract, the arbitrator should not be permitted to reach a result that the parties could not have reached themselves by simply contracting for it.

[1] 9 U.S.C. §§1–16 (2000).
[2] 9 U.S.C. §§201–08, 301–07 (2000).
[3] International arbitration is discussed in Chapter 6 of this book.
[4] 9 U.S.C. §2 (2000).

The FAA very much embodies this contractual approach to arbitration law, as do most of the Supreme Court's arbitration decisions over the last twenty years or so.[5] Therefore, I see little to change in arbitration law generally or, more specifically, in the FAA. However, there are some reforms to the FAA that would be worthwhile to advance the three just-stated principles of the contractual approach to arbitration law.

One reform, repeal of the separability doctrine, would correct the Supreme Court's one departure from the first principle – a court should not send a dispute to arbitration unless the parties have formed an enforceable contract requiring arbitration of that dispute.

Four reforms would advance the second principle – arbitration agreements should be enforced "save upon such grounds as exist at law or in equity for the revocation of any contract." One of these reforms would advance this principle by repealing the FAA's exclusion of some employment agreements from its scope. The other three would advance this principle by resolving in favor of enforceability issues about which the FAA and/or current case law are unclear. These issues are: (1) the enforceability of agreements to arbitrate disputes that do not arise out of the contract containing the arbitration clause, (2) the enforceability of electronic agreements to arbitrate, and (3) the enforceability of agreements specifying grounds for vacating arbitration awards.

Two reforms are necessary to effectuate the third principle stated earlier – the principle that, because an arbitrator's power derives from the parties' contract, the arbitrator should not be permitted to reach a result that the parties could not have reached themselves by simply contracting for it. One of these reforms would eliminate court enforcement of arbitration subpoenas, while the other would institute de novo judicial review of arbitrator's rulings on claims arising out of mandatory law.

Finally, the last reform would both strengthen the contractual approach to arbitration law and clarify the scope of the FAA. This reform would clarify

[5] *See, e.g., Green Tree Financial Corp. v. Bazzle*, 539 U.S. 444 (2003); *PacifiCare Health Systems, Inc. v. Book*, 538 U.S. 401 (2003); *Howsam v. Dean Witter Reynolds, Inc.*, 537 U.S. 79 (2002); *Circuit City Stores, Inc. v. Adams*, 532 U.S. 105 (2001); *Green Tree Financial Corp. v. Randolph*, 531 U.S. 79 (2000); *Doctor's Assocs, Inc. v. Casarotto*, 517 U.S. 681 (1996); *Vimar Seguros y Reaseguros, S.A. v. M/V Sky Reefer*, 515 U.S. 528 (1995); *First Options of Chicago, Inc. v. Kaplan*, 514 U.S. 938 (1995); *Mastrobuono v. Shearson Lehman Hutton, Inc.*, 514 U.S. 52 (1995); *Allied-Bruce Terminix Cos., Inc. v. Dobson*, 513 U.S. 265 (1995); *Gilmer v. Interstate/Johnson Lane Corp.*, 500 U.S. 20 (1991); *Volt Info. Sciences, Inc. v. Board of Trustees*, 489 U.S. 468 (1989); *Shearson/American Express Inc. v. McMahon*, 482 U.S. 220 (1987); *Perry v. Thomas*, 482 U.S. 483 (1987); *AT&T Technologies, Inc. v. Communications Workers of Am.*, 475 U.S. 643 (1986); *Mitsubishi Motors Corp. v. Soler Chrysler-Plymouth, Inc.*, 473 U.S. 614 (1985); *Southland Corp. v. Keating*, 465 U.S. 1 (1984).

that the FAA's first two sections apply in state and federal court but that its remaining sections apply only in federal court.

In sum, this chapter proposes several reforms to the FAA. These reforms are based on the contractual approach to arbitration law. Thus, they are unlikely to satisfy those who oppose the contractual approach with the belief that enforcement of arbitration agreements is a way for Big Business to oppress consumers, employees, and other "little guys."[6] Nor are these proposed reforms likely to satisfy those who want arbitration to be governed by a comprehensive statutory code addressing the full range of issues in arbitration law. The FAA is a concise statute that addresses some of the most important questions of arbitration law, while leaving many other questions open for courts to resolve through developing case law. These proposals are written with an eye to keeping it that way, and even to preserving the organization and style of the original FAA.

What follows is a discussion of each of these proposals to reform various portions of FAA Chapter 1. Appendix A consists of a draft statute, "Ware's Revised Federal Arbitration Act," incorporating these proposed reforms.

Section 4.2 Ensure the Contractual Basis of Arbitration

4.2(1) Current Law: The "Separability" Doctrine

The first principle of the contractual approach to arbitration law is that a court should not send a dispute to arbitration unless the parties have formed an enforceable contract requiring arbitration of that dispute. Current law fails to live up to this principle because current law contains the separability doctrine.[7] The separability doctrine was adopted by the Supreme Court in

[6] *See, e.g.*, Jean R. Sternlight, *Panacea or Corporate Tool?: Debunking the Supreme Court's Preference for Binding Arbitration*, 74 Wash. U. L.Q. 637, 637 (1996) (*Attention All Consumers, Employees, Franchisees, and 'Little Guys'*). *See also* Paul D. Carrington & Paul H. Haagen, *Contract and Jurisdiction*, 1996 Sup. Ct. Rev. 331 (describing consumer arbitration agreements, not as products of mutual consent, but as "predation" by those with "economic power" on those lacking such power); Jere Beasley, *The Jere Beasley Consumer Report* 1 (Sept. 1, 1999) ("The spread of binding arbitration in consumer transactions is absolutely the worst possible attack on all Alabamians that I have experienced in recent years. Our political leaders have a moral duty to right this wrong.")

[7] The related doctrine of competence-competence, at least as adopted by some countries, also violates the principle that a court should not send a dispute to arbitration unless the parties have formed an enforceable contract requiring arbitration of that dispute.

> The concept referred to as compétence-compétence (literally "jurisdiction concerning jurisdiction") links together a constellation of disparate notions about when arbitrators can rule on the limits of their own power. In its simplest formulation, compétence-compétence means no more than that arbitrators can look into their own jurisdiction without waiting

Prima Paint Corp. v. Flood & Conklin Manufacturing Co.[8] The facts of that case are as follows. F&C sold to Prima Paint a list of F&C's customers and promised not to sell paint to these customers for six years. F&C also promised to act as a consultant to Prima Paint during these six years. This consulting agreement included an arbitration clause which called for arbitration of any disputes arising out of the agreement. Prima Paint did not make the payments required by the consulting agreement. Prima Paint's defense to nonpayment was that F&C had fraudulently represented that it was solvent and able to perform its duties under the contract, but, in fact, was insolvent and intended to file for bankruptcy shortly after executing its consulting agreement with Prima Paint.

F&C served upon Prima Paint a demand for arbitration. Prima Paint then sued in federal court seeking rescission of the consulting agreement (due to the alleged misrepresentation) and an order enjoining F&C from proceeding with arbitration. F&C cross-moved to stay the suit pending arbitration. The trial court granted F&C's motion, staying Prima Paint's suit pending arbitration. The Supreme Court affirmed.

> for a court to do so. In other words, there is no need to stop arbitral proceedings to refer a jurisdictional issue to judges. However, under this brand of compétence-compétence, the arbitrators' determination about their power would be subject to judicial review at any time, whether after an award is rendered or when a motion is made to stay court proceedings or to compel arbitration.
>
> French law goes further and delays court review of arbitral jurisdiction until after an award is rendered. If an arbitral tribunal has already begun to hear a matter, courts must decline to hear the case. When an arbitral tribunal has not yet been constituted, court litigation will go forward only if the alleged arbitration agreement is clearly void (manifestement nulle).

William W. Park, *Bridging the Gap in Forum Selection: Harmonizing Arbitration and Court Selection*, 8 TRANS'L L. & CONTEMP. PROBS. 19, 46–7 (1998). The French version of competence-competence may be inconsistent with the principle that a court should not send a dispute to arbitration unless the parties have formed an enforceable contract requiring arbitration of that dispute. The French version is inconsistent with this principle to the extent the French version prevents a court from considering challenges to an arbitration agreement's existence or scope until after the arbitrator has done so. *See* Note 27, *infra*, and accompanying text.

By contrast, the simple version of competence-competence (in the first quoted paragraph) is consistent with the principle. Also consistent with this principle is court enforcement of agreements submitting to the arbitrator the power to decide the arbitrator's jurisdiction. Such enforcement is blessed by *First Options of Chicago, Inc. v. Kaplan*, 514 U.S. 938, 946–47 (1995), and *AT&T Technologies, Inc. v. Communications Workers of Am.*, 475 U.S. 643 (1986). On the other hand, if the parties dispute whether their agreement *does* submit to the arbitrator the power to decide the arbitrator's jurisdiction, then a court must resolve *that* dispute or its risks sending a dispute to arbitration even though the parties have not formed an enforceable contract requiring arbitration of that dispute.

These issues in international arbitration are discussed in Section 6.4(5), *infra*.

[8] 388 U.S. 395 (1967). Lower courts had adopted it earlier. *See, e.g.*, Arthur Nussbaum, *The Separability Doctrine in American and Foreign Arbitration*, 17 N.Y.U.L.Q. 609, 615 (1940) ("On the whole, it may be said that the separability doctrine has gained a solid footing in this country.") *See* Section 2.4(2)(B)(6), *supra*, discussing the separability doctrine.

Although the Court ruled against Prima Paint, the Court did not address Prima Paint's argument that F&C fraudulently induced Prima Paint to sign the consulting agreement. The Court held that this argument should be addressed by the arbitrator, rather than a court. In other words, the Court held that Prima Paint must go to arbitration to defend against F&C's claim for breach of contract and to assert its defense that the allegedly-breached contract was induced by F&C's fraudulent misrepresentation.

The Court stated that this result is required by FAA Section 4, which provides that if

> [a] party [claims to be] aggrieved by the alleged failure . . . of another to arbitrate . . . [t]he court shall hear the parties, and upon being satisfied that the making of the agreement for arbitration or the failure to comply therewith is not in issue, the court shall make an order directing the parties to proceed to arbitration. . . . If the making of the arbitration agreement or the failure, neglect, or refusal to perform the same be in issue, the court shall proceed summarily to the trial thereof.[9]

This provision says that the court shall not order the parties to arbitration if "the making of the arbitration agreement" is in issue. If the making of the arbitration agreement is in issue then the court proceeds to trial on that issue. If the trial determines that an arbitration agreement was made then the court orders the parties to arbitration. Conversely, if the trial determines that an arbitration agreement was not made then the court does not order the parties to arbitration.

The Supreme Court held that Prima Paint was not entitled to a trial on the question of whether an arbitration agreement was made.[10] Prima Paint was not entitled to such a trial because its allegations of fraudulent inducement did not put in issue the question of whether an "arbitration agreement" was made. The term "arbitration agreement," as used in FAA Section 4, refers specifically to the arbitration clause itself, not more broadly to the consulting contract of which the arbitration clause was a part. The Supreme Court held that if Prima Paint had argued there was fraud "directed to the arbitration clause itself,"[11] then the making of the arbitration agreement would have been at issue and Prima Paint would have been entitled to a trial on that issue, but FAA Section 4 "does not permit the court to consider arguments of fraud in the inducement of the contract generally."[12]

[9] 9 U.S.C. §4 (2000).
[10] *Prima Paint*, *supra* Note 8, 388 U.S. at 404.
[11] 388 U.S. at 402.
[12] 388 U.S. at 404.

This holding is known as the "separability doctrine" because it treats the arbitration clause as if it is a separate contract from the contract containing the arbitration clause, that is, the "container contract."[13] The *Prima Paint* Court endorsed the view that

> arbitration clauses as a matter of federal law are "separable" from the contracts in which they are embedded, and that where no claim is made that fraud was directed to the arbitration clause itself, a broad arbitration clause will be held to encompass arbitration of the claim that the contract itself was induced by fraud.[14]

Although *Prima Paint* is the only Supreme Court case applying the separability doctrine, lower courts have expanded the doctrine beyond fraudulent misrepresentation. Many courts agree with the First Circuit's understanding that

> [t]he teaching of Prima Paint is that a federal court must not remove from the arbitrators consideration of a substantive challenge to a contract unless there has been an independent challenge to the making of the arbitration clause itself. The basis of the underlying challenge to the contract does not alter the severability principle.[15]

Following this understanding, courts have applied the separability doctrine to order to arbitration parties who allege defenses to contract enforcement other than misrepresentation (such as duress, undue influence or overreaching, mistake, frustration of purpose) and even parties who allege that no contract was formed at all because of illegality or lack of capacity.[16] The Supreme Court has indicated, however, that courts should not order to arbitration a party who says that he never manifested assent to the alleged arbitration agreement.[17]

[13] *Id.* at 402. In international arbitration, the separability doctrine is generally known as the "autonomy" principle. *See, e.g.*, W. Laurence Craig, William Park & Jan Paulsson, INTERNATIONAL CHAMBER OF COMMERCE ARBITRATION §5.04 (3d ed. 2000).

[14] 388 U.S. at 402.

[15] *Unionmutual Stock Life Insurance Co. of America v. Beneficial Life Insurance Co.*, 774 F.2d 524, 529 (1st Cir. 1985).

[16] Ian R. Macneil, Richard E. Speidel, & Thomas Stipanowich, FEDERAL ARBITRATION LAW: AGREEMENTS, AWARDS AND REMEDIES UNDER THE FEDERAL ARBITRATION ACT §15.3.2 (1994 & Supp. 1999) (hereafter cited as Macneil et al., FEDERAL ARBITRATION LAW).

[17] *First Options of Chicago, Inc. v. Kaplan*, 514 U.S. 938 (1995). *See also Howsam v. Dean Witter Reynolds, Inc.*, 537 U.S. 79, 82 (2002) ("a gateway dispute about whether the parties are bound by a given arbitration clause raises a 'question of arbitrability' for a court to decide," citing *First Options*).

There has been controversy over whether *First Options* is inconsistent with, or at least in tension with, *Prima Paint.* Compare, e.g., Richard C. Reuben, *First Options, Consent*

4.2(2) Recommendation

The separability doctrine should be repealed because it violates a principle of the contractual approach to arbitration law, the principle that no dispute should be sent to arbitration unless the parties have formed an enforceable contract requiring arbitration of that dispute.[18] If F&C did, in fact, fraudulently induce Prima Paint to sign the consulting agreement, then the Court sent Prima Paint to arbitration even though Prima Paint did not form an *enforceable* contract to arbitrate. The only way to avoid this problem is for courts to hear challenges to the enforceability of the contract to arbitrate, that is, the container contract. Courts should send cases to arbitration only after rejecting any such challenges.

This repeal of the separability doctrine can be accomplished by changing the wording of FAA Section 4.[19] Instead of Section 4 sending cases to arbitration when the court is "satisfied that the making of the agreement for arbitration . . . is not in issue," a Revised Section 4 should send cases to arbitration when the court is "satisfied that the making of the *contract containing the* agreement for arbitration . . . is not in issue."[20]

4.2(3) Argument

Among those who specialize in international arbitration, a common defense of the separability doctrine is that it "permits arbitrators to invalidate the main contract (e.g., for illegality or fraud in the inducement) without the risk that their decision will call into question the validity of the arbitration clause

to Arbitration, and the Demise of Separability: Restoring Access to Justice for Contracts with Arbitration Provisions, 56 S.M.U.L. Rev. 819 (2003) (tension between these cases), with Alan Scott Rau, *The Arbitrability Question Itself*, 10 Am. Rev. Int'l Arb. 287, 311 (1999) ("[t]here is not the slightest conflict between *Kaplan* and *Prima Paint* as properly understood").

18 Other criticisms of the separability doctrine are found in Richard C. Reuben, *First Options, Consent to Arbitration, And the Demise of Separability: Restoring Access to Justice for Contracts with Arbitration Provisions*, 56 S.M.U.L. Rev. 819 (2003).

19 No change in the wording of FAA Section 3 is necessary because *Prima Paint* held that the procedures of Section 4 also apply to stay motions under Section 3. *Prima Paint, supra* Note 8, 388 U.S. at 404.

20 Under this anti-separability procedure, courts would continue to hear, as they currently do, challenges focused only on the arbitration clause, e.g., an argument that only the arbitration clause is unconscionable. Although such challenges focus only on the arbitration clause, they are arguments that the contract containing the arbitration clause is unenforceable. If the court agrees, then it has to choose among remedies such as: (1) "reforming" the contract to rewrite the offending term in a way that makes the contract enforceable, (2) not enforcing the offending term, but otherwise enforcing the contract as written, or (3) enforcing none of the contract. These are basically the same remedial choices a court has when it finds some non-arbitration clause of a contract unconscionable or otherwise unenforceable.

from which they derive their power."[21] Suppose, for example, that when Prima Paint receives F&C's demand for arbitration, Prima Paint decides not to go to court to allege F&C's fraudulent inducement, but instead complies with F&C's demand to submit the case to arbitration. Suppose further that the arbitrator concludes that F&C fraudulently induced Prima Paint to sign the consulting agreement so the arbitrator issues an award rejecting F&C's claim for payment from Prima Paint and even awarding damages to Prima Paint. Separability defenders seem to worry that – without the separability doctrine – this arbitration award in favor of Prima Paint would have no legal force (that is, could not be confirmed and enforced by a court) because the arbitrator's only power to render the award came from a contract, the consulting agreement, that the arbitrator held unenforceable.

In fact, however, the arbitrator's power came, not just from the consulting agreement, but also from a post-dispute agreement to arbitrate. When F&C demanded arbitration and Prima Paint complied with that demand by participating in arbitration, the parties formed a post-dispute agreement to arbitrate. The agreement was formed, not by mutual assent to a writing, but by conduct. More importantly, this post-dispute agreement is not an executory agreement, but rather one that has been performed; both sides participated in the arbitration and the arbitrator rendered an award. What could be the ground for vacating such an award? None of the grounds in FAA Section 10 applies.[22] And even before enactment of the FAA, when courts generally refused to enforce executory arbitration agreements, they did enforce arbitration awards.[23] It is hard to imagine a contemporary court refusing to enforce an arbitration award – rendered after both sides manifested assent to arbitration by participating in it – on the ground that the arbitrators deprived themselves of the power to render the award by the very act of rendering it, that is, holding that the container contract is

[21] William W. Park, *Determining Arbitral Jurisdiction: Allocation of Tasks Between Courts and Arbitrators*, 8 AM. REV. INT'L ARB. 133, 143 (1997). *See also* Gary B. Born, INTERNATIONAL COMMERCIAL ARBITRATION 68 (2d ed. 2001) ("Another possible consequence of the separability doctrine is that, if an arbitral tribunal or court concludes that the parties' entire underlying contract was void, that conclusion would not necessarily deprive the parties' arbitration agreement – and hence, in a Catch 22 turn, the arbitrators' award – of validity."); Robert H. Smit, *Separability and Competence-Competence in International Arbitration: Ex Nihilo Nihil Fit? Or Can Something Come from Nothing?*, 13 AM. REV. INT'L ARB. 19 (2002) ("separability means that . . . a party's challenge to the validity of the underlying contract does not automatically deprive the arbitral tribunal of jurisdiction to resolve the parties' dispute concerning the challenged contract").

[22] 9 U.S.C. §10 (2000).

[23] Macneil et al., FEDERAL ARBITRATION LAW, Chapter 4. *See also* Ian R. Macneil, AMERICAN ARBITRATION LAW: REFORMATION, NATIONALIZATION, AND INTERNATIONALIZATION 19 (1992) (hereafter cited as Macneil, AMERICAN ARBITRATION LAW).

unenforceable. So the separability doctrine is not necessary to ensure avoid that unfortunate quandary.

Perhaps in response to such arguments, William Park writes:

> Occasionally one hears suggestions that an estoppel doctrine could achieve the same goal [as the separability doctrine], by deeming a party who participated in the arbitration to have waived the right to challenge the award. Such an approach, however, would not deal adequately with the common situation in which an arbitrator rules on several claims and/or counterclaims, but has jurisdiction only over some of them. Moreover, an estoppel or waiver doctrine would likely encourage boycott of arbitral proceedings.[24]

Whether the arbitrator has jurisdiction over some or all claims is determined by interpreting the agreement submitting the dispute to arbitration.[25] In the case of an agreement formed by conduct, rather than assent to a writing, the parties take the risk that the arbitrator and any reviewing court will interpret the agreement to give the arbitrator jurisdiction over all claims the arbitrator thought to rule on. If a party does not like that risk then it should not participate in arbitration without a written agreement specifying which claims are, and are not, being submitted to the arbitrator. Similarly, in the absence of the separability doctrine, a party who does not want to comply with the arbitrator's rulings on challenges to the enforceability of the container contract should not participate in arbitration until a court rules on such challenges.[26] If this is what Professor Park calls "encourag[ing] boycott of arbitral proceedings," then – at least in the context of domestic arbitration – such

[24] William W. Park, *Arbitration in Banking and Finance*, 17 ANN. REV. BANKING L. 213, 270 n.224 (1998).

[25] *First Options of Chicago, Inc. v. Kaplan*, 514 U.S. 938 (1995); *AT&T Technologies, Inc. v. Communications Workers of Am.*, 475 U.S. 643 (1986).

[26] *First Options, supra* Note 25, 514 U.S. at 946–7, can be read to the contrary. However, the facts of *First Options* differ in an important respect from the hypothetical facts discussed in the text. In the hypothetical, Prima Paint's participation in arbitration (arguing the merits of the case without questioning the arbitrator's power to decide the case) is a manifestation of assent to the arbitrator deciding, among other things, whether Prima Paint formed an enforceable contract containing an arbitration clause. In *First Options*, by contrast, the Kaplans' participation in arbitration consisted primarily of arguing that they had never manifested assent to the arbitrator deciding whether they had formed an enforceable contract to arbitrate. *Id.* Thus *First Options*' holding that the Kaplans' participation in arbitration did not constitute a waiver of the right to have a court decide whether they had formed an enforceable contract to arbitrate can be reconciled with a holding in the hypothetical that Prima Paint has waived its right to have a court decide whether it had formed an enforceable contract to arbitrate. That said, under the anti-separability procedure I propose, the safer course for those in the Kaplans' position is to stay out of arbitration because any participation in arbitration could be (mis?)interpreted by a court as waiver of the right to have a court decide whether an enforceable contract to arbitrate was formed.

encouragement is positive. After all, it ensures that parties who want a court to rule on the enforceability of the container contract get such a ruling,[27] and rightly allocates to parties who go to arbitration without such a ruling the consequences of leaving the question to the arbitrator.[28]

However, this "anti-separability" procedure I have proposed – a court available for resolving disputes over whether the parties have formed an enforceable container contract before an arbitrator resolves the merits of the claims – has downsides. It would add an extra step that would often make arbitration slower and costlier than it is under the separability doctrine, which resolves in one forum disputes both about the enforceability of the container contract and about the merits.[29] In addition, this procedure

[27] It thus vindicates the first principle of the contractual approach to arbitration law – the principle that a court should not send a dispute to arbitration unless the parties have formed an enforceable contract requiring arbitration of that dispute.

[28] In the international arbitration context, some argue, this reasoning does not apply "[f]or normally there is no international court with compulsory jurisdiction to determine and enforce the validity of the international/arbitration agreement." Stephen M. Schwebel, International Arbitration: Three Salient Problems 4 (1987). But surely the national court of the party opposing arbitration has jurisdiction over that party.

The worry of separability defenders is that that national court would be biased in favor of the party opposing arbitration, and thus refuse to enforce an executory arbitration agreement that it really should enforce. But avoiding that biased court at the stage of enforcing an executory arbitration agreement does no good if that same biased court can later prevent enforcement of an arbitration award against its preferred party.

In some cases, of course, a biased court cannot prevent enforcement of an arbitration award because, for example, the assets necessary to satisfy the award are outside that court's jurisdiction and within the jurisdiction of a court willing to enforce the award (the "good court"). But if the good court is willing to defy the biased court at the award-enforcement stage, it should also be willing to defy the biased court at the executory-agreement stage. Ultimately, whether international arbitration decisions are more than hortatory turns on whether good courts are willing and able to enforce such decisions, not whether courts get involved only at the end of the process (as required by the separability doctrine) or also earlier. There is no reason for courts to apply different standards of personal jurisdiction in actions to enforce executory arbitration agreements and actions to enforce arbitration awards.

The reasoning of the previous two paragraphs also responds to other arguments for separability in the international context. An example is the argument that in cases

> in which the agreement runs not between two persons or companies of different nationality but between a foreign contractor and a government, not only would the contractor be loath to seek enforcement of his arbitral remedy [enforcement of the executory arbitration agreement] in national courts; often national courts would lack the authority to require the executive branch to arbitrate contrary to its will, its executive order or national legislation.

Id. Again, whether international arbitration decisions are more than hortatory turns on whether good courts are willing and able to enforce such decisions, not whether courts get involved only at the end of the process (as required by the separability doctrine) or also earlier.

[29] The anti-separability procedure would allow a party who expects to lose in arbitration to delay arbitration by fabricating an allegation that the container contract is unenforceable. *See* W. Michael Reisman et al., International Commercial Arbitration 540 (1997)

would have a court resolving issues that will often be intertwined with the merits that will go to the arbitrator if the court finds that the parties have formed an enforceable container contract.[30] In short, repealing the separability doctrine will come at a price to both disputants and adjudicators. That price, however, must be paid to ensure that parties are sent to arbitration only when they have formed an enforceable contract to be there.

Those who believe that this is too high a price to pay may be attracted to a compromise position that preserves the separability doctrine with respect to the sort of fraud allegations in *Prima Paint* but allows a court to hear other challenges to the container contract. For example, many courts distinguish between challenges alleging that no contract was formed at all (due to illegality or lack of capacity, assent or consideration) and challenges alleging that an admittedly formed contract was voidable (due to misrepresentation, duress, mistake, or the like).[31] As Lord Chancellor Simon put it:

> If the dispute is as to whether the contract which contains the [arbitration] clause has ever been entered into at all, that issue cannot go to arbitration under the clause, for the party who denies that he has ever entered into the contract is thereby denying that he has ever joined in the submission [to

("it is all too easy for a party seeking to derail an arbitration at its inception to claim that the main agreement was or had become invalid.") Perhaps parties who refuse to go to arbitration without a court's determination that the container contract is enforceable should, if they lose on that determination, be required to pay the other side's legal fees and costs. Additional sanctions might also be imposed. *See* Fed. R. Civ. P. 11.

30 For example, in *Prima Paint, supra* Note 8, if a court had sent F&C's claim for payment to arbitration only after determining that Prima Paint's consent to the consulting agreement was not induced by misrepresentation, the court would have already decided much of the dispute it was sending to arbitration because Prima Paint's argument on the merits, its defense to payment, was misrepresentation.

In the absence of the separability doctrine, courts deciding whether to send disputes to arbitration often would, as in this example, become entangled with the merits of the dispute. If the court sent a dispute to arbitration after effectively ruling on the merits, the arbitrator would have two choices. The arbitrator could reconsider the merits de novo, which would require the parties to adjudicate the merits twice and create the possibility of inconsistent results. Or the arbitrator could rubber-stamp the court's view of the merits, which would make the arbitration agreement effectively unenforceable because the parties would get a court's, rather than an arbitrator's, decision on the merits.

31 *See, e.g., Burden v. Check Into Cash of Kentucky, LLC,* 267 F.3d 483, 488 (6th Cir. 2001) ("[t]he void/voidable distinction is relevant for the *Prima Paint* analysis because a void contract, unlike a voidable contract, was never a contract at all."); *Three Valleys Mun. Water Dist. v. E. F. Hutton & Co.*, 925 F.2d 1136, 1140–1 (9th Cir. 1991) ("If the dispute is within the scope of an arbitration agreement, an arbitrator may properly decide whether a contract is 'voidable' because the parties have agreed to arbitrate the dispute. But . . . a party who contests the making of a contract containing an arbitration provision cannot be compelled to arbitrate the threshold issue of the existence of an agreement to arbitrate. Only a court can make that decision.").

> arbitration]. Similarly, if one party to the alleged contract is contending that it is void ab initio (because, for example, the making of such a contract is illegal), the arbitration clause cannot operate, for on this view the clause itself is also void.[32]

This confined version of the separability doctrine only precludes courts from hearing arguments that the contract is voidable at a party's option, not from hearing arguments that there was never any contract at all.

Confining the separability doctrine so that it only applies to voidable-contract arguments is an improvement over cases that also apply it to no-contract arguments like illegality[33] and lack of capacity,[34] but why stop there?

[32] *Heyman v. Darwins, Ltd.*, 1 All E.R. 337, 343 (H.L. 1942). *See also Sphere Drake Ins. Ltd. v. All American Ins. Co.*, 256 F.3d 587 (7th Cir. 2001) (Easterbrook, J.).

> Fraud in the inducement does not negate the fact that the parties actually reached an agreement. That's what was critical in *Prima Paint.* But whether there was any agreement is a distinct question. *Chastain* [*v. Robinson-Humphrey Co.*, 957 F.2d 851 (11th Cir.1992)] sensibly holds a claim of forgery must be resolved by a court. A person whose signature was forged has never agreed to anything. Likewise with a person whose name was written on a contract by a faithless agent who lacked authority to make that commitment. This is not a defense to enforcement, as in *Prima Paint*; it is a situation in which no contract came into being; and as arbitration depends on a valid contract an argument that the contract does not exist can't logically be resolved by the arbitrator (unless the parties agree to arbitrate this issue after the dispute arises).

Id. at 590–1.

[33] *See, e.g., Lawrence v. Comprehensive Business Servs. Co.*, 833 F.2d 1159, 1161–2 (5th Cir. 1987). Many scholars of international arbitration argue that the separability doctrine should apply to illegality. *See* Robert H. Smit, *supra* Note 21 at 38–9.

> Application of the separability doctrine should not depend upon the existence or validity of the underlying contract because the doctrine is predicated on the notion that the arbitration agreement and underlying contract are separate and distinct agreements – thus, one can come into existence or force without the other. Separability does not, in fact, presume an existing underlying contract, as most U.S. courts have held. Nor, however, is an arbitration clause always immune to challenges to the existence of the underlying contract. Rather, the appropriate inquiry is whether the particular challenge to the existence (or validity ab initio) of the contract is such as necessarily also to put the existence (or validity ab initio) of the arbitration agreement in issue – to use the language of §4 of the FAA. In other words, would the particular challenge to the existence of the contract at issue, if well-founded, also necessarily mean that the arbitration agreement could not exist?

Id. at 36–7. Accord Tanya J. Monestier, *"Nothing Comes of Nothing"... Or Does it??? A Critical Re-Examination of the Doctrine of Separability in American Arbitration*, 12 Am. Rev. Int'l Arb. 223, 241 (2001) ("The only issue for a court should be the threshold determination: Is the challenge leveled at the contract one which necessarily places in issue the existence of the agreement to arbitrate therein contained?"); William W. Park, *supra* Note 24 at 270 ("The notion that an arbitration clause is 'separable' or autonomous from the commercial agreement in which it is encapsulated permits arbitrators to invalidate the main contract (e.g., for illegality or fraud in the inducement) without the risk that their decision will also invalidate the source of their power."); Alan Scott Rau, *Everything You Really Need to Know About "Separability" in Seventeen Simple Propositions*, 14 Am. Rev. Int'l Arb. 1, 45–6 (2003).

[34] *Primerica Life Ins. Co. v. Brown*, 304 F.3d 469 (5th Cir. 2002).

Why distinguish between no-contract arguments and voidable-contract arguments? A practical reason not to preserve the separability doctrine for voidable-contract arguments is that it is often difficult to distinguish no-contract arguments from voidable-contract arguments.[35]

More importantly, preserving the separability doctrine for voidable-contract arguments undermines what the grounds for voidability (such as misrepresentation and duress) protect. An example of a voidable contract is an arbitration agreement someone signs with a gun to her head.[36] Preserving the separability doctrine for voidable-contract arguments imposes upon her a duty to arbitrate whether a gun was in fact used as alleged. Imposing such a duty violates a fundamental principle of contract law. It enforces a duty assumed through coerced, not voluntary, consent.

To avoid this result, some would further confine the separability doctrine so that it applies only to some voidable-contract arguments (such as misrepresentation) but not others (such as duress). For example, Alan Rau supports a separability doctrine that distinguishes between misrepresentation and duress on the ground that "There is simply no agreement to anything, for example, where a signature has been forged, or where an authentic signature was obtained at gunpoint."[37] While this is true with respect to forgery, it is not with respect to the signature obtained at gunpoint. The person who signs with a gun to her head does agree, does manifest assent to the terms on the paper she is signing; it is just that she does so under circumstances in which the law properly declines to enforce her agreement. Just as when

[35] *See* Macneil et al., FEDERAL ARBITRATION LAW, *supra* Note 16 at §15.3.3.2.

[36] *See id.* §15.3.4, n.74 (discussing ramifications of the *Prima Paint* holding with respect to duress-at-gunpoint example).

[37] Alan Scott Rau, *Everything You Really Need to Know About "Separability" in Seventeen Simple Propositions*, 14 AM. REV. INT'L ARB. 1, 4–5 (2003) (quoting Alan Scott Rau, *The New York Convention in American Courts*, 7 AM. REV. INT'L ARB. 213, 253, n.173 (1996)). Rau's approach is endorsed by John J. Barceló III, *Who Decides the Arbitrators' Jurisdiction? Separability and Competence-Competence in Transnational Perspective*, 36 VAND. J. TRANS'L L. 1115 (2003).

Approaches similar to Professor Rau's have come from several scholars of international arbitration. For example, Professor Park writes:

> One occasionally hears scholarly attacks on separability suggesting that the doctrine facilitates enforcement of agreements that are unconscionable or not based on informed consent Properly understood, however, separability should not prevent a party from resisting arbitration on the grounds of duress, unconscionability, lack of informed consent or arbitrator excess of authority. Notwithstanding the separability doctrine, courts can and do refuse to enforce an arbitration agreement tainted by duress, unconscionability, or a signatory's lack of authority, which render the clause itself void, voidable or otherwise inoperative.

William W. Park, *Arbitration in Banking and Finance*, 17 ANN. REV. BANKING L. 213, 271–2. (1998). Unlike Rau, whose argument for distinguishing between duress and misrepresentation is addressed in the text following this footnote, Park provides no argument for his view that the separability doctrine should apply to misrepresentation but not duress.

she signs in reliance on a misrepresentation regarding, say, F&C's financial condition: she does agree, but she does so under circumstances in which the law properly declines to enforce her agreement.

In this regard, the case of the signature with a gun to the head is different from the example in which "A grasps B's hand and compels B by physical force to write his name" to the signature line of an arbitration agreement.[38] As the current Restatement of Contracts says, "B's signature is not effective as a manifestation of his assent, and there is no contract."[39] By contrast to this example, in which there is no contract because there is no agreement, the signature obtained at gunpoint is an agreement, albeit one induced by an improper threat, and there is a contract, albeit one voidable at the option of the victim. The Restatement treats the A-grasps-B's-hand example in its Section 174 and the gunpoint example in its Section 175 for good reason; they are conceptually quite distinct, with the A-grasps-B's-hand example far more analogous to fraud in the factum and the gunpoint example far more analogous to the sort of fraud alleged in *Prima Paint*, fraud in the inducement.[40] In the A-grasps-B's-hand example and in fraud in the factum, there is no agreement. In the gunpoint example, as in *Prima Paint*, there is an agreement.

This foray into the doctrinal nuances of contract-law defenses is important for the light it sheds on the intuition that there is somehow less of an agreement to arbitration in the gun-to-the-head example than in a fraud-in-the-inducement case like *Prima Paint*. I think this intuition is captured by Professor Alan Rau's suggestion that it is "perfectly plausible . . . that [F&C and Prima Paint] might have chosen to submit to arbitration – not only questions with respect to the quality of F&C's performance – but also questions with respect to whether F&C had misrepresented the quality of its performance."[41]

Rau suggests that if Prima Paint did choose to arbitrate the question of whether F&C misrepresented the quality of its performance then Prima Paint should be bound by this choice. The problem, however, is that Prima Paint may have made this choice while under the influence of F&C's misrepresentation. For that reason, Prima Paint should not be bound by this choice until a court determines that Prima Paint made this choice free of influence from misrepresentation. Similarly, Prima Paint might have chosen to arbitrate the question of whether F&C obtained Prima Paint's signature through

[38] Restatement (Second) of Contracts §174, cmt. a, illus. 1 (1979).

[39] *Id.*

[40] See *id.* §§163 & 164 (distinguishing between misrepresentation that prevents formation of a contract and misrepresentation that makes a contract voidable).

[41] Rau, *supra* Note 37, 14 Am. Rev. Int'l Arb. at 18.

duress. The problem is that Prima Paint may have made this choice while under the influence of F&C's duress. For that reason, Prima Paint should not be bound by this choice until a court determines that Prima Paint made this choice free of influence from duress. The separability doctrine's bootstrapping problem is the same with respect to misrepresentation (*Prima Paint*) and duress (the gun to the head). There is no more or less of an agreement to arbitration in either case. Thus the question is not, as Rau insists, whether "the parties might have wished to make a binding submission to the arbitrators of this issue of the enforceability of the container contract."[42] The parties' wishes on this issue should not matter unless they expressed those wishes in an agreement formed under circumstances in which contract law enforces their agreement, that is, circumstances in which neither misrepresentation nor duress is present.[43] A distinction by which the separability doctrine applies to misrepresentation but not duress denigrates the misrepresentation defense and what it operates to advance, honesty.

The separability doctrine should be repealed in its entirety to ensure that no dispute is sent to arbitration unless the parties have formed an *enforceable* contract requiring arbitration of that dispute. It is not enough to say that "'a party cannot be required to submit to arbitration any dispute which he has not agreed so to submit.'"[44] It is necessary to say that a party cannot be required to submit to arbitration any dispute which he has not agreed *in an enforceable contract* so to submit.

Section 4.3 Enforce Arbitration Agreements

The second principle of the contractual approach to arbitration law is that arbitration agreements should be enforced, as FAA Section 2 states, "save

[42] *Id.* 14 Am. Rev. Int'l Arb. at 27. *See also* Schwebel, *supra* Note 28 at 3 ("[t]he will of the parties [on this issue] should be given effect").

[43] The timing of such an agreement can vary. For example, suppose that parties X and Y form two contracts a year apart, and in the second contract there is no arbitration clause, but in the first contract there is a clause providing for arbitration, not only of disputes arising out of that contract, but also disputes arising out of any later contracts between the parties. What if X and Y have a dispute about the second contract and whether X fraudulently induced Y to enter the second contract? Each party should have the duty to arbitrate that dispute because Y has alleged a misrepresentation defense only to the second contract, but not to the first contract, the one through which Y assumed the duty arbitrate.

Parties who want to contract around the anti-separability doctrine I have proposed should follow this procedure. They should enter a truly separate contract.

[44] *Howsam v. Dean Witter Reynolds, Inc.*, 537 U.S. 79, 82 (2002)(quoting *Steelworkers v. Warrior & Gulf Nav. Co.*, 363 U.S. 574 (1960)).

upon such grounds as exist at law or in equity for the revocation of any contract."[45] The following four reforms would advance this principle. One would do so by repealing the FAA's exclusion of some employment agreements from its scope. The other three would do so on issues about which the FAA and/or current case law are unclear. These issues are: (1) the enforceability of agreements to arbitrate disputes that do not arise out of the contract containing the arbitration clause, (2) the enforceability of electronic agreements to arbitrate, and (3) the enforceability of agreements specifying grounds for vacating arbitration awards.

4.3(1) Repeal the Employment Exclusion

FAA Section 1 says "nothing herein contained shall apply to contracts of employment of seamen, railroad employees, or any other class of workers engaged in foreign or interstate commerce."[46] Arbitration agreements falling within this "employment exclusion" are not governed by the FAA and are, therefore, governed by state law. There was until recently a circuit split on the interpretation of the FAA's employment exclusion. The Ninth Circuit held that the FAA did not apply to any employment contracts,[47] while other federal circuit courts held that the FAA applied to all employment contracts except for those of employees who work directly in interstate commerce, that is, those actually transporting things across state lines.[48] The Supreme Court overruled the Ninth Circuit on this issue in the 2001 decision of *Circuit City Stores, Inc. v. Adams*.[49]

Current law thus presents the strange picture of a federal statute, enacted pursuant to Congress' power to regulate interstate commerce,[50] governing the agreements of all employees except those most directly involved in interstate commerce, transportation workers, whose agreements are governed by state law. One might say that this is the opposite of what the law should be.[51] But – aside from constitutional federalism, which is discussed

[45] 9 U.S.C. §2 (2000).

[46] 9 U.S.C. §1 (2000).

[47] *Craft v. Campbell Soup Co.*, 177 F.3d 1199 (9th Cir. 1998).

[48] *Id.* at 1202, n.5 (citing cases).

[49] 532 U.S. 105 (2001).

[50] *Southland Corp. v. Keating*, 465 U.S. 1 (1984). This holding of *Southland* is controversial and is discussed subsequently in Section 4.5 of this chapter. *See also* Section 3.2, *supra*.

[51] "Under current law, the right answer is that the FAA keeps to its 1925 contours, so that employment arbitrations are governed by state law, save to the extent that they involve interstate commerce as that phrase was understood in 1925." Richard A. Epstein, *Fidelity Without Translation*, 1 Green Bag 2d 21 (Fall 1997).

subsequently[52] – there is no policy reason for treating the arbitration agreements of transportation workers differently from those of other employees. The FAA should apply to the agreements of all employees or none. "All" is better than "none" because some states have law rejecting, with respect to employees, the FAA's rule that arbitration agreements should be enforced "save upon such grounds as exist at law or in equity for the revocation of any contract."[53] Thus, bringing all individual employment arbitration agreements within the scope of the FAA brings more law in line with the contractual approach to arbitration law. The employment exclusion of FAA Section 1 should be repealed.[54]

4.3(2) Repeal the "Arising Out of Such Contract or Transaction" Requirement

FAA Section 2 makes enforceable only "A written provision in any maritime transaction or a contract evidencing a transaction involving commerce to settle by arbitration a controversy thereafter arising out of such contract or transaction, or the refusal to perform the whole or any part thereof." By contrast, the Revised Uniform Arbitration Act (RUAA) makes enforceable "An agreement contained in a record to submit to arbitration any existing or subsequent controversy arising between the parties to the agreement."[55]

One difference between these provisions is how they treat an agreement to arbitrate disputes that do not arise out of the contract containing the agreement to arbitrate. For example, suppose that parties X and Y form two

[52] The proper scope of federal (as opposed to state) arbitration law is discussed later in Section 4.5 of this chapter. *See also* Sections 3.4 and 3.6, *supra.*

[53] *See, e.g.*, Iowa Code Ann. §679A.1 (West 1987); *Baxter v. John Weitzel, Inc.*, 871 P.2d 855 (Kan. Ct. App. 1994); Ky. Rev. Stat. Ann. §336.700 (Michie 1995) (employment contracts); R.I. Gen. Laws §10-3-2 (Supp. 1995); S.C. Code Ann. §15–48–10 (Law. Co-op. Supp. 1995). For more on the merits of the contractual approach with respect to employment arbitration in particular, *see* Stephen J. Ware, *The Effects of Gilmer: Empirical and Other Approaches to the Study of Employment Arbitration*, 16 Ohio St. J. on Disp. Resol. 735(2001); Stephen J. Ware, *Employment Arbitration and Voluntary Consent*, 25 Hofstra L. Rev. 83 (1996).

[54] Repealing the employment exclusion might also have the salutary effect of bringing labor arbitration within the coverage of the FAA. The Supreme Court has not clearly stated whether its treatment of labor arbitration as outside the scope of the FAA rests on the employment exclusion or something else. For a good discussion of the "puzzling" and "cryptic" decisions of the Court, including *Textile Workers Union v. Lincoln Mills*, 353 U.S. 448 (1957), *see* Macneil et al., Federal Arbitration Law, *supra* Note 16 at §11.3.1 (1994). A similar recommendation is made for international commercial arbitration. *See* Section 6.2(1)(B)(3), *infra.*

[55] Revised Uniform Arbitration Act §6(a) (2000) (hereafter cited as RUAA).

contracts a year apart, and in the second contract there is no arbitration clause, but in the first contract there is a clause providing for arbitration, not only of disputes arising out of that contract, but also disputes arising out of any later contracts between the parties. What if X and Y have a dispute about performance of the second contract? As a matter of standard contract law, each party should have the duty to arbitrate the dispute about the second contract because each party assumed this duty in the first contract and nothing later occurred to discharge, modify or excuse this duty. But it is not clear that this duty is enforced by the FAA because the FAA limits its enforcement mandate to "controvers[ies] arising out of such contract," with "such" contract referring to the contract containing the arbitration clause.[56] By contrast, the duty to arbitrate the dispute about the second contract is clearly made enforceable by RUAA's language covering "any existing or subsequent controversy arising between the parties to the agreement." Therefore, the FAA should adopt RUAA's broad coverage of "any existing or subsequent controversy," to advance the second principle of the contractual approach to arbitration law, the principle that arbitration agreements should be enforced "save upon such grounds as exist at law or in equity for the revocation of any contract."

Although FAA Section 2 should adopt RUAA's broad coverage of "any existing or subsequent controversy," it should not adopt RUAA's language limiting enforcement to a controversy "arising between the parties to the agreement." Suppose, for example, that the contract between X and Y contains a clause in which each party promises to arbitrate disputes they have with each other or with Z. Although, depending on how one defines "party," Z might not technically be a party to the contract, Z is an intended third-party beneficiary of the arbitration clause and thus, under standard contract law, has the right to compel X and Y to arbitrate any disputes with

[56] Similarly, it is not clear that the FAA requires courts to enforce the arbitration agreement in the opposite fact pattern in which the second contract contains a clause providing for arbitration, not only of disputes arising out of that contract, but also disputes arising out of any earlier contracts between the parties. Courts, nevertheless, generally seem to enforce these agreements. *See* Macneil et al., FEDERAL ARBITRATION LAW §20.3.6 (1994 & Supp. 1999). In discussing one such case, the authors say:

> Although the origins of the dispute in *Zink* were in the earlier bond transaction, it is unclear that the dispute existed when the [later] account agreement [containing the arbitration clause] was executed. If it did, the agreement to arbitrate is explicitly covered by FAA §2. The result should not change simply because the potential dispute had not yet materialized.

Id. §20.3.6 (Supp. 1999)(discussing *Zink v. Merrill Lynch, Pierce, Fenner & Smith, Inc.*, 9 F.3d 1060 (10th Cir. 1993)). The authors are correct both (1) that FAA §2 does not "explicitly" require enforcement of agreements to arbitrate not-yet-existing disputes arising out of contracts preceding the arbitration agreement and (2) that it should.

Z.[57] Cases under the FAA currently recognize the rights of third-party beneficiaries to compel arbitration,[58] and a Revised FAA should endorse this case law.

4.3(3) Enforce Electronic Agreements

As noted previously, FAA Section 2 makes enforceable only "A written provision in any maritime transaction or a contract . . . ," while the RUAA makes enforceable "An agreement contained in a record. . . . " RUAA says "'Record' means information that is inscribed on a tangible medium or that is stored in an electronic or other medium and is retrievable in perceivable form."[59] By bringing this language from RUAA into the FAA, a Revised FAA would adapt to the change in technology from written to electronic agreements.

Much of what this reform would accomplish has already been accomplished by the Electronic Signatures in Global and National Commerce Act, better known as "E-SIGN," which says:

> Notwithstanding any statute, regulation, or other rule of law (other than this subchapter and subchapter II of this chapter), with respect to any transaction in or affecting interstate or foreign commerce – a signature, contract, or other record relating to such transaction may not be denied legal effect, validity, or enforceability solely because it is in electronic form.[60]

However, E-SIGN's exceptions[61] are broad enough to cover many arbitration agreements so reforming the FAA to enforce electronic agreements is worthwhile to advance the second principle of the contractual approach to arbitration law, the principle that arbitration agreements should be enforced "save upon such grounds as exist at law or in equity for the revocation of any contract."

4.3(4) Enforce Contractual Grounds for Vacating Arbitration Awards

Some parties to arbitration agreements try to add grounds for vacating arbitration awards to the grounds already found in the law. For instance, the

[57] Restatement (Second) of Contracts §§302 & 304 (1979).
[58] Macneil et al., Federal Arbitration Law §18.3.2.
[59] RUAA §1(6) (2000). *See* Timothy J. Heinsz, *The Revised Uniform Arbitration Act: Modernizing, Revising, and Clarifying Arbitration Law*, 2001 J. Disp. Resp. Res. 1, 9-11 (discussing electronic arbitration under the RUAA).
[60] 15 U.S.C. §7001(a)(1).
[61] *See id.* §7003.

arbitration agreement in *Kyocera Corp. v. Prudential-Bache Trade Services, Inc.*,[62] provided that "The Court shall vacate, modify or correct any award: (i) based upon any of the grounds referred to in the Federal Arbitration Act, (ii) where the arbitrators' findings of fact are not supported by substantial evidence, or (iii) where the arbitrators' conclusions of law are erroneous."[63] Courts are split on whether to enforce such clauses.[64] Such clauses should be enforced to advance the principle that arbitration agreements should be enforced "save upon such grounds as exist at law or in equity for the revocation of any contract."[65] Accordingly, a Revised FAA should instruct

[62] 341 F.3d 987 (9th Cir. 2003) (en banc).

[63] *Id.* at 990–1.

[64] *Compare Kyocera, supra* Note 62, 341 F.3d at 994 (refusing to enforce expanded review provision); *Bowen v. Amoco Pipeline Co.*, 254 F.3d 925 (10th Cir. 2001) (same); *Chicago Typographical Union No. 16 v. Chicago Sun Times, Inc.*, 935 F.2d 1501, 1505 (7th Cir.1991) (Posner, J.) ("If the parties want, they can contract for an appellate arbitration panel to review the arbitrator's award. But they cannot contract for judicial review of that award; federal jurisdiction cannot be created by contract."), *with Harris v. Parker College of Chiropractic*, 286 F.3d 790 (5th Cir. 2002) (enforcing expanded review provision); *Hughes Training Inc. v. Cook*, 254 F.3d 588 (5th Cir. 2001) (same); *Syncor Int'l Corp. v. McLeland*, 120 F.3d 262, 1997 WL 452245 (4th Cir. Aug. 11, 1997) (per curiam) (same); *Gateway Tech., Inc. v. MCI Telecommunications Corp.*, 64 F.3d 993 (5th Cir. 1995) (same); *Fils et Cables d'Acier de Lens v. Midland Metals Corp.*, 584 F. Supp. 240 (S.D.N.Y. 1984) (same); *New England Utils. v. Hydro-Quebec*, 10 F. Supp. 2d 53 (D. Mass. 1998) (same); *Collins v. Blue Cross Blue Shield of Michigan*, 579 N.W.2d 435 (Mich. App. 1998) (same). *Cf. Roadway Package Sys., Inc. v. Kayser*, 257 F.3d 287, 293 (3d Cir. 2001) ("We . . . hold that parties may opt out of the FAA's off-the-rack vacatur standards and fashion their own."); *Green v. Ameritech Corp.*, 200 F.3d 967 (6th Cir. 2000). *See also* Sections 3.5 and 6.2(2) of this text, where this issue is also discussed.

[65] Margaret M. Maggio & Richard A. Bales, *Contracting Around the FAA: The Enforceability of Private Agreements to Expand Judicial Review of Arbitration Awards*, 18 Ohio St. J. on Disp. Resol.151 (2002); Edward Brunet, *Replacing Folklore Arbitration With a Contract Model of Arbitration*, 74 Tul. L. Rev. 39, 73 (1999); Alan Scott Rau, *Contracting Out of the Arbitration Act*, 8 Am. Rev. Int'l Arb.225 (1997); Stephen J. Ware, *"Opt-In" for Judicial Review of Errors of Law Under the Revised Uniform Arbitration Act*, 8 Am. Rev. Int'l Arb. 263, 270 (1997); Tom Cullinan, Note, *Contracting for an Expanded Scope of Judicial Review in Arbitration Agreements*, 51 Vand. L. Rev. 395, 422 (1998). For analyses more equivocal about treating Section 10's grounds as a default, *see* Christopher R. Drahozal, *Contracting Around RUAA: Default Rules, Mandatory Rules, and Judicial Review of Arbitral Awards*, 3 Pepp. Disp. Resol. L.J. 419 (2003); Sarah Rudolph Cole, *Managerial Litigants? The Overlooked Problem of Party Autonomy in Dispute Resolution*, 51 Hastings L. J. 1199 (2000). And there are those who oppose treating Section 10's grounds as a default. *See* Andreas F. Lowenfeld, *Can Arbitration Coexist With Judicial Review? A Critique of LaPine v. Kyocera*, ADR Currents 1, 12 (Sept. 1998); Amy J. Schmitz, *Ending a Mud Bowl: Defining Arbitration's Finality Through Functional Analysis*, 37 Ga. L. Rev.123, 189–202 (2002); Abby Cohen Smutny, *Judicial Review of Arbitral Awards: Comment on the Ninth Circuit Decision in LaPine Technology Corp. v. Kyocera Corp .*, Mealey's Int'l Arb. Rep. 18, 22 (Feb. 1998); Hans Smit, *Contractual Modification of the Scope of Judicial Review of Arbitral Awards*, 8 Am. Rev. Int'l Arb. 147 (1997).

courts to vacate the award where doing so would enforce the agreement submitting the controversy to arbitration.

Section 4.4 Confine Arbitrators' Powers to Those Delegated by the Parties

The third principle of the contractual approach to arbitration law is that, because an arbitrator's power derives from the parties' contract, the arbitrator should not be permitted to reach a result that the parties could not have reached themselves by simply contracting for it. Effectuating this principle requires two changes to the FAA.

4.4(1) End Court Enforcement of Arbitration Subpoenas

FAA Section 7 authorizes arbitrators to "summon in writing any person to attend before them or any of them as a witness and in a proper case to bring with him or them any book, record, document, or paper which may be deemed material as evidence in the case." This section goes on to say:

> if any person or persons so summoned to testify shall refuse or neglect to obey said summons, upon petition the United States district court for the district in which such arbitrators, or a majority of them, are sitting may compel the attendance of such person or persons before said arbitrator or arbitrators, or punish said person or persons for contempt in the same manner provided by law for securing the attendance of witnesses or their punishment for neglect or refusal to attend in the courts of the United States.

In sum, Section 7 treats arbitration subpoenas much like litigation subpoenas.

Section 7 conflicts with the contractual approach to arbitration law because Section 7 gives the arbitrator the power to reach a result that the parties could not have reached themselves by simply contracting for it. A contract can impose duties on the parties to that contract but not on others.[66] An arbitration agreement between X and Y should not be held to impose duties on Z, even the duty to provide evidence to X and Y's arbitration and even if Z would have to provide that evidence in litigation if X and Y later rescind their arbitration agreement. No party should have a duty to provide evidence in arbitration unless that party has agreed to do so.

[66] To be more precise, one might say that a contract can impose *contract-law* duties on the parties to that contract but not on others. Tortious interference with contract might be an example of a contract imposing non-contract-law duties on those who are not parties to that contract.

4.4(2) Strengthen and Clarify Judicial Review of Arbitrator's Legal Rulings[67]

4.4(2)(A) The Arbitration Award as the Parties' Contract

Judicial review of arbitration awards is a topic on which some are tempted to disregard the principle that, because an arbitrator's power derives from the parties' contract, the arbitrator should not be permitted to reach a result that the parties could not have reached themselves by simply contracting for it. Perhaps this disregard is because, when arbitrators are making decisions and rendering awards, they look more like courts doing the same things than like parties forming a contract. But this similarity of arbitrators to courts – both adjudicators issuing legally-binding rulings – should not obscure the fact that the arbitrator's power to issue such rulings derives from the parties' contract. "In the main, an arbitrator acts as the parties' agent and as their delegate may do anything the parties may do directly,"[68] but may not do what the parties could not have done directly. As the Supreme Court said in a labor arbitration case, "we must treat the arbitrator's award as if it represented an agreement between" the parties themselves.[69]

Accordingly, the FAA and case law generally treat arbitration awards the way the law treats contracts. Conceptually, "judicial enforcement of arbitration awards is an example of courts enforcing contracts. The parties agreed to comply with the arbitrator's decision and if the losing party refuses to do so then that party is in breach of contract. When a court vacates an arbitration award, the court is refusing to enforce a contract."[70] Thus, the grounds for vacating an arbitration award should correspond to the grounds for denying enforcement to contracts generally. And the FAA's grounds for vacatur do this quite well. The FAA lists the following grounds for vacatur:

> (1) Where the award was procured by corruption, fraud, or undue means.
> (2) Where there was evident partiality or corruption in the arbitrators, or either of them.

[67] This proposal is based on Stephen J. Ware, *Default Rules from Mandatory Rules: Privatizing Law Through Arbitration*, 83 Minn. L. Rev. 703 (1999).

[68] *George Watts & Son, Inc. v. Tiffany and Co.*, 248 F.3d 577, 580 (7th Cir. 2001) (Easterbrook, J.).

[69] *Eastern Associated Coal Corp. v. United Mine Workers*, 531 U.S. 57, 62 (2000).

[70] Stephen J. Ware, Alternative Dispute Resolution §2.43 (2001).

(3) Where the arbitrators were guilty of misconduct in refusing to postpone the hearing, upon sufficient cause shown, or in refusing to hear evidence pertinent and material to the controversy; or of any other misbehavior by which the rights of any party have been prejudiced.
(4) Where the arbitrators exceeded their powers, or so imperfectly executed them that a mutual, final, and definite award upon the subject matter submitted was not made.[71]

With respect to the first ground, just as courts should not enforce contracts "procured by corruption, fraud, or undue means," courts should not enforce arbitration awards so procured, either. The second and third grounds also fit the model of the parties' contract delegating to the agent, the arbitrator, the power to do what the parties chose not to do themselves. It is hard to imagine a case in which the arbitrator-agent is acting within the scope of his authority delegated by the party-principals' contract if he "eviden[ces] partiality or corruption," or is "guilty of misconduct" or "misbehavior." And if a rare contract did authorize such things, that contract might well be unenforceable under the standard contract-law ground of violating public policy.[72] Finally, the fourth ground – "Where the arbitrators exceeded their powers" – also endorses the contract-delegating-powers-to-the-arbitrator model.[73] This model and the contractual approach to arbitration law that underlies it, require a court to vacate the award if any of these four grounds is present. Accordingly, a Revised FAA Section 10 should change the language preceding these grounds from the permissive, a court "*may* make an order vacating the award,"[74] to the directive, a court "*shall* make an order vacating the award."[75]

[71] 9 U.S.C. §10(a) (2000).

[72] Courts do vacate awards, especially in labor arbitration, that violate public policy. Stephen J. Ware, Alternative Dispute Resolution §2.45(b) (2001). *See also Eastern Associated Coal Corp. v. United Mine Workers,* 531 U.S. 57 (2000). This should continue to be a ground, albeit a narrowly confined one, for vacatur.

[73] *See* Macneil et al., Federal Arbitration Law §40.5.2.2.

> [T]he primary foundation of the arbitrators' powers is the intention of the parties manifested in their agreement to arbitrate. This principle is subject, however, to limitations imposed on the parties' freedom of contract by the legal system. There are thus two fundamental principles to test whether in any given instance the arbitrators have exceeded their powers within the meaning of FAA §10(d).
>
> ...The first, and most commonly in issue, is whether what the arbitrators have done is within the scope of the power the parties intended to confer upon them....
>
> ...The second question is whether the parties have the legal power to confer such intended powers on the arbitrators.

[74] 9 U.S.C. §10(a) (emphasis added).

[75] This would accord with the directive language in RUAA §23(a) (emphasis added).

4.4(2)(B) Grounds for Vacatur in Context: Default Rules and Mandatory Rules

To ensure that arbitrators reach only results that the parties could have, by contract, reached themselves requires vacating awards on the four grounds in FAA Section 10. And this is all that is required when the arbitrator is hearing only breach-of-contract claims, the claims which have long been the bulk of what is resolved in arbitration. When certain claims other than breach-of-contract are resolved in arbitration, however, an additional ground for vacatur is required to prevent arbitrators from exercising power not derived from the parties' contract and thus possibly reaching results that the parties could not have reached themselves when they agreed to arbitrate.

For a long time, the claims sent to arbitration were primarily breach-of-contract claims. As late as 1985, a United States Supreme Court Justice could refer to "the undisputed historical fact that arbitration has functioned almost entirely in either the area of labor disputes or in 'ordinary disputes between merchants as to questions of fact.'"[76] Arbitrators in these two contexts hear almost nothing but breach-of-contract claims. In the labor context, a union or employee asserts breach of a collective bargaining agreement. In the commercial context, merchants allege breach of contracts for the sale of goods and raise "questions of fact – quantity, quality, time of delivery, compliance with terms of payment, excuses for non-performance, and the like."[77]

When hearing breach-of-contract claims, the arbitrator is not so much applying the law as applying the contract. Put another way, the arbitrator is clearly resolving questions that the parties could have resolved when they drafted the contract. The arbitrator is resolving questions that arise because the parties chose to draft a contract in broad, general terms, rather than detailed, specific terms. For example, a collective bargaining agreement might say only that the employer must have "just cause" before terminating an employee, and the labor arbitrator may be called upon to decide whether shouting obscenities at a supervisor is "just cause." The parties could have resolved this question themselves by specifically defining "just cause" in the agreement to include "using foul language" or "shouting at a supervisor." But the parties' broad, general language left a gap in the agreement and it is the arbitrator's job to fill that gap by interpreting or applying the

[76] *Mitsubishi Motors Corporation v. Soler Chrysler-Plymouth Inc.*, 473 U.S. 614, 650 (1985) (Stevens, J., dissenting).

[77] *Id.* at 646, n.11 (quoting Cohen & Dayton, *The New Federal Arbitration Law*, 12 Va. L. Rev. 265, 281 (1926)).

agreement. Case law emphasizes that courts should not substitute their own judgment for that of the arbitrators on such questions of contract interpretation.[78] Contracts are private matters between the parties and the parties have hired the arbitrator as their agent to interpret and apply their contract. It is a model of self-governance.[79] This all supports the FAA's narrow grounds for vacating arbitration awards., that is, grounds for vacatur that correspond to the grounds for denying enforcement to contracts generally. If the arbitrator is resolving a contract-interpretation issue, the arbitrator is reaching a result that the parties could have reached themselves (by simply contracting for it) when they agreed to arbitrate, and thus the arbitrator is acting within powers derived solely from the parties. The same is true when the arbitrator is deciding many other issues of contract and commercial law.[80]

By contrast, the same is not necessarily true when arbitrators are deciding claims based on other areas of law. Some claims arise out of law consisting of mandatory rules, as opposed to default rules. A default rule is one that

[78] "[A]s long as the arbitrator is even arguably construing or applying the contract and acting within the scope of his authority, that a court is convinced he committed serious error does not suffice to overturn his decision." *United Paperworkers Int'l Union v. Misco, Inc.*, 484 U.S. 29, 38 (1987).

[79] *See, e.g., United Steelworkers of America v. Warrior & Gulf Nav. Co.*, 363 U.S. 574 (1960).

> A collective bargaining agreement is an effort to erect a system of industrial self-government.... Gaps may be left to be filled in by reference to the practices of the particular industry and of the various shops covered by the agreement. Many of the specific practices which underlie the agreement may be unknown, except in hazy form, even to the negotiators... [The arbitration] grievance machinery under a collective bargaining agreement is at the very heart of the system of industrial self-government. Arbitration is the means of solving the unforeseeable by molding a system of private law for all the problems which may arise and to provide for their solution in a way which will generally accord with the variant needs and desires of the parties. The processing of disputes through the grievance machinery is actually a vehicle by which meaning and content are given to the collective bargaining agreement.

Id. at 580–1.

[80] *Cf.* Alan Scott Rau, Edward F. Sherman & Scott R. Peppet, Process of Dispute Resolution 745 (3d ed. 2001).

> Of course, in thinking about judicial review [of arbitration] on matters of "law" we should distinguish between mere rules of construction, which come into play in the absence of a contrary agreement, and mandatory rules. After all, most "rules" of contract or commercial law are nothing more than "gap-fillers." They supply a term where the parties have not expressly supplied one themselves; modern commercial law looks in particular to industry custom and course of dealing to furnish the "framework of common understanding controlling any general rules of law which hold only when there is no such understanding." But where the parties have bargained for dispute resolution through arbitration, the method *they* have chosen to fill any gaps in the agreement is the arbitrator's interpretation. His interpretation *is* their bargain. In contrast, legal "rules" in other areas may reflect stronger and overriding governmental or societal interests. In such cases, obviously, some greater degree of arbitral deference should be expected.

governs unless the parties contract out of it. In contrast, a mandatory rule is one that governs despite a contract term to the contrary, that is, a rule that cannot be avoided by contract. One can identify which laws are default and which are mandatory by examining the sorts of contract terms that are, and are not, enforceable.[81] For example, the legal rule that the place for delivery in a sale of goods is the seller's place of business is a default rule because parties can make an enforceable contract requiring delivery at some other location.[82] In contrast, the legal rule giving a consumer the right that goods purchased not be "in a defective condition unreasonably dangerous to the user"[83] is mandatory because it applies no matter what the contract terms say.[84] The distinction between mandatory and default rules is fundamentally important because it reveals the extent of contractual freedom. Mandatory rules limit the freedom of contract, while default rules permit it.[85]

As discussed previously, the rationale for limiting vacatur of arbitration awards to grounds that correspond to the grounds for denying enforcement to contracts generally is that the arbitrator, as the parties' agent, is resolving questions that the parties could have resolved themselves when they drafted the contract. That rationale does not apply when the arbitrator is resolving issues the parties could not have resolved themselves when they drafted the contract. Those are issues about violations of rights conferred by mandatory rules. For example, just as the parties' contract could not have established, in a legally-binding way, that Consumer has no right to recover for personal injury from Seller's "unreasonably dangerous" goods, the parties' agent, the arbitrator, should not be permitted to enter a legally-binding award depriving Consumer of her right to recover for personal injury from Seller's "unreasonably dangerous" goods.

[81] Default rules can also be avoided by consensual legal devices that are not technically contracts. Examples include deeds, wills and trusts, and commercial devices, such as negotiable instruments and letters of credit. Default rules can also be avoided by the doctrine of consent in tort law.

[82] Uniform Commercial Code §2-308.

[83] Restatement of Torts (Second) §402A (1975).

[84] *Id.* comment m. *See generally* Richard C. Ausness, *"Waive" Goodbye to Tort Liability: A Proposal to Remove Paternalism from Product Sales Transactions*, 37 San Diego L. Rev. 293 (2000).

[85] One can distinguish among default rules by the process parties must use to opt out of them. Some default rules require more elaborate processes than others. *See, e.g.*, Ian Ayres & Robert Gertner, *Filling Gaps in Incomplete Contracts: An Economic Theory of Default Rules*, 99 Yale L. J. 87 (1989) (contrasting penalty, tailored and untailored default rules); Stephen J. Ware, *Consumer Arbitration As Exceptional Consumer Law (with a Contractualist Reply to Carrington & Haagen)*, 29 McGeorge L. Rev. 195, 219 (1998) (contrasting contractual and "knowing and voluntary" standards).

How can we know if the arbitration award effects such a deprivation? Surely, that does not necessarily occur any time an arbitrator rules against a consumer in a product-liability action. Sometimes, the consumer-plaintiff will fail to prove her case and should lose under a correct application of product-liability law. But whenever the arbitrator rules against a consumer in a product-liability action, it is possible that the arbitrator is not applying the law correctly and thus depriving the consumer of her right to recover for personal injury from Seller's "unreasonably dangerous" goods. The only way to prevent this deprivation is for a court to review the award to ensure that the consumer's loss resulted from a correct application of the law by the arbitrator. And this applies not just to product liability cases but to the arbitration of any claims asserting rights conferred by mandatory law.[86] Therefore, a Revised FAA should instruct courts to vacate an arbitration award that was based on the arbitrators' error of law if the parties could not have formed an enforceable contract to avoid such law, that is, if such law is mandatory. In other words, when arbitrators hear claims arising out of mandatory rules, courts should review de novo the arbitrators' legal rulings on such claims.[87]

4.4(2)(C) Arbitration Arising Out of Post-Dispute Agreements

While courts should vacate awards based on errors of law that deprive parties of rights conferred by mandatory law, this conclusion applies only to awards rendered in arbitration pursuant to pre-dispute arbitration agreements. It does not apply to awards rendered in arbitration pursuant to post-dispute arbitration agreements. Post-dispute arbitration agreements are like post-dispute settlement agreements except that, instead of the parties settling themselves, they delegate their settlement decision to their agent, the arbitrator. Post-dispute settlement agreements are, of course, routinely enforced

[86] The Supreme Court has several times come close to recognizing this point. When the Court has enforced agreements to arbitrate claims arising under mandatory law, it has said "'although judicial scrutiny of arbitration awards necessarily is limited, such review is sufficient to ensure that arbitrators comply with the requirements of the statute.'" *Gilmer v. Interstate/Johnson Lane Corp.*, 500 U.S. 20, 32 n.4 (1991) (quoting *Shearson/American Express, Inc. v. McMahon*, 482 U.S. 220, 232 (1987)). *See also Mitsubishi Motors Corporation v. Soler Chrysler-Plymouth Inc.*, 473 U.S. 614 (1985).

Unfortunately, the Court's assertion is more aspirational than descriptive. Current judicial review is not "sufficient to ensure that arbitrators comply with the requirements of the statute." *See* Sections 4.4(2)(E)–(F).

[87] Judicial review would have to extend to arbitrators' factual rulings to the extent necessary to prevent a dishonest arbitrator from making incorrect factual findings that compel the arbitrators' desired legal rulings.

without any judicial review over how the parties chose to resolve claims arising out of mandatory rules. Awards rendered in arbitration pursuant to post-dispute agreements to arbitrate should not be reviewed for errors of law anymore than courts review settlement agreements for "errors of law." For example, in arbitration pursuant to a post-dispute agreement, the parties' agent (the arbitrator) can hold that Consumer has no right to recover for personal injury from Seller's "unreasonably dangerous" goods because the parties' post-dispute contract (settlement agreement) could have established the same thing. In sum, post-dispute arbitration agreements are like post-dispute settlement agreements, while pre-dispute arbitration agreements are like pre-dispute settlement agreements.[88]

4.4(2)(D) Claims Arising Out of Default Rules

Although courts should engage in de novo review of arbitration awards with respect to claims arising under mandatory law, courts should not at all review the legal rulings of arbitration awards with respect to claims arising under default law. Even arbitration awards that result from a "manifest disregard of law" should be confirmed if it was default law that the arbitrator disregarded. Because parties could have directly avoided default law by simply contracting around it, the parties should be free to indirectly avoid default law by agreeing to arbitrate before an arbitrator who has the discretion to disregard such law or, for that matter, is required by the arbitration agreement to disregard such law.

While arbitrators should be free to disregard default law, because the parties were free to disregard it, the parties can – in their arbitration agreement – constrain the arbitrator's discretion with respect to matters of default law. For example, the agreement can specify that the arbitrator must apply the law of a particular state. Or the agreement can specify that the arbitrator must apply, instead of the law any state, the privately-created law of a

[88] Here lies the answer to Judge Easterbrook's question: "If [the parties] may resolve their differences [in a settlement agreement] without [conforming to mandatory law], why can't an arbitrator, as their agent, prescribe the same outcome?" *George Watts & Son, Inc. v. Tiffany and Co.*, 248 F.3d 577, 580 (7th Cir. 2001) (Easterbrook, J.). The answer is that the settlement agreement to which Judge Easterbook refers is a post-dispute agreement, while the arbitration outcome to which he refers arises out of a pre-dispute agreement. It is true that "[i]n the main, an arbitrator acts as the parties' agent and as their delegate may do anything the parties may do directly," *id.*, but it is crucial to add the pre-/post-dispute distinction so the sentence reads: in the main, an arbitrator acts as the parties' agent and as their delegate may do anything the parties may *have done* directly *when they agreed to arbitrate.*

particular trade association.[89] Either way, the arbitrator's failure to apply the contractually-specified law would be a ground for vacatur under the proposal made earlier in Section 4.4(4) of this chapter.

4.4(2)(E) Perspective

The sharp distinction I have drawn – between arbitration of claims arising out of mandatory law and claims arising out of default law – would be a significant change from current case law, which generally authorizes courts to vacate awards resulting from a "manifest disregard of the law" by the arbitrator,[90] regardless of whether the law disregarded is mandatory or default.[91] I justify this change on the merits argued previously and with the historical point that, at the time the FAA was enacted and for generations thereafter, arbitration tended to resolve claims arising out of default law,

[89] Stephen J. Ware, *supra* Note 67 at 744–54. Within the bounds in which government-created law permits freedom of contract, the parties and their arbitrators can produce entire bodies of privately created law.

> Not only can agreements require arbitrators to apply rules, agreements can require arbitrators to write reasoned opinions. As the Widget Dealers Association arbitrators build a supply of precedents, they can be contractually required to follow precedents in future cases. So the privately-created law consists of not only unwritten norms and/or written rules, but also decisional law. In short, arbitration can produce a sophisticated, comprehensive legal system.
>
> Even better, it can produce many such systems. The law – unwritten norms, written rules and decisional law – of the Widget Dealers Association may differ from the law of the Gadget Dealers Association. Both may differ from the laws of the Sierra Club, the Alabama Baptist Convention, the American Association of Retired People, the Rotary Club, or the Saab Owners Association. Thus emerges privatized law in the fullest sense. There is diversity because what is best for some is not best for others. But there is also a process of experimentation in which lawmakers learn from each other and copy laws which seem better. There may even be open competition among different lawmakers to earn money by producing better laws. A market for law develops. This privatized system produces better law than does a system in which government monopolizes lawmaking. The principles animating privatization around the world apply to lawmaking just as they apply to coal mining or mail delivery.

Id. at 746–7.

[90] *See, e.g.*, Macneil et al., Federal Arbitration Law §40.7; Stephen L. Hayford, *A New Paradigm for Commercial Arbitration: Rethinking the Relationship Between Reasoned Awards and the Judicial Standards for Vacatur*, 66 Geo. Wash. L. Rev. 443, 466–6 (1998).

Although it was nearly impossible, until about 1997, to find a case vacating an arbitration award in reliance on the "manifest disregard of law" doctrine, since that time some courts have begun to apply the doctrine more aggressively. Ware, Alternative Dispute Resolution, *supra* Note 72 at §2.45(a)(2).

[91] Courts do seem more willing to find a manifest disregard of law when the law in question is statutory and when the party harmed by the disregard is a consumer or other party thought to lack bargaining power. *See, e.g., Halligan v. Piper Jaffray, Inc.*, 148 F.3d 197 (2d Cir. 1998); *Cole v. Burns International Security Services*, 105 F.3d 1465 (D.C. Cir. 1997). The flaw in these distinctions is discussed infra. *See* text at Notes 94–101.

rather than mandatory law.[92] Had the drafters of the original FAA foreseen both the growth of mandatory law and the expansion of arbitration to resolve claims arising out of it, the original FAA might have instructed courts to vacate awards that would otherwise avoid the strictures of mandatory law. Or those drafters might have written the FAA so that it did not require enforcement of pre-dispute agreements to arbitrate claims arising out of mandatory law. Either would accomplish the goal of ensuring that parties cannot do indirectly, through a pre-dispute arbitration agreement, what they cannot do directly in a pre-dispute contract lacking an arbitration clause, forego rights conferred by mandatory law.[93]

In addition to being a significant change from current law, the sharp distinction between arbitration of claims arising out of mandatory and default law is also a significant change from what several other commentators have advocated. While I am hardly the only commentator whose call for tightened judicial review of arbitration awards focuses on mandatory law,[94] some

[92] *See supra* Note 76 and accompanying text.

[93] As an aside, I feel compelled to add that I oppose much of the mandatory law enacted since the FAA so I am sort of pleased that arbitration now allows parties to opt out of such law. But I believe candor and logical consistency require those of us who oppose mandatory law to seek to repeal it outright, not to use arbitration to make an end run around it.

[94] I proposed this distinction between claims arising out of mandatory and default law in a 1999 law review article, Stephen J. Ware, *Default Rules from Mandatory Rules: Privatizing Law Through Arbitration*, 83 Minn. L. Rev. 703 (1999), which focused on domestic arbitration. In the same year, Dean Phillip McConnaughay published an excellent article that, although focused on international arbitration, made similar arguments based on this distinction. *See* Philip J. McConnaughay, *The Risks and Virtues of Lawlessness: A "Second Look" at International Commercial Arbitration*, 93 Nw. U. L. Rev. 453, 514–15 (1999) ("Achieving the compliance objectives of mandatory U.S. law – at least to the extent those objectives remain achievable in a private arbitral context – would require courts to refuse recognition or enforcement of a mandatory law award unless the award was both (1) rendered pursuant to arbitral procedures and rules of discovery and evidence closely approximating those that would have applied had the mandatory law claim been resolved in U.S. court, and (2) demonstrably correct.")

Others, often writing on international arbitration, have also used the distinction between claims arising out of mandatory and default law in recommending different approaches to judicial review of arbitration awards. See Andrew T. Guzman, *Arbitrator Liability: Reconciling Arbitration and Mandatory Rules*, 49 Duke L. J. 1279 (2000) ("existing rules governing judicial review of arbitral decisions are not only inadequate to ensure that mandatory rules are applied, but they actually encourage arbitrators to ignore such rules"; recommending that the losing party in an arbitration be able to sue the arbitrator on the ground that a mandatory rule was ignored); Eric A. Posner, *Arbitration and Harmonization of International Commercial Law: A Defense of Mitsubishi*, 39 Va. J. Int'l L. 647, 651 (1999) ("The dilemma can be stated succinctly. If domestic courts enforce arbitration awards, rather than subjecting them to de novo review, arbitrators will ignore local mandatory rules. However, if courts subject arbitration awards to de novo review in order to ensure that mandatory rules are respected, the benefits of arbitration – predictability, neutrality, and other commentators have focused on the arbitration of *statutory* claims, as opposed to the arbitration of claims arising out of *mandatory law*. These commentators argue that if statutory claims are arbitrable then courts should review arbitrators' decisions more aggressively than they do under the current, deferential "manifest disregard of law" standard.[95] "Framed for contractual disputes, the 'manifest disregard' standard may be too deferential for arbitration of public law claims,"[96] suggests Samuel Estreicher. Similarly, Richard Speidel argues that "courts should have clear authority, when statutory claims are involved, to vacate or modify an arbitrator's award where arbitral procedures denied an adequate hearing or where the arbitrator made an error of law."[97]

Both Professor Estreicher and Professor Speidel expressly distinguish between contract claims (which should receive deferential judicial review), and statutory claims (which should receive heightened judicial review). There is, of course, substantial overlap between the default/mandatory categories and the contract/statutory categories, with mandatory rules more prevalent in the statutory context. The contract/statutory distinction does not work as well, however. First, the contract/statutory distinction leaves unaddressed claims arising out of common law other than contract law; for example, much of tort law. Mandatory common law rules deserve no less fidelity from arbitrators than mandatory statutory rules.[98] Therefore,

minimization of litigation cost – are lost." "The main contribution of the paper is a proof that the optimal strategy of courts, under plausible conditions, is to engage in random de novo review of arbitration decisions"). Professor Rogers says "anxiety over arbitrators applying mandatory law has become something of a mania, often producing extreme proposals." Catherine A. Rogers, *Context and Institutional Structure in Attorney Regulation: Constructing an Enforcement Regime for International Arbitration*, 39 Stan. J. Int'l L. 1, 53 n.282 (2003) (citing Guzman, 49 Duke L.J. at 1316).

On the more general topic of mandatory rules in international arbitration, see Guidetta Cordero Moss, International Commercial Arbitration: Party Autonomy and Mandatory Rules (1999).

95 That standard is summarized in Macneil et al., Federal Arbitration Law §40.7.

96 Samuel *Estreicher, Predispute Agreements to Arbitrate Statutory Employment Claims*, 72 N.Y.U. L. Rev. 1344, 1375 n.22 (1997) (apparently treating "statutory" and "public law" as synonymous, at least in the employment law context).

97 Richard E. Speidel, *Arbitration of Statutory Rights Under the Federal Arbitration Act: The Case for Reform*, 4 Ohio St. J. Disp. Resol. 157 (1989).

98 My reason for rejecting the contract/statutory distinction is somewhat different from that of Professor Park, who says:

> "Statutory right" is a problematic label. In a civil law system, contract rights may be statutory, and in a common law system "core public policies" may be embedded in common law doctrines as important as those underpinning statutes. Whether the claim is based on statute or common law is less significant than whether the enforcement of the right directly protects the interest of non-contracting parties. Reference to "statutory claims" may be shorthand for claims which cannot be abrogated consensually by the parties. This begs the

courts should review de novo arbitrators' legal rulings on claims arising out of mandatory law, whether the source of that law is a statute or the common law. Second, not all statutory law is mandatory. When arbitrators resolve claims arising under default rules, whether of a statute or the common law, courts should not review the award for legal error, but only under the grounds otherwise found in the FAA or the parties' arbitration agreement.[99]

While Estreicher and Speidel propose a distinction between deferential review of contract claims and heightened review of statutory claims, Professor Sternlight proposes a distinction based on the type of parties rather than the type of claim. She distinguishes between deferential judicial review of arbitration between "two large companies that had bargained for the arbitration clause" and the need for heightened judicial review of arbitration arising out of consumer form contracts. Sternlight says:

> By limiting their review of arbitrators' decisions courts are simply furthering the policy of sacrificing consumer interests to achieve judicial economy. The FAA was written to limit, not eliminate, appeal. Although courts should refuse to conduct de novo review on many arbitration decisions, they should not be reluctant to set aside arbitral awards that are clearly unfounded and inconsistent with applicable law.[100]

There is, of course, substantial overlap between the default/mandatory categories and the business/consumer categories, with mandatory rules more prevalent in the consumer context. But the (relatively few) mandatory rules

> question of how claims whose resolution affects principally the parties to the arbitration agreement are to be distinguished from claims whose settlement has a direct and important impact on the community at large, which includes persons not signatories to the arbitration agreement.

William W. Park, *Private Adjudicators and the Public Interest: The Expanding Scope of International Arbitration*, 12 Brook J. Int'l L. 629, 630, n.3 (1986). To determine whether a right is conferred by default or mandatory law, a court need not determine "whether the enforcement of the right directly protects the interest of non-contracting parties" or "has a direct and important impact on the community at large." To determine whether a right is conferred by default or mandatory law, a court determines whether it would enforce a pre-dispute contract giving up the right conferred by that law. If the answer is no, that might be because the right directly protects the interest of non-contracting parties, or it might be for some other reason, such as protecting the contracting party herself by preventing her from giving up a right that she may want later. It is commonly said that "[t]here are two justifications for mandatory rules: paternalism and externalities." Steven L. Schwarcz, *Rethinking Freedom of Contract: A Bankruptcy Paradigm*, 77 Tex. L. Rev. 515, 535 (1999). Park understandably focuses on externalities in writing on international arbitration, a context in which the sophistication of the parties makes paternalism (or "parentalism") unlikely.

99 *See* Section 4.4(2)(D).

100 Jean Sternlight, *Panacea or Corporate Tool?: Debunking the Supreme Court's Preference for Binding Arbitration*, 74 Wash. U. L. Q. 637, 711 (1996).

in the business context deserve no less fidelity from arbitrators than mandatory rules in the consumer context. Therefore, courts should review de novo arbitrators' legal rulings on claims arising out of mandatory law regardless of the parties involved. Second, not all law governing consumers and other individuals is mandatory. When arbitrators resolve claims arising under default rules, regardless of the parties involved, courts should not review the award for legal error, but only under the grounds otherwise found in the FAA or the parties' arbitration agreement.[101]

4.4(2)(F) Practical Concerns

One practical concern about the sharp distinction I have drawn – between arbitration of claims arising out of mandatory law and claims arising out of default law – is that courts would have trouble controlling their understandable desire to do justice.

> Once the barndoor is open, so to speak, to review some of an arbitrator's legal rulings, will a court be tempted to review all the legal rulings in that case, even though the court should confine itself to rulings on claims arising under mandatory rules? This concern is heightened by the timing of judicial review after arbitration, in contrast to the arbitrability decision made before arbitration. A court making an arbitrability decision prior to arbitration might be worried about whether the arbitrators might do an injustice. But that worry seems less likely to motivate a court than a completed arbitration award in which the arbitrators actually did injustice.
>
> Another practical concern arises from the fact that arbitration pleadings often do not identify discrete causes of action. There may be nothing resembling what is standard in litigation – a complaint with discrete counts alleging discrete legal claims. Arbitration pleadings are often so informal that there is ambiguity about what claims are asserted or even if the concept of "claims" applies. Thus, parties who lose at arbitration may move to vacate the award on the ground that the arbitrator did not apply mandatory law when there is much doubt about whether claims arising under mandatory law were even asserted in arbitration.
>
> To counter this, courts may need to require parties to announce at the outset of arbitration whether they are asserting any claims arising under mandatory law. This would alert other parties to the risk of a motion to vacate for failure to apply the law and to the need for a record of the arbitration proceedings. Requiring arbitration pleadings to announce whether they assert claims arising under mandatory law would partially "judicialize" arbitration procedure, adding legalistic formalities that may make the process less attractive

[101] *See* Section 4.4(2)(D).

to many parties. Requiring arbitration pleadings to announce whether they assert claims arising under mandatory law would also contravene the freedom to contract for the procedures of arbitration. Thus it should be imposed only to the extent needed to ensure that parties who, post-dispute, demand an application of mandatory law receive that application. Accordingly, parties who do not announce at the outset of arbitration that claims under mandatory law are being asserted should be precluded from seeking judicial review of the arbitrators' legal rulings. They have waived such review.[102]

Section 4.5 Clarify the Scope of the FAA: Only Sections 1 and 2 Apply in State Court

4.5(1) Introduction

For a long time after its enactment in 1925, only federal courts applied the FAA.[103] It was not until the 1984 case of *Southland Corp. v. Keating*,[104] that the Supreme Court concluded that the FAA also applies in state court. Scholars debate whether *Southland* transformed the FAA into something more sweeping than its drafters wanted,[105] and at least one Supreme Court justice stands ready to overrule it.[106] Regardless of whether *Southland* best interpreted the original FAA, its result is good policy so a Revised FAA should codify it and thus greatly reduce the chance of it being overruled as the Court's membership changes.

4.5(2) A Revised FAA's Reach into State Court

4.5(2)(A) The Basic Rule that Sections 1 and 2 Apply in State Court

While *Southland* applied the FAA to a state court case, the Court was careful to note that not all of the FAA applies in state court. In particular, *Southland* indicated that FAA Sections 3 and 4 do not apply in state court. In 1983,

[102] Ware, *supra* Note 89, 83 Minn. L. Rev. at 740–1.

[103] Macneil, American Arbitration Law, Chs. 7–12.

[104] 465 U.S. 1, 11 (1984).

[105] This is the view of Ian Macneil, who criticizes *Southland* as a results-oriented decision at odds with the FAA's legislative history. Macneil, *supra* Note 103. *See also* David S. Schwartz, *Correcting Federalism Mistakes in Statutory Interpretation: The Supreme Court and the Federal Arbitration Act*, 67 Law & Contemp. Prob. 5 (2004). By contrast, a recent article by Christopher Drahozal argues that, as a matter of legislative history, *Southland* "reached the correct conclusion." Christopher R. Drahozal, *In Defense of Southland: Reexamining the Legislative History of the Federal Arbitration Act*, 78 Notre Dame L. Rev. 101, 169 (2002).

[106] *Allied-Bruce Terminix Cos. v. Dobson* 513 U.S. 265, 285 (1995) (Scalia, J., dissenting).

the year preceding *Southland*, the Court said that "state courts, as much as federal courts, are obliged to grant stays of litigation under §3 of the Act."[107] But *Southland* backtracked: "we do not hold that §§3 and 4 of the Arbitration Act apply to proceedings in state courts."[108] And in 1989, the Supreme Court stated: "we have never held that §§3 and 4, which by their terms appear to apply only to proceedings in federal court, are nonetheless applicable in state court."[109] This distinction between Section 2, which does apply in state court, and Sections 3 and 4, which seem not to, remains the last word from the Supreme Court.

A Revised FAA should codify the results of the case law just discussed. FAA Sections 1 and 2 should apply in both federal and state court, while Sections 3–16 should apply only in federal court. This result strikes a reasonable balance between federal and state interests. On the one hand, arbitration agreements involving interstate commerce are made enforceable. This vindicates the federal interest in promoting interstate commerce pursuant to the United States Constitution's Commerce Clause. Of course, the enforcement of contracts generally promotes commerce, but there is a reason why the enforcement of arbitration agreements in particular is especially closely connected to the *federal* interest in promoting *interstate* commerce. State courts have incentives to favor their own citizens over out-of-state businesses,[110] and some states' courts have earned reputations for bias against outsiders.[111] Arbitration agreements are often used by these outsiders to avoid that bias. Arbitration is often a way to replace the provincial, hostile-to-outsiders norms of some state courts with the cosmopolitan norms of interstate commerce. Thus, there is a very rational reason why the enforcement of arbitration agreements should be part of federal law, rather than left up to the states.

On the other hand, confining FAA Sections 3–16 to federal court respects state sovereignty in a federal system. Sections 3–16 are less about the

[107] *Moses H. Cone Memorial Hospital v. Mercury Construction Corp.*, 460 U.S. 1, 26, n.34 (1983).

[108] *See Southland, supra* Note 104, 465 U.S. 1, 16, n.10 (1984).

[109] *Volt Information Sciences, Inc. v. Board of Trustees of the Leland Stanford Junior University*, 489 U.S. 468, 477, n.6 (1989).

[110] The following words of Judge Richard Neely from the West Virginia Supreme Court of Appeals are often quoted:

> As long as I am allowed to redistribute wealth from out-of-state companies to injured in-state plaintiffs, I shall continue to do so. Not only is my sleep enhanced when I give someone else's money away, but so is my job security, because the in-state plaintiffs, their families, and their friends will reelect me.

Richard Neely, The Product Liability Mess 4 (1988).

[111] The bias to which I refer is not a bias in the legal rules themselves, but in their application by judges and juries. It is bias found, not in the law in the books, but in the law in action.

substantive question of what contracts should be enforced than about procedural questions of how courts should conduct themselves. For example, Sections 3–16 go into such details as the manner in which certain court papers must be served and the number of days notice that must be given.[112] There is no need for federal mandates on such topics. Principles of federalism counsel for state courts to make their own rules on these essentially procedural subjects.

It is true that leaving only Sections 1 and 2 applicable in state court leaves many federal-preemption issues unresolved. Suppose, for instance, that a state vacates arbitration awards on grounds not found in FAA Section 10. Since Section 10 does not apply in state court, one might assume that there is no federal preemption of the state grounds for vacatur. On the other hand, suppose that the state's grounds for vacatur are so extensive that they apply to nearly all arbitration awards. This would effectively convert the binding arbitration agreed to by the parties into non-binding arbitration. And that would plainly be preempted by FAA Section 2's requirement that arbitration agreements be "valid, irrevocable and enforceable."[113] There will be other similar issues, issues on which states may depart to some degree from FAA Sections 3–16 but on which too much of a departure is preempted by Section 2. These questions of degree will and should be resolved on a case-by-case basis, rather than with the broad brush of legislation.

4.5(2)(B) Specific Performance in State Court

Applying FAA Section 2, but not Sections 3 and 4, in state court raises an issue highlighted by Justice Thomas's dissent in the 1995 case, *Allied-Bruce Terminix Cos. v. Dobson.*[114] *Allied-Bruce* held that the FAA preempts an Alabama statute prohibiting courts from enforcing arbitration agreements with the remedy of specific performance, that is, orders to arbitrate.[115] Justice Thomas's dissent in *Allied-Bruce* pointed out that this Alabama statute does not, by its terms, make arbitration agreements unenforceable but merely limits the remedies courts can use in enforcing arbitration agreements.[116] For example, the Alabama statute permits courts to award money damages for

[112] 9 U.S.C. §§4, 9 & 12.

[113] 9 U.S.C. §2 (2000).

[114] 513 U.S. 265, 281 (1995).

[115] Ala.Code §8-1-41(3)(1975)("The following obligations cannot be specifically enforced:. . . An agreement to submit a controversy to arbitration").

[116] *See* 513 U.S. at 293 (Thomas, J., dissenting) ("A contract surely can be 'valid, irrevocable, and enforceable' even though it can be enforced only through actions for damages."); *id.* at 294 ("the [Alabama] statute does not itself make executory arbitration agreements invalid, revocable, or unenforceable").

breach of an arbitration agreement. Therefore, Justice Thomas concluded, the Alabama statute does not conflict with the FAA Section 2's requirement that arbitration agreements be "valid, irrevocable and enforceable."[117] It only conflicts with the FAA's requirement that the remedy for enforcement be specific performance, but that requirement is found in FAA Sections 3 and 4 and those sections do not apply in state court so they could not preempt the Alabama statute.

In reply to Justice Thomas (and on behalf of the *Allied-Bruce* majority), one can note that it is virtually impossible to calculate money damages for breach of arbitration agreements and so, in the days prior to specific performance of arbitration agreements, courts generally awarded no more than nominal damages of a dollar or so.[118] Such a minimal remedy might well conflict with – indeed make a mockery of – FAA Section 2's requirement that arbitration agreements be "valid, irrevocable and enforceable."[119] So one could conclude that FAA Section 2, alone, requires state courts to enforce arbitration agreements with the remedy of specific performance. But to avoid debate on this issue, a Revised FAA should clarify in the text of Section 2 that courts should enforce arbitration agreements with the remedy of specific performance.

4.5(2)(C) FAA Creates No Federal Jurisdiction

While the line of cases culminating in *Southland* establishes that the FAA (particularly Section 2) is substantive, as opposed to procedural law, it is unusual federal substantive law in that it creates no federal jurisdiction. Ordinarily, a party asserting its federal rights is entitled to have a federal court hear its claims. But that is not true of parties asserting their FAA rights. These parties are relegated to state court unless they can point to some other source of federal jurisdiction.[120] As *Southland* put it,

> While the Federal Arbitration Act creates federal substantive law requiring the parties to honor arbitration agreements, it does not create any independent federal-question jurisdiction under 28 U.S.C. §1331 (1976) or otherwise. This seems implicit in the provisions in §3 for a stay by a "court in which such suit

[117] 9 U.S.C. §2 (2000).

[118] *See, e.g., Munson v. Straits of Dover S. S. Co.*, 102 F. 926, 928 (2d Cir. 1900) (holding that plaintiff, who sought damages in the form of lawyer's fees and costs incurred in defending a lawsuit for breach of agreement to arbitrate, was entitled to nominal damages only); Macneil, American Arbitration Law 20 (1992) (damages remedy was "largely ineffective").

[119] 9 U.S.C. §2 (2000).

[120] See Macneil et al., Federal Arbitration Law §9.2.1.

> is pending" and in §4 that enforcement may be ordered by "any United States district court which, save for such agreement, would have jurisdiction under Title 28, in a civil action or in admiralty of the subject matter of a suit arising out of the controversy between the parties."[121]

A Revised FAA should continue to create no federal jurisdiction because experience has not a shown a significant or widespread problem with state court application of the FAA.

Section 4.6 Conclusion

The FAA generally embodies the contractual approach to arbitration law and most Supreme Court decisions are faithful to this approach, as well. The reforms proposed in this chapter would further advance the progress of arbitration law in the United States toward a consistently contractual approach. To recap, that approach consists of at least three principles:

> **First Principle:** a court should not send a dispute to arbitration unless the parties have formed an enforceable contract requiring arbitration of that dispute.
>
> **Second Principle:** arbitration agreements should be enforced "save upon such grounds as exist at law or in equity for the revocation of any contract."[122]
>
> **Third Principle:** because an arbitrator's power derives from the parties' contract, the arbitrator should not be permitted to reach a result that the parties could not have reached themselves by simply contracting for it.

The reforms proposed in this chapter would advance these principles as follows.

The repeal of the separability doctrine would prevent courts from sending a dispute to arbitration unless the parties have formed an enforceable contract requiring arbitration of that dispute.

Enforcement of arbitration agreements "save upon such grounds as exist at law or in equity for the revocation of any contract" would be encouraged by repealing the FAA's employment exclusion and by changing the FAA's language to endorse enforcement of: (1) agreements to arbitrate disputes that do not arise out of the contract containing the arbitration clause, (2) electronic agreements to arbitrate, and (3) agreements specifying grounds for vacating arbitration awards.

Eliminating court enforcement of arbitration subpoenas and instituting de novo judicial review of arbitrator's rulings on claims arising out of

[121] *Southland, supra* Note 114, 465 U.S. 1, 16 n.9 (1984).
[122] 9 U.S.C. §2 (2000).

mandatory law would both effectuate the principle that, because an arbitrator's power derives from the parties' contract, the arbitrator should not be permitted to reach a result that the parties could not have reached themselves by simply contracting for it.

Finally, clarifying that the FAA's first two sections apply in state and federal court but that its remaining sections apply only in federal court would both strengthen the contractual approach to arbitration law and clarify the scope of the FAA.

CHAPTER FIVE

Consumer Arbitration

Jean R. Sternlight

Section 5.1 Introduction

The use of arbitration in the consumer context in the United States has been highly controversial. As one consumer organization put it: Mandatory, pre-dispute binding arbitration clauses in consumer contracts "are the single biggest threat to consumer rights in recent years, a de-facto rewrite of the Constitution that undermines a broad range of consumer protections painstakingly built into law."[1] The President of another consumer protection organization similarly stated: "[T]he use of mandatory pre-dispute arbitration clauses presents a grave problem for consumer rights and public safety."[2] This chapter will examine the nature and origin of this form of arbitration, why it has been so controversial, how it has been regulated to date, and what if any further regulation is desirable.

As has been discussed in Chapters 1 and 2, arbitration was traditionally agreed to, knowingly, by two or more business entities. Such businesses voluntarily traded the formality and publicity of litigation for the potentially cheaper, quicker, and more expert arbitration.

Historically, consumers and businesses did not enter into arbitration agreements with one another in the United States. Indeed, to the limited extent that the possibility of such arbitration was considered by Congress in 1925, when it passed the FAA, those few who spoke on the issue made clear that they did not view such a use of arbitration as appropriate. For example, when one Senator voiced a concern that arbitration contracts might be

[1] National Consumer Law Center Inc. Press Release July 28, 2003, *Consumer and Media Alert: The Small Print That's Devastating Major Consumer Rights* at www.consumerlaw.org, accessed on July 28, 2004.

[2] Joan Claybrook, President, Public Citizen, Testimony to House Judiciary Subcommittee on Commercial and Administrative Law re: H.R. 534, the Fairness and Voluntary Arbitration Act, June 7, 2000.

"offered on a take-it-or-leave-it basis to captive customers or employees," the Senator was reassured by the bill's supporters that they did not intend for the bill to cover such situations.[3]

Section 5.2 The Emergence of Consumer Arbitration

The first United States industry to attempt to impose arbitration on persons who might be deemed consumers was the securities field. Beginning in 1872, the New York Stock Exchange began to require its investors to sign form agreements stating that they would arbitrate, rather than litigate, any future disputes.[4] In subsequent years many other exchanges and brokerages have also established arbitration programs for settling security disputes.[5] Although many such investors may have been business entities or knowledgeable individual investors, some were no doubt neither rich nor knowledgeable. Nonetheless, these clauses were typically enforced by the courts, particularly after the passage of the Federal Arbitration Act in 1925.

However, the United States Supreme Court's 1953 decision in *Wilko v. Swan*[6] limited the types of claims that investors could be required to arbitrate with their brokers. *Wilko* was a case in which an individual sued partners at his brokerage house under Section 12(2) of the federal Securities Act of 1933 alleging that he had been fraudulently induced to buy 1,600 shares of a particular company. In response, the defendants asked the court to stay litigation in favor of the arbitration called for in the margin agreement entered into between the customer and the brokerage. By a seven to two majority the Supreme Court rejected the brokers' argument, instead holding that the Securities Act of 1933 must be interpreted to prohibit this use of arbitration. Relying on a provision of the Securities Act that voided "[a]ny condition, stipulation, or provision binding any person acquiring any security to waive compliance with any provision of this subchapter or of the rules and regulations of the Commission,"[7] the Court explained that the Act "was drafted

[3] *Prima Paint Corp v. Flood & Conklin Mfg. Co.*, 388 U.S. 407, 414 (1967) (Black, J., dissenting) (citing Hearing on S. 4213 and S. 4214 before the Subcommittee of the Senate Committee on the Judiciary, 67th Cong. 4th Sess. 9–11 (1923). *See also* David S. Schwartz, *Enforcing Small Print to Protect Big Business: Employee and Consumer Right Claims in an Age of Compelled Arbitration*, 1997 Wis. L. Rev. 33, 75 (1997).

[4] *See* Constantine N. Katsoris, *The Resolution of Securities Disputes*, 6 Fordham J. Corp. & Fin. L. 307, 310 (2001).

[5] *See* Katsoris, *supra* Note 4. *See also* Constantine N. Katsoris, *The Arbitration of a Public Securities Dispute*, 53 Fordham L. Rev. 279, 292 (1984).

[6] 346 U.S. 427 (1953).

[7] 346 U.S. at 429 & n.6, quoting 15 U.S.C. §77n.

with an eye to the disadvantages under which buyers labor,"[8] specifically that sellers of stock possess more relevant information than buyers. Thus, found the Court, it would be inappropriate to find that the customer had knowingly selected arbitration, and that the clause could not be enforced as to a claim brought under the Securities Act of 1933. The *Wilko* decision no doubt discouraged businesses from seeking to impose arbitration on consumers in other contexts as well.

As has been recounted at length in this book and elsewhere,[9] the Supreme Court's attitude toward commercial arbitration changed dramatically beginning in the 1980s. Although the earliest cases marking this shift involved arbitration between two business entities,[10] by 1989 the Supreme Court had applied these precedents to reverse *Wilko* and require courts to enforce arbitration clauses imposed by securities brokerage houses on their investors as to all claims.[11] In essence the Court has ruled that when parties assent to a so-called "broad" arbitration clause they agree to arbitrate all statutory claims arising out of or related to the contract unless Congress has expressly reserved such issues for the courts.

5.2(1) Scope and Features of Consumer Arbitration

The Supreme Court's dramatic and rapid embrace of arbitration in general soon led to the creation of the new field of consumer arbitration. Throughout the 1990s, companies in a wide array of areas followed the lead of the securities industry and began to use form agreements to require their customers to agree to resolve all future disputes through arbitration rather than litigation. Examining the decisions in reported cases, one can see that arbitration soon began to be mandated by a broad range of companies including financial institutions (as to personal accounts, house and car loans, payday loans, and credit cards); service providers (termite exterminators, gymnasiums, telephone companies, tax preparers); and sellers of goods (mobile homes, computers, E-Bay). Arbitration has even been mandated in connection with games sponsored by the McDonald's hamburger chain and with respect to a mail-in on a Cheerios cereal box. In this new millennium, consumer arbitration has quickly expanded as well to health care (hospitals,

[8] 346 U.S. at 435.

[9] *See, e.g.*, Jean R. Sternlight, *Panacea or Corporate Tool?: Debunking the Supreme Court's Preference for Binding Arbitration*, 74 Wash. U.L.Q. 637 (1996).

[10] *See, e.g.*, *Scherk v. Alberto-Culver*, 417 U.S. 506 (1974); *Moses H. Cone Memorial Hospital v. Mercury Const.*, 460 U.S. 1 (1983).

[11] *Rodriguez de Quijas v. Shearson/American Express, Inc.*, 490 U.S. 477, 481 (1989).

health maintenance organizations, and hospitals), nursing homes, and educational institutions. One study of the "average Joe" in Los Angeles in 2001 showed that approximately one third of the consumer transactions in his life were covered by arbitration clauses.[12]

The new consumer arbitration has some features that were not present even in the securities arbitration upon which it was based. First, whereas the arbitration clauses prepared by brokerage houses were typically included in documents required to be signed by investors, companies soon realized that an actual signature was not required in order for a consumer arbitration agreement to be enforced by many U.S. courts. Section 2 of the FAA requires that an arbitration agreement be written, but does not mandate it be signed, in order to be enforceable. Thus, companies often impose arbitration on their consumers by including an arbitration agreement in a document that is received by the consumer but not necessarily read and certainly not signed. Specifically, it is now common to include arbitration clauses in small print notices or envelope "stuffers" or warranties contained in boxes or sent to consumers in the mail. Some arbitration clauses are contained in web sites, and some arbitration clauses have even been e-mailed to customers. Although a few courts have refused to enforce particular unsigned arbitration clauses for various contractual reasons, in general, courts do enforce arbitration clauses contained in small print unsigned documents, even though they were not signed by the consumer and even though the company can't necessarily provide specific evidence that the specific customer actually received the notice.[13]

Second, whereas the arbitration imposed by securities brokers was typically required at the beginning of the business relationship, that is at the time that the customer opened the account, companies now commonly impose arbitration after the relationship has already commenced. Credit card companies, for example, often send their customers small print notices stating that all future disputes will be governed by arbitration. Although there are exceptions, courts have often enforced such clauses. Sometimes companies even attempt to use such clauses to replace ongoing litigation with arbitration. For example, a clause issued by Banana Republic in

[12] Linda Demaine & Deborah Hensler, *"Volunteering" To Arbitrate Through Predispute Arbitration Clauses: The Average Consumer's Experience*, 67 LAW & CONTEMP. PROBS. 55 (2004). (The study focuses on industries that provided what the authors terms "important purchases" – transactions that were expensive, ongoing, or with potentially large impact. For example, expensive transactions include automobile purchases, ongoing transactions include purchasing long-distance telephone service, and significant impact purchases include purchase of health care services.)

[13] *See infra* Section 5.5(2) for further discussion of how courts are treating contractual and other challenges to consumer arbitration clauses.

June 2004 states that "[t]he New Arbitration Provision applies to Claims previously asserted in lawsuits filed before the effective date of any previous arbitration provision."[14]

Third, the broad expansion of consumer arbitration has likely meant that a less educated cadre of persons is now covered by arbitration clauses. Though not all securities investors are well educated, it seems reasonable to assume that such investors are better educated than the general public. In contrast, virtually all consumers, whether well educated or not, have phones and credit cards, purchase termite extermination services, and so on. Thus, courts have had to face situations in which consumers to whom arbitration notices were provided denied that they were aware of the clause, understood the clause, were literate, or even could see. Nonetheless, although there are some exceptions, for the most part courts have held that even illiterate or blind consumers can be bound by unsigned small print arbitration notices. One case to this effect is *Washington Mutual Financial Group v. Bailey*,[15] in which the court found that a group of illiterate plaintiffs were bound by the arbitration clause they had signed in connection with obtaining loans together with insurance they subsequently said they did not want or need. The illiterate plaintiffs complained that even after they told the bank they "could not read and inquired as to the nature of the documents they were signing," the bank stated only that they were signing "insurance and finance papers."[16] The Fifth Circuit found this contention irrelevant, explaining that parties to contracts have a duty to read the contract or have it read to them.[17]

A fourth important feature of the new consumer arbitration is that companies are increasingly using the arbitration clause not only to require arbitration but also to further limit consumers' procedural and even substantive rights. For example, some companies have included clauses in the arbitration agreement that shorten statutes of limitations, limit or eliminate discovery, require claimants to file in a distant forum, prevent consumers from joining together in a class action, or bar consumers from recovering particular forms of relief (injunctive, compensatory damages, punitive damages, or attorney fees). As will be discussed, the harshest of these provisions have led some courts to invalidate at least portions of particular arbitration clauses, but not all such limits have been challenged or voided.[18]

[14] Clause on file with Professor Sternlight.

[15] 364 F.3d 260 (5th Cir. 2004).

[16] *Id.* at 265.

[17] *Id.* at 266.

[18] For one examination of these clauses *see* David S. Schwartz, *Understanding Remedy-Stripping Arbitration Clauses: Validity, Arbitrability and Preclusion Principles*, 38 U.S.F.L. Rev. 49 (2003).

5.2(2) Some Illustrative Arbitration Clauses

This section provides examples of consumer arbitration clauses. The specific clauses have been chosen to show readers that such clauses vary tremendously in their length, complexity, and terms. Some but not all of the clauses expressly deny the consumers remedies or procedures that would have been available in court. Some but not all of the clauses reference provider rules that the consumer would need to look up to be clear how his or her rights had been affected.

In *Szetala v. Discover Bank*,[19] the parties litigated with respect to a notice inserted inside the customer's billing statement that purported to amend the terms of the Cardmember Agreement to include an arbitration clause. The court reports that in relevant part the amendment stated as follows:

> Arbitration. We Are Adding a New Section to Read as Follows:
>
> Arbitration of Disputes. In the event of any past, present or future claim or dispute (whether based upon contract, tort, statute, common law or equity) between you and us arising from or relating to your Account, any prior account you have had with us, your application, the relationships which result from your Account or the enforceability or scope of this arbitration provision, of the Agreement or of any prior agreement, you or we may elect to resolve the claim or dispute by binding arbitration.
>
> If Either You or We Elect Arbitration, Neither You Nor We Shall Have the Right to Litigate That Claim in Court or to Have a Jury Trial on That Claim. Pre-Hearing Discovery Rights and Post-Hearing Appeal Rights Will Be Limited. Neither You Nor We Shall Be Entitled to Join or Consolidate Claims in Arbitration by or Against Other Cardmembers with Respect to Other Accounts, or Arbitrate Any Claims as a Representative or Member of a Class or in a Private Attorney General Capacity. Even if all parties have opted to litigate a claim in court, you or we may elect arbitration with respect to any claim made by a new party or any new claims later asserted in that lawsuit, and nothing undertaken therein shall constitute a waiver of any rights under this arbitration provision.

[19] 97 Cal. App. 4th 1094 (Cal. App. 2002), *rev'd and remanded sub nom. Discover Bank v. Superior Court*, 36 Cal. 4th 148 (Cal. 2005).

The arbitration clause at issue in *Leonard v. Terminix International Co.*[20] was contained in a document the homeowners received in the mail and which was entitled "Termite Protection Plan." Section 9 of the Plan provided as follows:

> ARBITRATION. The Purchaser and Terminix agree that any controversy or claim between them arising out of or relating to this agreement shall be conducted in accordance with the Commercial Arbitration Rules then in force of the American Arbitration Association. The decision of the arbitrator shall be a final and binding resolution of the disagreement which may be entered as a judgment by any court of competent jurisdiction. Neither party shall sue the other where the basis of the suit is this agreement other than for enforcement of the arbitrator's decision. In no event shall either party be liable to the other for indirect, special or consequential damages or loss of anticipated profits.

Citibank also imposed on its customers a much longer arbitration clause, which read as follows:

> **Notice of Change in Terms Regarding Binding Arbitration to Your Citibank Card Agreement**
>
> Effective on the day after the Statement/Closing Date indicated on your November 2001 billing statement, we are amending your existing Citibank Card Agreement to include the following provision regarding binding arbitration. The binding arbitration provision does not apply to individual Claims of named parties in any lawsuit served on us before the effective date, or to Claims by unnamed members of a class in any certified class action if notice has been provided to the class by court direction before the effective date.
>
> **ARBITRATION:**
>
> **PLEASE READ THIS PROVISION OF THE AGREEMENT CAREFULLY. IT PROVIDES THAT ANY DISPUTE MAY DE RESOLVED BY BINDING ARBITRATION. ARBITRATION REPLACES THE RIGHT TO GO TO COURT, INCLUDING THE RIGHT TO A JURY AND THE RIGHT TO PARTICIPATE IN A CLASS ACTION OR SIMILAR PROCEEDING. IN ARBITRATION, A**

[20] 854 So.2d 529 (Ala. 2002).

DISPUTE IS RESOLVED BY AN ARBITRATOR INSTEAD OF A JUDGE OR JURY. ARBITRATION PROCEDURES ARE SIMPLER AND MORE LIMITED THAN COURT PROCEDURES.

Agreement to Arbitrate:

Either you or we may, without the other's consent, elect mandatory, binding arbitration for any claim, dispute, or controversy between you and us (called "Claims").

Claims Covered:

What Claims are subject to arbitration? All Claims relating to your account or a prior related account, or our relationship are subject to arbitration, including Claims regarding the application, enforceability, or interpretation of this Agreement and this arbitration provision. All Claims are subject to arbitration, no matter what legal theory they are based on or what remedy (damages, or injunctive or declaratory relief) they seek. This includes Claims based on contract, tort (including intentional tort), fraud, agency, your or our negligence, statutory or regulatory provisions, or any other sources of law; Claims made as counterclaims, cross-claims, third-party claims, interpleaders or otherwise; and Claims made independently or with other claims. A party who initiates a proceeding in court may elect arbitration with respect to any claim advanced in that proceeding by any other party. Claims and remedies sought as part of a class action, private attorney general or other representative action are subject to arbitration on an individual (non-class, non-representative) basis, and the arbitrator may award relief only on an individual (non-class, non-representative) basis.

Whose Claims are subject to arbitration? Not only ours and yours, but also Claims made by or against anyone connected with us or you or claiming through us or you, such as a co-applicant or authorized user of your account, an employee, agent, representative, affiliated company, predecessor or successor, heir, assignee, or trustee in bankruptcy.

What time frame applies to Claims subject to arbitration? Claims arising in the past, present, or future, including Claims arising before the opening of your account, are subject to arbitration.

Broadest interpretation. Any questions about whether Claims are subject to arbitration shall be resolved by interpreting this arbitration provision in the broadest way the law will allow it to be enforced. This arbitration provision is governed by the Federal Arbitration Act (the "FAA").

What about Claims filed in Small Claims Court? Claims filed in a small claims court are not subject to arbitration, so long as the matter remains in such court and advances only an individual (non-class, non-representative) Claim.

How Arbitration Works:

How does a party initiate arbitration? The party filing an arbitration must choose one of the following three arbitration firms and follow its rules and procedures for initiating and pursuing an arbitration: American Arbitration Association, JAMS, and National Arbitration Forum. Any arbitration hearing that you attend will be held at a place chosen by the arbitration firm in the same city as the U.S. District Court closest to your then current billing address, or at some other place to which you and we agree in writing. You may obtain copies of the current rules of each of the three arbitration firms and forms and instructions for initiating an arbitration by contacting them as follows:

American Arbitration Association • Web site: www.adr.org
335 Madison Avenue, Floor 10, New York, NY 10016-4605
JAMS Web site: www.jamsadr.com
1920 Main Street, Suite 300, Irvine, CA 92610
National Arbitration Forum • Web site: www.arbitration-forum.com
P.O. Box 50191, Minneapolis, MN 55405

At any time you or we may ask an appropriate court to compel arbitration of Claims, or to stay the litigation of Claims pending arbitration, even if such Claims are part of a lawsuit, unless a trial has begun or a final judgement has been entered. Even if a party fails to exercise these rights at any particular time, or in connection with any particular Claims, that party can still require arbitration at a later time or in connection with any other Claims.

What procedures and law are applicable in arbitration? A single, neutral arbitrator will resolve Claims. The arbitrator will be either a lawyer with at least 10 years experience or a retired or former judge, selected in accordance with the rules of the arbitration firm.

The arbitration will follow procedures and rules of the arbitration firm in effect on the date the arbitration is filed unless those procedures and rules are inconsistent with this Agreement, in which case this Agreement will prevail. Those procedures and rules may limit the discovery available to you or us. The arbitrator will take reasonable steps to protect customer account information and other confidential information if requested to do so by you or us. The arbitrator will apply applicable substantive law consistent with the FAA and applicable statutes of limitations, will honor claims of privilege recognized at law, and will have the power to award to a party any damages or other relief provided for under applicable law. You or we may choose to have a hearing and be represented by counsel. The arbitrator will make any award in writing and, if requested by you or us, will provide a brief statement of the reasons for the award. An award in arbitration shall determine the rights and obligations between the named parties only, and only in respect of the Claims in arbitration, and shall not have any bearing on the rights and obligations of any other person, or on the resolution of any other dispute.

Who pays? Whoever files the arbitration pays the initial filing fee. If we file, we pay; if you file, you pay, unless you get a fee waiver under the applicable rules of the arbitration firm. If you have paid the initial filing fee and you prevail, we will reimburse you for that fee. If there is a hearing, we will pay any fees of the arbitrator and arbitration firm for the first day of that hearing. All other fees will be allocated as provided by the rules of the arbitration firm and applicable by law. However, we will advance or reimburse your fees if the arbitration firm or arbitrator determines there is good reason for requiring us to do so, or if you ask us and we determine there is good reason for doing so. Each party will bear the expense of that party's attorneys, experts, and witnesses, and other expenses, regardless of which party prevails, but a party may recover any or all expenses from another party if the arbitrator, applying applicable law, so determines.

Who can be a party? Claims must be brought in the name of an individual person or entity and must proceed on an individual (non-class, non-representative) basis. The arbitrator will not award relief for or against anyone who is not a party. If you or we require arbitration of a Claim, neither you, we nor any other person may pursue the Claim in arbitration as a class action, private attorney general action or other representative action, nor may such Claim be pursued on your or our behalf in any litigation in any court. Claims, including assigned Claims, of two or more persons may not be joined or consolidated in the same arbitration. However, applicants, co-applicants, authorized users on a single account and/or related accounts, or corporate affiliates are here considered as one person.

When is an arbitration award final? The arbitrator's award is final and binding on the parties unless a party appeals it in writing to the arbitration firm within fifteen days of notice of the award. The appeal must request a new arbitration before a panel of three neutral arbitrators designated by the same arbitration firm. The panel will consider all factual and legal issues anew, follow the same rules that apply to a proceeding using a single arbitrator, and make decisions based on the vote of the majority. Costs will be allocated in the same way they are allocated for arbitration before a single arbitrator. An award by a panel is final and binding on the parties after fifteen days has passed. A final and binding award is subject to judicial review and enforcement as provided by the FAA or other applicable law.

Survival and severability of terms:

This arbitration provision shall survive: (i) termination or changes in the Agreement, the account, and the relationship between you and us concerning the account; (ii) the bankruptcy of any party; and

(iii) any transfer, sale or assignment of your account, or any amounts owed on your account, to any other person or entity. If any portion of this arbitration provision is deemed invalid or unenforceable, the remaining portions shall nevertheless remain in force. Any different agreement regarding arbitration must be agreed to in writing.

This binding arbitration provision applies to your Citibank card account ending in the last four numbers that appear after your name on the front of this mailing.

NON-ACCEPTANCE INSTRUCTIONS

If you do not wish to accept the binding arbitration provision contained in this change in terms notice, you must notify us in writing within 26 days after the Statement/Closing date indicated on your November 2001 billing statement stating your non acceptance. Include your name, address, and account number and mail to: Customer Service Center, P.O. Box 44121, Jacksonville, Florida, 32231–4121. If you notify us by that time that you do not accept the binding arbitration provision contained in this change in terms notice, you can continue to use your card(s) under your existing terms until the end of your current membership year or the expiration date on your card(s), whichever is later. At that time your account will be closed and you will be able to pay off your remaining balance under your existing terms.

Any consumer in the United States can check their files or daily mail to review additional variations on arbitration clauses.

5.2(3) A Uniquely U.S. Phenomenon

For now, at least, the mandatory imposition of pre-dispute binding arbitration on consumers by companies appears to be a uniquely U.S. phenomenon. Indeed, as will be discussed, policies issued by the European Union preclude companies from replacing consumers' litigation option with binding arbitration. However, it is important to further explain this statement, to prevent confusion.

Consumer arbitration does exist outside the United States, but it is not imposed on a pre-dispute mandatory basis. For example, in Britain the

Chartered Institute of Arbitrators offers a number of arbitration "schemes" to resolve disputes in an array of industries including travel, internet service providers, mortgages, and home construction.[21] After the dispute has arisen, consumers can elect to take their disputes to arbitration, rather than litigation. In some instances, if arbitration is elected by the consumer, the company must accept an arbitral forum.

In addition, in many countries consumer disputes are resolved by a special governmental agency. Sometimes these processes are called "arbitration," because they are relatively informal. However, these processes are unlike what we call "arbitration" in the United States in several respects. First, there is a great difference between a legislature mandating arbitration and a private company doing the same. Second, whereas U.S. arbitration permits disputants to pick their own private arbitrator, other countries' processes provide a government salaried employee as the arbitrator. Third, although U.S. arbitration is typically conducted privately and often creates no public record or precedent, most countries' government agencies would likely provide at least some access to their determinations.

Thus, what is apparently unique to the U.S., at least so far, is the phenomenon of private companies requiring their customers to agree to resolve future disputes through private binding arbitration rather than in court. Although it is very difficult to conduct research that covers the entire world, especially research that confirms the absence of a phenomenon, to date this author has not found mandatory binding consumer arbitration in use in other countries.[22]

Indeed, it seems that the use of mandatory pre-dispute arbitration would be prohibited in the consumer context, at least in the European Union. In 1993, the Council of the European Union issued a directive entitled "Unfair Terms in Consumer Contracts."[23] An annex to the Directive listed specific practices, including mandatory binding arbitration, that "may"

[21] Dispute Resolution Services, Chartered Institute of Arbitrators, International Arbitration and Mediation Centre. http://www.arbitrators.org/DRS/Schemes/chartered_surveyors.htm, accessed on July 20, 2004.

[22] Note, however, that there may be some use of mandatory employment arbitration in Canada. *See generally* John-Paul Alexandrowicz, *A Comparative Analysis of the Law Regulating Employment Arbitration Agreements in the United States and Canada*, 23 Comp. Lab. L. & Pol'y J. 1007, 1008 (2002) (stating that "arbitration agreements between employers and individual non-union employees are still relatively uncommon in Canada" but implying that at least a few do exist).

[23] Council Directive 93/13 of 5 April 1993 on Unfair Terms in Consumer Contracts, 1993 O.J. (L 95) 29, WL OJ 1993 L95/29. For further discussion of the European approach to consumer arbitration *see* Jean R. Sternlight, *Is the U.S. Out on a Limb? Comparing the U.S. Approach to Mandatory Consumer and Employment Arbitration to that of the Rest of the World*, 56 U. Miami L. Rev. 831, 844–8 (2002).

be regarded to be unfair if they significantly and detrimentally impact consumers' rights.[24] Although the Directive, by its terms, would not seem to unequivocally bar all mandatory consumer arbitration, subsequent interpretive documents reveal that EU bodies have effectively prohibited the practice. For example, a 1998 European Commission "Recommendation" states that "out-of-court alternative[s] may not deprive consumers of their right to bring the matter before the courts unless they expressly agree to do so, in full awareness of the facts and only after the dispute has materialised."[25] Apparently based on these documents, a number of EU countries have proscribed companies' imposition of binding arbitration on consumers. Similarly, Section 89(1) of the English Arbitration Act of 1997 extends the Unfair Terms in Consumer Contracts Regulations of 1994 (revised in 1999) to a "term that constitutes an arbitration agreement."

Section 5.3 The Controversy Surrounding U.S. Mandatory Consumer Arbitration

5.3(1) Is Consumer Arbitration Really Mandatory?

The controversy surrounding mandatory arbitration begins with its name. Although critics of the process feel comfortable labeling it "mandatory" or even "cram down" arbitration, defenders suggest this nomenclature is inappropriate and unfair. Such defenders urge that as consumers always have the option to refuse the services or products connected to binding arbitration, such arbitration is not mandatory at all.

In this author's view it makes no sense to dwell a great deal on the nomenclature, given the practical reality that consumers have little if any choice but to accept the arbitration mandated by the company. The typical consumer will not be aware of the fact that arbitration is being imposed by small print, nor will the typical consumer even know what arbitration is, nor that it takes the place of an opportunity to bring claims in court.[26] Even in those rare

[24] Council Directive 93/13, annex (1)(q), 1993 O.J. (L 95) 29, WL OJ 1993 L95/29.

[25] Commission Recommendation 98/257 of 30 March 1998 on the Principles Applicable to the Bodies Responsible for Out-Of-Court Settlement of Consumer Disputes (Text with EEA relevance), 1998 O.J. (L 115) 31, 33 WL OJ 1998 L115/31. The Recommendation relies on Article 6 of the European Human Rights Convention, which it characterizes as providing that "access to the courts is a fundamental right that knows no exceptions." *Id.* at 32. Commission Recommendations are commonly referred to as "soft law." Although they are not technically binding on member countries, they do have a strong practical effect.

[26] *See* Alan M. White & Cathy Lesser Mansfield, *Literacy and Contract*, 13 Stan. L. & Pol'y Rev. 233. *See also* Todd D. Rakoff, *Contracts of Adhesion: An Essay in Reconstruction*, 96 Harv. L. Rev. 1174, 1179 (1983).

instances when a consumer has read and understood the arbitration clause being required by the company, she likely has little choice but to accept the provision. In many instances competitor companies will require the same or similar clause. Even if a competitor existed that did not mandate arbitration, it likely would not be worth the consumer's time to conduct the research necessary to identify the competitor and compare the arbitration clauses. After all, even the rare well-informed consumer (such as this author) would take into account the likelihood that they would need to bring a claim against the company (small), the cost of conducting a search to find a competitor that did not offer arbitration (high), and quite possibly conclude that she might as well just accept the clause.[27] Further, the reality is that consumers are typically not this rational and will predictably underestimate the risk of having to sue the company.[28] So, for both rational and irrational reasons the companies' decision to impose arbitration on consumers will almost inevitably result in the creation of an "agreement" to arbitrate. Thus, this chapter will continue to call the process "mandatory" arbitration.

The dispute over the fairness and propriety of mandatory consumer arbitration can be boiled down as follows: critics charge the process is unfair to individual consumers, detrimental to the public interest, and potentially unconstitutional. Defenders urge that mandatory consumer arbitration offers consumers a quicker, cheaper, fair alternative to litigation and thus benefits both individual consumers and the public at large. These contrasting perspectives will be set out below, but it seems appropriate to disclose that the author ultimately sides with the critics.

5.3(2) Criticisms of Mandatory Arbitration

Critics' attacks on mandatory consumer arbitration have been impassioned, as illustrated by the following excerpt from one of the most colorful court opinions:

> The reality that the average consumer frequently loses his/her constitutional rights and right of access to the court when he/she buys a car, household

[27] *See* Russell Korobkin, *Bounded Rationality, Standard Form Contracts and Unconscionability*, 70 U. Chi. L. Rev. 1203, 1206 (2003) (pointing out that non-drafting parties are "boundedly rational" and take into account only a limited number of salient product attributes, such as price, while ignoring terms they deem less critical).

[28] *See, e.g.*, Christine Jolls et al., *A Behavioral Approach to Law and Economics*, 50 Stan. L. Rev. 1471, 1541–3 (1998) (explaining that individuals' inability to accurately assess risks may undermine 'consumer sovereignty' arguments opposing paternalist and government regulation).

> appliance, insurance policy, receives medical attention or gets a job rises as a putrid odor which is overwhelming to the body politic.[29]

Academic and journalistic critics have been harsh as well. One well-known article states:

> As architecture, the arbitration law made by the Court is a shantytown. It fails to shelter those who most need shelter. And those it is intended to shelter are ill-housed. Under the law written by the Court, birds of prey will sup on workers, consumers, shippers, passengers, and franchisees; the protective police power of the federal government and especially of the state governments is weakened; . . .[30]

Another academic critic urges that

> The Supreme Court has created a monster. With the Court's enthusiastic approval, pre-dispute arbitration clauses – agreements to submit future disputes to binding arbitration – have increasingly found their way into standard form contracts of adhesion. . . . Given the Supreme Court's blessing in the name of a "national policy favoring arbitration," adhesive pre-dispute arbitration clauses should expand beyond their current strongholds in consumer contracts in health insurance, banking and securities investing to other areas of the economy and society. . . . The doctrine of rigorous enforcement of adhesive pre-dispute arbitration clauses – what I call "compelled arbitration" – has given large firms the power to displace the judiciary from its role in enforcing common law claims and statutory rights.[31]

Journalists from many of the most prestigious U.S. newspapers have critically described the practice as well, including articles in the New York Times, Washington Post, Wall Street Journal, and San Francisco Chronicle.[32] At least one British journalist has also focused on the U.S. phenomenon of mandatory arbitration, criticizing Americans for failing to focus on the huge importance of the practice. The Financial Times article characterizes the growth of arbitration as "a silent revolution" through which "[l]arge

[29] *In re Knepp*, 229 B.R. 821, 827 (Bankr. N.D. Ala. 1999).

[30] Paul D. Carrington & Paul H. Haagen, *Contract and Jurisdiction*, 1996 Sup. Ct. Rev. 331, 401–2 (1997).

[31] David S. Schwartz, *Enforcing Small Print to Protect Big Business: Employee and Consumer Rights Claims in an Age of Compelled Arbitration*, 1997 Wis. L. Rev. 33, 36–7 (1997).

[32] *See, e.g.*, Jane Spencer, *Signed Away Your Right to Sue, In Significant Legal Shift Doctors, Gyms, Cable Services Start to Require Arbitration*, Wall St. J. Oct. 1, 2003, at D1; Reynolds Holding, *Private Justice; Millions are Losing Their Legal Rights; Supreme Court Forces Disputes from Court to Arbitration – a System with No Laws*, S. F. Chron. Oct. 7, 2001, at A1; Caroline E. Mayer, *Hidden in Fine Print: 'You Can't Sue Us'; Arbitration Clauses Block Consumers from Taking Companies to Court*, Wash. Post, May 22, 1999, at A1; Barry Meier, *In Fine Print, Customers Lose Ability to Sue*, N.Y.Times, Mar. 10 1997, at A1.

areas of US life and commerce have silently been insulated from the lawsuit culture."[33] Yet, to understand the critiques (and defense) of mandatory arbitration one must move beyond the level of rhetoric.

5.3(2)(A) Unfair to Individual Consumers

(1) Consumers Do Not Read or Understand Arbitration Clauses

One argument critics frequently make is that mandatory consumer arbitration is detrimental and thus unfair to individual consumers. This argument has many sub-parts. First, critics urge that the non-consensual nature of mandatory consumer arbitration is itself a problem, per se. As discussed in Chapters 1 and 2, consent is generally thought to lie at the core of arbitration. Yet, as has been noted, only a minute percentage of consumers read form agreements, and of these, only a smaller number understand what they read.[34] Some companies may even deliberately design their arbitration clauses in a manner geared to decrease the likelihood that the consumer will focus on the arbitration clause.[35] Moreover, even to the extent that consumers might read and understand an arbitration clause imposed on a pre-dispute basis, psychologists have shown that predictable irrationality biases will prevent them from properly evaluating the costs and benefits of accepting such a clause. For example, because people tend to be overly optimistic they will often under-predict the need they might have to bring a claim against the company and thus undervalue what they are losing by giving up a right to sue.[36] Similarly, psychologists have shown that people are risk-seeking with respect to certain prospective losses.[37] Given the

[33] Patti Waldmeir, *How America is Privatising Justice by the Back Door*, FINANCIAL TIMES 12 (June 30, 2003). While the author offers praise as well as criticism for the phenomenon, she urges Americans to focus on how arbitration "threatens to transform their experience as consumers and employees."

[34] *See supra* Note 26.

[35] *See, e.g., Ting v. AT & T*, 182 F. Supp. 2d 902, 911–13 (N. D. Cal. 2002), *aff'd in part, rev'd in part*, 319 F.3d 1126 (9th Cir.), *cert. denied*, 540 U.S. 811 (2003) (showing AT & T spent substantial resources determining how best to implement their binding arbitration provision so that it would not be opposed by consumers).

[36] *See, e.g.,* Christine Jolls et al., *A Behavioral Approach to Law and Economics* in Cass Sunstein, ed., BEHAVIORAL LAW AND ECONOMICS (2000).

[37] Cognitive psychologists Daniel Kahneman and Amos Tversky developed the widely accepted account of decision making known as "prospect theory." Under this theory, people are often risk seeking with respect to moderate-to-high probability losses, and risk averse with respect to low probability losses. *See, e.g.,* Daniel Kahneman and Amos Tversky, *Judgment Under Uncertainty: Heuristics and Biases*, in Daniel Kahneman et al., eds., JUDGMENT UNDER UNCERTAINTY: HEURISTICS AND BIASES 3 (1982).

motivation for profit maximization it seems inevitable that, absent regulation, companies will seek to take advantage of consumers' irrational behavior by manipulating arbitration clauses together with other aspects of consumer contracts.[38]

In short, under most reasonable definitions mandatory consumer arbitration is non-consensual, given that consumers don't typically read or understand the clauses. Critics urge that pre-dispute mandatory arbitration is wrong as a matter of policy on that basis alone. By definition, arbitration eliminates rights consumers would otherwise have had to a trial before a judge or jury. It almost certainly limits the amount of pretrial discovery available to consumers and also limits their opportunity for appeal, by comparison to the rights they would have had in court. Critics assert that it is fundamentally wrong and unfair to deprive consumers of their access to court on an involuntary unknowing basis.

(2) Substance of Arbitration Clause Favors Drafter

Critics often point out that many (although admittedly not all) consumer arbitration agreements also slant the odds in companies' favor from a substantive standpoint. There are virtually an infinite number of ways in which the company, as drafting party, can try to use the arbitration clause to gain the upper hand, including arbitrator selection, imposition of high costs, and limitations of remedies. Although it would be wrong to suggest that most of these excesses are included in most arbitration clauses, some of them are quite common.

The drafter of the arbitration clause has the opportunity to select the arbitrator or the arbitration provider. In the most egregious situations, companies have selected arbitrators who might clearly be expected to be biased, such as a representative of management of the company against whom a claim might be made. Some medical clauses have required that the arbitrator be a specialist in the same field as the doctor accused of malpractice, and critics suspect this will lead to few findings of malpractice. A few clauses have named arbitration providers that sound, by their names, like independent organizations but turn out to be an alter ego of the company against which a claim would be made.

Selection bias can also be more subtle. Arbitration critics frequently discuss a phenomenon known as the "repeat provider" problem. Arbitration providers, such as the American Arbitration Association or the National

[38] *See* Jon D. Hanson & Douglas A. Kysar, *Taking Behavioralism Seriously: The Problem of Market Manipulation*, 74 N.Y.U.L. Rev. 630, 747 (1999) ("Manufacturers, to survive, *must* behave 'as if' they are attempting to manipulate consumer risk perceptions.") (emphasis added).

Arbitration Forum, are now competing to provide arbitration services for particular companies that require their consumers to arbitrate future disputes. Companies and providers often sign agreements to the effect that a particular company will be named as the provider in a particular arbitration clause. Obviously, once a company is named as the provider, financial benefits accrue to that company. Although arbitrator fees may be paid to individual arbitrators, rather than the company, the company itself at minimum earns fees for administering the disputes. Thus, charge the critics, providers have a financial incentive to make sure that the company is pleased with the results in arbitration. If the company is displeased with the results secured through a particular provider it may well switch providers. Needless to say, providers and arbitrators vehemently deny the charge that they are biased. Providers urge that they have no direct influence over their arbitrators. Yet, critics maintain that, consciously or unconsciously, arbitrators may slant the result in companies' favor.

A related purported phenomenon is known as the "repeat player" bias.[39] Whereas a given company will tend to arbitrate many consumer disputes, a given consumer will typically arbitrate, at most, one. Thus, the companies have far greater experience with and exposure to the arbitration process than do the consumers. There is some limited empirical evidence that the repeat player does somewhat better in arbitration than the non-repeat player.[40]

Companies can also use arbitration clauses to impose costs on consumers and thereby discourage them from bringing claims against the company. Using the lingo of economics, companies can impose terms that increase customers' transaction costs.[41] Examples of the ways in which companies can impose high costs on consumers include selecting an arbitrator or provider

[39] The "repeat player" concept was first introduced by Marc Galanter, in the context of litigation. *See* Marc Galanter, *Why the "Haves" Come out Ahead: Speculations on the Limits of Legal Change*, 9 Law & Soc'y Rev. 95 (1974) (discussing multiple advantages of "repeat players" over "one shotters" in our legal system).

[40] *See* Lisa Bingham, *On Repeat Players, Adhesive Contracts, and the Use of Statistics in Judicial Review of Employment Arbitration Awards*, 29 McGeorge L. Rev. 223, 238 (1998) ("The repeat player effect is a cause for concern because in dispute resolution, sometimes the perception of fairness is as important as the reality. There is undeniably a repeat player effect in employment arbitration;"). Of course, the original point of Galanter's work is that repeat players also have an advantage in litigation, so it is unclear whether the non-repeat players do relatively worse in arbitration as compared to litigation.

[41] *See* Lisa B. Bingham, *Control Over Dispute-System Design and Mandatory Commercial Arbitration*, 67 Law & Contemp. Probs. 221 (2004) (explaining that by controlling dispute system design one party can impose transaction costs on the other, thereby dramatically altering the available settlement range or making it no longer cost effective for the opposing party to bring a claim). *See also* Marc Galanter, *The Quality of Settlements*, 1988 J. Disp. Resol. 55, 70–2 (pointing out that when one party imposes high transaction costs on the other, it may encourage a settlement that would not otherwise have been desirable).

with high fees, locating the arbitration in a distant forum, and limiting available discovery and thereby requiring consumers to try to gather evidence through more expensive means.

Another method companies increasingly use to increase consumers' costs is to bar them from proceeding jointly with other consumers in a class action either in litigation or arbitration.[42] Indeed, companies' lawyers have admitted that the elimination of class actions is, for them, one of the great attractions of consumer arbitration. One study showed that such prohibitions were contained in one third of the consumer arbitration clauses studied in Los Angeles in 2001.[43] It is likely that this percentage has increased in recent years. Proscribing consumers from using class actions increases consumers' costs and decreases their ability to prevail in a variety of ways. Many consumer claims are not viable, from a financial standpoint, if brought individually. A single consumer who has been harmed to the extent of a few dollars or even perhaps a few hundred dollars would not rationally bring a claim in arbitration to recover those damages. The costs in terms of time, travel, expenses, and attorney fees would not be worthwhile in view of the likely recovery. The Supreme Court and many other lower courts have repeatedly explained this rationale for allowing class actions. In addition, and somewhat less obvious, class actions permit claims that would not otherwise be brought due to lack of information. Many consumers may be unaware that they have been treated illegally. Nor, given the small sum of money involved, might it even be worth their while to try to investigate whether they are being treated illegally, even assuming they had a suspicion. Yet, if one knowledgeable consumer figures out that a company is acting illegally with respect to a group of consumers, she can bring a class action to protect her less informed fellow consumers. Similarly, whereas an individual consumer may be unaware how to bring a claim, from a procedural standpoint, class actions allow the more knowledgeable consumers and their attorneys to assist the less educated. Given these benefits of class actions, it is clear that by eliminating the class action option companies increase consumers' costs of pursuing a claim and thereby make it more difficult if not impossible for consumers to bring claims against the company.

The third main argument critics make to attack mandatory consumer arbitration is that some companies use their arbitration clauses as a means

[42] For further discussion of the class action issue *see* Jean R. Sternlight & Elizabeth J. Jensen, *Using Arbitration to Eliminate Consumer Class Actions: Efficient Business Practice or Unconscionable Abuse?*, 67 Law & Contemp. Probs. 75 (2004); Jean R. Sternlight, *Arbitration Meets the Class Action, Will the Class Action Survive?* 42 Wm. & Mary L. Rev. 1 (2000).

[43] Linda Demaine & Deborah Hensler, *supra* Note 12 at 10.

to limit consumers' access to substantive relief. That is, at the same time that they mandate arbitration, such clauses may shorten consumers' statute of limitations; bar recovery of punitive damages, compensatory damages, or attorney fees; or bar recovery of injunctive relief. The Terminix clause, reprinted earlier, provides an example of some of these limits. Although, as will be discussed, courts have stricken or rewritten a number of arbitration clauses containing these sorts of provisions, it is not easy or cheap to attack clauses on these grounds. To the extent such clauses exist and are enforced they may impact consumers adversely not only by diminishing their recovery, but also by making it more difficult for them to secure legal representation. Presumably when attorneys make a determination as to whether to represent a particular client, particularly on a contingent fee basis, they take into account the extent of the client's likely recovery, if successful. To the extent that a consumer's relief has been substantially limited by an arbitration clause the consumer may find it difficult or impossible to secure legal representation, and this in turn may make it difficult or impossible for the consumer to win their case.

Indeed, although proponents of mandatory consumer arbitration argue that this process will allow more consumers to file claims against companies, it is not clear whether more claims are indeed being filed. One credit card company, First USA, revealed that in the two years since it implemented its mandatory arbitration clause in early 1998, only four consumers had filed arbitration claims against the company.[44] In contrast, First USA itself filed 51,622 arbitration claims against consumers in the same period.[45] Companies are increasingly using arbitration, affirmatively, as a means to secure default judgments against their customers.

5.3(2)(B) Detrimental to the Public Interest

In addition to arguing that mandatory consumer arbitration is detrimental to individual consumers, opponents argue that it is detrimental to the public interest. Although the arguments are related to one another, the public interest critique focuses on the fact that arbitration is typically private and usually does not yield public precedent. Therefore, to the extent that consumers' claims are resolved privately, other consumers and members of the public will not be able to benefit from the public exposition that would occur

[44] See Caroline E. Mayer, *Win Some, Lose Rarely?: Arbitration Forum's Rulings Called One-Sided*, Wash. Post, Mar. 1, 2000, at E1.
[45] *Id.*

through litigation. Specifically, if claims regarding defective tires or fraudulent financial practices or dangerous medical practices were all resolved through private arbitration, illegal practices might continue longer than would have been the case had such claims been litigated. Public litigation helps serve the public purposes of deterring illegal conduct and educating companies and potential consumers regarding the permissibility (or not) of particular practices. The replacement of public litigation with private arbitration can therefore be seen as detrimental to the public.

Often the critique that mandatory arbitration is detrimental to the public interest is phrased with respect to the constitutional right to jury trial. That is, it is argued that mandatory consumer arbitration is undesirable because it impairs the jury trial right. From a technical standpoint, the jury trial argument is somewhat complex and will be discussed later in this chapter. However, from a policy standpoint it is clear that any dispute that is required to be presented in arbitration will not be presented to a jury. For those who treasure the civil jury trial right, this is a loss not only for the parties but also for the public-at-large.

Mandatory consumer arbitration can also be critiqued on the ground that it is fundamentally undemocratic to compel people to resolve their disputes in arbitration, rather than in court. Professor Richard Reuben has argued that such a process may diminish public trust in the rule of law and erode the social capital necessary for effective democracy.[46] However, as this author has argued elsewhere, in greater detail, it is important not to let familiarity with the status quo hinder a complete analysis of the propriety or impropriety of mandatory binding arbitration. The mere fact that the imposition of binding arbitration would, per se, eliminate jury or bench trials, ought not in and of itself be sufficient to support a conclusion that mandatory binding arbitration is unjust. Rather, we should look more deeply at whether mandatory binding arbitration has features, such as privacy or its imposition by a single private party, that lead us to conclude it is unjust.[47]

5.3(3) The Defense of Mandatory Consumer Arbitration

"Mandatory" arbitration also has its advocates. Although few, if any, would defend the most unfair arbitration clauses in which companies impose non-neutral arbitrators or greatly limit possible recoveries, some contend that fair

[46] Richard C. Reuben, *Democracy and Dispute Resolution: The Problem of Arbitration*, 67 Law & Contemp. Probs. 279 (2004).

[47] *See* Jean R. Sternlight, *Creeping Mandatory Arbitration: Is it Just?* 57 Stan. L. Rev. 1631 (2005).

binding arbitration is better for claimants than the alternative of litigation. They urge that when companies include arbitration in form contracts they help consumers and employees by providing them with a forum that is cheaper, quicker, and more accessible than litigation. The argument made is that the litigation system is simply not affordable by or accessible to most consumers, and that arbitration provides much better access. As one defender has colorfully put it, better to provide a decent car like a Saturn for all consumers than to provide a Cadillac for a very few and rickshaws for the vast majority[48]

Some defenders also urge that to the extent companies reduce their own dispute resolution costs, market forces will ensure that they pass on such savings to their customers in the form of lower prices. To the extent that sufficient competition exists, any company that did not pass on these savings would be driven out of the market by the lower-priced competitors who did pass on the savings.[49] Of course, critics of mandatory arbitration dispute that the conditions of perfect competition exist in many markets, and therefore dispute the proposition that all profits will be passed on to the consumers.[50] Defenders, responding to this point, may urge that at least *some* of companies' savings will be passed on to consumers, even absent all the features of perfect competition. In response the debate will then turn to the question of whether such savings are zero, minuscule, or large, and whether any such savings justify any costs in terms of fairness or justice that are imposed by mandatory arbitration.

Another defense of mandatory arbitration is philosophical. Whereas critics attack the phenomenon as denying consumers choice, some defenders paradoxically contend that regulation or elimination of mandatory arbitration restricts consumers' freedom to reduce their prices by purchasing products and services governed by arbitration provisions.[51] In response, critics will argue that there is no true freedom to choose when clauses are imposed in small print, using terms few consumers understand, and in

[48] Samuel Estreicher, *Saturns for Rickshaws: The Stakes in the Debate of Predispute Employment Arbitration Agreements*, 16 OHIO ST. J. ON DISP. RESOL. 559, 563–4 (2001).

[49] This argument is spelled out in Stephen J. Ware, *Paying the Price of Process: Judicial Regulation of Consumer Arbitration Agreements*, 2001 J. DISP. RESOL. 89 (2001).

[50] See Jean R. Sternlight & Elizabeth J. Jensen, *Using Arbitration to Eliminate Consumer Class Actions: Efficient Business Practice or Unconscionable Abuse?* 67 LAW & CONTEMP. PROBS. 75, 92–8 (2004).

[51] *See* Stephen J. Ware, *Consumer Arbitration As Exceptional Consumer Law With A Contractualist Reply to Carrington & Haagen*, 29 MCGEORGE L. REV. 195, 213 (1998) (urging that consumers should have an alienable right "to get consideration for the right to government adjudication").

circumstances in which consumers often have no real ability to elect the same or similar product unburdened by an arbitration clause. Further, critics will assert that the benefits of consumer protection outweigh whatever slight loss of liberty might be imposed on that rare knowledgeable consumer who actually would prefer to purchase products or services encumbered with a mandatory arbitration clause.

Defenders of mandatory arbitration are frequently queried "if arbitration is so great, why do you need to force it on consumers? Why not just let consumers and companies agree to take disputes to arbitration rather than litigation after the dispute has arisen?" Defenders do have an answer, albeit one that is somewhat complex. They respond that as a practical matter, few if any agreements to arbitrate would be reached on a post-dispute basis. They assert that in strong cases, consumers or their lawyers would insist on taking the claim to litigation, where they could likely secure a greater recovery. By contrast, the argument goes, in weak cases the company would refuse to take the case to arbitration, instead preferring to force the client with a weak case to try to find a lawyer to litigate the matter, which they likely could not.[52] Thus, defenders propound a sort of deal whereby companies should be permitted to mandate arbitration with respect to all consumer claims as a means of assuring that they will arbitrate the weaker consumer claims. Of course, this argument accepts as given critics' idea that from a plaintiffs' standpoint, stronger cases will do better in litigation than in arbitration. The argument also does not consider the possibility that perhaps it would be fairer to require companies to arbitrate certain cases than it would be to permit companies to require consumers to arbitrate all cases.

From a public policy standpoint, defenders of mandatory consumer arbitration contend that the practice will save public dollars by keeping more disputes out of the publicly funded courts. Certainly this argument has proved attractive to many legislators. Of course, one could take other steps to reduce the budget such as eliminating public schools or paved roads, and thus the real question should be whether the publicly funded service (courts) is worth the money spent on that service.

Finally, the defenders seek to rebut many of the critics' strongest arguments. For example, when critics point to egregiously unfair clauses, defenders state that these clauses are aberrations that courts would not enforce. When critics bemoan the loss of the jury trial, defenders respond that juries often behave irrationally and add unnecessary cost to the legal process. When critics emphasize the potential loss of public precedent, defenders reply that

[52] *See* Samuel Estreicher, *supra* Note 48 at 567–8.

more than sufficient cases are still litigated so as to provide ample information to the public. And when critics point to the elimination of class actions, defenders say "good riddance."

While some of the policy differences between critics and defenders are philosophical and theoretical, others rest on different impressions of the empirical world. Unfortunately, scant empirical work has been done regarding the positive and negative aspects of mandatory consumer arbitration.

Section 5.4 Empirical Studies on Mandatory Consumer Arbitration

Given the fierce controversy over mandatory consumer arbitration, one would hope that empirical studies could be used to evaluate the process. Unfortunately, researchers have found it very difficult to evaluate mandatory arbitration, for a number of reasons. First, to a large extent researchers cannot obtain access to the data they need to perform good studies. As we have seen, one of the fundamental traits of arbitration is that it is typically private. Thus, researchers can only obtain data on arbitration to the extent that disputants or arbitration providers make the data available, which they often do not. A second problem researchers face is that even if they had data regarding results of claims filed in arbitration and in court, it would be difficult to know how to compare that data. After all, the same case is never brought in both processes, and one cannot simply assume that claims brought in arbitration were otherwise identical to those brought in litigation. Third, to the extent researchers look only at who wins or loses or even at how much they obtain when a claim goes to trial/arbitration, they are missing a large part of the dispute resolution picture. For example, it seems likely that the choice between arbitration and litigation may also affect such things as whether a disputant can obtain a lawyer, whether a disputant chooses to bring a claim at all, whether a claim settles and if so for how much, and whether a claim is resolved by motion, prior to a hearing. Studies that focus only on results at trial as compared to arbitration miss all of this bigger picture. For example, as noted earlier one credit card company's statistics showed that in the two years after it imposed mandatory arbitration, only four customers filed claims against the company.[53] The imposition of mandatory arbitration may well have a significant deterrent effect on the filing of claims that would be missed by studying only success rates in arbitration.

[53] Caroline E. Mayer, *Win Some, Lose Rarely?: Arbitration Forum's Rulings Called One-Sided*, Wash. Post, March 1, 2000, at E1 (discussing policy implemented in early 1998).

Frustrated by the lack of data on consumer arbitrations, the California Legislature recently mandated that all arbitration providers keep and publish certain information regarding consumer arbitrations that they administer.[54] At least three major providers, AAA, JAMS, and NAF have now published reports pursuant to this legislation,[55] as have at least two other providers, Kaiser Health and Alternative Resolution Centers, more focused on California.[56] The hope is that this data, once thoroughly analyzed, might help to provide additional insights into the negative and positive aspects of mandatory consumer arbitration. For example, the published information might help us to learn about how often consumers win or lose arbitrations, and how much they win or lose. Equally or more important, this information might also provide insights as to the percentage of consumer claims that are settled or withdrawn prior to an arbitration ruling, the percentage that are resolved through a paper hearing rather than live testimony, the percentage of arbitrations in which consumers are represented by attorneys, the respective win rates of represented and unrepresented consumers, and the fees charged by arbitrators in such cases and by whom they are paid.

Unfortunately, preliminary reviews of the data by this author and others show that analysis will be difficult. As a report by the California Dispute Resolution Institute notes, "there are inconsistencies, ambiguities, and gaps in the data" that "limit the utility of the information in presenting a clear picture of consumer arbitration in California."[57] The various providers report the data in different ways from one another, often provide the mere minimum of required information, and typically rely on arbitrator self-reporting that may not be reliable.[58]

[54] *See* Cal. Code Civ. P. 1281.96, effective Jan. 1, 2003.

[55] The AAA data is available at http://www.adr.org (follow link for "California Consumers"). The JAMS data is available at http://www.jamsadr.com (follow link for arbitration, then consumer arbitration, and the "Disclosures for California Consumer Arbitrations"). The NAF data is available at http://www.arb-forum.com (follow link for focus areas, then consumers, and the Cal. CCP 1281.96 reports). Note that NAF was sued by consumer groups for its alleged failure to provide information required by California law. The lawsuit, *Corbett v. National Arbitration Forum*, was ultimately dismissed for lack of standing. NAF placed additional data on its web site subsequent to the dismissal of that suit.

[56] The Kaiser data is available at http://www.oia-kaiserarb.com (follow link for disclosures). The Alternative Resolution Centers data is available at http://www.arc4adr.com (follow link for "consumer arbitration reporting").

[57] "Consumer and Employment Arbitration in California: A Review of Website Data Posted Pursuant to Section 1281.96 of the Code of Civil Procedure" (California Dispute Resolution Institute Aug. 2004) at 5 (noting that few cases reported all three of the amount of initial claims, the amount of the arbitration award, and the amount of the arbitration fee).

[58] *Id.* at 33.

Further, the California data will not be sufficient to answer some of the most important questions outlined previously, such as whether the imposition of mandatory arbitration makes it more difficult for consumers to obtain representation, or whether the existence of mandatory arbitration affects the rate or amount of settlements.

In addition to the California data, a few studies have been done of consumer arbitration in the securities setting. Securities arbitration is more public than most forms of consumer arbitration, and is also governmentally regulated. The consumers involved with securities arbitration are presumably wealthier than many consumers. Thus, although the availability of data permits the study of securities arbitration, big questions exist as to whether it is proper to assume that securities arbitration results are applicable in other areas. Several studies done by the General Accounting Office show that customers win slightly more than 50 percent of their claims against brokers.[59] Although this sounds promising, several caveats must be noted. First, although investors prevail they may be awarded just a small percent of the relief to which they claim they were entitled.[60] Second, even to the extent investors win at arbitration they may not be able collect on their awards.[61] Third, investors may need to secure legal representation to have a chance of making a good recovery.[62] Fourth, one study has shown that "repeat player" brokers tended to do better in arbitration than those companies which had less experience with the arbitration process.[63]

In addition, the American Bankers Association funded a study that was done by the Ernst & Young consulting company on data provided by the National Arbitration Forum. The study showed that consumers were doing

[59] Gen. Accounting Office, Securities Arbitration: How Investors Fare, GAO/GGD-92–74, at 7 (May 11, 1992) (approximately 60% of investors prevail); *Public Customer Award Survey*, Securities Arbitration Commentator, May 1996, at 1, 3 (investors prevail 54% of the time); Gen. Accounting Office, Actions Needed to Address Problem of Unpaid awards, GAO/GGD-00–115, at 7 (June 15, 2000) (investors prevailed 51% of the time between 1992 and 1996); Richard A. Voytas, Jr., *Empirical Evidence of Worsening Conditions for the Investor in Securities Arbitration*, Securities Arbitration Commentator, June 2002 at 5 (finding investors prevailed 51% of the time according to 1999–2000 data and that rate of investor success had decreased over the years since 1992).

[60] Several GAO studies showed investors who prevailed won approximately 25%–28% of the amount they sought. Voytas, *supra* Note 59 at 5. However, it is also true that investors may be claiming more than the amount to which they are really entitled.

[61] The 2000 GAO report, *supra* Note 59, discusses this problem extensively.

[62] Voytas, *supra* Note 59 at 7 (showing represented investors did substantially better than non-represented investors).

[63] Voytas, *supra* Note 59 at 6 (showing that brokers who are repeat players did significantly better than non-repeat player brokers both in defending themselves against investor claims and also in bringing counterclaims against investors).

well and pleased with mandatory arbitration. However, as the data has not been made available to independent researchers, this study has not been given a great deal of weight by most researchers.

Some empirical studies have also been done on employment arbitration, but the results here are inconclusive as well. For example, Professor Lisa Bingham's study of employment arbitration has shown that "repeat player" companies gain an advantage in arbitration, but that the voluntary imposition of fairness requirements through due process protocols may diminish this advantage.[64] On the other hand, a study comparing litigated non-discrimination employment claims to those arbitrated before the AAA found that higher level employees, (those most likely to have negotiated arbitration clauses rather than have had them imposed upon them), received similar results in both fora.[65] However, the study was careful to note that the results might well not be generalizable to other types of claims or claims brought before other arbitrators, and further recognized many of the methodological problems noted previously. It seems that we will not soon be able to resolve the debate over mandatory arbitration using empirical studies.

Section 5.5 The Enforceability of Mandatory Consumer Agreements to Arbitrate in the Courts

With policy debates raging in the background and empirical studies inconclusive, a number of consumers have sought relief from mandatory arbitration in the courts. Of course, only a minute percentage of those consumers subject to mandatory arbitration have attempted to litigate the legitimacy of these clauses. Some consumers are no doubt content to take their claims to arbitration; other consumers may be displeased with the arbitration requirement but may determine that it would not be practical or advisable to try to challenge the clause.

In that small group of cases in which consumers decide to challenge the enforceability of an arbitration clause, consumers rely on one of four

[64] See Lisa B. Bingham, *Self-Determination in Dispute System Design and Employment Arbitration*, 56 U. Miami L. Rev. 873, 893–7 (2002).

[65] Theodore Eisenberg & Elizabeth Hill, *Employment Arbitration and Litigation: An Empirical Comparison*, 58 Disp. Res. J. 44–55 (2004). The study could not compare arbitrated and litigated civil rights claims, because too few such claims were arbitrated. *Id.* at 45. Similarly, the study could not compare arbitrated and litigated non-civil rights claims by lower paid employees because too few such claims were litigated. *Id.*

types of arguments: that the imposition of arbitration violates the federal Constitution; that the arbitration is inconsistent with one or more federal statutes; that the arbitration clause is void as a matter of state statute or constitution; or that the arbitration clause is void as a matter of state common law. Each of these kinds of arguments will be discussed, below. However, before courts can reach these arguments they must decide two threshold issues: (1) should it be the court or instead the arbitrator who should rule on the validity of an arbitration clause; and (2) is a particular arbitration clause governed by federal or instead state arbitration law.

5.5(1) Preliminary Questions

5.5(1)(A) Who Decides Arbitrability?

The question of who decides the validity of an arbitration provision has previously been discussed in Chapter 2. Although this question may seem technical, as a practical matter it can be critical when consumers seek to challenge the validity of arbitration provisions. It is generally believed that courts are more likely to hold a matter non-arbitrable than is an arbitrator. After all, if an arbitrator finds a dispute non-arbitrable she rules herself out of a paycheck. Although ethically it would be inappropriate for an arbitrator to take her own financial benefit into account, such factors may at least have a unconscious impact. Often referred to as the "arbitrability" question, the issue of "who decides" the validity of an arbitration provision is often said to be one of the murkiest and most confusing issues in arbitration.

The Supreme Court's 1967 decision in *Prima Paint Corp. v. Flood & Conklin Mfg., Co.*[66] poses one hurdle for U.S. consumers seeking to challenge arbitration provisions. As discussed earlier in Chapter 2, the Supreme Court held in that case that where the parties had agreed to a broad arbitration clause, and one party claimed that the contract as a whole was fraudulent, the party must present the challenge to the arbitrator rather than to the court.[67] Quite a few courts have relied on *Prima Paint* to reject consumers' attempts to attack arbitration clauses on such grounds as fraud or unconscionability, finding that because the consumers' attacks were directed to the contract as a whole, and not merely to the arbitration

[66] 388 U.S. 395 (1967).

[67] By contrast, had the consumer been arguing only that the arbitration clause was fraudulent, the consumer would have made that argument to the court.

agreement itself, the claims ought to be heard by the arbitrator rather than the court.[68]

A series of more recent Supreme Court cases also discuss the arbitrability issue and illustrate how the doctrine of arbitrability can sometimes be used to defeat consumers' claims. On the one hand, the Court's decision in *First Options of Chicago Inc. v. Kaplan*[69] sets a limit, holding that a court rather than an arbitrator must generally decide whether the parties ever contracted to arbitrate at all.[70] On the other hand, *First Options* also made clear that if the arbitration agreement explicitly provides that such determinations must be made by the arbitrator, then such a contractual allocation of duties will be enforceable. Since that decision, many mandatory consumer arbitration agreements have explicitly provided that the arbitrator rather than the court shall decide all attacks on the clause.

To the extent that arbitrators make initial rulings as to the validity of arbitration clauses in consumer cases, courts will have to determine what degree of deference should be given to such rulings. In *First Options* the Court suggested that where parties had agreed to have arbitrability decisions made by the arbitrator, the arbitrator's determination of validity would be subject to a "deferential" rather than a de novo review in the courts.[71] Although it is not yet clear whether special rules might be developed in the consumer setting, three of the Court's 2002–2003 Term decisions provide increasing

[68] *See, e.g., Hawkins v. Aid Ass'n for Lutherans*, 338 F.3d 801, 807 (7th Cir. 2003) (holding that argument that arbitration agreement was unconscionable, in that clause denied plaintiffs opportunity to recover punitive damages or attorney fees, must be resolved by arbitrator rather than court). However, some state courts have chosen not to apply the rule enunciated by the Supreme Court in *Prima Paint*, to the extent they conclude state rather than federal law is relevant. *See, e.g., Fox v. Tanner*, 101 P.3d 939 (Wyo. 2004); *Frizzell Const. Co v. Gatlinburg, LLC*, 95 S.W.3d 79, 84 (Tenn. 1979). The Florida Supreme Court recently limited the scope of *Prima Paint*, holding that the case did not apply where consumers claimed that the underlying contract was illegal and void ab initio in that it was usurious. However, the U.S. Supreme Court granted certiorari in this case and may reverse. *Cardegna v. Buckeye Check Cashing Inc.*, 894 So.2d 860 (Fla. 2005), *cert. granted*, 125 S. Ct. 2937 (2005). For a critique of *Prima Paint*, *see* Richard C. Reuben, *First Options, Consent to Arbitration, and the Demise of Separability: Restoring Access to Justice for Contracts with Arbitration Provisions*, 56 SMU L. Rev. 819 (2003).

[69] 514 U.S. 938 (1995).

[70] In that case, Manuel and Carol Kaplan argued that while their wholly owned company had agreed to arbitrate certain claims, the Kaplans had never agreed to arbitrate their personal claims. The Court found that the court rather than an arbitrator must decide this issue.

[71] 514 U.S. at 943. In contrast, in cases under the New York Convention and Convention Act the courts have given a de novo review to decisions by the arbitral tribunal that the alleged agreement to arbitrate satisfied the requirement of Article II of the Convention that the agreement be in writing. In these cases the parties had clearly conferred power on the tribunal to decide questions of arbitrability. *See infra* at Section 6.4(5).

evidence that the Court is willing to interpret contracts in favor of arbitrator's power to decide questions involving or relating to arbitrability.[72]

5.5(1)(B) Federal or State Arbitration Law

A number of states' arbitration laws are designed to protect consumers from mandatory pre-dispute arbitration. One state, Alabama, provides that pre-dispute arbitration agreements are not enforceable.[73] A number of other states prohibit or limit the application of mandatory pre-dispute arbitration provisions to certain claims that might be made by consumers.[74] Still others impose particular procedural requirements, such as that the arbitration clause must be signed or contain particular font size or titles.[75] Other

[72] *Howsam v. Dean Witter Reynolds Inc.*, 537 U.S. 79 (2002), was a case in which an investor sued a brokerage house for securities fraud. The brokerage defended on the ground that the dispute was untimely, and argued that a court rather than the arbitrator should rule on the timeliness question. However the Supreme Court rejected the argument, holding that procedural issues such as timeliness should be resolved by the arbitrators. The second case, *PacifiCare Health Systems, Inc. v. Book*, 538 U.S. 401 (2003), did not involve consumers, but will likely impact consumer challenges. A group of doctors sought to void the arbitration clause imposed on them by a health care provider. They argued that because the clause prohibited the recovery of "punitive damages" it was inconsistent with the federal RICO statute under which they sued, in that RICO allows for recovery of treble damages. The Court found that an arbitrator rather than a court should determine whether the contractual exclusion would prevent the doctors from fully vindicating their rights under RICO. Finally, *Green Tree Fin. Corp. v. Bazzle*, 539 U.S. 444 (2003), involved fraud claims brought by consumers against a commercial lender. The case had gone through arbitration, where the arbitrator permitted the consumers to proceed by way of a class action and awarded them approximately $20 million. The company then sought to vacate the award, arguing that the arbitrator had erred by permitting the consumers to proceed in a class action. In a confusing plurality decision the Court found that it was up to the arbitrator, rather than the court, to determine whether a class action was permitted by the contractual language of the clause. Together all of these decisions will likely lead to more and more interpretive questions being routed to the arbitrator, rather than the court.

[73] Ala. Code 1975 §8-1-41 (West 2004).

[74] For example, an Alaska statute provides that a medical patient may enter into a pre-dispute mandatory arbitration agreement with the health care provider, but that the patient has thirty days from the execution of the agreement (tollable for persons rendered incapable by medical injury) to revoke, in writing to the provider, the agreement to arbitrate . Alaska Stat. §09.55.535 (West 2004). Furthermore, health care providers are prohibited from making arbitration agreements a prerequisite to health care services. *Id.*

[75] For example, a Montana statute, Mont. Code Ann. 27-5-114(4) provided that a pre-dispute arbitration provision must be typed, in underlined capital letters, and contained on the first page of the contract. However, this provision was withdrawn in 1997 after the Supreme Court held that it was preempted as applied to contracts involving interstate commerce. *See Doctor's Assocs. Inc. v. Casarotto*, 517 U.S. 681 (1996). Similarly, the Alaska statute, mentioned earlier, also requires that any arbitration provision must be on the first page of the written agreement, in bold print, with the disclaimer that agreement to arbitrate is not a prerequisite to receiving medical attention. Alaska Stat. §09.55.535(b) (West 2004).

procedural requirements include statutorily mandated processes for selecting arbitrators as well as statutorily prescribed rules that shall govern the arbitration proceedings.[76]

Despite some states' eagerness to protect their consumers from the perceived evil of mandatory arbitration, many regulatory limitations on contracts to arbitrate are subject to the sweeping scope of the FAA, and have been rendered substantially irrelevant by the series of Supreme Court decisions discussed earlier in this book.[77] Even though state law in general applies to questions of contractual validity arising under Section 2 of the FAA, state laws that are in conflict with the FAA or single out the contract to arbitrate for treatment different from that given to contracts generally are

[76] *See, e.g.*, Ala. Code §6-5-485 (West 2004) (providing that AAA rules shall govern any arbitration arising out of mandatory arbitration provisions between health care providers and patients, and further providing that the claimant shall choose one arbitrator, the respondent shall choose a second, and the third arbitrator is chosen by the first two arbitrators); Alaska Stat. §09.55.535 (West 2004) (providing that, in arbitration arising from arbitration agreements between health care providers and patients, the claimant shall choose one arbitrator, the respondent shall choose a second, and the two parties must agree on a third or, in the alternative, have a third arbitrator court-appointed). With respect to health care disputes, Alabama enforces mandatory arbitration agreements only if they have been entered into *after* the provision of medical services giving rise to the claim. Ala. Code 1975 §6-5-485 (West 2004). Furthermore, the statute provides the manner in which arbitrators are to be selected and which arbitration rules shall govern. *Id.* New York law specifically forbids personal injury attorneys, physicians, dentists, hospital, and HMO personnel from serving as arbitrators for health care disputes. N.Y. CLS CPLR §7554 (West 2004). Arbitrators in some states are given broad powers over the proceedings, including judging the relevancy and materiality of all evidence without deference to any rules of evidence, and ordering the arbitration to proceed even if one party is absent. Cal. Bus. & Prof. Code §7085.5 (West 2004).

[77] In *Allied-Bruce Terminix Cos. v. Dobson*, 513 U.S. 265 (1995), a consumer case, the Court held that the FAA would be applied as broadly as possible. A consumer in Alabama had sought to sue a termite exterminator for breach of a contract to eradicate termites. The company argued that the claim must be arbitrated, pursuant to the form agreement signed by the consumer, but the consumer responded that agreements to arbitrate future disputes were impermissible under Alabama law. The company countered that the transaction was governed by the FAA, rather than Alabama law, and the Supreme Court agreed. The Court found that even though the transaction merely involved an Alabama homeowner contracting for termite extermination services, it involved sufficient "interstate commerce" to bring the FAA into play. Specifically, held the Court, the FAA applies to the broadest possible reach of the commerce clause, including circumstances of the case at bar. Similarly, in *Doctor's Associates, Inc. v. Casarotto*, 517 U.S. 681 (1996), a case involving arbitration imposed on a franchisee, the Supreme Court voided a Montana state law mandating certain notice requirements be contained in arbitration clauses. It found that so long as the transaction involved interstate commerce, the FAA would preempt all state law targeted only to invalidate arbitration provisions.

preempted.[78] Given these decisions, most all consumer attacks on arbitration will be decided under the FAA rather than state arbitration statutes. A few exceptions will, however, be discussed below.

5.5(2) Potential Defenses to Enforceability

5.5(2)(A) Constitutional Arguments

When a consumer contends she has improperly been mandated to resolve her claims through binding arbitration, rather than in court, she sometimes attempts to argue that her rights under the U.S. Constitution have been violated. Although these arguments have intuitive appeal, and have been championed by some scholars, they have not to date been particularly successful.

In order to establish a violation of the Due Process Clause of the Fifth or Fourteenth Amendments arbitration opponents would have to first demonstrate the existence of "state action." The Due Process Clauses only limit actions taken by governmental entities, and not by private parties. In those rare cases in which binding arbitration is being imposed directly by a state legislature or other government entity, it is not difficult to show state action. Thus, were a state to require consumers to resolve all medical malpractice claims through binding arbitration rather than in court, Due Process requirements would apply.[79] By contrast, it is much more difficult to establish state action with respect to binding arbitration imposed by a private party. Although some scholars have urged that state action can be found either in the entanglement between private parties and the courts or in courts' reliance on a "preference" for arbitration over litigation,[80] these

[78] For example, in *Southland Corp. v. Keating*, 465 U.S. 1 (1984), the Court ruled that the FAA preempted a state arbitration law that would have required claims brought under the California Franchise Investment Law to be litigated. In *Doctor's Associates Inc. v. Casarotto*, 517 U.S. 681 (1996), a case involving arbitration imposed on a sandwich shop franchisee, the Supreme Court voided a state law mandating certain notice requirements be contained in arbitration clauses. It found that so long as the transaction involved interstate commerce, the FAA would preempt all state law targeted only to invalidate arbitration provisions. For an analysis of these and other decisions, *see* David S. Schwartz, *Correcting Federalism Mistakes in Statutory Interpretation: The Supreme Court and the Federal Arbitration Act*, 67 Law & Contemp. Probs. 5 (2004).

[79] *Cf. Morris v. Metriakoo*, 344 N.W.2d 736, 738–41 (Mich. 1984) (applying Due Process Clause to state mandated medical malpractice arbitration but finding no violation); *Murray v. Wilner*, 325 N.W. 2d 422, 427 (Mich. Ct. App. 1982) *rev'd on other grounds*, 348 N.W.2d 6 (Mich. 1984) (finding state mandated arbitration violated Due Process Clause).

[80] *See* Richard C. Reuben, *Public Justice: Toward a State Action Theory of Alternative Dispute Resolution*, 85 Cal. L. Rev. 577, 615–19 (1997) (arguing that intertwining of public and

arguments have not been accepted by the courts.[81] Moreover, even once state action is established, the challenger would have to demonstrate that the arbitration process is sufficiently unfair as to violate the norms of due process. This may not be easy, as the Supreme Court has held that due process concepts are flexible and do not always require a traditional adversarial process. In short, the Due Process Clause of the U.S. Constitution is not a strong basis upon which to challenge mandatory arbitration.

Challengers may also attempt to argue that a binding arbitration provision violates their rights to a jury trial under the Seventh Amendment. It is well accepted that the right to a civil jury trial, in appropriate cases, is one of the fundamental elements of the United States system of justice. Although the Seventh Amendment only applies in certain cases, specifically those cases brought in federal court, "at common law," claiming damages of at least $20, it would seem to offer a powerful weapon for defeating mandatory arbitration in those cases. No state action need be proven, and in the non-arbitration context courts have upheld jury trial waivers only when the waivers are made knowingly, voluntarily, and intelligently.

Many mandatory arbitration provisions would not pass the test of having been accepted on a knowing, voluntary, and intelligent basis. Specifically it would seem that the jury trial argument ought to defeat arbitration clauses imposed in small print clauses, particularly when those clauses are unsigned, and when the recipients of the clauses are consumers who are not particularly well educated or well informed.

Nonetheless, the Seventh Amendment argument has rarely succeeded in the arbitration context. For the most part courts simply fail to address the jury trial argument, perhaps because it has not typically been presented by the party challenging the arbitration agreement. The Supreme Court, in particular, has never focused on whether or how jury trial arguments should be applied to arbitration clauses. To the extent that courts have focused on the jury trial argument, some have rejected it by stating simply that arbitration

private processes in enforcement of contractual arbitration gives rise to state action); Jean R. Sternlight, *Rethinking the Constitutionality of the Supreme Court's Preference for Binding Arbitration: A Fresh Assessment of Jury Trial, Separation of Powers, and Due Process Concerns*, 72 Tul. L. Rev. 1, 40–7 (1997) (arguing that state action exists at least to the extent courts are relying on a preference for arbitration over litigation to interpret validity and scope of arbitration agreements).

[81] *See, e.g.*, *Duffield v. Robertson Stephens & Co.*, 144 F.3d 1182, 1200–1 (9th Cir. 1998), *overruled on other grounds in EEOC v. Luce, Forward, Hamilton, and Scripps*, 345 F.3d 742 (9th Cir. 2003). *See also* Sarah Rudolph Cole, *Arbitration and State Action*, 2005 B.Y.U. L. Rev. 1 (agreeing with courts' position that no state action exists when private companies impose arbitration).

is "favored" under federal law. Yet, purported statutory favoritism cannot legitimately trump a constitutional argument. Some courts have found that jury trial arguments are inapplicable in that by "agreeing" to present their claims in arbitration consumers waived their right to present jury trial arguments.[82] Yet, this position makes no sense, since the "agreement" to arbitrate was not knowing, voluntary, and intelligent.[83] As will be discussed, a jury trial argument can also be made under state constitutions.[84]

5.5(2)(B) Federal Statutory Arguments

Consumer challenges made to arbitration agreements under federal statutes have been far more successful than Constitutional attacks. Although the Supreme Court has found that claims under most federal statutes are generally subject to arbitration, it has always recognized the possibility that Congress might exempt certain claims from arbitration. Two particular statutes warrant special discussion in the consumer context. First, it is widely recognized that the McCarran Ferguson Act[85] gives states the right to invalidate the use of arbitration to resolve insurance claims. This statute in effect "reverse-preempts" the FAA by providing in relevant part that "no Act of Congress shall be construed to invalidate, impair, or supersede any law enacted by any State for the purpose of regulating the business of insurance." For these purposes insurance includes not only life insurance by also insurance with respect to disability, health, and other matters.[86] Thus, to the extent states have legislation proscribing the arbitration of insurance claims, insurance claims are not arbitrable.[87] Although some states do currently prohibit companies from mandating the use of arbitration to resolve insurance disputes,[88] many do not, thus the power of this exception lies

[82] For a recent example of this sort of decision, *see McKenzie Check Advance of Mississippi, LLC v. Hardy*, 866 So.2d 446, 454–5 (Miss. 2004) (rejecting consumers' jury trial argument in payday loan case and observing that plaintiffs had an obligation to read the written contract, and that jury trial right only attaches where, unlike in the case at bar, there is a right to trial).

[83] For discussion of the Seventh Amendment argument, *see* Jean R. Sternlight, *Mandatory Binding Arbitration and the Demise of the Seventh Amendment Right to a Jury Trial*, 16 Ohio St. J. on Disp. Resol. 669 (2001).

[84] See Jean R. Sternlight, *The Rise and Spread of Arbitration as a Substitute for the Jury Trial*, 38 U.S.F. L. Rev. 17 (2003).

[85] 15 U.S.C. §§1011, 1012(b) (2000).

[86] *See, e.g., Rush Prudential HMO Inc. v. Moran*, 536 U.S. 355 (2002) (recognizing that state law regulating HMOs constituted regulation of insurance for purposes of McCarran Ferguson Act and ERISA).

[87] *See, e.g., Standard Sec. Life Ins. Co. v. West*, 267 F.3d 821, 823–4 (8th Cir. 2001).

[88] *See, e.g.*, Mo. Rev. Stat. §435.350 (2004).

mostly in state legislation that may be adopted in the future. No doubt there will be some controversy over whether particular business practices, such as home warranties, should be categorized as " insurance."

Second, consumers have argued that they cannot be forced to arbitrate claims brought under the federal Magnuson-Moss Warranty Act.[89] This statute prohibits a number of unfair consumer practices, and also discusses the establishment of internal dispute resolution mechanisms by companies. The relevant federal regulatory agency, the Federal Trade Commission issued regulations interpreting the statute to prohibit the imposition of mandatory arbitration with respect to claims brought under that statute. Several courts followed these regulations, and prohibited the mandatory arbitration.[90] However, the more recent trend is to permit companies to mandate arbitration of claims brought under the Magnuson-Moss Warranty Act.[91]

Other federal statutes may potentially be construed to bar mandatory arbitration of claims brought under those statutes. For example, it has recently been argued that the federal Medicaid Act bars mandatory arbitration with respect to nursing home contracts. However, it is not clear whether these arguments will succeed.

Even to the extent consumers are unable to convince courts that claims brought under particular federal statutes are completely exempt from mandatory arbitration, they may still be able to use federal law to defeat the imposition of mandatory arbitration in particular cases. The Supreme Court has frequently explained that "[b]y agreeing to arbitrate a statutory claim, a party does not forgo the substantive rights afforded by the statute; it only submits to their resolution in an arbitral, rather than a judicial, forum."[92] Thus, where a challenger can show that the arbitration clause was written in such a way as to effectively prevent the challenger from vindicating her rights under a particular federal statute, the Court has explained that the arbitration clause should not be enforced. For example, in *Green Tree Financial Corp. – Alabama v. Randolph*,[93] consumer Larketta Randolph purchased a mobile home and financed the purchase through Green Tree Financial Corporation. When Randolph later sued Green Tree, alleging violation of the federal Truth in Lending Act and the Equal Credit Opportunity

[89] 15 U.S.C. §2301 et seq. (2000).

[90] *See, e.g., Wilson v. Waverlee Homes, Inc.*, 954 F. Supp. 1530, 1537–8 (M. D. Ala. 1997), *aff'd*, 127 F.3d 40 (11th Cir.1997); *Raesly v. Grand Housing, Inc.*, 105 F. Supp. 2d 562 (S. D. Miss. 2000).

[91] *See, e.g., Walton v. Rose Mobile Homes*, 298 F.3d 470, 478 (5th Cir. 2002); *Davis v. South. Energy Homes Inc.*, 305 F.3d 1268, 1272 (11th Cir. 2002).

[92] *Mitsubishi Motors Corp. v. Soler Chrysler-Plymouth, Inc.*, 473 U.S. 614, 628 (1985).

[93] 531 U.S. 79 (2000).

Act, Green Tree responded that the contract required Randolph to arbitrate the claims. Randolph, in turn, urged that she was not required to arbitrate because the arbitration would be so expensive as to prevent her from vindicating her rights under the federal statutes. The Supreme Court accepted plaintiff's basic argument but found she had failed to make an adequate factual showing regarding the alleged high cost of arbitration. Thus, although Randolph was required to arbitrate, the decision makes clear that when the costs of arbitration are proven to be excessive courts may not mandate arbitration of federal claims. A number of courts have rejected particular arbitration clauses on this basis in subsequent cases.[94]

Consumers have pointed to other problems in addition to high costs in attempting to void arbitration statutes as failing to allow them to vindicate their rights under federal statutes. Some features courts have or may find problematic include shortening consumers' statute of limitations, preventing consumers from recovering relief (e.g., punitive or compensatory damages or attorney fees) that would have been available in court, requiring consumers to present their claims in a distant forum, or preventing consumers from presenting their claims in a class action. These arguments are very similar to consumers' claims of unconscionability, which will be discussed in the following section.

5.5(2)(C) Common Law Contractual Arguments

(1) State Law Grounds for Invalidation

Consumers' chances of defeating arbitration clauses have been greatest to the extent they have relied on contractual and other common law attacks. As Section 2 of the Federal Arbitration Act makes clear, as the Supreme Court has frequently stated, and has previously been discussed in this book, arbitration clauses can be invalidated "upon such grounds as exist at law or in equity for the revocation of any contract."[95]

Although the language of Section 2 of the FAA seems straightforward, it has spawned an interesting policy debate, particularly in the consumer context, regarding how standard contract law is or should be applied to

[94] For an article summarizing case law on this point in the employment context, *see* Michael H. Leroy & Peter Feuille, *When Is Cost An Unlawful Barrier To Alternative Dispute Resolution? The Ever Green Tree of Mandatory Employment Arbitration*, 50 UCLA L. Rev. 143 (2002).

[95] 9 U.S.C. §2 (2000). *See, e.g., Allied-Bruce Terminix Cos., Inc. v. Dobson*, 513 U.S. 265, 281 (1995) (stating "[s]tates may regulate contracts, including arbitration clauses, under general contract law principles and they may invalidate an arbitration clause 'upon such grounds as exist at law or in equity for the revocation of any contract'").

arbitration clauses. Specifically, should arbitration clauses be treated just like other contracts? Or, should they be easier or harder to vacate than other contracts? At one extreme, some companies have argued that the federal policy of "favoring" arbitration means that arbitration clauses must be enforced "as written."[96] Taken literally, this position would seem to exempt arbitration clauses from standard contract law regarding fraud, unconscionability, and other matters. At the other end of the spectrum, some such as this author point out that an arbitration clauses is an unusual type of contract in that it implicates important legal rights including the right to jury trial. As has been discussed previously and will be discussed further below, with regard to state constitutional jury trial rights, the special nature of arbitration contracts may warrant special protection. Most courts have taken an intermediate position, finding that the same contractual doctrines can be used to attack arbitration clauses as can be used to attack other kinds of contracts.[97]

What contractual challenges are typically made? The challenger may argue that the agreement was invalid due to lack of consideration,[98] that the clause did not cover the particular claim,[99] that it was invalid due to fraud,[100] or that the clause was unconscionable.[101]

Clauses most likely to be defeated as unconscionable are those that impose excessive costs, require claimants to travel to distant locations, limit remedies, impose a biased arbitrator, and/or eliminate the opportunity for class

[96] This argument was made by the company and amici in the *Bazzle* case, recently decided by the Supreme Court. *See Green Tree Financial Corp. v. Bazzle*, 593 U.S. 444 (2003). But, the Court did not accept the argument.

[97] One author argues that judges are applying an arbitration-specific version of unconscionability that leads courts to void arbitration agreements under circumstances when they would not otherwise void a contract. Susan Randall, *Judicial Attitudes Toward Arbitration and the Resurgence of Unconscionability*, 52 Buff. L. Rev. 185 (2004). *See also* Stephen J. Ware, *Consumer Arbitration As Exceptional Consumer Law (With A Contractualist Reply to Carrington & Haagen)*, 29 McGeorge L. Rev. 195 (1998) (urging that it is inappropriate to provide special protections in arbitration that are not available with respect to other types of contracts and labeling various consumer-protection measures as "anti-contract"). However, it is difficult to distinguish between whether judges are being unduly tough on arbitration clauses or whether companies are seeking to use their arbitration clauses to take especially unfair advantage of consumers.

[98] *See, e.g.*, *Gibson v. Neighborhood Health Clinics, Inc.*, 121 F.3d 1126, 1131–2 (7th Cir. 1997); *Piano v. Premier Distributing Co.*, 107 P.3d 11 (N. Mex. 2005).

[99] *See, e.g.*, *Seifert v. U.S. Home Corp.*, 750 So.2d 633, 642–3 (Fla. 1999) (holding arbitration clause in construction contract does not cover tort claim).

[100] *See, e.g.*, *Engalla v. Permanente Med. Group, Inc.*, 15 Cal. 4th 951, 974–81 (Cal. Ct. App. 1997).

[101] *See, e.g.*, *Ting v. AT & T*, 182 F. Supp. 2d 902, 939 (N. D. Cal. 2002), *aff'd in relevant part*, 319 F.3d 1126 (9th Cir. 2003), *cert. denied*, 504 U.S. 811 (2003).

actions. Indeed, the most vulnerable clauses are those that combine a number of these problems. *Ting v. AT & T*[102] provides a good example of this sort of clause. In that case phone provider AT & T chose to impose binding arbitration on its existing phone customers. AT & T sent customers a new "legal remedies" provision that not only required customers to take future disputes to arbitration, but also prohibited them from proceeding in class actions, curtailed damages available to the customers, shielded AT & T from liability for intentional and fraudulent conduct, shortened the applicable statute of limitations, and imposed upon consumers additional costs associated with arbitration.[103] Holding the clause unconscionable the district court stated:

> This lawsuit is not about arbitration. If all AT & T had done was to move customer disputes that survive its informal resolution process from the courts to arbitration, its actions would likely have been sanctioned by the state and federal policies favoring arbitration. While that is what it suggested it was doing to its customers, it was actually doing much more; it was actually rewriting substantially the legal landscape on which its customers must contend. Aware that the vast majority of service related disputes would be resolved informally, AT & T sought to shield itself from liability in the remaining disputes by imposing Legal Remedies Provisions that eliminate class actions, sharply curtail damages in cases of misrepresentation, fraud, and other intentional torts, cloak the arbitration process with secrecy and place significant financial hurdles in the path of a potential litigant. It is not just that AT & T wants to litigate in the forum of its choice – arbitration; it is that AT & T wants to make it very difficult for anyone to effectively vindicate her rights, even in that forum. That is illegal and unconscionable and must be enjoined.[104]

Yet, many decisions reject consumers' attempts to defeat arbitration clauses as unconscionable, often on the ground that the consumers have failed to present sufficient evidence to prove bias or lack of choice. A recent decision by the Alabama Supreme Court exemplifies this type of decision. In *Briarcliff Nursing Home, Inc. v. Turcotte*,[105] the Alabama Court forced the survivors of two deceased residents to bring their wrongful death claims in arbitration, rather than in court. The court explained that plaintiffs have failed to show bias on behalf of the relevant arbitral organization (which plaintiffs called a "puppet for the health care and long term care industries"); and that plaintiffs had failed to show a lack of real options because they had

[102] 182 F. Supp. 2d 902, 939 (N. D. Cal. 2002), *aff'd in relevant part*, 319 F.3d 1126 (9th Cir. 2003).

[103] *Id.*

[104] *Id.* at 938–9.

[105] 894 So.2d 661 (Ala. 2004).

not considered residents' options for nursing home care outside their own county.[106]

The class action issue is particularly interesting and important for consumer claims. As has been discussed, companies are increasingly seeking to use arbitration clauses to prevent consumers from pursuing class action claims against the company, either in litigation or in arbitration. Thus, in a number of cases consumers have brought challenges arguing that the class action prohibition is unconscionable. A few of these challenges have succeeded, but quite a few have not. Although companies have attempted to argue that such unconscionability arguments are preempted by the FAA, to date such arguments have failed.[107] To prevail in an unconscionability challenge it is key for consumers to present a strong factual showing, and not to rely exclusively on mere facial legal arguments.[108] Where consumers can use affidavits, depositions, and expert testimony to show that the class action is critical to their chance of success, courts may well accept their argument that the class action prohibition is unconscionable.[109] In contrast,

[106] The court also found that the transaction sufficiently involved interstate commerce to bring the FAA into play (important since Alabama law rejects mandatory arbitration). Without discussion, the majority also rejected the argument that wrongful death claims do not arise until the victim's death and thus cannot be waived in advance. For other recent cases rejecting consumers' arguments of unconscionability with respect to an imposed arbitration clause *see McKenzie v. Hardy*, 866 So. 2d 446 (Miss. 2004) (emphasizing that all parties to contracts have a legal obligation to read that document, and asserting that the customers "would have easily understood the language of the agreement" had they read it); *Crippen v. Central Valley RV Outlet Inc.*, 22 Cal. Rptr. 3d 189 (Cal. App. 2004) (finding that plaintiff, purchaser of used motor home, failed to show imposed contract was procedurally unconscionable in that plaintiff presented no extrinsic evidence of unconscionability but rather relied exclusively on inferences that might be drawn from the document itself).

[107] *See, e.g., Discover Bank v. Superior Court*, 30 Cal. Rptr. 3d 76, 87–91 (Cal. 2005) (holding that class action prohibitions could be unconscionable, and that FAA would not preempt such determination, but remanding to lower court for determination of choice of law issue regarding which jurisdiction's unconscionability doctrines should apply).

[108] *See* F. Paul Bland, Jr., *Is That Arbitration Clause Unconscionable? PROVE IT!*, The Consumer Advoc.(National Association of Consumer Advocates, Washington, D.C.), July–Aug. 2002, at 1, 5 (observing that the one common thread in cases where the plaintiffs failed to show that class action prohibitions were unconscionable was "that the plaintiffs treated the cases principally as posing legal rather than factual issues"); James C. Sturdevant, *The Critical Importance of Creating an Evidentiary Record to Prove that a Mandatory, Pre-Dispute Arbitration Clause is Unconscionable*, Forum, Oct. 2002 at 18 (urging that attorneys seeking to defeat motions to compel arbitration engage in substantial discovery and seek to amass factual cases showing that the clause is illegal and unconscionable, rather than relying on purely legal arguments that are likely to fail).

[109] For some examples of federal and state court decisions holding that class action prohibitions contained in arbitration clauses either contributed to a finding that the clause was unconscionable or must be severed, due to their unfairness *see ACORN v. Household Int'l, Inc.*, 211 F. Supp. 2d 1160 (N. D. Cal. 2002); *Comb v. Paypal, Inc.*, 218 F. Supp. 2d 1165

consumers have generally failed in their attempts to argue that every exclusion of class actions prevents them from adequately protecting their rights under the Truth in Lending Act, even though that statute specifically references class actions.[110] Of course, by requiring consumers to make a strong factual showing in order to defeat a class action prohibition, courts are imposing a substantial financial burden on the consumers and their counsel that may prove insurmountable.[111]

Consumers and others have successfully challenged mandatory arbitration clauses on a number of other grounds as well. For example, arbitration clauses have been voided on such grounds as lack of mutuality, that insufficient notice of the arbitration provision was afforded, or that the party urging arbitration waived that right by participating in litigation. Some clauses have also been defeated on the ground that the company waived its right to impose arbitration by failing to assert the arbitration clause early enough in the litigation.

(2) Judicial Reluctance to Invalidate

Although arbitration clauses have been defeated on each of these grounds, most mandatory arbitration clauses are upheld, even in the consumer context. Why do so many challenges fail? First, as noted earlier, courts are increasingly refusing to consider challenges to arbitration clauses, holding instead that the purported invalidity of the clause must be ruled on by the arbitrator.[112] Second, as previously mentioned with regard to class actions,

(N. D. Cal. 2002); *Luna v. Household Finance Corp. III*, 236 F. Supp. 2d 1166 (W. D. Wash. 2002); *Ting v. AT & T*, 182 F. Supp. 2d 902 (N. D. Cal. 2002), *aff'd in rel. part*, 319 F.3d 1126 (2003); *Lozada v. Dale Baker Oldsmobile, Inc.*, 91 F. Supp. 2d 1087, 1104–5 (W. D. Mich. 2000); *In re Knepp*, 229 B. R. 821, 842 (N. D. Ala. 1999); *Leonard v. Terminix Int'l Co.*, 854 So. 2d 529 (Ala. 2002); *Szetela v. Discover Bank*, 97 Cal. App. 4th 1094 (Cal. App. 2002), *aff'd in relevant part*, 30 Cal. Rptr.3d 76 (Cal. 2005); *Powertel, Inc. v. Bexley*, 743 So. 2d 570, 576 (Fla. App. 1999); State *ex rel. Dunlap v. Berger*, 567 S.E.2d 265 (W. Va. 2002). Note that a number of arbitrators have now similarly ruled that construing an arbitration clause that is silent as to class actions to preclude arbitral class actions would be unconscionable. *See* American Arbitration Association Class Arbitration Case Docket, http://www.adr.org (follow link to Class Arbitration Policy, Rules & Docket).

110 Truth in Lending Act, 15 U.S.C. §§1601 et seq. (2000) (specifically the Truth in Lending Class Action Relief Act of 1995, 15 U.S.C. §1640 (2000)).

111 For further discussion of the question of whether prohibiting class action remedies renders arbitration clauses unconscionable, *see* Jean R. Sternlight & Elizabeth J. Jensen, *Using Arbitration to Eliminate Consumer Class Actions: Efficient Business Practice or Unconscionable Abuse?* 67 Law & Contemp. Probs. 75 (2004).

112 *See, e.g., Hawkins v. Aid Ass'n for Lutherans*, 338 F.3d 801, 807 (7th Cir. 2003) (ruling, in case where group of insureds argued that clause unconscionably denied them access to appropriate relief, that decision as to alleged unconscionability must be made by arbitrator).

courts typically void only those clauses where challengers have presented substantial evidence of unfairness. Courts have frequently stated that they are unwilling to assume that an arbitration clause would operate unfairly or be biased, even though the consumer claims such a result is likely.[113] Thus, courts generally seem to employ a strong presumption in favor of arbitration that creates a difficult hurdle for consumers seeking to challenge clauses to which they have seemingly assented.

The mere fact that arbitration has been mandated in a small print form agreement is certainly not sufficient to defeat such a clause. For example, in *Hill v. Gateway 2000, Inc.*,[114] consumer Enza Hill purchased a Gateway computer by phone. When Hill subsequently sought to bring a lawsuit, arguing that the computer was defective, Gateway argued that the claim must be brought in arbitration pursuant to the rules of the International Chamber of Commerce. At minimum this process would have cost several thousand dollars, and likely more than the cost of the computer itself.[115] The arbitration clause was contained on page 3, paragraph 10 of the warranty booklet, which was packed with the computer and delivered to Hill. The Seventh Circuit Court of Appeals held that there was a contract to arbitrate because Hill accepted the clause by failing to return the computer within thirty days, although Hill never signed an agreement or knowingly agreed to arbitration.[116]

In seeking to void arbitration clauses on contract grounds consumers also face the problem that even assuming that the court finds an aspect of the clause to be improper, it may well sever or rewrite that portion of the clause, rather than void the arbitration provision in its entirety.[117] In contrast, some

[113] *See, e.g.*, *Green Tree Financial Corp.-Alabama v. Randolph*, 531 U.S. 79 (2000) (refusing to void arbitration clause based on mere "speculation" that arbitration would be excessively costly); *Gilmer v. Interstate/Johnson Lane Corp.*, 500 U.S. 20 (1991) (generalized attacks on arbitration are out of step with Court's strong endorsement of arbitration).

[114] 105 F.3d 1147 (7th Cir. 1997), *cert. denied*, 522 U.S. 808 (1997).

[115] *See* Jean R. Sternlight, *Gateway Widens Doorway to Imposing Unfair Binding Arbitration on Consumers*, 71 FLA. B. J. 8 (1997).

[116] 105 F.3d 1147 (7th Cir. 1997). However, Hill might have been more successful had he attempted to invalidate the clause using a different argument. In a subsequent case, a New York court held that the Gateway arbitration provision was unconscionable to the extent that it mandated arbitration pursuant to the rules of the International Chamber of Commerce. *Brower v. Gateway 2000, Inc.*, 676 N.Y.S.2d 569 (App. Div. 1998).

[117] For examples of cases in which courts merely severed the offending portion of the clause *see Gannon v. Circuit City Stores, Inc.*, 262 F.3d 677, 683 (8th Cir. 2001) (holding that the punitive damages clause in arbitration agreement should be severed); *Wilmott v. McNabb*, 269 F. Supp. 2d 1203 (N. D. Cal. 2003) (granting motion to compel arbitration on the condition that the unconscionable venue provision be severed from the arbitration clause); *Wright v. Circuit City Stores, Inc.*, 82 F. Supp. 2d 1279, 1287–88 (N. D. Ala. 2000)

courts do void the entire clause, reasoning, for example, that its problems permeate the entire provision.[118]

Finally, consumers' claims sometimes fail because companies choose to "cure" the unfairness of their arbitration clause on the courthouse steps. That is, a company that had imposed a clause imposing high fees on a customer might agree to pay those fees, or a company that had imposed a clause barring recovery of punitive damages might agree to lift that bar. Although, at first glance, such a move by the company might sound fair, a number of courts have recognized that allowing companies to cure the problems with their clauses in fact gives an unfair advantage to the company. This approach allows companies to use the unfair clause to deter arbitration by most consumers, while avoiding liability with respect to the rare consumer who manages to challenge the clause. In other words, allowing companies to cure the problems with their arbitration clauses takes away an incentive companies would otherwise have had to draft clauses that are fair in the first instance.[119]

In short, although contractual and other common law arguments have proved more successful for consumers than other approaches, even those arguments fail far more often than they succeed. Some courts are proving willing to strike the most obviously unfair arbitration clauses on such grounds as unconscionability,[120] but many other courts are upholding

(holding that the "arbitration clause at issue should be modified in accordance with the severability/conflict of law provision" of the contract); *Gutierrez v. Autowest, Inc.*, 7 Cal. Rptr.3d 267 (Cal. App. 2003) (holding that unconscionable terms within an arbitration provision may be severed for the purpose of granting a motion to compel arbitration).

[118] *See, e.g., Alexander v. Anthony Crane Int'l*, 341 F.3d 256, 270–3 (3d Cir. 2003) (voiding entire clause, rather than severing unfair portions, because unfair portions so permeated the entire agreement rendering it fundamentally unfair); *Hooters of America, Inc. v. Phillips*, 173 F.3d 933, 940 (4th Cir. 1999) (holding that "rescission [of the entire contract] is the proper remedy"); *Torrance v. Ames Funding Corp.*, 242 F. Supp. 2d 862 (D. Or. 2002) (finding three of the arbitration clause's provisions unconscionable, and holding that the clause was so permeated by unconscionability that the entire arbitration clause was unenforceable); *Armendariz v. Found. Health Psychcare Servs., Inc.*, 6 P.3d 669, 697 (Cal. 2000) (holding that the court "must void the entire agreement").

[119] For a decision providing a similar analysis, *see Morrison v. Circuit City Stores, Inc.*, 317 F.3d 646, 676–7 (6th Cir. 2003).

[120] For a somewhat more upbeat take on courts' willingness to strike down arbitration clauses as unconscionable *see* Jeffrey W. Stempel, *Arbitration, Unconscionability and Equilibrium: The Return of Unconscionability Analysis as a Counterweight to Arbitration Formalism*, 19 Ohio St. J. Disp. Res. 757, 764–5 (2004) (finding lower courts more willing than once was the case to strike arbitration clauses as unconscionable). *See also* Susan Randall, *Judicial Attitudes Toward Arbitration and the Resurgence of Unconscionability*, 52 Buff. L. Rev. 185, 186 (2004) (arguing that a number of trial courts, hostile to arbitration, have stretched unconscionability doctrine beyond its usual and appropriate limits to strike arbitration clauses).

similar clauses. Moreover, only rarely do consumers have the knowledge, financial wherewithal, or assistance needed to challenge an arbitration clause that might fail on contractual grounds.

5.5(2)(D) State Statutory and Constitutional Arguments

In addition to raising contractual arguments consumers may also seek to invalidate arbitration clauses on the ground that they are void under a state statute or state constitution. As noted earlier, a number of states have adopted legislation seeking to protect consumers from mandatory arbitration in particular contexts. Also, consumer protection groups are asking state legislatures to adopt additional such legislation, particularly in the context of states' consideration of the proposed Revised Uniform Arbitration Act.

To prevail on a claim brought under a state statute or constitution the consumer would usually have to defeat the argument that the relevant state provision was preempted by the FAA. Although preemption is only an issue to the extent that the transaction at issue involves interstate commerce, the Supreme Court's broad definition of interstate commerce assures that preemption will be an issue in most consumer cases involving state law. Unfortunately, however, as has also been discussed in prior chapters, the scope of FAA preemption of state laws and constitutions is not entirely apparent.

A few things are clear. Given the Supreme Court's decisions in *Southland Corp. v. Keating*[121] and *Allied-Bruce Terminix Cos., Inc. v. Dobson,*[122] we *know* that the FAA preempts those state laws that entirely proscribe arbitration of particular claims. For example, the Court held preempted the statute in *Southland* providing that franchise claims were not arbitrable and the statute in *Terminix* providing that no pre-dispute arbitration agreements were enforceable. In addition, the Supreme Court's decision in *Doctor's Assocs., Inc. v. Casarotto*[123] shows that the preemption doctrine extends much further. In that case an 8–1 majority of the Court held that the FAA preempted a Montana statute requiring that arbitration clauses in franchise agreements be "typed in underlined capital letters on the first page of the contract."[124] The Justices explained that "[c]ourts may

[121] 465 U.S. 1 (1984).
[122] 513 U.S. 265 (1995).
[123] 517 U.S. 681 (1996).
[124] *Id.* at 683. The preempted provision was Mont. Code Ann. §27-5-114(4), subsequently withdrawn by the Montana legislature.

not . . . invalidate arbitration agreements under state laws applicable *only* to arbitration provisions."[125]

Some have suggested that the preemption doctrine goes even further. For example, co-author Stephen Ware argues that states may only legislate as to arbitration if the legislation would cover *all* contracts in the state, and not, for example, merely consumer contracts.[126] Professor Ware also argues it would be appropriate for the Supreme Court to review state uses of unconscionability doctrines to ensure they are not "nullifying the FAA with respect to a huge class of contracts."[127]

Courts' approach to the preemption question has varied. The Ninth Circuit employed a very broad interpretation of preemption law in *Bradley v. Harris Research, Inc.*,[128] holding that a state statute prohibiting franchisors from mandating out-of-state dispute resolution was preempted to the extent it purported to void a portion of an arbitration clause mandating out-of-state proceedings. The court reasoned that the statute was preempted as applied to an arbitral agreement, although it would have been valid in the litigation context. In contrast, other courts have held that state laws are valid, even when they result in the voiding of an arbitration provision, so long as the state law was not targeted specifically to arbitration.[129] Also, courts have generally found that state arbitration laws are not preempted to the extent that they deal with procedural issues such as the appealability of decisions with respect to arbitration.[130]

This confused body of law leaves open many important questions as to the extent to which states can regulate arbitration.[131] For example, if a statute generally prohibits the contractual elimination of class actions would such a statute be preempted as applied to arbitration clauses? If a state statute provides that the right to pursue judicial remedies for violations of a particular state law can only be waived knowingly and voluntarily, or with a

[125] *Id.* at 687 (emphasis in original).

[126] Stephen J. Ware, Alternative Dispute Resolution §2.13–2.14 (2001).

[127] *Id.* at §2.25.

[128] 275 F.3d 884 (9th Cir. 2001).

[129] *See, e.g., Mitchell v. Am. Fair Credit Ass'n, Inc.*, 122 Cal. Rep.2d 193 (Cal. App. 2002) (invalidating arbitration provision under California Credit Services Act of 1984 because, contrary to requirements of Act, the arbitration provision was not signed by the credit consumer).

[130] *See* F. Paul Bland et al., Consumer Arbitration Agreements: Enforceability and Other Topics §2.2.2.2 (National Consumer Law Center, 2d ed., 2002).

[131] For an excellent discussion of preemption and a critique of courts' current approach *see* David Schwartz, *Correcting Federalism Mistakes*, *supra* Note 78.

signed document, would such a provision be preempted?[132] These questions are not merely hypothetical, as will be shown in the discussion, later in this chapter, regarding specific state laws and regulations.

Section 5.6 Regulation of Mandatory Consumer Arbitration

Mandatory consumer arbitration is clearly alive and well in the United States, although it apparently does not exist elsewhere in the world at this point. Those who oppose such arbitration or who think that its use should be limited have used or considered five means of regulating the practice. First, as has already been discussed, opponents of mandatory consumer arbitration have used existing case law to rein in abusive arbitration clauses. Second, opponents have encouraged arbitration providers to regulate themselves. Thus, a number of providers have created a series of "due process protocols" geared to ensure that mandatory consumer arbitration is fair. Third, as has been discussed briefly, some states have sought to regulate consumer arbitration. Fourth, powerful third party organizations may put pressure on companies not to mandate arbitration. Finally, the most effective means of eliminating or regulating mandatory consumer arbitration would be federal legislation. Such legislation has been proposed but, to date, not adopted. This section will discuss the latter four approaches, as case law has already been examined.

5.6(1) Due Process Protocols and Provider Self-Regulation

Some providers of arbitration services have responded to the critique of mandatory arbitration by themselves attempting to ensure that arbitration is fair. The most well known such exercise in self-regulation commenced in 1995, when a number of arbitration providers began to adopt policies known collectively as "due process protocols." Although the phrase "due process" is used, it is meant to denote general fairness and not technical compliance with the Due Process Clause of the Constitution. Some of the

[132] *See, e.g.*, *Garfinkel v. Morristown Obstetrics & Gynecology Assocs.*, 773 A.2d 665 (N.J. 2001) (holding that employees may waive the right to judicial remedy for violation of the New Jersey Law Against Discrimination in favor of binding arbitration only if waiver is clear and unequivocal so as to ensure waiver was knowing and voluntary); *Mitchell v. Am. Fair Credit Ass'n, Inc.*, 122 Cal. Rptr. 2d 193 (Cal. App. 2002) (invalidating arbitration provision under California Credit Services Act of 1984 because, contrary to requirements of Act, the arbitration provision was not signed by the credit consumer).

protocols are known by other names. For example, the National Arbitration Forum has its equivalent, the "Arbitration Bill of Rights."

In general these protocols do not prohibit the practice of mandatory arbitration, but instead try to insure that if a company imposes arbitration, it is fair. The protocols address such issues as neutrality, cost, location, and availability of remedies. The protocol that has received the most widespread attention is "A Due Process Protocol for Mediation and Arbitration of Statutory Disputes Arising out of the Employment Relationship," released in 1995. The American Arbitration Association played a key role in drafting the Protocol, though representatives of labor, management, individual employees, arbitration providers, and arbitrators also collaborated in its development. This protocol was adopted by a broad range of organizations from all these perspectives.[133]

The next major protocol to be adopted was the Consumer Due Process Protocol. Again, this protocol did not proscribe mandatory pre-dispute arbitration, but rather specified what kinds of provisions are and are not fair to include in such a clause. Generally, the Consumer Due Process Protocol suggests that the agreement include provisions assuring that any costs associated with the arbitration be reasonable, and that the clause also provide for a reasonably convenient location, reasonable time limits in which to conduct the proceedings, clear and adequate notice of the provision and its consequences (including whether the provision is voluntary or mandatory), and the availability of fair remedies (specifically providing that all remedies available in court under law or in equity be available to parties submitting their consumer claims to arbitration).[134]

In contrast to any of the other protocols, the AAA Health Care Due Process Protocol actually proscribes mandatory arbitration of certain disputes. Principle 3 states: "In disputes involving patients, binding forms of dispute resolution should be used only where the parties agree to do so after a dispute arises."[135] In deference to this policy, both the AAA and the American Health Lawyers Association ADR Service have announced that they will not administer cases involving medical claims by consumers without a post-dispute agreement to arbitrate.

Sometimes providers also take important steps to ensure fairness without incorporating such measures into a broader protocol. In November 2004

[133] It can be viewed on the AAA web site, http://www.adr.org.

[134] The Consumer Due Process Protocol can also be viewed on the AAA web site, http://www.adr.org.

[135] The Health Care Due Process Protocol can also be viewed on the AAA web site, http://www.adr.org.

provider JAMS announced that it would no longer enforce clauses in arbitration agreements that precluded class actions, unless the claimants agreed at the time of submission to arbitration that the claim should proceed on an individual basis. This announcement was extremely controversial. It was praised enthusiastically by consumer advocates and harshly criticized by business interests, some of whom asserted it violated federal law. JAMS subsequently withdrew its prior policy, in March 2005, and that withdrawal has been equally controversial. Consumer advocates claimed JAMS caved in to financial pressure imposed by companies seeking to use binding arbitration to eliminate class actions.

Although the Health Care Due Process Protocol has proved to be effective in discouraging some providers from administering clauses that violate the protocol, some important caveats must be noted with respect to all of the protocols and self-regulation measures. Because the protocols are simply policies adopted by arbitration providers, there is no clear enforcement mechanism. Although a disputant may bring a supposed violation of a protocol to the attention of a provider, the disputant has limited recourse if the provider chooses to administer the clause, notwithstanding the violation of the protocol. In addition, many have raised the concern that if major and reputable arbitration providers all choose to adopt fairness protocols, other less reputable providers may enter the field, offering companies an alternative that is beneficial to the company, but not its opponents. That is, the Protocols could prompt a classic "race to the bottom." Indeed, when JAMS for a time refused to enforce class action prohibitions some businesses threatened to and perhaps did strike JAMS from their arbitration clauses.

Unless courts cite to protocols in determining whether a particular arbitration clause is unconscionable, there will be no direct way to ensure that good practices are followed. Yet, only a very few courts have explicitly relied on the protocols to define fair practices.[136] Indeed, in one case where the designated arbitration provider, JAMS, refused to administer the clause because it violated its protocol, the court nonetheless ordered the parties to arbitration before a different provider.[137]

[136] Actually, it is more common for courts to cite lack of violation of the protocols, to support upholding a clause, than it is for courts to cite a violation of the protocols as a justification for voiding a clause.

[137] *See Great W. Mortgage Corp. v. Peacock*, 110 F.3d 222, 232 & nn. 40–6 (3d Cir. 1997). For a contrary decision, *see Martinez v. Master Protection Corp.*, 12 Cal. Rptr.3d 663 (Cal. App. 2004) (prohibiting substitution of alternative provider after AAA refused to administer clause due to shortened statute of limitations).

Further, even to the extent that the protocols were enforceable, only the Health Care Protocol actually bans pre-dispute arbitration provisions. By contrast, the Consumer Protocol bans neither mandatory arbitration nor clauses that would eliminate consumers' rights to proceed in class actions. As a practical matter, if companies can use arbitration to eliminate class actions the remaining provisions of the arbitration clause will not be important, in that virtually no consumer will choose to bring an individual claim against a company.

5.6(2) State Regulation

As has been discussed, many actions states have taken or might take to prohibit mandatory arbitration would be preempted under the FAA to the extent a party attempted to apply the state prohibition to a transaction involving interstate commerce. Nonetheless, a few states have taken steps to proscribe or at least regulate mandatory arbitration. At minimum their laws are effective for those transactions involving only intrastate commerce or also for those transactions in which consumers have elected to be covered by state rather than federal law. In addition, a number of states have attempted to craft legislation that would curb some of the worst excesses of mandatory consumer arbitration without falling subject to the preemption problem.[138]

5.6(2)(A) RUAA as a Bargaining Chip

Some recent state legislative efforts have been inspired by the adoption of a new uniform law regarding arbitration. The Revised Uniform Arbitration Act (RUAA), adopted by the National Conference of Commissioners of Uniform State Law in 2000,[139] does not directly address the question of the permissibility of mandatory consumer arbitration, instead opining in its Reporter's Notes that state attempts to deal with the subject would likely be preempted.[140] Thus, in some states opponents of mandatory consumer arbitration have sought to block adoption of the RUAA, whereas other states have adopted modified versions of the RUAA designed to protect consumers from mandatory arbitration.

[138] A consumer organization, the National Consumer Law Center Inc., has crafted draft legislation intended to help states in this endeavor. *See* http://www.consumerlaw.org.

[139] *See* http://www.law.upenn.edu/bll/ulc/ulc.htm#uaa.

[140] *See* RUAA, Prefatory Note, available at http://www.law.upenn.edu/bll/ulc/uarba/arbitrat1213.htm.

State legislation or potential state legislation can be broken down into several categories. First, a state might entirely prohibit the use of mandatory arbitration in the consumer context. However, such legislation would be preempted except as applied to purely local transactions, insurance transactions, or those transactions in which the parties elected to be governed by state rather than federal arbitration law.

5.6(2)(B) Regulating Arbitration

Second, a state might attempt to regulate the procedures under which consumers agree to arbitration or the nature of the arbitration itself. For example, a state might (and several have) require that arbitration agreements be signed or appear in a particular font size. However, the Supreme Court's decision in *Casarotto*[141] shows that these laws, too, will largely be preempted. As an example of more substantive regulation, in 2001, New Mexico adopted a revised Uniform Arbitration Act providing that arbitration clauses are voidable where, as compared to litigation, they require consumers, borrowers, tenants, or employees to assert claims in a less convenient or more costly forum; assume a risk of liability for the legal fees of the party preparing the contract; forego access to discovery; present evidence to a purported neutral who may "regard the party preparing the contract as more likely to be a future employer of the neutral person"; forego access to appeal; preclude participation in a class action; or forego awards to attorney fees or multiple damages.[142] No New Mexico court has yet addressed whether the FAA preempts this statute.

5.6(2)(C) Regulating Content of Contract to Arbitrate

Third, a state might opt to regulate arbitration in a manner similar to the way it regulates other dispute resolution processes. For example, in Kentucky a bill was introduced that would prohibit contract provisions, whether in arbitration or litigation, that impose a non-Kentucky forum on Kentucky residents.[143] States might, similarly, pass legislation barring predispute agreements to waive classwide relief, injunctive relief, or punitive damages, whether contained in arbitration clauses or other documents. Although courts have split on whether these sorts of clauses ought to be

[141] *See* discussion *supra* Notes 75–8, 121–32.

[142] New Mexico Uniform Arbitration Act, N. M. Stat. Ann. §44-7A-1 et seq. (2003).

[143] House Bill 523 was introduced in February 2004. It can be viewed at http://www.lrc.state.ky.us/record/04rs/hb523.htm.

held preempted, this author contends that they should survive, as they are not targeted to arbitration clauses in particular.

5.6(2)(D) State Constitutions

Fourth, consumers may also attempt to rely on preexisting state constitutional provisions to challenge mandatory arbitration. Most states' constitutions include a civil jury trial guarantee that, like the federal Seventh Amendment, permits waiver of the jury trial right only where such waiver is knowing, voluntary, and intelligent. These provisions might be used to attack mandatory arbitration clauses in cases in which the Seventh Amendment would not apply (such as cases brought in state court). If consumers attempt to use state constitutional jury trial provisions to attack mandatory arbitration, companies will no doubt argue that the state jury trial provision is preempted. The resolution of this dispute will turn on the court's interpretation of the preemption doctrine. Consumers will argue that the jury trial requirements are not preempted because they do not single out or target arbitration clauses for elimination.[144] By contrast, companies may argue that the provisions are preempted to the extent they have the effect of voiding an arbitration clause.[145]

5.6(2)(E) Regulating Arbitration Service Providers

Fifth, some states have chosen to regulate the provision of arbitration services rather than to attempt to block consumer arbitration directly. California has taken the lead in this trend, having recently both passed legislation and adopted new court rules regulating arbitration in an attempt to prevent potential arbitration abuses. In particular, Section 1281.5 of the California Code of Civil Procedure required California's Judicial Council to create and enact ethics standards for arbitrators that became effective July 1, 2002. The new standards, for example, require arbitrators to disclose information pertaining to a variety of personal and professional relationships, potential conflicts of interest, and prior service as an arbitrator. In addition, other legislation passed in California requires arbitration providers to collect and publish a range of data, prohibits an arbitration provider from administering

[144] For an example of this reasoning, *see Kloss v. Edward D. Jones & Co.*, 54 P.3d 1 (Mont. 2002).

[145] For further discussion of jury trial arguments that might be made under state constitutions, *see* Jean R. Sternlight, *The Rise and Spread of Mandatory Arbitration as a Substitute for the Jury Trial*, 38 U.S.F. L. Rev. 17 (2003).

a consumer arbitration if it had a financial interest in a participant, proscribes "loser pays" provisions in consumer arbitration, and requires a private arbitration company to waive the fees and costs of arbitration, exclusive of arbitrator fees, for an indigent consumer, as defined in the statute.[146] Other states now seem poised to follow California's lead on regulating arbitration and requiring disclosure of certain information with respect to arbitration. A Texas agency, for example, has required that certain information be published regarding construction defect arbitrations handled in that state.

5.6(3) Third Party Pressure

A third potential mode of regulation is that powerful entities may directly or indirectly prevent companies from imposing arbitration on their customers. The best example of this sort of regulation has occurred in the mortgage industry, where two federally-sponsored stockholder-owned corporations, Freddie Mac[147] and Fannie Mae,[148] have refused to purchase mortgages that impose mandatory arbitration provisions on home owners. These entities have stated that while they are not opposed to arbitration, they believe that home owners should have the option to choose the forum in which they will bring a claim.[149] This decision is putting substantial pressure on the companies that deal directly with home owners not to mandate binding arbitration, as doing so means that their mortgage does not qualify for purchase by these two giants in the secondary mortgage market. If other powerful entities were to announce similar policies, companies might change their practice in other areas as well.

5.6(4) Federal Legislation

For those who oppose the use of mandatory arbitration in the consumer context it is clear that federal legislation is the most powerful tool by which such arbitration might be eliminated or regulated. The Supreme Court has repeatedly made clear that Congress has the power to eliminate the use of

[146] Cal. Code Civ. Proc. §§1284.3, 1281.92, & 1281.96 (2002). For a decision holding that the new California disclosure rules were preempted by both the New York Stock Exchange Rules and also by the Federal Arbitration Act, *see Mayo v. Dean Witter Reynolds, Inc.*, 258 F. Supp. 2d 1097 (N. D. Cal. 2003).

[147] Federal Home Loan Mortgage Corporation.

[148] Federal National Mortgage Association.

[149] Freddie Mac's policy is set out at http://www.freddiemac.com/news/archives/afford_housing/2003/consumer˙120403.html. Fannie Mae's policy is set out at http://www.fanniemae.com/initiatives/pdf/adc/background.pdf.

arbitration in general or in specific situations, should it so choose. Such laws would effectively repeal the Federal Arbitration Act in whole or in part.

Although an array of legislative approaches are possible and a number of specific proposals have been made, it should be noted from the outset that Congress has not, to date, proved eager to pass laws regulating or prohibiting mandatory arbitration. There is, however, one interesting and rather odd exception to this general rule. The Motor Vehicle Franchise Contract Arbitration Fairness Act of 2001[150] protects automobile franchisees from mandatory arbitration imposed by automobile franchisors. This legislation was passed after the franchisees mounted a substantial lobbying effort complaining about how unfair it is for large automobile manufacturers to force their franchisees to resolve disputes through arbitration rather than in court. Most ironically, however, the legislation does nothing to prohibit automobile franchisees from requiring their customers to arbitrate future disputes, even though it has now become common for automobile dealers to force arbitration on their customers.[151] It is hard not to be cynical about the fact that this is the only law regulating mandatory arbitration that earned substantial support from both Republicans and Democrats.[152]

What kinds of legislation has been or might be proposed to protect consumers? The first and most aggressive approach would be to use federal law to prohibit the use of mandatory arbitration in particular consumer contexts. Such legislation would be comparable to the approach of the European Union, which, as noted earlier, has issued a series of directives and statements barring binding consumer arbitration unless if it has been agreed to knowingly and voluntarily after the dispute has arisen.[153] In recent years, opponents of mandatory arbitration have introduced a series of such proposals, although, to date, none of these bills have garnered substantial support. One set of bills has focused on eliminating the use of mandatory arbitration with respect to consumer lending and credit cards. For example, the Consumer Credit Fair Dispute Resolution Act,[154] provides that "a written

[150] This bill was signed into law as Section 11028 of the 21st Century Department of Justice Appropriations Authorization Act, Pub. L. No. 107–273, §11028, 116 Stat. 1758, 1835–6 (2001).

[151] *See* Kelly K. Spors, *Tip of the Week: Don't Sign Car Clause*, Wall St. J., Jan. 11, 2004, at 1.

[152] Along the same lines, a bipartisan coalition of mid-Western senators introduced a bill that would amend the Federal Arbitration Act to bar the use of mandatory pre-dispute arbitration clauses in livestock contracts, but this one has not yet passed. S. 91, 108th Cong. (2003) was introduced on January 7, 2003.

[153] *See supra* Section 5.2(3). For more detail *see* Jean R. Sternlight, *Is the U.S. Out on a Limb*, *supra* Note 23 at 836.

[154] S. 192, 107th Cong. (2001).

provision in any consumer credit contract evidencing a transaction involving commerce to settle by arbitration a controversy thereafter arising out of the contract . . . shall not be valid or enforceable." More recently a series of bills have been proposed in the U.S. House and Senate that would bar the inclusion of mandatory arbitration clauses in certain home loan contracts.[155] Typically such bills permit arbitration agreements that are entered into post-dispute, while prohibiting arbitration proposed on a mandatory basis, pre-dispute.[156]

Law professor Paul Carrington has proposed a sweeping piece of federal legislation that would protect consumers, employees, and local franchisees.[157] "Consumer" is defined as "any person purchasing goods or services delivered for personal use in the United States, and includes passengers and shippers of goods on common carriers in commerce." The draft bill declares that contracts between consumers and providers of goods or services are illegal to the extent that they purport to deny consumers access to courts that would otherwise have been available. The bill would, however, allow for post-dispute agreements to arbitrate, and would also allow for

[155] The proposed Predatory Lending Consumer Protection Act of 2003, S. 1928, 108th Cong. §4 (2003) and the proposed Save Our Homes Act, H.R. 3322, 108th Cong. §3 (2003), sought to make mandatory arbitration clauses in high cost mortgage contracts invalid and unenforceable. The proposed Responsible Lending Act, H.R. 833, 108th Cong. (2003), included a provision which would have prohibited, in high cost mortgage contracts, mandatory arbitration agreements that were "oppressive, unfair, unconscionable, or substantially in derogation of the rights of consumers." It also provided that any arbitration clause should establish an arbitration venue in the jurisdiction in which the mortgaged property would be located, the proceedings should comply with the standards set forth by a nationally recognized arbitration association, and that the creditor should bear the costs of the arbitration proceedings. The proposed Predatory Mortgage Lending Practices Reduction Act, H.R. 1663, 108th Cong. (2003), sought to amend the Consumer Credit Protection Act, 15 U.S.C. §§1601 et seq., to make unenforceable any consumer pre-dispute mandatory arbitration agreement on which fulfillment of the contract would be contingent.

[156] Quite a number of bills prohibiting or limiting the use of pre-dispute mandatory arbitration in the employment context have also been proposed in the U.S. Congress, but as with the consumer bills, none have been successful. One example is the Preservation of Civil Rights Protections Act, which stated that "any agreement between an employer and an employee that requires arbitration of a claim arising under the Constitution or laws of the United States shall not be enforceable." H.R. 2282, 107th Cong. (2001), WL 2001 CONG US HR 2282. S. 2088, 108th Cong. §513 (2004), sought to impose the same restriction on pre-dispute arbitration provisions appearing in employment contracts, while providing an exception for terms of collective bargaining agreements. The Civil Rights Procedures Protection Act of 1999, S. 121, 106th Cong. (1999), sought to amend the FAA by adding a provision stating that the chapter did not apply to claims for unlawful employment discrimination based on race, religion, sex, national origin, color, age, or disability.

[157] Paul D. Carrington, *Regulating Dispute Resolution Provisions in Adhesion Contracts*, 35 Harv. J. on Legis. 225 (1998).

mandatory pre-dispute arbitration regarding claims brought by securities investors and with respect to breach of warranty claims.

Taking a second and very different approach, a bill proposed by Alabama Senator William ("Jeff") Sessions in 2000 would have legalized mandatory binding arbitration so long as it met certain minimal criteria. In essence this proposal would legislate the requirements of some of the now-voluntary due process protocols.[158] Upon initial consideration such legislation sounds attractive to many, in that it would purportedly bar unfair mandatory consumer arbitration while allowing those forms of arbitration that are fair. Closer analysis has, however, led many to oppose the approach. First, such a law would legitimize the unknowing involuntary loss of the right to take a legal claim to trial, and many assert this approach is inherently wrong and unfair, no matter the specific nature of the arbitration process. Second, although the bill would proscribe certain egregiously unfair forms of arbitration, it would inevitably fail to list every unfair practice that companies might envision. For example, the specific legislation proposed in 2000 by Senator Sessions would not have prevented companies from using arbitration clauses to insulate themselves from class actions. Third, to the extent that the burden is placed on the consumer to prove the unfairness of an arbitration clause, rather than on the company to defend the fairness of a clause, most consumers will find it financially infeasible to mount a challenge. Thus, even clauses that failed to comply with the standards of the legislation would be left standing, because consumers could not afford to bring the legal challenge to prove they violated the statute.

A third type of federal legislation would shift the opportunity to regulate or proscribe consumer arbitration to the individual states. As has been discussed, the FAA has been interpreted to block much potential state legislation. However, the FAA could be revised to allow states to regulate with respect to consumer arbitration, just as they regulate with respect to most consumer issues. The main advantage of this approach is political, in that it will appeal to those legislators who favor states' rights and oppose extensive federal interference with business matters. However, there are also several disadvantages to this type of federal law. Taking the perspective of those who oppose mandatory arbitration, such a law clearly would not accomplish as much as a federal law banning the practice in all fifty states. Some

[158] The bill referred to is the Consumer and Employee Arbitration Bill of Rights, 146 Cong. Rec. S10619–08 (daily ed. Oct. 17, 2000), 2000 WL 1532688. Although, based on its title, one might assume that such a bill would receive wide support from organizations geared to protect consumers and employees, in fact such groups were staunchly opposed to the legislation, as it would legitimize mandatory arbitration.

states would undoubtedly choose to allow mandatory arbitration, at least in a regulated form. Taking the mandatory arbitration battle to all fifty states would be expensive, and the pro-consumer forces would likely lose to the pro-business interests in many states. Also, allowing all fifty states to regulate consumer arbitration individually might lead to some confusion or inefficiency. Since many companies provide their goods and services on a national basis, it could be costly and inconvenient for them to redraft their contracts for each of the fifty states. Although companies already have to adjust to multi-state regulation with respect to many matters, it can be argued that imposing an additional such burden would be undesirable.

Section 5.7 A Policy Recommendation

Having considered the broad array of policy arguments pertaining to mandatory consumer arbitration, this author concludes that the practice should be prohibited in the United States, and that this prohibition is best accomplished through federal legislation. Although arbitration has numerous potentially valuable features and our litigation system is itself far from perfect, we invite bias and overreaching by permitting companies to impose arbitration on unconsenting unknowledgeable consumers. Given the opportunity to design their own dispute resolution process, it is only to be expected that companies would create a process geared to minimize their own liability exposure and public embarrassment. Further, by allowing companies to take away consumers' right to go to court we not only harm individual consumers but also harm the public at large. Our public open system of justice is important to deter harmful conduct and to foster faith in our system of justice. We must not allow private companies to redesign our system of justice.

Ironically, although the defenders of mandatory consumer arbitration tend also to defend the free market and resist government regulation in other contexts, they resist the idea that consumers and companies might voluntarily and knowledgeably consent to arbitration on a post-dispute basis. Surely to the extent that arbitration is truly cheaper, quicker, and better than litigation it will be selected by both sides knowingly on a post-dispute basis? The retort that companies and consumers will not want to arbitrate the same cases does not withstand further analysis. Although it is often urged that consumer lawyers would resist arbitration that might be desired by their clients, this makes no economic sense. If the arbitration is fair and cheap and quick, plaintiffs' lawyers operating on a contingent fee will flock to that process. By contrast, if the arbitration offers lower awards than would be available in litigation in many cases then it is not fair to allow companies to unknowingly deprive consumers of the opportunity to litigate. Although some argue that the supposed benefits (improved access, low cost) offered to many consumers outweigh the detriment caused to other consumers (lower awards), this kind of calculation should properly be made by a legislature, not private companies. Some other countries have chosen to use intensive regulatory or administrative mechanisms to protect consumers, rather than relying on private causes of action as we have done in this country. Although those choices may be defensible, they are not comparable to providing potential defendants with the unfettered right to conveniently redesign the system under which they operate.

Similarly, to the extent it is argued that companies will refuse to arbitrate cases in which they have a strong defense, instead hoping to force plaintiffs to drop weak cases or small claims for which they will not be able to find lawyers, such an argument should not protect mandatory arbitration imposed by the companies. If plaintiffs' cases are very weak, then plaintiffs should not be encouraged to bring such claims in any forum. We should not favor a "deal" in which companies are allowing weak claims to be brought in arbitration in return for forcing strong claims to be brought there as well. Further, if the problem is that plaintiffs cannot afford legal representation for claims that might be strong, perhaps the answer is additional support for class actions or legal services lawyers, rather than mandatory arbitration.

To the extent that mandatory arbitration is seen as desirable because it provides a forum for weaker or less lucrative claims, perhaps we should be considering a different type of mandatory arbitration than currently exists. Maybe *companies* should be required to arbitrate any claim that consumers would prefer to resolve through arbitration rather than litigation? Such a law would truly improve consumers' access to justice. Yet this is a form of mandatory arbitration that business interests do not seem eager to support.

Federal regulation makes more sense than any of the alternatives that have been discussed because mandatory consumer arbitration has become a national phenomenon in our globalized economy. State-by-state regulation may be the most feasible to the extent that business interests control the national legislature, but from a pure policy perspective it is clear that federal legislation is best. Once the American public awakens to the fact that their rights to sue over medical services, health, personal injury, and education have been eroded, they may create the political climate necessary to pass legislation limiting mandatory consumer arbitration. Such legislation should clearly and simply proscribe the use of mandatory pre-dispute arbitration with respect to consumer transactions. An example of such potential legislation is set out in Appendix C.

There are, of course, aspects of this draft statute as to which reasonable persons might differ. For example, some might choose to permit mandatory arbitration in the federally regulated securities field, or with respect to claims arising solely out of the contract creating the arbitration clause. However, I have chosen the simpler and broader approach, because I believe it is better, because it matches the approach taken by European Union regulatory authorities, and because legislators choosing to urge passage of this Act will of course be free to make their own modifications.

In rejecting mandatory consumer arbitration I am not asserting that our current litigation system is perfect, nor am I rejecting other forms of alternative dispute resolution. As defenders of mandatory consumer arbitration have asserted, our system of litigation is often too slow, too costly, and too inaccessible. People with valid claims cannot necessarily get relief. Thus, we should be considering an array of solutions including voluntary post-dispute binding arbitration, voluntary mediation, creation of stronger federal or state administrative agencies, and reform of our litigation system. I do not have fixed views on which of these solutions (or others) is best, but I am convinced that one approach to consumer disputes is clearly detrimental: mandatory binding arbitration.

CHAPTER SIX

International Commercial Arbitration: Implementing the New York Convention

Richard E. Speidel

Section 6.1 The Case for Revision

6.1(1) Introduction

In this chapter, you will be exposed to the views of a law professor working in Chicago and San Diego and looking at international commercial arbitration from an American perspective.[1] Although I have written extensively about American arbitration law and have taught international arbitration on a regular basis, I am not part of any arbitration "inner circle."[2] In that sense, I am free from the preferences that might evolve from association with a particular arbitration institution, serving regularly as an arbitrator, or being a partner in a major law firm representing clients who do commercial arbitration. I do have my preferences, however, and will state them up front.

First, I believe that arbitration is a vital ingredient in the continuing globalization of commerce. Whether conducted in the conventional manner or in cyberspace, arbitration will be the primary method of resolving disputes in an era where individuals and entities will, because of technological advances, be able to "conduct their affairs across a world without

[1] This does not mean that I favor the "Americanization" of international arbitration law, whatever negative connotations that term may invoke. *See* Symposium, *The Americanization of International Dispute Resolution*, 19 Oh. St. J. Disp Res. 1 (2003).

[2] *See* Yves Dezalay & Bryant G. Garth, Dealing in Virtue (1996) (describing existence and negative effects of "inner circle" in international arbitration). *See also* Tom Ginsburg, *The Culture of Arbitration*, 36 Vand. J. Transn'l L. 1335, 1340 (2003), commenting that in "arbitration, perhaps more than any other field of law, the line between scholar and practitioner is blurred so that many leading scholars are involved in arbitrations, and many arbitrators take the time to write academic articles and books."

reference to nationality, government authority, time of day or physical environment."[3]

Second, I believe that the United States and other signatories of the New York Convention should work to achieve de-localized arbitration within the Convention framework through the interpretation of the Convention by the courts and the enactment of harmonious legislation to implement and supplement the Convention. By de-localized arbitration I mean a "species of international arbitration not derived from or based on a municipal legal order."[4] Unlike the more extreme theory of A-National arbitration,[5] however, de-localized arbitration within the Convention depends upon support at the place of arbitration under harmonized international principles enforced by the courts. The goal, then, is to minimize the role of domestic arbitration law and policy in international arbitration.[6]

Third, conceding that American courts have developed a strong policy favoring domestic and international arbitration, the current legislation

[3] Richard Langhorne, THE COMING OF GLOBALIZATION, ITS EVOLUTION AND CONTEMPORARY CONSEQUENCES 2 (2001).

[4] De-localized arbitration is detached from the procedural rules and the substantive law of the place of arbitration. It is premised on a written agreement by the parties and general principles of substantive law and procedure acceptable to the parties. Unlike denationalized arbitration, however, de-localized international arbitration agreements and awards depend upon support at the place of arbitration from harmonized international arbitration law enforced by the courts. *See* Olakunle O. Olatawura, *Delocalized Arbitration Under the English Arbitration Act 1996: An Evolution or a Revolution*, 30 SYRACUSE J. INT'L L. & COM. 49, 51–5 (2003) (collecting authorities). *See also* Alan Redfern & Martin Hunter, LAW & PRACTICE OF INTERNATIONAL COMMERCIAL ARBITRATION 89–93 (3d ed. 1999) (hereafter cited as Redfern & Hunter).

[5] As one commentator put it:

> It is possible to envisage an ideal world in which country or place in which a particular arbitration is held make no difference to the legal principles applied or the procedure followed. In such a world, the arbitral tribunal would be guided by the agreement of the parties, or failing such agreement, by its own judgment: it would decide the substantive matters in issue before it on the basis of the applicable law or legal rules, or if the parties so wished, ex aequo et bono; and it would make an award which was enforceable on the same conditions in any state in which the losing party had assets. Moreover, its award would be the same, uninfluenced by national laws or attitudes of mind, in which ever state the arbitral tribunal happened to sit for the purpose of conducting arbitration.

Theodore C. Theofrastous (student author), *International Commercial Arbitration in Europe: Subsidiary and Supremacy in Light of the De-Localization Debate*, 31 CASE W. RES. J. INT'L L. 455, 456 (1999).

[6] Professor Hans Smit described A-National theory as an effort escape from the arbitration law and policy at the "seat" of the arbitration. He argues that to the extent the theory could exist outside of a legal context (dubious, he thought) it really wasn't needed because in an international arbitration the parties could contract for international arbitration law principles. Hans Smit, *A-National Arbitration*, 63 TUL. L. REV. 629 (1989).

implementing the Convention, namely the Chapter 2 of the Federal Arbitration Act (Convention Act) and Chapter 1 of the Federal Arbitration Act, is, because of age, fragmentation, and omission, sadly deficient. Accordingly, in the balance of this section I will identify those deficiencies in more detail and in the remainder of this chapter will suggest through text and "draft" legislation the directions an appropriate revision might take. The primary objective of this revision will be to further harmonize American internationalize arbitration law with emerging international norms[7] while protecting the core values of the arbitration process. These revisions are needed so the United States can continue to play a leading role in what Professor Tom Carbonneau has called the "Ballad of Transborder Arbitration": a "ballad" where the number of arbitration claims and the number of new arbitration institutions is steadily increasing.[8]

6.1(1)(A) Critical First Questions

Assume that an American seller and a German buyer have entered into a contract for the sale of goods. Because their places of business are in different countries, the transaction is an international sale. During the negotiations, however, the seller argued that the contract should contain an arbitration clause agreeing to arbitrate all disputes arising out of or relating to the sales contract. Although arbitration is common in international transactions, there are some choices to be made. First, should the parties agree to arbitrate future disputes at all or should the resolution of those disputes be left to the courts? Second, if the parties agree to arbitration, should the arbitration be ad hoc or should the arbitration be administered by an arbitration institution, such as the International Chamber of Commerce (ICC) under the ICC's international arbitration rules? Third, where should the arbitration be held? This is a critical question, because the place or "seat" of arbitration, without more, determines the applicable arbitration law.

[7] For a discussion of these norms, *see* Elena V. Helmer, *International Commercial Arbitration: Americanized, "Civilized," or Harmonized*, 19 Oh. St. J. Disp Res. 35, 49–66 (2003). *See also* Claudia Salomon, *The Conduct of an International Arbitration: Do the Rules Make a Difference*, 21 J. Int'l Arb. 103 (2004) (extracting norms from comparison of international arbitration rules).

[8] Thomas C. Carbonneau, *The Ballad of Transborder Arbitration*, 56 U. Miami L. Rev. 773 (2002) (hereafter cited as Carbonneau, *Ballad*). Another commentator has concluded that in light of the increase numbers of claims and arbitral institutions "arbitration has become widely recognized as the normal, rather than the alternative, way of settling international commercial disputes." Helmer, *supra* Note 7 at 38–40 (reviewing data).

(1) Why Arbitrate?

It is probable that the parties will agree to arbitrate. Why?

The attributes of and expectations for international arbitration are, at first glance, the same as any other arbitration. Arbitration depends on an agreement under which the parties submit defined disputes, either existing or future, to private arbitrators with the expectation of a fair hearing and a final decision on the merits. A presumed objective of the parties is to remove the dispute from the courts to a neutral forum with the hope that private adjudication will achieve a fair award made by persons with expertise in a confidential procedure where there is less formality and an opportunity to resolve the dispute quicker and at a lower cost than in court. In the United States, these are frequently stated objectives which are common to international, interstate, and intrastate arbitration.[9]

Unfortunately, there are very few empirical studies on international (or for that matter, domestic) arbitration practice to confirm what the expectations of the parties really are and whether they are in fact being achieved.[10]

In one significant study, however,[11] the advantages to international arbitration as perceived by participants in the process were surveyed with some interesting results. The four greatest perceived advantages were (1) the reliability of agreement and award enforcement under international treaties, (2) a neutral forum removed from the courts of country where the arbitration is to take place, (3) the procedural factors of arbitrator expertise, confidentiality, and limited discovery, and (4) the finality of awards. Less important were amicable proceedings, cost savings, quicker proceedings,

[9] *See* Chapter 1, The Core Values of Arbitration, *supra*. Section 1 of the English Arbitration Act of 1996 states the basic principles upon which the act shall be construed:
(a) the object of arbitration is to obtain the fair resolution of disputes by an impartial tribunal without unnecessary delay or expense;
(b) the parties should be free to agree how their disputes are resolved, subject only to such safeguards as are necessary in the public interest;
(c) the court should not intervene except as provided by this Part.

[10] According to Christopher R. Drahozal, however, the existing empirical studies in this area, even though sparse, are "just the beginning." He claims:

> The potential benefits are enormous: for parties, who will know more about what to expect from their dispute resolution choices; for practitioners, who can better represent their clients; for arbitrators, who can make more informed decisions on both procedural and substantive matters; for policy-makers, who can legislate on the basis of better information; and for academics, who not only can develop and test theories in a more systematic way, but who also can better train future generations of lawyers for the practice of international commercial arbitration.

Christopher R. Drahozal, *Of Rabbits and Rhinoceri: A Survey of Empirical Research on International Commercial Arbitration*, 20(1) J. INT'L ARB. 23, 33–4 (2003).

[11] *See* Christian Buhring-Uhle, ARBITRATION AND MEDIATION IN INTERNATIONAL BUSINESS 127–215 (Kluwer, 1996).

voluntary compliance, and predictability.[12] Studies like this provide some insight into why parties choose to arbitrate international disputes rather than leave them to the courts, what arbitration features are prized in the process, and the extent to which courts under arbitration law should step in (when asked) to support or regulate the process.[13]

(2) Institutional v. ad hoc Arbitration

It is not our intent to enter the debate on whether an international arbitration should be ad hoc or administered by an arbitral institution. Except in countries where ad hoc arbitration is not permitted, this is a choice the parties must make.[14]

One consequence of institutional arbitration is that the parties agree to incorporate the institution's international arbitration rules into the contract to arbitrate. Because there is competition for business among the various arbitral institutions, these comprehensive rules are regularly revised and do not vary dramatically in content from institution to institution.[15] It is

[12] In the subsequent chart, the so-called advantages of ICA, found by Burhing-Uhle, are listed in the order of importance (HR + S), with HR = Highly Relevant, S = Significant, and NA = No Significant Advantage.

	HR	S	NA
Award enforced	64%	27%	–
Neutral forum	72%	11%	–
Arbitrator expertise	32%	32%	–
Confidential procedures	32%	32%	–
Limited discovery	29%	35%	21%
Award finality	37%	23%	23%
More amicable	11%	24%	41%
Voluntary compliance	7%	33%	47%
Less time than courts	11%	24%	37%
Less costly than courts	8%	13%	51%
Predictable results	0	0	75%

See also Richard W. Naimark, *What Do Parties Really Want from International Commercial Arbitration,* 57 Disp. Res. J. 78 (2003) (parties want fairness and justice rather than quicker and lower cost).

[13] According to Professor Carbonneau, in "transborder commercial matters, choosing to arbitrate goes almost without saying, because international arbitration is instrumental to neutrality, the provision of the necessary expertise, effective dispute resolution, and the enforcement of awards." Thomas E. Carbonneau, *The Exercise of Contract Freedom in the Making of Arbitration Agreements,* 36 Vand J. Transn'l L. 1189, 1205 (2003) (hereafter cited as Carbonneau, *Exercise of Contract Freedom*).

[14] Factors in this choice, including cost, are discussed in Carbonneau, *Exercise of Contract Freedom, supra* Note 13 at 1207–9.

[15] *See* Salomon, *supra* Note 7.

assumed, of course, that the chosen institution will administer the arbitration in an impartial and efficient manner.

In an ad hoc arbitration the parties are expected to "do it themselves." They may, of course, adopt the UNCITRAL Arbitration Rules, which were drafted with ad hoc international arbitration in mind,[16] or draft a set of rules that are tailor-made to the situation. But the responsibility for setting up and administering the arbitration and selecting an arbitral tribunal is theirs.

In either case, however, the parties should agree to a comprehensive set of arbitration rules for the conduct of the international arbitration. These rules become part of the contract to arbitrate and will cover most of the issues that may arise in the middle ground between commencement of the arbitration and the final award. When properly applied during the arbitral proceedings, these rules contribute to de-localized arbitration by reducing the risk that the non-mandatory arbitration law of the forum will be directly involved. Without these rules, however, the parties may be left to the vagaries of local arbitration law with the risk that there will be few or no default rules to supplement the contract.

(3) The "Seat" of Arbitration

The parties may select the place or the "seat" of the arbitration by agreement. Two practical considerations in this choice are first, the neutrality of the place selected, and second, the convenience of the place chosen to the parties, the transaction, and the evidence that must be adduced.

A third consideration is that unless otherwise agreed, choice of the place of arbitration chooses the arbitration law of the country within which the arbitration is to be held. The consequences of this choice are somewhat fictional, because the transaction may have no links with the seat of the arbitration and the arbitration hearings may be held and the award made in other places.[17] Nevertheless, if the parties choose to arbitrate in a country adopting the UNCITRAL Model Law on International Commercial Arbitration (Model

[16] These rules can be found at the United Nations Website, http://www.un.org.at/Uncitral. *See* Jacomijn J. van Hof, Commentary of the UNCITRAL Arbitration Rules: The Application by the Iran-U.S. Claims Tribunal (1991). The London Court of International Arbitration will assist parties arbitrating under the UNCITRAL Rules, with fees depending upon the degree of assistance contracted for.

[17] *See* Gabrielle Kaufmann-Kohler, *Globalization of Arbitral Procedure*, 36 Vand. J. Transn'l L. 1313, 1315–20 (2003) (discussing tests for choice of arbitration law). Professor Kaufman-Kohler argues that despite the obvious fiction, choice of a particular "seat" of arbitration can produce de-localization because both the arbitration rules selected and the applicable lex arbitri are increasingly harmonized. *Id.* at 1320–2.

Law), that law will apply.[18] Similarly, if the "seat" of an arbitration is in London, the English Arbitration Act of 1996 (EAA) will apply.[19] In both of these choices the parties will benefit from modern statutes that are relatively in tune with developing international norms.

Suppose, however, that the seller in the United States proposes to the German buyer that the place of arbitration shall be in New York City. If the buyer agrees to this and there is no other choice of law clause, what sort of international arbitration law will govern?[20] What law governs international arbitrations conducted in the United States?

6.1(2) International Arbitration Law in the United States

6.1(2)(A) Some History

In the long history of international arbitration practice there has been recurring disagreement on the role of arbitration law. To what extent should private agreements to arbitrate be authorized or empowered by the law of any country? To what extent should any country impose its law upon private parties who engage in international arbitration? Because arbitration is a "creature of contract,"[21] why not simply permit private parties to contract for international arbitration with minimal intrusions by the law of any country?

Between the extremes of those theorists who espouse an A-National theory of arbitration and countries with a history of hostility toward arbitration or extensive control over arbitration through mandatory rules are countries like the United States, Great Britain, and other Western democracies that support and to a lesser extent regulate international arbitration.[22] The reality is that arbitration agreements may be resisted, arbitration procedures may break down, and the loser may refuse to comply with an arbitral award.

[18] Model Law Art. I(2) (Model Law applies "only if the place of arbitration" is in the territory of the enacting state).

[19] EAA §2(1). Under the EAA, the "seat of the arbitration" means the "juridical seat of the arbitration" designated by the agreement of the parties or the tribunal. EAA §3.

[20] If, however, the agreed place of arbitration was Berlin, the applicable arbitration law would be the New York Convention as supplemented by the German Arbitration Law of 1998. *See* G.A.L §1025(1). The G.A.L is based upon the Model Law.

[21] According to Judge Bruce Selya, the "abecedarian tenet" of arbitration law is that "a party cannot be forced to arbitrate if it has not agreed to do so." *InterGen N.V. v. Grina*, 344 F.3d 134, 137 (1st Cir. 2003) (international arbitration).

[22] For a brief but helpful history, *see* Carbonneau, *Ballad*, *supra* Note 8 at 777–92.

To protect the parties and the agreed processes, some legal intervention, usually through the courts, may be required. When cooperation and voluntary compliance break down, the key questions are at what point and for what purposes should courts intervene?

6.1(2)(B) The Federal Arbitration Act

Until the ratification of the New York Convention in 1970, the United States enforced international arbitration agreements and awards through Chapter 1 of the Federal Arbitration Act, enacted by Congress in 1925. The incomplete and fragmented coverage of the FAA has already been discussed.[23] Nevertheless, the FAA as implemented by the courts offers strong support in both international and interstate arbitration to the enforcement of agreements to arbitrate and the confirmation of arbitral awards.

Prior to ratification of the Convention, Chapter 1 of the FAA applied to international arbitration agreements if the place of arbitration was in the United States and the agreement evidenced a transaction in interstate or foreign commerce.[24] In sum, the FAA empowers federal courts with jurisdiction to order the arbitration of controversies under written agreements to arbitrate existing and future disputes "save on grounds as exist at law or in equity for the revocation of any contract."[25] In addition, courts are empowered to stay litigation pending in courts on "any issue referable to arbitration under an agreement in writing for such arbitration."[26] Sections 9–11 facilitate the enforcement of arbitral awards by stating that a court must, upon timely application, confirm an arbitral award unless the limited grounds to vacate or modify or correct the award are satisfied. But, as discussed in Section 5 of Chapter Two, many issues arising in the enforcement stages are not answered and only two sections in Chapter 1 of the FAA deal with issues arising in the middle ground between the commencement of the arbitration and the final award. For example, if the parties have initiated arbitration but failed to agree upon the place for arbitration, there are no default rules in the FAA to fill the gap in agreement.

Over time the courts have repeatedly said that the purpose of Congress in enacting the FAA "was to make arbitration agreements as enforceable as other contracts but not more so." Further, they have stressed that the

[23] *See* Section 2.5, *supra.*

[24] *See* FAA §§1, 2. The same test now applies to arbitration agreements not preempted by the Convention and the Convention Act.

[25] FAA §§2, 4.

[26] FAA §3.

FAA creates a "body of federal substantive law of arbitrability, applicable to any arbitration agreement within the coverage of this act" but "in evaluating whether the parties have entered into a valid arbitration agreement, the court must look to state law principles, including applicable contract defenses such as fraud, duress, and unconscionability."[27] The thrust of this policy is more local than international.

In applying Chapter 1 of the FAA, American courts have also stated on the one hand that arbitration is a "creature of contract" and on the other hand that there is a "strong" federal policy in favor of arbitration.[28] In most cases, these statements are consistent; they support the power of private parties to contract for arbitration and to obtain enforcement of the contract to arbitrate and the final award. Both derive from the presumed goals and objectives of arbitration, with the latter operating to resolve doubts in interpreting and applying the contract in favor of arbitration. Care must be taken, however, to prevent the policy tail from wagging the arbitration dog. Many commentators have criticized the Supreme Court for utilizing the so-called "strong federal policy favoring arbitration" to extend the scope and preemptive effect of the FAA beyond that originally intended by Congress.[29]

6.1(2)(C) The New York Convention

The Convention, completed in 1958 and ratified by the United States in 1970, is now in force in 134 countries.[30] The Convention established international standards for the enforcement of international arbitration agreements and the recognition of foreign arbitral awards. For example, a written agreement to arbitrate future disputes is valid unless certain defenses stated in Article II of the Convention are established and the parties can be referred to arbitration by a court.[31] Similarly, a foreign or non-domestic arbitration award in proper form is to be given recognition and enforcement by a court without further inquiry unless one party raised one or more of the limited

[27] *Cap Genini Erst & Young, U.S., L.L.C v. Nackel*, 346 F.3d 360, 364–5 (2d Cir. 2003). *See also Circuit City Stores, Inc. v. Adams*, 279 F.3d 889, 892–3 (9th Cir.), *cert. denied*, 535 U.S. 1112 (2002).

[28] *See Will-Drill Resources, Inc. v. Samson Resources Co.*, 352 F.3d 211, 214 (5th Cir. 2003) ("strong" federal policy does not apply to "determination of whether there is a valid agreement to arbitrate between the parties").

[29] *See* Ian R. Macneil, American Arbitration Law: Reformation, Nationalization, Internationalization 134–55 (1992). *See also* David S. Schwartz, *Correcting Federalism Mistakes in Statutory Interpretation: The Supreme Court and the Federal Arbitration Act*, 67 L. & Contemp. Prob. 5 (2004).

[30] *See* Section 2.5(1), *supra*.

[31] Convention Art. II.

grounds in Articles IV–VI to deny recognition and enforcement. But the Convention does not fully divorce the enforcement process from the law of the country where enforcement was sought. To the contrary, under Article II the law of the forum country can be invoked to determine whether the arbitration agreement was "null and void" or whether the dispute was "capable" of submission to arbitration. Similarly, a foreign arbitration award can be denied recognition and enforcement under Article V(2) if the dispute was not capable of arbitration or the award was against public policy under the law of the country where recognition and enforcement was sought.

Thus, the Convention reflects a compromise between the need for uniformity and certainty in the enforcement of international arbitration agreements and awards and the varying interests and differing laws of the countries in whose courts enforcement is sought. The important task of mediating that compromise is left to the courts of the country where enforcement is sought under whatever domestic arbitration law and procedure is applicable.

As previously noted,[32] the Convention provides no default rules for the middle ground. All is reasonably well if the parties have adopted a set of international arbitration rules as part of the contract. But suppose they have not. Is there any other applicable arbitration law?

6.1(2)(D) Chapter 2 of the FAA: The Convention Act

Chapter 2 of the FAA was enacted by Congress to implement the Convention. As Section 201 states, the "Convention . . . shall be enforced in United States courts in accordance with this chapter."[33] Unfortunately, the Convention Act provides no help for those mired in the middle ground. Rather, Section 202 clarifies, in the light of United States reservations,[34] when an agreement or award falls under the Convention and the next three sections deal with jurisdiction (the Convention Act creates federal jurisdiction), venue (broad), and removal from state to federal courts.

Section 206 provides:

> A court having jurisdiction under this chapter . . . may direct that arbitration be held in accordance with the agreement at any place therein provided for, whether that place is within or without the United States. Such court may also appoint arbitrators in accordance with the provisions of the agreement."

[32] *See* Section 2.5(3), *supra*.

[33] 9 U.S.C. §§201 et seq.

[34] The reservations of the United States were that the transaction between the parties must be "commercial" and that the place of arbitration or award must be in a country that has ratified the Convention.

Having covered the arbitrability issues raised in Article II of the Convention, Section 207 then provides:

> Within three years after an arbitral award falling under the Convention is made, any party to the arbitration may apply to any court having jurisdiction . . . for an order confirming the award as against any other party to the arbitration. The court shall confirm the award unless it finds one of the grounds for refusal or deferral of recognition or enforcement of the award specified in said Convention.

Our German buyer may now ask, "Is that all?" Suppose, for example, that we have not agreed on a place for arbitration or have failed to appoint an arbitrator. Does the arbitration founder because of that failure? No default rules exist to answer these questions in either the Convention or the Convention Act.

A possible solution exists, because Section 208 provides that "Chapter 1 [of the FAA] applies to actions and proceedings brought under this chapter to the extent that chapter is not in conflict with this chapter . . . or the Convention as ratified by the United States." But Chapter 1 is the FAA, virtually unamended since 1925, which says nothing about the "place of arbitration" problem and little else about issues in the middle ground.

6.1(2)(E) Interpretation of the Convention and the Convention Act

It has been stated that the "strong federal policy in favor or arbitration" applies "with special force in the field of international commerce."[35] In a leading case, the Supreme Court enforced an international agreement to arbitrate a securities fraud claim arising from subject matter that, arguably, was not (at that time) capable of arbitration under domestic arbitration law.[36] And in *Mitsubishi Motors Corp. v. Soler Chrysler-Plymouth, Inc.*,[37] the Court famously said:

> [W]e conclude that concerns of international comity, respect for the capacities of foreign and transnational tribunals, and sensitivity to the need of the international commercial systems for predictability in the resolution of disputes

[35] *Restoration Preservation Masonry v. Grove Europe Ltd.*, 325 F.3d 54, 60 (1st Cir. 2003) (citing authorities).

[36] In *Scherk v. Alberto-Culver Co.*, 417 U.S. 406 (1974), the Court enforced an agreement to arbitrate a securities fraud claim that, at that time, was not arbitrable under domestic law. The Court stressed the importance of arbitration in "truly international" agreements in achieving order and predictability and avoiding the submission of claims to hostile or uninformed forums. It lauded arbitration clauses as specialized forum selection clauses that both created the forum and stated the rules for dispute resolution. 417 U.S. at 515.

[37] 473 U.S. 614 (1985).

require that we enforce the parties' agreement, even assuming that a contrary result would be forthcoming in a domestic context.[38]

It is no surprise that this strong preference for international arbitration meshes well with the objectives of the Convention as implemented by the Convention Act. For example, in *InterGen N. V. v. Grina*,[39] the court noted that the Convention was an international treaty designed to "encourage the recognition and enforcement of commercial arbitration agreements in international contracts and to unify the standards by which agreements to arbitrate are observed and arbitral awards enforced."[40] For disputes within its ambit, a "district court's duty to enforce arbitration clauses that so qualify cannot seriously be questioned" and that "enforcing arbitration clauses under the New York Convention is an obligation, not a matter of discretion."[41] The same pro-arbitration policies also apply when the question involves giving recognition and enforcement to an arbitral award governed by the Convention.[42]

6.1(3) Other Legislative Models

In sum, international arbitration law in the United States is derived from a fifty-six-year-old treaty, implemented by thirty-five-year-old legislation (the Convention Act), and supplemented, when there is no conflict, by Chapter 1 of the FAA, which was eighty years old in 2005. Although arbitration is clearly favored, this legal regime, on the face of it, is fragmented, outdated, and incomplete and depends upon the courts to interpret and fill the gaps. What other models are available?

[38] 473 U.S. at 629. In essence, the Court ordered the parties to arbitrate in Japan an antitrust claim that was not, at that time, arbitrable under United States law. *See* Susan L. Karamanian, *The Road to the Tribunal and Beyond: International Commerical Arbitration and United States Courts*, 34 G.W. Int'l L. Rev. 17, 43–52 (2002) (discussing *Mitsubishi*). (hereafter cited as Karamanian, *Road to the Tribunal*).

[39] 344 F.3d 134 (1st Cir. 2003).

[40] 344 F.3d at 141.

[41] *Id.*

[42] *See Karaha Bodas Co. v. Perushaan Pertambangan Minyak*, 364 F.3d 274 (5th Cir.), *cert. denied*, 125 S. Ct. 59 (2004). *See also* Macneil, American Arbitration Law, *supra* Note 29 at 159–66, who traces the "internationalization" of American arbitration law. He concludes, quite accurately, that the Supreme Court has subordinated certain aspects of American public policy to the perceived needs of international arbitration and commerce. His sketchy proposed solution would be to apply common arbitration principles to both interstate and international arbitration to the extent possible without violating treaty obligations. *Id.*. at 178–80. This solution is consistent with the approach of the English Arbitration Act but appears to be inconsistent with the goal of de-localized international arbitration. *See* Section 6.1(2)(A), *supra*.

6.1(3)(A) The UNCITRAL Model Law on International Arbitration

The Model Law, approved by UNCITRAL in 1985, was designed to supplement the Convention and has been an important influence in the harmonization of international arbitration law.[43] Thus, the Model Law is consistent with the Convention on the critical questions of agreement and award enforcement in international arbitration. Put differently, a country can enact the Model Law to implement the Convention and to supply suppletive rules in and around the middle ground. If enacted in the United States,[44] it could provide comprehensive legislation for international arbitration that would replace the Convention Act and displace Chapter 1 of the FAA.[45]

The Model Law supplements the Convention in several respects. First, it clearly states when the law applies and when an arbitration is international. Second, it defines a limited role for courts in cases other than where enforcement of an arbitration agreement or award are involved. For example, a court can grant interim measures of relief and can be appealed to in the "middle ground" from decisions by the tribunal on its jurisdiction or challenges to arbitrators. Third, it provides a series of default rules for the "middle ground," default rules the effect of which can, in most cases, be varied by agreement and which have strongly influenced the development of institutional arbitration rules. Finally, the Model Law provides in Articles 34 and 35 the same limited grounds available to deny recognition and enforcement to an award under Article V of the Convention. Moreover, if the losing party seeks recourse against an award made in a Model Law country,

[43] As previously noted, at least forty-four countries and five states of the United States have enacted legislation based on the Model Law. *See* Section 2.5, *supra*.

[44] There is no current movement to adopt the Model Law as federal law. Just the opposite appears to be true. Professor Park, however, sees the Model Law as a possible "springboard" for reform but concludes that it "should not be imported wholesale." Any amendment to the FAA "must take account of homegrown arbitration concerns and precedents." William W. Park, *The Specificity of International Arbitration: The Case for FAA Reform*, 38 Vand. J. Transn'l L. 1241, 1243 (2003) (hereafter cited as Park, *Specificity*).

[45] For helpful background *see* Aron Broches, Commentary on the UNCITRAL Model on International Commercial Arbitration (1990). *See also* Peter Binder, International Commercial Arbitration in UNCITRAL Model Law Jurisdictions (2000); Henri C. Alvarez, Neil Kaplan, & David W. Rivkin, Model Law Decisions: Cases Applying the UNCITRAL Model Law on International Commercial Arbitration (1985–2001) (2003).

The Model Law has been criticized for its highly general and minimal standards; it finds the "lowest common denominator" and does not "advance the state of art." Further, it is myopic, concentrating on a few selected problems and is beginning to show its age. Alan S Reid, *The UNCITRAL Model Law on International Commercial Arbitration and the English Arbitration Act: Are the Two Systems Poles Apart*, 21 J. Int'l Arb. 227, 237 (2004).

Article 34 applies. Under Article 34, there is no difference in outcome depending on whether the winner seeks recognition and enforcement of an award made in another country or whether the loser seeks recourse against a non-domestic award made at home.[46]

6.1(3)(B) The English Arbitration Act of 1996

The English Arbitration Act of 1996 applies "where the seat of the arbitration is in England and Wales or Northern Ireland."[47] The English Act deals with both international and domestic arbitration without drawing sharp distinctions between the two. Thus, when the "seat" of the arbitration is in London and the award is to be made there, a commercial arbitration between two British corporations and a commercial arbitration between a British and an American corporation would be subject to the same legislative rules in all stages of the arbitration. If, however, recognition and enforcement of an award made in another country is sought in England the enforcement provisions of the Convention clearly apply.[48] The English Act was influenced by the Model Law and many principles, such as "separability" and "competence," correspond to or are derived from the Model Law.[49] The English Arbitration Act, however, did not adopt the Model Law because it was "incomplete in many respects" and not needed in a "country such as England, where the law of arbitration is up to date and where there is extensive current practice."[50] Because of this close link to domestic arbitration law, some commentators have concluded that the goal of de-localization for international arbitration law has not been achieved in England.[51]

6.1(4) The Prospects for Reform

Against this fragmented, ageing, and incomplete framework for international arbitration law in the United States, it is appropriate to consider whether it is time for reform and, if so, what changes are appropriate in a

[46] This problem of concurrent jurisdiction is discussed and resolved in Section 6.5(3), *infra*.
[47] EAA §2(1).
[48] *See* Sections 100–4 dealing with New York Convention Awards.
[49] *See* EAA §§7 (separability), 30(1) (competence). Compare Model Law Art. 16.
[50] *See* Bruce Harris, Rowan Planterose, & Jonothan Tecks, The Arbitration Act of 1966: A Commentary 1 (2d ed.1999).
[51] The English Act has been criticized for failing to achieve "true globalization" because it exists in a context of national law. *See* Reid, *supra* Note 45 at 237.

country where, like England, there is an extensive and current arbitration practice but, unlike England and many other countries, the legal framework is not up to date. If change is required, what should be the source of the revision, the Model Law, the English Arbitration Act, the Revised Uniform Arbitration Act, or a blend from all three sources?

For the following reasons, I think that a prima facie case exists for a critical assessment of international arbitration law in the United States. What revisions, if any, will depend upon the results of that assessment in the sections that follow.[52]

6.1(4)(A) Defining International Commercial Arbitration

A preliminary problem is one of definition. How is it determined whether a dispute resolution procedure is arbitration and, if arbitration, by what standard do we know whether it is "international" and "commercial?"

For now let us assume (quite properly) that an arbitration is international and commercial if there is a written agreement to arbitrate contained in a contract for sale or construction entered into by corporations doing business in different countries.[53] But what is arbitration and why do we need to know?

Unfortunately, there is no accepted definition of arbitration in American law. Although the Convention, the Convention Act, and Chapter 1 of the FAA apply to arbitration, none define it. The elements can be teased from relevant arbitration law but the exact scope is fuzzy.

Why do we need to know? In general, we need to know because existing and proposed treaties and legislation purport to support and to regulate "arbitration." If a dispute procedure is not arbitration then this legal framework does not apply.[54] For example, suppose an agreement provides that the parties are not required to arbitrate if a dispute arises but if they do the award is final. Or suppose that the agreement requires the parties to arbitrate

[52] Professor William W. Park has undertaken a similar but less ambitious revision project. *See* Park, *Specificity, supra* Note 44. Although I agree with the thrust of his limited recommendations, I am not nearly so timid as he in proposing broader reforms.

[53] We discuss these issues in more detail at Section 6.2(1), *infra.*

[54] For example, the ICANN Domain Name Dispute Resolution Process is not arbitration because parties who consent to it are not bound to use it and decisions by the "arbitrators" are not final. *See, e.g., Parisi v. Netlearning, Inc.*, 139 F. Supp. 2d 745 (E.D. Va. 2001). Similarly, an appraisal procedure where the third party decision does settle the dispute is not arbitration. *See Salt Lake Tribune v. Management Planning*, 390 F.3d 684, 690 (10th Cir. 2004). *But see Dow Corning Corp. v. Safety National Cas. Corp.*, 335 F.3d 742, 745–8 (8th Cir. 2003), *cert. denied*, 540 U.S. 1219 (2004), where the court held that FAA §10 applied to a mandatory but not binding arbitration.

a dispute but provides that the award is not final. Are these agreements to arbitrate which are subject to applicable arbitration law?[55]

This question raises three somewhat different issues about the scope of private autonomy. Assume we can agree on a working definition of arbitration. The first issue is the extent to which the parties can choose applicable arbitration law that differs from the place where the arbitration is to be held. For example, suppose the "seat" of the arbitration was in London but the parties choose the arbitration law of Germany. The second issue is the extent to which the parties can avoid or "opt out" of otherwise applicable arbitration law by designing a dispute resolution mechanism that resembles but is not arbitration. For example, suppose the parties agree that the arbitral award is not final. The third issue is the extent to which the parties can vary the effect of applicable arbitration law by, say, expanding the scope of judicial review of arbitration awards. For now it suffices to say that the answers to these issues depend in part upon the existence of a satisfactory definition of arbitration.[56]

6.1(4)(B) Scope of Mandatory Arbitration Law

Even with a working definition of arbitration, it is assumed that private parties can by agreement create a dispute resolution procedure that has some but not all of the features of arbitration. If core features are omitted, the parties have in fact contracted out of relevant arbitration law. Thus, if the parties agree to submit certain disputes to arbitrators but also state that neither party is bound to do so or any award is not final, the procedure is (probably) not arbitration.[57]

If the dispute procedure is arbitration, however, and the applicable legal regime is determined, one must decide which parts of that framework can be varied by agreement and which parts cannot. This is a controversial question in the United States under Chapter 1 of the FAA.

Current federal law gives no explicit guidance on the extent to which the effect of the Convention or Chapter 1 of the FAA can be varied by agreement of the parties or waived. Arbitration is a creature of contract and the parties have considerable power to shape the terms of that contract. But are there mandatory arbitration rules that cannot be waived or varied? The issue is

[55] These issues and others are explored in Amy J. Schmitz, *Ending a Mud Bowl: Defining Arbitration's Finality through Functional Analysis*, 37 Ga. L. Rev. 123 (2002).

[56] A definition is proposed in Section 6.2(1)A, *infra*.

[57] On the other hand, it is assumed that parties who are subject to one body of arbitration law can contract for another body of arbitration law.

sharply raised by the disagreement among the federal courts over whether private parties have power by contract to expand the grounds for vacating an award stated in Section 10 of the FAA.[58] This issue should be clearly resolved. For example, let us assume that such agreements are enforceable under the FAA[59] and that such agreements are not enforceable under the Convention and the Convention Act. As we shall see, if a non-domestic arbitration award is made in the United States the losing party can move to vacate the award under Section 10 of the FAA. If there is an enforceable agreement to permit vacatur for errors of fact or law, the tension with Article V of the Convention, where such grounds are not permitted, is palpable and casts doubt over the goal of de-localization.[60]

These developments raise two questions: (1) what should the mandatory arbitration rules be, and (2) how should those mandatory rules be expressed in the treaty or legislation? Both the English Arbitration Act of 1996 and the Revised Uniform Arbitration Act assume that the parties have power to waive or vary the effect of their provisions by agreement unless a contrary rule is stated and provide elaborate lists of sections the effect of which cannot be varied by agreement.[61] The Model Law, on the other hand, seems to assume that its provisions are not waivable or the effect variable by agreement unless the particular section so provides with permissive language or a phrase like "unless otherwise agreed." Under both the English Act and the Model Law, however, the parties have no power to vary the effect of the provisions dealing with grounds to vacate or deny recognition and enforcement to an arbitral award.

[58] *See Kyocera Corp. v. Prudential-Bache*, 341 F.3d 987, 1000 (9th Cir.), *cert. dismissed*, 540 U.S. 1098 (2003), where the court held en banc that "private parties have no power to determine the rules by which federal courts proceed, especially when Congress has explicitly prescribed those rules." The parties, however, have "complete freedom to contractually modify the arbitration process by designing whatever procedure and systems they think will best meet their needs–including review by one or more appellate arbitration panels." The court noted that "once a case reaches the federal courts . . . the private arbitration process is complete, and because Congress has specified standards for confirming an arbitration award, federal courts must act pursuant to those standards." Other circuits disagree. *See* Victoria L.C. Holstein, *Co-opting the Federal Judiciary: Contractual Expansion of Judicial Review of Arbitral Awards*, 1 J. Amer. Arb. 127 (2002) (discussing cases). Note that courts may enforce contracts to arbitrate subject to the FAA where the parties clearly intend to adopt or borrow state standards for vacating arbitral awards. *See Roadway Package System, Inc. v. Kayser*, 257 F.3d 287 (3d Cir.), *cert. denied*, 534 U.S. 1020 (2001).

[59] This is Professor Ware's conclusion. *See* Section 4.4(4), *supra*.

[60] This issue with a proposed solution is discussed in Section 6.5(3), *infra*.

[61] The mandatory provisions of the English Arbitration Act are stated in Schedule 1. The mandatory provisions for the R.U.A.A are stated in Section 4.

Are limitations on private autonomy of this sort appropriate for international arbitration subject to the Convention? Drawing a line between private autonomy in and government control of arbitration law is a "first order" problem for any proposed revision.[62]

6.1(4)(C) Modernization

The law of international arbitration in the United States is old, incomplete, and fragmented. On those grounds alone some modernization is required. Although it is difficult to be sure, the quality of the arbitration law at the "seat" of the arbitration is arguably a factor in deciding whether to choose the United States as the place for the arbitration.[63]

(1) Age

The New York Convention was approved in 1958, ratified by the Senate in 1970, and became effective in the United States in 1972. Chapter 2 of the Federal Arbitration Act (the Convention Act), implementing the Convention, became law in 1972 and Chapter 1 of the Federal Arbitration Act, which supplements Chapter 2 when there is no conflict, became law in 1925. There have been no significant revisions or amendments to either the Convention or the FAA in all of that time.[64] Not surprisingly, a large body of frequently conflicting case law has built up within and among the federal courts in the eleven circuits in the United States. At the same time, a consensus on basic norms has gradually emerged in international arbitration, derived from the Model Law and the evolving international arbitration rules. On this ground alone, an effort to better harmonize United States law with the emerging international consensus should be made.

Another problem of particular concern is the growing use of electronic commerce to create agreements to arbitrate, exchange documents and information, and, in some cases, actually conduct the arbitration through teleconferencing. Current federal arbitration law says nothing about international

[62] *See* Section 6.2(2), *infra*.

[63] *See* Christopher R. Drahozal, *Regulatory Competition and the Location of International Arbitration Proceedings*, 24 INT'L REV. L. & ECON. 371 (2004) (concluding that there was a statistically significant increase in ICC arbitrations in countries that had enacted modern arbitration law but that the economic benefit from increased arbitration is smaller than predicted).

[64] Two sections have been added to Chapter 1 of the FAA, Section 15 making the Act of State doctrine inapplicable to the enforcement of agreements and awards and Section 16 stating when appeals may or may not be taken from orders of the federal district court.

arbitration in cyberspace.[65] Although the United States has not ratified the UNCITRAL Model Laws on Electronic Commerce (1996) and Electronic Signatures (2001), Congress has enacted a law validating electronic documents and signatures[66] and most states have enacted the Uniform Electronic Transactions Act. Under these laws it is unlikely that any federal arbitration agreement or award will be invalidated because the document or signature is in electronic form. Nevertheless, it is worth considering whether a more direct approach to cyberspace arbitration should be taken.[67]

Nevertheless our German buyer, in evaluating the situation, might still be appalled. Not only does our creaking legal framework depend upon a "common law" of arbitration, but it is out of sync with emerging international norms found in the Model Law and has not directly confronted the potential use of electronic commerce in the international arbitral process.

(2) Incomplete

As noted, the primary source of international arbitration law in the United States is the New York Convention as implemented by Chapter 2 of the FAA. Chapter 1 of the FAA, dealing with interstate arbitration, may apply to supplement the Convention where there is no conflict but the extent (and sometimes the wisdom) of this supplementation is not always clear. Moreover, this legal framework is limited to the enforcement of arbitration agreements and awards and depends heavily upon judicial interpretation to clarify meaning and fill gaps the middle ground.[68] On the procedural front, it is unclear whether the FAA permits class action arbitrations[69] or the consolidation of arbitration claims without the consent of the parties.[70] These omissions were identified and briefly discussed in Chapter 2.

[65] For an excellent discussion of cyberspace arbitration, *see* Katherine Lynch, THE FORCES OF ECONOMIC GLOBALIZATION: CHALLENGES TO THE REGIME OF INTERNATIONAL COMMERCIAL ARBITRATION 345–401 (Kluwer 2003). *See also* Mohamed Wahab, *The Global Information Society and Online Dispute Resolution: A New Dawn for Dispute Resolution*, 21 J. INT'L ARB. 143 (2004): Neicolas de Witt, *Online International Arbitration: Nine Issues Crucial to its Success*, 12 AM. REV. INT'L ARB. 441 (2001).

[66] Electronic Signatures in Global and National Commerce Act, 15 USCA §7001(a).

[67] Section 7031 requires the Secretary of Commerce to promote the acceptance and use "on an international basis" of the principles stated in Section 7001(a) of the E-Sign legislation.

[68] This dependence is illustrated in Karamania, *Road to the Tribunal*, *supra* Note 38. Given this incomplete structure, the incentive is high for the parties to adopt some set of modern arbitration rules.

[69] In *Green Tree Financial Corp. v. Bazzle*, 539 U.S. 444 (2003), the Court did not decide whether class action arbitration was permitted by the FAA and remanded the case to determine whether the parties, under state contract law, had agreed to permit class actions.

[70] Section 10 of the Revised Uniform Arbitration Act permits a court to consolidate separate arbitration proceedings under stated conditions.

Our German buyer, aware of these gaps and omissions, would surely insist upon the adoption in the contract of modern international arbitration rules for arbitrations held in the United States.[71] To further reduce the uncertainty, the parties might agree to arbitrate in a state of the United States that has enacted the UNCITRAL Model Law on International Commercial Arbitration as state law. These statutes, which are drafted to be consistent with the Convention, do not apply unless the place of arbitration is in the enacting state.[72] Thus, the parties would have to agree to arbitrate in Hartford, or Chicago, or Los Angeles to insure that these state versions of the Model Law apply.

Again, the basic problem lies in the middle ground. Under current law there is little statutory guidance when a party petitions the court to intervene in the arbitration before the award is made.[73] For example, most courts conclude that they have no power to intervene to remove an arbitrator: the petitioner's remedy for claimed bias or partiality is to attack the award.[74] On the other hand, although federal courts have intervened to provide interim relief in support of arbitration[75] and to aid the arbitral process by compelling the attendance of witnesses and documents, the exact grounds for and scope of the intervention are not always clear.[76]

These gaps and ambiguities arguably do not create incentives for foreign nationals to arbitrate in the United States and, at the same time, induce those parties to bargain for the application of international arbitration law that is more in tune with emerging norms.

[71] Issues in the middle ground covered by modern arbitration rules include appointment of arbitrators, disclosure by and challenges to arbitrators, organizing and conducting the hearing, and making the award. *See* American Arbitration Association International Rules of 2003.

[72] These states include California, Connecticut, Illinois, Oregon, and Texas. Litigation involving these statutes is sparse. *See H.S.M.V. Corp. v. ADI Ltd.*, 72 F. Supp.2d 1122 (C. D. Cal. 1999) (applying sections of California International Dispute Resolution Act dealing with duty of arbitrator to disclose).

[73] FAA §5 gives the court power to appoint an arbitrator when all else fails and FAA §7 permits the court to compel the attendance of witnesses (along with relevant documents).

[74] The leading case is *Aviall Inc. v. Ryder System, Inc.*, 110 F.3d 892 (2d Cir. 1997) (FAA does not provide for the pre-award removal of an arbitrator).

[75] For an example of the issues and disagreements, *see Deiulemar v. Allegra*, 198 F.3d 473 (4th Cir. 1999), *cert. denied*, 529 U.S. 1109 (2000) (order preserving evidence pending arbitration hearing); *China Nat. Metal Prod. Import/Export v. Apez Digital, Inc.*, 141 F. Supp.2d 1013, 1022–8 (C. D. Cal. 2001), order set aside, 155 F. Supp.2d 1174 (C. D. Cal. 2001 (court refuses to issue attachment in aid or arbitration after tribunal appointed).

[76] Under FAA §7, most courts will order non-parties to produce documents prior to the hearing, *see In Re Security Life Ins. Co. of America*, 228 F.3d 865, 870–1 (8th Cir. 2000), but it is an "open question" whether arbitrators and courts have power to order and compel pre-hearing depositions from non-party witnesses. *See Nat'l Broadcasting Co., Inc. v. Bear Stearns & Co.*, Inc., 165 F.3d 184, 187–8 (2d Cir. 1999).

(3) Fragmented

(a) Tension between international and interstate arbitration law. Arbitration may be viewed as a unitary method of dispute resolution in that the elements and objectives of arbitration are relatively constant even though the parties and the nature of the transactions involved may vary. This is especially true in international commercial arbitration.[77]

Despite this, the coverage of international arbitration law in the United States is somewhat fragmented. It is possible for an international arbitration to be governed by both the Convention and the Convention Act and interstate arbitration law found in Chapter 1 of the FAA.

Consider the problem of concurrent jurisdiction in the enforcement of an award in our potential arbitration between the seller from the United States and the buyer from Germany. Suppose, first, that the award was made in Berlin for the buyer and the buyer sought recognition and enforcement against the seller in New York. In this case, Section 207 of the Convention Act directs the court to "confirm the award unless it finds one of the grounds for refusal or deferral of recognition or enforcement of the award" specified in the said Convention. These are, I would argue, the exclusive grounds for refusal or deferral and any attempt to interject the grounds stated in Section 10 of Chapter 1 of the FAA is in conflict with the Convention and the Convention Act. On the other hand, if the award (a non-domestic award) was made in New York City, the seller could move to vacate under Section 10 of the FAA even though the grounds asserted differ from those in the Convention. It is, arguably, permissible to make this motion because Article V(1)(e) of the Convention permits a court to deny recognition and enforcement is the award "has been set aside . . . by a competent authority in the country in which, or under the law of which, that award was made." But why should the standards for the enforceability of an international award vary depending upon where the award was made? The answer, I believe, is that they should not and that this disparate treatment requires a change in American law.[78]

(b) Other sources of international arbitration law: The Panama Convention. In addition to arbitrations governed by the Convention as

[77] It is also true of arbitration law within the United States. For example, despite a common conception of arbitration, there is a different legal framework for commercial arbitration and labor arbitration and there is a different legal framework for interstate arbitration and intrastate arbitration. Recently, doubts have been expressed on whether the unitary model of arbitration developed for commercial transactions works as well in contexts where the agreement is between commercial entities and individuals, such as consumers, employees, and patients. *See* Chapter 5, *supra*.

[78] *See* discussion at Section 6.5(3), *infra*. Professor Park and I agree that this problem needs resolution.

implemented by the Convention Act, there are several other sources of international arbitration law. Some involve arbitration between private parties and others involve disputes between private parties and sovereign states.[79] I will briefly discuss one source governing disputes between private parties, the Panama Convention.[80]

The Panama Convention. The United States and eighteen countries in Central and South America have ratified the Inter-American Convention on International Commercial Arbitration, to so-called Panama or IAC Convention.[81] The IAC Convention is implemented by Chapter 3 of the Federal Arbitration Act,[82] which draws heavily on the Convention Act.[83]

The Panama Convention was drafted to be compatible with the New York Convention.[84] Thus, an agreement to arbitrate future disputes is valid,[85] the arbitration agreement must be in writing, the burden of proof is placed

[79] There are two notable treaties governing arbitral disputes between private parties and sovereign states. The first is the International Convention on the Settlement of Investment Disputes between States and Nationals of Other States (ICSID). *See* Moshe Hirsch, The Arbitration Mechanism of the International Centre for the Settlement of Investment Disputes (1993). The second is the arbitration mechanism established under Chapter 11 of the North American Free Trade Agreement (NAFTA). *See* Guillermo A. Alvarez & William W. Park, *The New Face of Investment Arbitration: NAFTA Chapter 11,* 28 Yale J. Int'l L. 365 (2003). I will not discuss these interesting and complex procedures in this chapter.

[80] A fourth source is ICANN's procedures for the resolution of disputes over domain names registered on the Internet. The rules and procedures are complex and controversial. *See* A. Michael Froomkin, *ICANN's "Uniform Dispute Resolution Policy" – Causes and (Partial) Cures*, 67 Brook. L. Rev. 605 (2002). Because participants who agree to the procedures are not obligated to use the procedure and awards made are not final, the process is not arbitration. *See* Richard E. Speidel, *ICANN Domain Dispute Resolution, the Revised Uniform Arbitration Act, and the Limitations of Modern Arbitration Law,* 6 J. Small & Emerg. Bus. L. 129 (2002) (describing procedure and concluding that it is not arbitration).

[81] The Panama Convention was completed in 1975. It was signed by the United States in 1978, ratified by the Senate in 1986, and became effective in 1990. The Panama Convention can be found at the website of the Organization of American States, http://www.oas.org.

[82] 9 U.S.C. §§301–7.

[83] Section 302 states that Sections 202, 203, 204, 205, and 207 of FAA Chapter 2 "shall apply to this chapter . . . as if specifically set forth herein."

[84] *See* John P. Bowman, *The Panama Convention and its Implementation under the Federal Arbitration* Act, 11 Am. Rev. Int'l Arb. 1, 11 (2000) (hereafter cited as Bowman, *The Panama Convention*). In fact, all of the nineteen signatories of the Panama Convention except Nicaragua and Uruguay have ratified the New York Convention.

[85] A court with jurisdiction "may direct that arbitration be held in accordance with the agreement at any place therein provided for, whether that place is within or without the United States." 9 U.S.C. §303(a). Under Section 303(a), the court may also appoint arbitrators "in accordance with the provisions of the agreement." If the agreement does not provide for the "place of arbitration or the appointment of arbitrators," the court "shall direct that the arbitration shall be had and the arbitrators be appointed" in accordance with the arbitration rules incorporated through Article 3 of the IAC. 9 U.S.C. §303(b).

upon the party opposing the confirmation of an award, and nearly identical grounds are provided for denying recognition and enforcement of an award.[86] Differences include provisions on the appointment of arbitrators[87] and the rules of procedure under which the arbitration is to be conducted[88] and a pronouncement that an "arbitral decision or award that is not appealable under the applicable law or procedural rules shall have the force of a final judicial judgment" enforceable "in accordance with the procedural laws of the country where it is to be executed and the provisions of international treaties."[89]

The relationship between the IAC Convention and the New York Convention is spelled out in Section 305 of the FAA. If the requirements for the application of both conventions are met,[90] the IAC Convention applies if a "majority of the parties to the arbitration agreement are citizens of a State or States that have ratified or acceded to the Inter-American Convention and are members States of the Organization of American States." Otherwise, the New York Convention applies.

6.1(4)(D) A Proposed Model for Reform

If you agree that a critical assessment of American international arbitration law is justified, the questions of what revisions are needed and how should those revisions be expressed remains. In the remainder of Chapter 6, I will attempt to answer both questions. Anticipating that many revisions will be required, the ultimate objective of this section is to propose and justify a self-contained, exclusive federal international arbitration statute that will (1) implement and supplement the United Nations Convention on the Recognition and Enforcement of Foreign Arbitral Awards of 1958 (the Convention), (2) replace current Chapter 2 of the FAA (the Convention Act), and (3) displace any state arbitration law that purports to deal with international arbitration. Moreover, it will not depend upon Chapter 1 of the FAA,

[86] Art. 1, 5. *See* Bowman, *The Panama Convention, supra* Note 84 at 22–4.

[87] Art. 2.

[88] Article 3 states that unless otherwise agreed, "the arbitration shall be conducted in accordance with the rules of procedure of the Inter-American Commercial Arbitration Commission." Effective January 1, 1978, the IACAC adopted the UNCITRAL Arbitration Rules. *See* Bowman, *The Panama Convention, supra* Note 84 at 29.

[89] Art. 4.

[90] It is not clear when the requirements for application of the IAC Convention are met. *See* Bowman, *The Panama Convention, supra* Note 84 at 35–40. Presumably, the IAC Convention applies to a commercial arbitration between parties who are citizens of countries, which have ratified the Convention.

dealing with interstate arbitration law, for supplementation in cases where there is no conflict. The new Act, however, does not, as does the English Arbitration Act of 1996, cover domestic arbitration law in the United States, whether that law deals with intrastate or interstate arbitration.

The new legislation draws on the UNCITRAL Model Law on International Commercial Arbitration of 1985 (Model Law), the English Arbitration Act of 1996, and the Revised Uniform Arbitration Act. It will restate and clarify the relationship between the arbitration process (parties to the arbitration agreement and the tribunal), arbitration law, and the role of courts. It will identify the issues arising from the arbitration process[91] where a petition for judicial intervention should be granted and provide standards (and procedures) for that intervention.

In addition, the new legislation will provide basic "default" rules for the arbitration process in the middle ground between commencement of the arbitration process and the final award. Current American arbitration law ignores this "middle ground" and focuses on enforcing arbitration agreements and awards within the framework of the Convention. Fortunately, international arbitration practice in the "middle ground" is frequently covered by modern arbitration rules, whether those of an arbitral institution or in ad hoc arbitration under the UNCITRAL Arbitration Rules. These rules constitute arbitration law because they are part of the contract to arbitrate. Nevertheless, the new legislation will state basic rules for the middle ground, indicate which rules can be varied by agreement and which cannot, and clarify when a court is justified to intervene before the award is made and for what purpose. For example, one important question involves the competence of a tribunal to decide its own jurisdiction and, if so, when may a court review that decision and by what standards? Other categories include the appointment of arbitrators, challenges to and removal of arbitrators, interim judicial relief, and assistance in the evidence process.

In the proposed Act (see Appendix B), the sources of the law and references to sections of the text where the section is discussed are stated. The general objectives of this revision of Chapter 2 of the FAA are to:

1. Harmonize federal law on international commercial arbitration with developments in the rest of the world, including default rules reflecting

[91] Those points include disputes over whether an alleged arbitration agreement should be enforced, disputes arising in the "middle ground" between the commencement of the arbitration and the award, and disputes over the recognition and enforcement of the award.

the consensus emerging from the Model Law and competitive International Commercial Arbitration rules.

2. Amplify and clarify the content of federal international commercial arbitration law and resolve the tension with Chapter 1 of the FAA and state international commercial arbitration laws.
3. Make corrections to and revisions in the content of federal international commercial arbitration law with the goal of protecting private autonomy, fostering other important arbitration values, and clarifying the relationship between the parties and the tribunal and the tribunal and the courts.[92]

[92] Some of the specific issues to be considered and the relevant sections of this Act contained in Appendix B are:

1. Define arbitration. §2(1)
2. Electronic commerce. §§2(6), (7), 4.
3. Clarify when the Convention applies in general and what arbitrations are excluded in particular. §1(b), (c).
4. Clarify the extent to which the parties can vary the effect of or opt out of applicable ICA law. §3.
5. State the extent to which a court can intervene under the Act. §6.
6. State the scope of immunity for the arbitral tribunal and the arbitral institution. §8.
7. State when and by whom separate arbitrations between the same parties can be consolidated. §21.
8. Clarify the scope of the writing requirement under Art. II and the relationship to Art. IV of the Convention. §9.
9. Provide legislative default rules on such things as the place of arbitration and selection of the Tribunal. §§12–16.
10. Clarify when an alleged agreement to arbitrate is enforceable and how. §10(a).
11. Authorize when a court may stay litigation pending arbitration and when decisions by a court on arbitrability issues are appealable. §10(b), (d).
12. Clarify the relationship between separability and competence and state when the tribunal has power to decide competence and the standard of judicial review. §17.
13. State the test for determining which arbitration rules are mandatory, the effect of which cannot be varied by agreement §3.
14. State the duty of confidentiality and its scope. §26.
15. State clearly when and for what purpose a court, when petitioned, may intervene on issues other than enforcement of the arbitration agreement or award. §§6, 10(e), passim.
16. State what mandatory legislative rules should govern the conduct of the arbitration and making the award. *See* §§19–28.
17. Clarify when an award is final and under what circumstances a court can thereafter direct the tribunal to correct the award or to make changes that avoid possible defenses under Article V. §25, 29, 31(c).
18. Clarify the scope and proper application of Articles V(1)(e) and VII(1) of the Convention. §32(6).
19. Resolve the concurrent jurisdiction problem when a non-domestic award is made in the US. §31.
20. State general policies to guide courts in granting recognition and enforcement of awards under Articles III–VII of the Convention. §32.

SECTION 6.2 THE SCOPE OF INTERNATIONAL COMMERCIAL ARBITRATION

Part One of my proposed Revised Chapter 2 of the Federal Arbitration Act (the Convention Act) contains eight general provisions, most of which will be discussed in this section. It should be clear that the proposed revision (hereinafter called "this Act") is designed to replace the Chapter 2 of the Federal Arbitration Act (the Convention Act), displace Chapter 1 of the Federal Arbitration Act, and preempt any state law dealing with international arbitrations within the scope of this Act.[93] Again, the proposed revision is contained in Appendix B and should be read along with the text that follows in Chapter 6.

6.2(1) SCOPE: WHAT IS INTERNATIONAL COMMERCIAL ARBITRATION?

This Act deals with international commercial arbitration (ICA) and applies, unless otherwise agreed, if the "place of arbitration is in a state or territory of the United States."[94] Nevertheless, if the place of an ICA is in another country that has ratified the Convention, this Act will apply to implement the enforcement provisions of the Convention. Thus, if the place of arbitration was England, an action in a court of the United States to refer the parties to arbitration or to obtain recognition and enforcement of an award made in London would be enforced under the Convention and this Act in the United States.[95]

Regardless of where the place of arbitration is, the scope of this Act should be clear. What is ICA? Are there any international arbitrations that should be excluded from this Act and left to domestic arbitration law? The answer turns on a policy judgment: to what extent should the goal of de-localized international arbitration be implemented?

6.2(1)(A) When is an Arbitration International?

Suppose that Party A, a Filipino citizen, has entered a contract of employment with Party B, owner of a vessel chartered under Liberian law. The employment contract contains a clause requiring arbitration of all disputes

[93] Section 1(b)(2) of this Act. Please review Section 2.5, *supra*.

[94] Section 1(b)(1). This Act follows Article I(2) of the Model Law and Section 2(1) of the English Arbitration Act of 1996, which applies when the "seat" of the arbitration is in "England and Wales and Northern Ireland."

[95] *See* Sections 10 and 30 of this Act.

"arising out of or relating to" the contract in the Philippines at a named arbitration institution. Party A is injured on the job in the United States and sues Party B for damages in a federal district court. Party B moves to stay the law suit pending arbitration and seeks an order under Article II of the Convention referring the dispute to arbitration in the Philippines. Is this an international arbitration to which the Convention applies?

There is some confusion under current law. Although Article II of the Convention deals with the enforcement of arbitration agreements, Article I, a scope provision, talks only of arbitral awards. Under Article I(1), the Convention applies to "arbitral awards" made in a state other than where enforcement is sought or awards that are not "domestic awards" in the state where recognition and enforcement are sought. In addition, the award must arise from "differences between persons, whether physical or legal." Finally, Article I(3) gives ratifying states an option to make two reservations: (1) on the basis of reciprocity, a state may declare that "it will apply the Convention to the recognition and enforcement of awards made only in the territory of another contracting state," and (2) a state may declare that it will apply the Convention to "differences arising out of legal relationships, whether contractual or not, which are considered as commercial under the national law of the State making such declaration." The United States made both reservations. But what about agreements to arbitrate? When are they subject to the Convention?

Section 202 of the Convention Act attempts to state when an arbitration "agreement" is subject to the Convention:

> An arbitration agreement or award arising out of a legal relationship, whether contractual or not, which is considered commercial, including a transaction, contract, or agreement described in section 2 of this title [9 U.S.C. §2],[96] falls under the Convention. An agreement or award arising out of such a relationship which is entirely between citizens of the United States[97] shall be deemed not to fall under the Convention unless the relationship involves property located abroad, envisages performance or enforcement abroad, or has some other reasonable relation to one or more foreign states.

How relevant is the place of arbitration to this test? Struggling with the ambiguity where agreements are concerned, the courts have held that when a motion to refer a dispute to arbitration is made in a federal district court, the arbitration agreement is subject to the Convention if the agreement

[96] These include a "maritime transaction or a contract evidencing a transaction involving commerce."

[97] For purposes of this section a "corporation is a citizen of the United States if it is incorporated or has its principal place of business in the United States." *See* Section (1)(c)(2) of this Act.

(1) is in writing and provides for arbitration in a country that has ratified the Convention, (2) involves a legal relationship that is considered "commercial" under the law of the place of arbitration, and (3) involves an arbitration where one of the parties is not an American citizen, or if both are American citizens, the arbitration is not a domestic arbitration, that is, that the relationship between the two American citizens "involves property located abroad, envisages performance or enforcement abroad, or has some other reasonable relation with one or more foreign states."[98]

A somewhat clearer statement of this scope principle is found in proposed Section 1(c) of this Act, which is drawn from the Model Law.

Section (1)(c). An arbitration is international if:

(i) the parties to an arbitration agreement have, at the time of the conclusion of that agreement, their citizenship or places of business in different States; or

(ii) one of the following places is situated outside the State in which the parties have their places of business:

the place of arbitration if determined in, or pursuant to, the arbitration agreement;

any place where a substantial part of the obligations of the commercial relationship is to be performed or the place with which the subject matter of the dispute is most closely connected; or

(iii) the parties have expressly agreed that the subject matter of the arbitration agreement relates to more than one country; and

(iv) the places stated in (b)(1)(ii) or the place where the award was made are in a country that has ratified the New York Convention.[99]

Thus, the arbitration between Party A and Party B is within the scope of the Convention as implemented by the Convention Act for at least two reasons – the parties are citizens of two different countries and the arbitration

[98] *See, e.g., Francisco v. Stolt Achievement MT*, 293 F.3d 270, 273 (5th Cir.), *cert. denied*, 537 U.S. 1030 (2002); *U.S. Titan, Inc. v. Guanghou Zhen Hua Shipping Co., LTD*, 241 F.3d 135, 146 (2d Cir. 2001); *DiMercurio v. Sphere Drake Ins., PLC*, 202 F.3d 71 (1st Cir. 2000); *Bautista v. Star Cruises*, 286 F. Supp.2d 1352, 1361–62 (S.D. Fla. 2003), *aff'd*, 396 F.3d 128 (11th Cir. 2005) *cert. dismissed*, 125 S. Ct. 2954 (2005); *Chloe Z. Fishing Co. v. Odyssey RE (London)*, 109 F. Supp. 1236, 1243 (S.D. Cal. 2000).

[99] Professor Park prefers a "residence" test under which an arbitration is international if the seat of the arbitration is in the United States and at "least one party is resident or incorporated outside of the United States at the time the agreement to arbitrate was concluded." William W. Park, *The Specificity of International Arbitration: The Case for FAA Reform*, 36 VAND. L. TRANSN'L L. 1241, 1259–60, 1307 (2003) (hereafter cited as Park, *Specificity*).

is to be held in another country (the Philippines) which has ratified the convention. We think that this definition of "international" nicely catches the variables of the transnational business transaction.[100]

But is an international employment contract between a seaman and the corporate owner of a vessel a "commercial" relationship?

6.2(1)(B) When is an Arbitration Commercial?

(1) In General

The Convention applies to "differences arising out of legal relationships, whether contractual or not, which are considered commercial under the national law of the State making such declaration."[101] There is no definition of "commercial" in the Convention Act, but in most exchange relationships between business entities no problems are posed. They are clearly commercial relationships.

The issue is complicated if one or both parties are individuals engaged in international commerce. Suppose, for example, that an individual in Canada assembles custom made computer systems and sells them to individuals in the United States for business purposes. If those contracts for sale included arbitration clauses, is this a international commercial arbitration? Under the Model Law, the answer is "yes." The focus is on the relationship rather than the parties to it. Thus, a "trade transaction for the supply or exchange of goods or services" is a commercial relationship even though both parties are individuals.[102] Similarly, a contract for sale between a large Canadian corporation of computer systems to an individual in the United States for use in a business would be a commercial relationship and an arbitration clause in the contract would also be covered by this Act.[103] It is not so clear, however, whether a contract of employment between a seaman and a corporation is a "relationship of a commercial nature."[104]

[100] If the place of arbitration was in the United States this Act would apply because the parties have their "places of business" in different states both of which have ratified the Convention. If the place of arbitration was in the Philippines, a signatory of the Convention, the arbitration is international under Section 1(c) of this Act but this Act would apply only if one party petitioned a federal district court to refer the parties to arbitration in the Philippines. Section 1(b) of this Act.

[101] Art. I(3). See FAA §202 (legal relationship which is "considered as commercial").

[102] Model Law Art. I(1), n.2. For background *see* Aron Broches, COMMENTARY ON THE UNCITRAL MODEL LAW ON INTERNATIONAL COMMERICAL ARBITRATION 18–20 (1990) (hereinafter cited as Broches, MODEL LAW).

[103] *See* Section 1(d), which adopts the Model Law test.

[104] Footnote 2 to Article 1 of the Model Law states that the term "commercial" should be given a "wide interpretation" and that the term "includes but is not limited to" the illustrative transactions provided. Employment contracts are not included.

(2) Consumer Contracts

Suppose, however, that the individual buys the computer from the Canadian seller for personal, family, or household purposes. This is a consumer transaction that is specifically excluded from the United Nations Convention on Contracts for the International Sale of Goods.[105] But does the sale still arise from a commercial relationship for purposes of international arbitration when the individual's purpose in buying is for personal not business purposes?

Although the issue is not free from doubt,[106] I have excluded arbitration clauses in international contracts between business entities and consumers from this Act.[107] For purposes of this Act, at least, we have left the controversial problems concerning consumer arbitration to domestic arbitration law. Even if the cost of arbitration is roughly the same under both regimes,[108] the special problems confronting consumers in the underlying transaction (lack of bargaining power, sophistication, and the like), the increased risk of litigation and judicial intervention, and the current concerns over the misuse of arbitration in consumer contracts pose a risk to the goal of de-localized international arbitration. These imbalances in the consumer contract argue for exclusion from this Act and for separate treatment in the United States under domestic arbitration law.[109]

(3) Employment Contracts

(a) In general. Should all international employment contracts also be excluded from this Act or should the issue be left to a judicial interpretation of whether an employment relationship is a "relationship of a commercial nature?"

Under domestic arbitration law, Chapter 1 of the FAA does not apply to arbitration clauses contained in collective bargaining agreements, even though the rights of individual employees are at stake. There is a specialized

[105] Article 2(a). Canada and the United States have ratified the CISG.

[106] Professor Ware argues that Chapter 1 of the FAA should treat consumer arbitration the same as any other arbitration where the parties have agreed to arbitrate. *See* Chapter 4, *supra*. Professor Sternlight, on the other hand, proposes amendments to Chapter 1 of the FAA to provide additional protection to consumers. *See* Chapter 5, *supra*.

[107] Section 1(b)(4), (e)(i). The line is difficult to draw, especially where an individual buys goods for both personal and business purposes.

[108] It is probably higher in international arbitration, especially institutional arbitration.

[109] Professor Park agrees in theory, although he prefers exclusion for transactions beneath a stated dollar amount. *See* Park, *Specificity, supra* Note 99 at 1289–95 (arguing for a less unitary model of arbitration for consumer and employment contracts). *See* Chapter 5, *supra*.

body of arbitration law that has developed for collective bargaining agreements.[110]

Except for "transportation workers," arbitration in all other employment contracts "evidencing a transaction in commerce" is covered by the Chapter 1 of the FAA.[111] In a series of controversial decisions, the Supreme Court has held that arbitration clauses in ordinary employment contracts between individuals and business employers are covered by the FAA rather than collective bargaining arbitration law and that only the employment contracts of "transportation workers" are excluded from the FAA under Section 1, to be covered, presumably, by state arbitration law.[112] Depending on the type of employment contract involved, therefore, there are three potentially applicable regimes of arbitration law: ordinary employment contracts, collective bargaining labor agreements, and contracts of transportation workers.

(b) Does the "transportation workers" exclusion in Section 1 of the FAA apply to the Convention? Return now to the international employment contract dispute between Party A and Party B. It is clear that Party A is a "transportation worker" whose arbitration agreement would be excluded from Chapter 1 of the FAA by the language of Section 1: "[N]othing herein contained shall apply to contracts of employment of seamen, railroad employees, or any other class of workers engaged in foreign or interstate commerce." But does this language also exclude the arbitration from coverage by the Convention and the Convention Act?

Concluding that an employment contract of this type was commercial and the arbitration agreement was international, the courts have refused to apply the exclusion in Section 1 of the FAA to the Convention. In the leading case, *Francisco v. Stolt Achievement MT*,[113] the court first concluded that the narrow exclusion in Section 1 of the FAA was in conflict with the broad language in the Convention and Section 202 of the Convention Act.[114] There was no suggestion that the international arbitration agreements in the employment

[110] *See, e.g., Major League Baseball Player's Ass'n v. Garvey*, 532 U.S. 504 (2001) (collective bargaining arbitration governed in part by Section 301 of the Labor Management Realtions Act of 1947, 29 U.S.C.A. §185(a)). *See* Professor Ware's discussion in Section 4.3(1), *supra.*

[111] Section 1 of the FAA excludes from coverage "contracts of employment of seamen, railroad employees, or any other class of workers engaged in foreign or interstate commerce."

[112] *See Circuit City, Inc. v. Adams*, 532 U.S. 105 (2001) (reviewing history and holding that exclusion in FAA Section 1 was limited to "transportation workers").

[113] 293 F.3d 270 (5th Cir. 2002), *cert. denied*, 537 U.S. 1030 (2002). *Accord: Acosta v. Norwegian Cruise Line, Ltd.*, 303 F. Supp.2d 1327 (S.D. Fla. 2003).

[114] Section 208 of the Convention Act states that Chapter 1 of the FAA applies to actions and proceedings under Chapter 2 "to the extent that chapter is not in conflict with this chapter . . . or the Convention as ratified by the United States."

contracts of seamen should be excluded.[115] The court embraced the policy that any doubts in defining the scope of the Convention should be resolved in favor of arbitration and noted that the "strong federal policy" in favor of enforcing arbitration agreements and that this policy "applies with special force in the field of international arbitration."[116] Thus, international employment contracts, whether or not contained in collective bargaining agreements, would appear to be commercial and arbitration clauses contained therein are subject to the Convention and the Convention Act. The parties, therefore, will be referred to arbitration at the agreed place unless the dispute is not capable of being arbitrated or the arbitration agreement is "null and void" under Article II of the Convention.[117]

(c) ***International employment contracts.*** Should this interpretation be preserved in this Act? Should any distinction be drawn between the type of worker or type of employment contract if the transaction is international and commercial? Put differently, if international arbitrations involving transportation workers are subject to the Convention, why not include all other employment contracts between and individual residing in one country and an employer doing business in another country?

The argument for inclusion is that the Convention provides enforcement policies that are available to both parties, subject to the permitted limitations imposed by domestic law. For example, a written agreement to arbitrate cannot be "null and void" under the law of the forum[118] and an award will not be enforced if the dispute is not capable of arbitration or against public policy.[119] Moreover, even if the employee is a citizen of the United States,

[115] Although FAA §202 states that the legal relationships covered by the Convention "include" those transactions covered by Section 2 of Chapter 1, the court concluded that the Convention Act does not "state that agreements falling under the Convention are exclusively limited to those which also fall under Section 2 of the Arbitration Act, and makes no mention of the exclusion for seaman employment contracts found in Section 1 of the Arbitration Act." 293 F.3d at 274.

[116] 293 F.3d at 274–75. The court rejected "two other arguments which favor Francisco's position but do not ultimately alter our conclusion."

[117] Some interesting public policy issues lurk on the fringes. Suppose, for example, that the seaman was an American citizen rather than a Filipino citizen. The Convention would still apply, but should the American seaman be sent to the Philippines to arbitrate? To do so would rob the seaman of the protection of the Jones Act and send him across the world to an uncertain fate. But unless the Jones Act states clearly that claims arising thereunder are not arbitrable (it does not so state), these concerns are not likely to block arbitration. *See Bautista v. Star Cruises*, 286 F. Supp.2d 1352 (S.D. Fla. 2003), *aff'd*, 396 F.3d 1289 (11th Cir. 2005), *cert. dismissed*, 125 S. Ct. 2954 (2005) (rejecting policy arguments where seaman was a Filipino citizen).

[118] Convention, Art. II(3).

[119] Convention, Art. V(2).

there is no evidence that the employee will obtain greater protection against exploitive arbitration agreements under Chapter 1 of the FAA as interpreted by the Supreme Court than under the Convention.

The difficulty is that many commentators argue that employees, like consumers, should receive greater protection under the FAA than that given to a commercial party.[120] Professor Park has warned that the available protection against exploitation derives from a body of domestic law tailored to the interests of individual consumers and employees and there is a risk that this law would spill over to other transactions subject to the Convention. This would create "uncertainty about the level of freedom from judicial intervention." He urges a "separate statute . . . to insulate arbitration from the undue judicial intervention that is inevitable in consumer and employment cases."[121] Given this warning and the political implications of change in this area, and the goal of de-localization, we have no hesitation in excluding all international employment contracts from the scope of this Act.[122]

6.2(2) Power of Parties to "Opt Out" of or Vary the Effect of This Act

6.2(2)(A) Choice of Arbitration Law

Section 2(1) of this Act defines "arbitration" to mean "an agreement in a record between two or more parties to submit an existing or a future dispute or controversy to an arbitral tribunal for a final decision on the merits." If the dispute resolution procedure agreed to by the parties does not fit within the definition this Act does not directly apply, although there should be room for the court to apply appropriate parts by analogy.[123]

If this Act applies, however, the parties still have power to choose the arbitration law of another country. Suppose, for example, that the place of

[120] *See* Erica F. Schohn *The Uncertain Future of Mandatory Arbitration of Statutory Claims in the Unionized Workplace*, 67 L. & Contemp. Prob. 321 (2004) (suggesting that "mandatory" arbitration is not justified in non-union arbitration). The issues are discussed in Chapter 7, *infra.*

[121] Park, *Specificity*, *supra* Note 99 at 1289–91.

[122] Section 1(b)(4), (e)(ii), (iii). This is a legislative choice. The somewhat arbitrary exclusion makes the most sense (from the standpoint of domestic policy) when one party to the employment contract is an individual who is a citizen of the United States dealing with a corporation doing business in another country.

[123] *See* discussion in Section 6.1(4)(A), *supra*. This may be too inflexible. For example, if the parties have agreed to submit a dispute to arbitration but agreed that the award is not final, the definition is not satisfied. Does this mean that one party cannot obtain an order referring the parties to arbitration? The issue can be resolved if the parties agree to "opt in" to portions of this Act.

an arbitration between a United States and a United Kingdom corporation was in New York City and the parties clearly chose the English Arbitration Act of 1996 to govern.[124] It is likely that a federal court would enforce this choice even though the *lex arbitri* of England differs in many respects from the international arbitration law of the United States. As one court put it:

> . . . [W]here the parties have chosen the governing body of law, honoring their choice is necessary to ensure uniform interpretation and enforcement of that agreement and to avoid forum shopping. This is especially true of contracts between transnational parties, where applying the parties' choice of law is the only way to ensure uniform application of arbitration clauses within the numerous countries that have signed the New York Convention. Furthermore, respecting the parties' choice of law is fully consistent with the purposes of the FAA.[125]

Given the goal of de-localization and the value of private autonomy, choices of this sort should be honored.[126]

6.2(2)(B) Agreements Varying the Effect of Applicable Arbitration Law

The more difficult question is the extent to which the parties should be permitted to vary the legal effect of the arbitration law which applies to the dispute? Should all provisions be classified as "default" rules subject to variance or should some be classified as "mandatory" rules that cannot be varied? And if some rules are "mandatory," which ones and why?

Despite the importance of private autonomy, modern ICA statutes do contain mandatory rules. Under the English Arbitration Act, for example, the parties have broad power to vary the effect of the EAA except for the

[124] This is to be distinguished from the choice of substantive law to govern the merits of the dispute. *See* Fabrizio Marrella, *Choice of Law in Third-Millennium Arbitrations: The Relevance of the UNIDROIT Principles of International Commercial Contracts*, 36 VAND. J. TRANSN'L L. 1137 (2003).

[125] *Motorola Credit Corp. v. Uzan*, 388 F.3d 39, 51 (2d Cir. 2004) (enforcing the choice of Swiss arbitration law). Under Chapter 1 of the FAA, private parties have power, within limits to select state arbitration law to govern an interstate arbitration. *See* Section 3.4, *supra*. *See also Volt Information Sciences, Inc. v. Board of Trustees of Leland Stanford Jr. Univ.*, 489 U.S. 468 (1989) (parties subject to FAA may choose California arbitration law even though it differs from FAA); Comment, *An Unnecessary Choice of Law: Volt, Mastrobuono, and Federal Arbitration Act Preemption*, 115 HARV. L. REV. 2250 (2002).

[126] *See generally* Alan Scott Rau, *Contracting Out of the Arbitration Act*, 8 AM. REV. INT'L ARB. 225 (1997).

twenty-six specific provisions listed in Schedule 1.[127] These include such things as the powers of the court to enforce agreements and awards and administer the arbitration, certain duties of the tribunal and the parties in the conduct of the arbitration, the immunity of the tribunal and the arbitral institution, and costs and fees. The Model Law adopts a different strategy toward the same result by creating a presumption of non-variability: the effect of no provision can be varied unless otherwise stated (by the phrase "unless otherwise agreed" or use the permissive word "may" in a particular section). Thus, under the Model Law the parties have no power to vary the effect of rules defining when an arbitration agreement shall be enforced or when an award shall be given recognition and enforcement by a court unless otherwise specifically provided. These are mandatory rules presumably rooted in the powers given to courts by the Convention and the Convention Act.[128]

In light of the controversy in the United States on the extent to which parties may vary the effect of Section 10 of the FAA to expand the grounds for vacatur,[129] some clear lines must be drawn for ICA by this Act. Rather than ceding the entire matter to private agreement, Section 3(a) of this Act provides that the parties "may not agree to derogate from or to vary the effect of this Act unless otherwise provided in a particular section by the phrase 'unless otherwise agreed' or by the word 'may' or other permissive language." This deviation from the principle of private autonomy is justified by the fact that the non-waivable sections contain common principles in international arbitration that are rooted in the Convention and the Model Law (as well as the English Arbitration Act) and are arguably essential for uniformity and certainty around the world. In effect, they promote de-localization

[127] EAA §4(1). The non-mandatory provisions of the EAA "allow the parties to make their own arrangements by agreement but provide rules which apply in the absence of agreement." §4(2).

[128] Depending how you count, there are 21 articles of the Model Law, the effect of which cannot be varied in whole or in part. Section 4(a) of the Revised Uniform Arbitration Act (RUAA) permits agreements varying or waiving the effect of the RUAA unless specifically stated in subsections 4(b) or 4(c). Subsection 4(b) lists sections that cannot be varied before a controversy arises and subsection 4(c) states sections that cannot be varied or waived in any circumstances. *See* Timothy J. Heinsz, *The Revised Uniform Arbitration Act: Modernizing, Revising, and Clarifying Arbitration Law*, 2001 J. Disp. Res. 1, 8 (2001).

[129] The circuit courts of appeal disagree on whether private parties have power to expand the scope of judicial review of arbitral awards under FAA §10. The cases and the issues are well discussed in Margaret Moses, *Can Parties Tell Courts What to Do? Expanded Judicial Review of Arbitral Awards*, 52 U. Kan. L. Rev. 429 (2004). Both Professor Brunet and Professor Ware have concluded that the parties should be able to vary the effect of FAA §10 by agreement. *See* Sections 3.5, 4.3(4), *supra*.

arbitration in that they are international mandatory rules protecting the power of parties to international contracts to arbitrate and the right to the enforcement of agreements and awards.[130] In this proposed Act, the non-variable principles include:

Section 1. Scope of application
Section 3. Rule against variation
Section 6. Extent of court intervention
Section 7. Jurisdiction, venue, removal, act of State
Section 8. Immunity of arbitrator and arbitral institution
Section 9. Definition and form of arbitration agreement
Section 10. Enforceability of arbitration agreement
Section 11. Interim measures by court
Section 14(b), (c) Appointment of arbitrators by court
Section 15. Disclosure and challenge
Section 16. Failure or impossibility of arbitrator to act
Section 17(b), (c). Competence of arbitral tribunal; separability
Section 19(a). Treatment of parties by tribunal
Section 19(b), (c). Conduct of hearings
Section 24. Rules applicable to substance of dispute and award
Section 25(b), (c), (d). Form and effect of award
Section 28(b). Termination of proceedings
Section 30. Confirmation of the arbitral award
Section 31. Recourse against or defenses to arbitral award
Section 32. Interpretive policies

In sum, an effort has been made in this Act to state fundamental principles most of which are not variable. These principles apply, primarily, to Stages One and Three of the arbitration. The "middle ground" in Stage Two is, for the most part, within the power of the parties to vary and define by agreement.

6.2(3) Extent of Court Intervention

Section 6 of this Act provides that "in matters governed by this Act, no court shall intervene except where so provided in this Act." This follows Section 5 of the Model Law and Section 1(c) of the English Arbitration Act and resolves an open question under American arbitration law: when and to

[130] Assuming that the core principles of the Convention are not variable, the parties can still contract for the supplementary arbitration law of a particular country without impairing international uniformity.

what extent may a court intervene in an arbitration after commencement and before the final award?

It is a given that courts may intervene upon request of a party to determine whether to enforce an arbitration agreement or to grant recognition and enforcement of an award. In what other cases should intervention be permitted and upon what grounds?

In this Act, intervention is permitted in five additional situations to facilitate or protect the arbitration process. Thus, a court may intervene upon petition to (1) stay litigation pending arbitration [Section 10(b)], (2) grant interim relief [Section 11], (3) appoint arbitrators or to hear appeals in disputes over challenges to arbitrators [Sections 14 and 15], (4) assist the arbitral tribunal in subpoenaing witnesses and obtaining documentary evidence [Section 22], and (5) remand an award to the arbitrators for action consistent with the agreement of the parties and applicable law [Section 30(c)]. We will discuss each section later in this chapter.

6.2(4) Electronic Commerce and Arbitration

As noted earlier,[131] electronic technology has outdated those sections of American arbitration law that require a written agreement or a writing and a signature. So what is the fate of an electronic agreement or an electronic signature? Does this mean that arbitration in cyberspace occurs outside of the protective confines of the Convention and the Convention Act?

Because of the federal "E-Sign" Law,[132] it is unlikely that any international arbitration agreement or award or signature will be invalidated solely because it is electronic form.[133] Nevertheless, because the United States has not yet ratified the draft United Nations Convention on the Use of Electronic Communications in International Contracts,[134] some of the issues have been resolved in this Act.[135]

[131] *See* Section 6.1(4)(C)(1), *supra*.

[132] Electronic Signatures in Global and National Commerce Act, 15 U.S.C. §§7001, 7002, which applies to international transactions.

[133] For the treatment of electronic arbitration under the Revised Uniform Arbitration Act, *see* Timothy J. Heinsz, *The Revised Uniform Arbitration Act: Modernizing, Revising, and Clarifying Arbitration Law*, 2001 Disp. Res. J. 1, 8–11 (2001) (discussing Section 8 and its impact on other provisions of the RUAA).

[134] One of the items on the Agenda for UNCITRAL Working Group II (Arbitration) at its meeting in Vienna in September, 2004 was to consider whether the New York Convention should be included on the list of international conventions to which the draft convention on Electronic Communications should apply. *See* United Nations Document, A/CN.9/WG.II/WP.130.

[135] Professor Ware proposes similar revisions for Chapter 1 of the FAA. *See* Section 4.3(3), *supra*.

First, throughout this Act the word "record" is used to replace the word "writing" or written. Record means "information that is inscribed on a tangible medium or that is stored in an electronic or other medium and is retrievable in perceivable form."[136] Thus, an arbitration agreement in either "a tangible medium" or stored on a computer hard drive with print-out potential is valid.

Second, a "signature" includes an "electronic signature," which means an "electronic sound, symbol, or process attached to or logically associated with a record and executed or adopted by a person with the intent to sign the record."[137]

Section 3(b), drawing on Section 15(b) of the Revised Uniform Arbitration Act, states when an electronic record is received.

These are but modest first steps in supporting on-line international arbitration. They apply primarily to enforcement of the arbitration agreement and the award. Within this legal framework, the real challenge will be to develop appropriate rules for the conduct of arbitration in cyberspace. Although such a development is inevitable, the scope and configuration of those rules are beyond the bounds of this chapter.[138]

6.2(5) Jurisdiction of the Court; Venue; Removal

Section 7 of this Act incorporates three sections of the Convention Act into one section, former Section 203 creating jurisdiction, former Section 204 stating where an action may be brought, and former Section 205 authorizing removal from state to federal courts. With the exception of Section 205, these sections are retained without change.[139]

Unlike Chapter 1 of the FAA, which depends upon diversity jurisdiction,[140] Section 7(a) of this Act provides that the district courts of the United

[136] Section 6.1(2)(7), *supra.*

[137] Section 6.1(2)(8), *supra.* The definitions of "record" and "signature" are taken from the Uniform Electronic Transactions Act, §7(c), (d).

[138] For an interesting discussion of the current scope of and potential problems for on-line arbitration, *see* Mohamed Wahab, *The Global Information Society and Online Dispute Resolution: A New Dawn for Dispute Resolution*, 21 J. Int'l Arb. 143 (2004).

[139] The relationship between the ambiguous language of former Section 205 and the removal procedures stated in 28 U.S.C. §§1141 and 1446 has created problems for the courts. For a critical assessment, *see* Susan L. Karamanian, *Road to the Tribunal, supra* Note 38, 34 G.W. Int'l L. Rev. 77–84. The revisions of this Act state the basic removal policy without resolving the complications discussed by Dean Karamanian.

[140] *See America's Moneyline, Inc. v. Coleman*, 360 F.3d 783, 784–7 (7th Cir. 2004) (Chapter 1 of the FAA does not grant jurisdiction to the federal courts). Professor Ware would retain the diversity jurisdiction requirement and clarify that only actions brought under Sections 1 and 2 can be decided in state courts. All other matters are for the federal courts with, of course, jurisdiction. *See* Section 4.5, *supra.*

States have "original jurisdiction" over actions of proceedings "authorized by or falling under the New York Convention and this Act" and shall "be deemed to arise under the laws and treaties of the United States."[141] Moreover, if the court has jurisdiction and there is no agreement to the contrary, "any action or proceeding ... may be brought in such court in which ... an action or proceeding with respect to the controversy between the parties could be brought ... " Nevertheless, the plaintiff must still obtain in personam jurisdiction over the defendant.[142]

The application of these sections and other "rules of procedure" under Article III of the Convention to the enforcement of awards will be treated in Section 6.5(2)(A)(1).

6.2(6) Foreign States and International Arbitration

Assume that a United States corporation enters a contract to buy machinery from Chinese entity owned by the People's Republic of China (PRC). The contract contains an agreement to arbitrate any and all disputes arising under or relating to the contract in Los Angeles under the AAA International Arbitration Rules. Assume further that the Chinese entity could not perform the contract because the PRC, in a move to stave off rampant inflation, shut down the only factory that could produce the machinery. When the Chinese entity refused to arbitrate, the American corporation petitioned a federal district court in California to refer the dispute to arbitration.

If the court has both subject matter and personal jurisdiction and the arbitration agreement is valid, there are two possible defenses that might still be raised if one of the parties to the arbitration agreement is a state entity: (1) the state entity is immune from suit in the United States, and (2) even if the court has jurisdiction, the arbitral tribunal, when appointed, cannot examine the merits of the PRC action to close the plant under the so-called "Act of State Doctrine." Neither of these defenses will work here, at least where the legal action or arbitration occurs in the United States.

6.2(6)(A) The Foreign Sovereign Immunities Act

A claim of sovereign immunity raises a jurisdictional defense. In an effort to control the exercise of the defense, the Foreign Sovereign Immunities Act (FSIA) provides that a "foreign state shall be immune from the jurisdiction of

141 *See Certain Underwriters v. Argonaut Insurance Co.*, 264 F. Supp.2d 926, 931–2 (N.D. Cal. 2003) (applying FAA §203).

142 *See Base Metal Trading, Ltd v. OJSC*, 283 F.3d 208 (4th Cir.), *cert. denied*, 537 U.S. 822 (2002).

the courts of the United States and of the States" unless one or more specific exceptions can be established. For example, a foreign state is not immune from the jurisdiction "of courts of the United States or of the States" if (1) the foreign state has "waived its immunity either explicitly or by implication," or (2) the action is "based upon a commercial activity carried on in the United States by the foreign state . . . "[143] Another exception, the so-called "arbitration" exception, applies to our case:

> A foreign state shall not be immune from the jurisdiction of courts of the United States or of the States in any case in which the action is bought, either to enforce an agreement made by the foreign state with or for the benefit of a private party to submit to arbitration all or any differences which have arisen or which may arise between the parties with respect to a defined legal relationship, whether contractual or not, concerning a subject matter capable of settlement by arbitration under the laws of the United States, or to confirm an award made pursuant to such an agreement to arbitrate, if (A) the arbitration takes place or is intended to take place in the United States, (B) the agreement or award is or may be governed by a treaty or other international agreement in force for the United States calling for the recognition and enforcement of arbitral awards, (C) the underlying claim, save for the agreement to arbitrate, could have been brought in a United States court under this section . . .[144]

In a case where both countries have ratified the Convention, the private party seeks to enforce the agreement to arbitrate in a United States court, and the underlying claim is for breach of contract, the sovereign immunity defense is not permitted by the FSIA.[145] But what of the Act of State Doctrine?

6.2(6)(B) The Act of State Doctrine

What is the Act of State Doctrine? According to the Supreme Court:

> Unlike a claim of sovereign immunity, which merely raises a jurisdictional defense, the act of state doctrine provides foreign states with a substantive

[143] 28 U.S.C. §§1604, 1605(a)(1), (2). *See Drexel Burnham Lambert Group, Inc. v. Committee of Receivers for Galadari*, 12 F.3d 317 (2d Cir. 1993), *cert. denied*, 511 U.S. 1069 (1994) (interpreting and applying statute).

[144] 28 U.S.C. §1605(a)(6). *See U.S. Titan, Inc. v. Guangzhou Zhen Hua Shipping*, 241 F.3d 135, 150–1 (2d Cir. 2001) (district court had subject matter jurisdiction in dispute over arbitrability between a corporation owned by the PRC and a U.S. corporation where China and the United States had ratified the Convention).

[145] The FSIA, which provides the exclusive standard for resolving sovereign immunity defense in United States courts, applies only if the foreign state has agreed to arbitrate in the United States. *See* Republic of Philippines, 309 F.3d 1143 (9th Cir. 2002). *See also Banco de Seguros del Estado v. Mutual Marine Office*, 344 F.3d 255, 260 (2d Cir. 2003).

> defense on the merits. Under the doctrine, the courts of one state will not question the validity of public acts (acts *jure imperii*) performed by other sovereigns within their own borders, even when such courts have jurisdiction over a controversy in which one of the litigants has standing to challenge those acts."[146]

Thus, if in a contract between a U.S. corporation and a state-owned entity, the People's Republic of China closed the plant of its state owned entity in China and prevented performance, this would appear to be a public act the validity of which that neither a court nor (presumably) an arbitrator could challenge in the United States. As a practical matter, the state-owned entity would have a defense on the merits.

To neutralize this defense in international arbitration, Section 7(d) of this Act adopts Section 15 of the FAA,[147] which provides that the "Act of State Doctrine" is not applicable to arbitrations under Chapter 1 of the FAA.

> Enforcement of arbitral agreements, recognition and enforcement of arbitral awards, and execution upon judgments based on orders confirming such awards subject to the Convention and this Act shall not be refused on the basis of the Act of State Doctrine.

According to the Practice Commentary, Section 15 of the FAA "precludes the use of the Act of State doctrine to undo the right to arbitrate, the right to confirm an award made on an already concludes arbitration, or the enforcement of a judgment rendered by a court on the award."[148] In practical terms, if an arbitrator has decided the merits of the claim against the foreign entity, the Act of State doctrine, whenever raised, will not preclude recognition and enforcement of the award.

6.2(7) Immunity of Arbitrators and Arbitral Institutions

Neither the Convention, the Convention Act, nor the Model Law provide immunity to arbitrators or an arbitral institution from liability to any person

[146] *Republic of Austria v. Altman*, 541 U.S. 677, 700, 124 S. Ct. 2240, 2254 (2004). A leading case is *Banco National de Cuba v. Sabbatino*, 376 U.S. 398, 401 (1964), holding that Cuba's nationalization of the sugar industry was an Act of State that prevented the court from reaching the merits of the dispute.

[147] Section 15 was added to the FAA in 1988. Pub. L. 100–669, §1, Nov. 16, 1988, 102 Stat. 3969.

[148] David D. Siegel, *Practice Commentary*, 9 USCA §15. According to Mr. Siegel, an agreement or award "falling under the convention and otherwise satisfying its requirements may by that very process attain a status insulating it from an attack based on the Act of State doctrine." Nevertheless, incorporating FAA §15 into this Act explicitly resolves that issue.

for acts or omissions in connection with the arbitration. This issue is typically covered in the contract, if at all.[149]

The English Arbitration Act of 1996, however, provides such immunity to an arbitrator and an arbitral institution.[150] Section 8 of this Act follows the English Act, endorsing a principle of broad immunity for arbitrators and arbitral institutions unless the challenged acts and omissions in connection with the arbitration were in bad faith. This is consistent with the case law in the United States.[151]

Section 6.3 Enforcing the Agreement to Arbitrate

6.3(1) Overview: The Concept of Arbitrability

Assuming that the Convention applies,[152] Article II deals with the question whether an alleged agreement to arbitrate shall be enforced by referring the parties to arbitration. Article II(3) of the Convention gives the court of a "contracting state" power to "refer the parties to arbitration" if the conditions stated in Article II are met. These conditions, which are discussed later, makeup the concept of arbitrability.[153] If the dispute is arbitrable, Section 206 of the Convention Act gives a court with jurisdiction power "to direct that arbitration be held in accordance with the agreement at any place therein provided for, whether that place is within or without the United States." Section 206 of the Convention Act is replaced by Sections 7 and 8 of this Act.

In Section 6.2(2) we argued that Article II of the Convention provides a set of mandatory arbitration rules for the enforcement of international agreements to arbitrate and awards. To the extent these rules define the

149 *See, e.g.,* ICC Art. 34; LCIA Art. 35; AAA Art. 35.

150 *See* EAA §§29 (arbitrators) & 74 (arbitral institutions).

151 Section 8 is consistent in principle with Section 14 of the Revised Uniform Arbitration Act. The American cases are discussed in Timothy J. Heinsz, *The Revised Uniform Arbitration Act: Modernizing, Revising, and Clarifying Arbitration Law,* 2001 J. Disp. Res. 1, 42–44 (2001).

152 *See* Section 6.2(1)(A), *supra*, and Section 1(b) of this Act. In *Freudensprung v. Offshore Technical Services, Inc.*, 379 F.3d 327 (5th Cir. 2004), the court applied the Convention to a dispute between two American citizens who had agreed to arbitrate in the United States where their commercial contract involved performance abroad: there was a reasonable connection between the parties' commercial relationship and a foreign state independent of the arbitration clause.

153 *See* Alan Scott Rau, *The Arbitrability Question Itself,* 10 Am. Rev. Int'l Arb. 287 (1999) (hereafter cited as Rau, *Arbitrability*). Professor Rau's primary focus is on the "separability" doctrine and who should decide the arbitrability question, the court or the tribunal. *See* Section 6.4(5), *infra*, where these questions are discussed in detail.

conditions of enforcement or confer power on the courts, the parties have no power to vary their legal effect by agreement. We argued that the uniform application of this international treaty and its implementing legislation was necessary for a theory of de-localized arbitration. Nevertheless, the concept of arbitrability under the Convention depends in part upon the law of the place where the petition to enforce the arbitration agreement is filed. Suppose, for example, that Congress creates a set of statutory claims or rights, the effect of which cannot be varied by agreement. Moreover, suppose that Congress clearly stated that these claims must be enforced in court and not through arbitration. Under Article II(1) of the Convention, these claims are not arbitrable because they are not "capable of settlement by arbitration."[154] Even if they were arbitrable, if the substantive rights created were "mandatory" in that the parties have no power to vary their legal effect, the arbitrators would be obligated to apply them in deciding the dispute.[155]

In the United States, however, there are few if any mandatory substantive rights that cannot be arbitrated. If the parties agree, say, to arbitrate an antitrust or a securities claim that Congress has not clearly excluded from arbitration, off they go to the tribunal. The unanswered question is the extent to which a court can review an award that purports to decide the mandatory statutory claim.[156] If there is no review on the merits, does this mean that a de-localized arbitration becomes a less acceptable A-National arbitration? If so, should the scope of judicial review reach the merits of mandatory claims that are arbitrable but which the parties cannot vary by agreement?[157] This is an important policy question for which a solution will be proposed in this Act.[158]

6.3(2) The Elements of Arbitrability

The concept of arbitrability involves several elements or conditions that must be satisfied before disputes arising under an arbitration agreement subject

[154] *See* Section 1(b)(3) of this Act. *See also* Section 6.3(2)(B), *infra.*

[155] A careful distinction should be drawn between "mandatory" arbitration law and "mandatory" substantive law. In the scheme of the Convention, "mandatory" substantive claims may be capable of arbitration (unless Congress has clearly said "no") even though the parties have no power to vary their legal effect by agreement.

[156] *See* Section 6.5(2)(B)(6), *infra.* Professor Ware discusses this point under Chapter 1 of the FAA in some detail. *See* Section 4.4(2), *supra.*

[157] Dean McConnaughay concludes that the answer is "yes." Philip J. McConnaughay, *The Risks and Virtues of Lawlessness: A "Second Look" at International Commercial Arbitration*, 93 Nw. U. L. Rev. 453 (1999). Professor Ware agrees. *See* Section 4.4(2), *supra.*

[158] *See* Section 30(9) of this Act.

to the Convention can be referred to arbitration. Although the conditions are easy to state, their content and application frequently cause problems.

6.3(2)(A) Agreement in Writing

Initially, Article II(1) of the Convention requires "an agreement in writing" between the parties under which they "undertake to submit to arbitration all or any differences which have arisen or which may arise between them. . . . " These differences must arise from a "defined legal relationship, whether contractual or not."[159] Note that the writing requirement is mandatory but that the parties have control over the nature and scope of the "differences" to be submitted to arbitration.

Although Article II(1) requires an "agreement" to arbitrate, it does not say what an agreement is, and the definition is left to local law.[160] Article II(2), on the other hand, attempts to state when an agreement "is in writing." Because the scope of the phrase "in writing" has caused trouble in the courts and been criticized by the commentators,[161] we will discuss it in some detail in Section 6.3(2)(B).

6.3(2)(B) Capability

Article II(1) states that the differences between the parties must concern "a subject matter capable of settlement by arbitration." The capability question is to be answered under the law of the place where enforcement is sought. Thus, the court must decide whether the particular dispute or claim has been reserved only for the courts under the law of the forum. In the United States, all differences and claims, whether involving contract rights or statutory

[159] Convention Art. II(1). The phrase "defined legal relationship" is intended to cover claims arising in tort. *See* Albert Jan Van den Berg, The New York Arbitration Convention of 1958 148–52 (1981)(hereafter cited as Van den Berg, New York Convention). The United States, upon ratifying the Convention, declared that the legal relationship must be "considered as commercial." Convention Act §206.

[160] As one court put it, under the Convention the courts "must treat agreements to arbitrate like any other contract . . . " A "contract is formed when there is a meeting of the minds of the parties on the essential terms of an agreement. . . . " and a court must "examine the parties's written communications to determine whether they have formed an agreement to arbitrate enforceable under the FAA and the Convention." *U.S. Titan, Inc. v. Guangzhou Zhen Hua Shipping*, 241 F.3d 135, 146 (2d Cir. 2001). For discussion of what law applies, *see* Section 6.3(4), *infra*.

[161] *See* Susan L. Karamanian, *The Road to the Tribunal and Beyond: International Commercial Arbitration and United States Courts*, 34 G.W. Int'l L. Rev. 17, 34–9 (2002) (hereafter cited as Karamanian, *Road to the Tribunal*). *See* Section 6.3(3)(B), *infra*.

rights, are capable of arbitration unless Congress has "expressly directed" that a particular claim must be resolved by the courts.[162]

A much debated "lightening rod" decision on the "capability" question in international arbitration is *Mitsubishi Motors Corp. v. Soler Chrysler-Plymouth, Inc.*[163] In this case, the Supreme Court, relying on both Chapter 1 of the FAA and the Convention, referred a dispute arising under a franchise agreement between a dealer in Puerto Rico and a partnership between Mitsubishi and Chrysler to arbitration in Tokyo. The rub was that the dispute involved a claim under the federal antitrust laws – a claim which at that time was not capable of arbitration under domestic arbitration law. To make matters worse, the contract provided that the arbitrators in Tokyo were to decide the antitrust claim under Swiss law, the place where one of the partners was incorporated. Expressing a strong policy in favor of international arbitration, the Court interpreted a "broad"[164] arbitration clause to include antitrust claims (even though those claims were not specifically mentioned), rejected the contention that arbitration was an inappropriate forum to decide complex antitrust claims, refused to consider in advance whether the arbitrators or the arbitral procedures in Tokyo were up to the job, and, in the absence of a clear congressional directive to the contrary, held that the claim was arbitrable "so long as the prospective litigant effectively may vindicate its statutory cause of action in the arbitral forum."[165] As for the prospect of judicial review of the award, the Court suggested that a reviewing court might properly consider, at a minimum, whether the tribunal actually decided the claim under applicable law.[166]

[162] *See Mitsubishi Motors Corp. v. Solar Chrysler-Plymouth, Inc.*, 473 U.S. 614, 639, n. 21 (1985); *Green Tree Financial Corp. v. Randolph*, 531 U.S. 79, 80 (2000) (has Congress "evinced an intention to preclude a waiver of judicial remedies for the statutory rights at issue").

[163] 473 U.S. 614 (1985). *See* Karamanian, *Road to the Tribunal*, *supra* Note 161 at 43–52.

[164] The parties agreed to arbitrate "all disputes, controversies or differences which may arise [between them] out of or in relation to [stated articles of the agreement] or for the breach thereof." 473 U.S. at 617.

[165] 473 U.S. at 637. A right cannot be vindicated, however, if there is a "prospective waiver" of the right in the arbitration agreement.

[166] The judicial review issue is discussed in Section 6.5(2)(B)(5), *infra*. *See Vimar Seguros y Reaseguros, S.A. v. M/V Sky Reefer*, 515 U.S. 528 (1995), where the question was whether the cost of complying with a forum selection clause requiring arbitration in Japan "lessened the liability" under Section 3(8) of the Carriage of Goods by Sea Act, 46 U.S.C. §1300. In holding "no" the Court followed the reasoning in *Mitsubishi Motors* and refused to consider whether the prospective arbitration panel would apply the correct law. The district court, which had retained jurisdiction, could later review whether the legitimate interests of the law were enforced. 515 U.S. at 540–1.

In sum, Article II(1) recognizes that a private agreement to arbitrate a particular claim can be trumped by a local determination that the claim or dispute is not "capable" of arbitration. The Supreme Court, however, has neutralized the trump by stating that, unless Congress has clearly said so, all claims created by or under federal statutes are arbitrable if the parties so agree.[167] The unanswered question is whether the tribunal's award on the merits of the claim is immune from judicial review for errors of fact or law.

6.3(2)(C) Scope of the Written Agreement to Arbitrate

The parties must also have "made an agreement" within the meaning of Article II(3) to arbitrate "all or any differences which have arisen or which may arise between them."[168] Assuming that some written agreement to arbitrate was reached, did it cover all of the disputes or differences between the parties? To answer this question, a court, aided by a presumption in favor of arbitration, must interpret the agreement to determine whether the dispute is within its scope. Although neither the Convention nor the Convention Act provide any principles for contract interpretation, the parties can avoid most disputes over scope by agreeing to a "broad" arbitration clause, that is, a clause that agrees to arbitrate "all disputes arising under or relating to" the contract.[169]

The power of the pro-arbitration policy in the Second Circuit is illustrated by *JLM Industries, Inc. v. Stolt-Nielsen SA*.[170] In an arbitration that was clearly international (even though the court applied Chapter 1 of the FAA), a series of shipping contracts between the owners of "parcel tankers" and the charterers of space contained a standard form contract agreeing to

[167] Given the continuing silence of Congress on these matters, the burden shifts to the parties who could presumably choose some other substantive or arbitration law or specifically exclude the statutory claim from the arbitration agreement. *See JLM Industries, Inc. v. Stolt-Nielsen SA*, 387 F.3d 163, 179–81 (2d Cir. 2004), where JLM conceded that antitrust claims in general were arbitrable but argued that the "type" of antitrust claim, a "horizontal" rather than a "vertical" claim, was excluded because of its complexity. This argument was rejected under *Mitsubishi*: "complexity . . . is not a reason to deny arbitrability." 387 F.3d at 181.

[168] Art. II(1).

[169] For an excellent example of the effect of a broad arbitration clause, *see Louis Dreyfus Negoce S.A v. Blystad Shipping & Trading Inc.*, 252 F.3d 218, 224–5 (2d Cir.), *cert. denied*, 534 U.S. 1020 (2001) (finding broad clause and holding dispute within scope). The parties, of course, could clearly agree to arbitrate only issue A in a dispute that involves issues A, B, and C. If all three issues arise out of or are related to the contract, the parties will probably arbitrate issue A first and then litigate issues B and C. The award on issue A will be res judicata on issues of fact and law common also to issues B and C.

[170] 387 F.3d 163 (2d Cir. 2004).

arbitrate "any and all differences and disputes of whatsoever nature *arising out of* this charter in either New York or the City of London" (emphasis added). JLM, a charterer, filed suit against the Owners alleging various horizontal arrangements between the owners and others that violated Section 1 of the Sherman Act and the Connecticut Antitrust Act. Even though the place of arbitration had not yet been selected, the Owners moved to compel arbitration of all JLM's claims. The district court held that the antitrust claims were outside the scope of the agreement to arbitrate but this decision was reversed on appeal. After going through an obligatory analytical litany,[171] the court classified the arbitration clause as "broad" even though the language "or relating to" was missing and held that the clause applied to "collateral matters" because an analysis of the factual allegations in the complaint revealed that the alleged "price-fixing conspiracy among the Owners undermined legitimate contractual relations between the parties."[172] Although the alleged price-fixing concerned "matters beyond the making of a particular contract between the parties and the performance of its terms," the damages allegedly suffered under these contracts resulted from the anti-competitive effects of agreements made by the Owners with others.[173] Thus, the phrase "arising under" was interpreted to mean "relating to" even though that latter phrase was not in the contract.

6.3(2)(D) Validity of the Written Agreement to Arbitrate

Finally, the court may not refer the parties to arbitration if it finds that the arbitration agreement is "null and void, inoperative or incapable of being performed."[174] This interesting collection of words surrounds the important question whether a written arbitration agreement is otherwise valid or

[171] The court first noted that it had jurisdiction under the Federal Arbitration Act, citing Chapter 1 and Chapter 2. The content of the Convention and the Convention Act were never mentioned. Next the court concluded that the district court's decision was appealable because it denied a motion to compel arbitration, 9 U.S.C. §16(a)(1)(A), (B), and held that the decision on arbitrability, although within the district court's power, was reviewable de novo. The court then stated that one of the questions for decision was whether the disputed claim was within the scope of the agreement to arbitrate. To reach this question, the court (1) noted the strong policy favoring arbitration, particularly in international transactions, (2) reiterated that despite the strong policy the scope question is a matter of agreement or consent, and (3) classified the arbitration agreement as "broad" rather than narrow. With this done and the goal clear, the court had no trouble fitting the claim into the arbitrability aura of *Mitsubishi Motors* and its progeny. 387 F.3d at 169, 171–7.

[172] 387 F.3d at 173.

[173] *Id.* at 175.

[174] Art. II(3). The same language appears in Article 8(1) of the UNCITRAL Model Law and Section 9(4) of the English Arbitration Act of 1996. *See* Section 10 of this Act.

enforceable under the law of the forum. Relevant questions might include whether a party was incapacitated, the agreement was unconscionable, a condition precedent to arbitration had failed, or changed circumstances made performance of an agreed arbitration impracticable.[175] Again, neither the Convention nor the Convention Act provides any guidance on how to interpret or apply this language.

6.3(2)(E) Enforcement of Written Agreement to Arbitrate

If the arbitrability requirements are met, Article II(3) states that "the court of a contracting state . . . shall at the request of one of the parties, refer the parties to arbitration." Section 206 of the Convention Act then provides:

> A court having jurisdiction . . . may direct that arbitration be held in accordance with the agreement at any place therein provided for, whether that place is within our without the United States.

Thus, if the dispute is arbitrable, the court may direct[176] the parties to arbitration in London, Moscow, Beijing, or wherever the parties have agreed.[177]

Under the Convention it is clear that a court with jurisdiction has competence to decide these questions of arbitrability, especially before the tribunal has been appointed.[178] An arbitral tribunal may also have power to determine its own jurisdiction. But concurrent jurisdiction on arbitrability questions does not normally pose a problem before the tribunal has been appointed. A court is unlikely to refer the arbitrability issue to the yet to

[175] *See* Van den Berg, New York Convention, *supra* Note 159 at 154–68. Van den Berg suggests that "null and void" covers "cases where the arbitration is affected by some invalidity right from the beginning." *Id.* at 156. Also, "inoperative" "can be deemed to cover those cases where the arbitration agreement has ceased to have effect," *id.* at 158, and "incapable of being performed" "would "seem to apply to those cases where the arbitration cannot be effectively set into motion." *Id.* at 159.

[176] It has been suggested that "refer" the parties to arbitration is the same as a "directive imposing arbitration." Van den Berg, New York Convention, *supra* Note 159 at 128–30. Similarly, the power of a court to "direct" the parties to arbitration under Section 206 of the Convention Act is tantamount to a specific performance order.

[177] *See, e.g., InterGenN.V. v. Grina*, 344 F.3d 134, 141–2 (1st Cir. 2003) (citing authorities). The court held that it had power to order the parties to arbitrate in London under Section 206 of the Convention Act even though it could not send an officer to London to enforce the command. The court had "other means at hand for enforcing such an order": it may "enter an default or an order of dismissal . . . or adjudge a recalcitrant party in contempt."

[178] *See* Section 6.4(5), *infra*. In *Howsam v. Dean Witter Reynolds, Inc.* 537 U.S. 79, 84 (2002), the Court stated that disagreements over the scope of an arbitration agreement are for the courts to decide.

be appointed tribunal, especially where the tribunal's decision on it own jurisdiction is ultimately subject to a de novo review.

Finally, the court may be asked to enjoin a party to the arbitration from filing or pursuing a lawsuit in a court within or without the United States on matters within the scope of the agreement to arbitrate.[179] This anti-suit injunction is not specifically authorized by the Convention or the Convention Act. Under Section 208 of the Convention Act, however, Chapter 1 of the FAA supplements to the extent not in conflict with the Convention. Section 3 of the FAA permits the injunction, and arguably does not conflict with the Convention. This matter is clarified in Section 10(b) of this Act.

6.3(3) Definition and Form of Arbitration Agreement

6.3(3)(A) Definition of Arbitration

Neither the Convention nor the Convention Act define arbitration. Nevertheless the scope of the Convention depends upon an "agreement in writing" to submit agreed differences "to arbitration." Section 9(a) of this Act, however, defines "arbitration agreement" and provides a working definition of arbitration that is consistent with the essential elements, express and implied, of that form of non-judicial dispute resolution.[180] Two key elements of this definition are that the agreement to arbitrate must commit both parties and the parties must intend the award to be final. If one or both of these elements are missing, neither party is subject to the Convention and the Convention Act.

6.3(3)(B) Form of Agreement to Arbitrate

Article II(1) of the Convention states that each contracting state "shall recognize an agreement in writing" to arbitrate and Article II(2) states that the term "'agreement in writing' shall include an arbitral clause in a contract or an arbitration agreement, signed by the parties, or contained in an exchange of letters or telegrams." In addition, Article IV(1)(b) of the Convention states that a party seeking recognition and enforcement of an award "shall at the time of the application supply: . . . The original agreement referred to in article II or a duly certified copy thereof." Thus, formality requirements exist at

[179] *See* Section 6.3(4), *infra.*

[180] *See also* Section 2(1) of this Act (defining "arbitration"). Section 6 of the English Arbitration Act defines "arbitration agreement" without defining arbitration.

the stages of enforcement for both arbitration agreements and arbitration awards.[181]

(1) Interpretation of Article II(1)

Assuming that the requirements of a "writing" and a "signature" can be satisfied by electronic means,[182] how should the language of Article II(1) be interpreted? Put differently, is Article II(1) ever satisfied if the parties have objectively assented to (by words or conduct) but not signed a written agreement to arbitrate?

Unfortunately, American courts have disagreed on the meaning of the phrase "an arbitral clause in a contract or an arbitration agreement, signed by the parties," one court concluding that the "signed by the parties" language refers only to "an arbitration agreement"[183] and another concluding that the language refers to both "an arbitral clause in a contract" and "an arbitration agreement."[184] Although one might prefer the literal interpretation of the second case, the question remains why an arbitration clause contained in a written contract objectively assented to by both parties should not be sufficient. This is particularly true if the writing requirement is intended to facilitate awareness and proof of the agreement rather than to protect against fraud.

Even more interpretive difficulty lurks in language "contained in an exchange of letters or telegrams." What is an "exchange" in this context? The easiest case is where the arbitration clause is contained in a signed written offer or counteroffer that is accepted by an signed telegram or letter that does not specifically mention arbitration. As one commentator put it, "the acceptance in writing by whatever means need not be directed specifically to the arbitral clause in the contract; the acceptance of the contract as a whole fulfils the exchange requirement of Article II(2)."[185] But suppose there is a written offer followed by a counteroffer in a letter containing an arbitration

[181] Section 2 of the FAA requires only that the agreement to arbitrate be in writing. No signature is required. Section 2, therefore, is in conflict with Article II(2) and is preempted. *See* Convention Act §208. For a discussion of Article IV(1) of the Convention, *see* Section 6.5(2)(A), *infra.*

[182] *See* Section 2(7), (8) of this Act.

[183] *Sphere Drake Insurance PLC v. Marine Towing, Inc.*, 16 F.3d 666 (5th Cir.), *cert. denied*, 513 U.S. 871 (1994) (arbitration clause in a contract assented to by both parties sufficient without signatures).

[184] *Kahn Lucas Lancaster, Inc. v. Lark Intern'l, Ltd.*, 186 F.3d 210 (2d Cir. 1999) (signature required on both an arbitral clause in a contract and an arbitration agreement).

[185] Van den Berg, New York Convention, *supra* Note 159 at 199.

clause followed by an acceptance by conduct. Or suppose there is conduct by one party sufficient to suggest an estoppel to deny the existence of an agreement in writing to arbitrate? In neither of these cases should the written agreement to arbitrate be enforceable if an exchange of signed writings is required, but there are cases to the contrary.[186]

Finally, neither Article II of the Convention nor the Convention Act say anything about the Model Law's view that "an exchange of statements of claim and defense in which the existence of an agreement is alleged by one party and not denied by another" is sufficient or the effect of an attempt to incorporate by reference an arbitration clause in another document into the writing.[187]

(2) Reducing the Formal Requirements of Article II(2)

According to an experienced judge and barrister, there are many informal international transactions where a party with knowledge objectively assents to a written arbitration clause. In these cases, he argues that the reasons for the writing requirement in the Convention and the Model Law are satisfied but the arbitration agreement is nevertheless not enforceable.[188] The result is a formality requirement that is out of touch with the international business transaction.

Section 5(2) of the English Arbitration Act apparently responds to this argument and transactional realities by stating that the agreement in writing requirement is satisfied "(a) if the agreement is made in writing (whether or not it is signed by the parties), (b) if the agreement is made by exchange of communications in writing, or (c) if the agreement is evidenced in writing." The Commentary, however, suggests that Section 5 "derives from the Model Law, Art. 7(2), and the writing requirements in prior English arbitration law." But although the Model Law and Article II(2) of the Convention are

[186] *See* Karamanian, *Road to the Tribunal, supra* Note 161 at 67–74 (reviewing conflicting cases).

[187] *See* Model Law Art. 7(2). The last sentence of Article 7(2) provides: "The reference in a contract to a document containing an arbitration clause constitutes an arbitration agreement provided that the contract is in writing and the reference is such as to make that clause part of the contract." There has been considerable litigation worldwide under Article 7 of the Model Law. *See* Henri C. Alvarez, Neil Kaplan, & David W. Rivkin, Model Law Decisions: Cases Applying the UNCITRAL Model Law on International Commercial Arbitration (1985–2001)37–55 (2003).

[188] *See* Neil Kaplan, *Is the Need for Writing as Expressed in the New York Convention and the Model Law Out of Step with Commercial Practice?* 12 Arb'n Int'l L. 27 (1996) (answering "yes").

similar, the English Arbitration Act "significantly differs from the Convention, providing very clearly . . . that no signature is necessary."[189]

On balance, the English Arbitration Act has got it right, provided that Article II(1) of the Convention does not state the exclusive methods to satisfy the "agreement in writing" requirement.[190] Thus, Section 9(b) of this Act provides:

> An arbitration agreement is in a record if it is contained in (1) a contract or document that is signed by the parties, (2) an exchange of letters, telex, telegrams or other means of communication which provide a record of the agreement, (3) a record to which the parties have otherwise assented, or (4) an exchange of statements of claim and defense in which the existence of an arbitration agreement is alleged by one party and not denied by the other.

Section 9(b), by expanding the methods by which the writing requirement can be satisfied, includes transactions where the arbitration agreement is "contained in a record to which the parties have otherwise assented" even though only one party or neither have signed it. Thus, a bill of lading containing an arbitration clause signed and issued by a carrier to a shipper is sufficient if the shipper assents to the bill of lading by conduct or otherwise but does not sign it. The conclusion is that a written agreement to arbitrate assented to by both parties, whether by signature or otherwise, is sufficient to satisfy the policy favoring informed consent implicit in Article II(1) of the Convention.[191]

To illustrate, assume that Seller and Buyer are negotiating toward the conclusion of a contract for the international sale of goods. Buyer makes a signed offer in a writing containing an arbitration clause. Seller accepts the offer on its own signed form which does not contain but does not object to an arbitration clause. Under the United Nations Convention on Contracts for the International Sale of Goods (CISG) there is a contract by offer and acceptance containing Seller's arbitration clause.[192] Also, this is arguably an "exchange of letters and telegrams" that satisfies the writing requirement in Article II(2) of the Convention and Article 9(b) of this Act.

[189] Bruce Harris, Rowan Planterose, & Jonothan Tecks, THE ARBITRATION ACT OF 1966: A COMMENTARY 72, 75 (2d ed. 2000).

[190] The argument is that the language "shall include" in Article II(1) does not foreclose other methods to satisfy the writing requirement without a signature.

[191] According to Van den Berg, the primary reason for the writing requirement was to insure that a party was aware of the arbitration clause. *See* Van den Berg, NEW YORK CONVENTION, *supra* Note 159 at 170–1.

[192] *See* CISG Articles 14(1) & 18(1).

To vary the facts, suppose that Buyer makes a written offer that does not contain an arbitration clause. Seller responds with a signed written counteroffer that contains an arbitration clause, which Buyer accepts by using and paying for the goods sent by Seller. Under Articles 18(1) and 19(1) of CISG, Buyer has accepted the counteroffer and, under CISG at least, there is a contract containing a written agreement to arbitrate. This transaction, however, probably does not satisfy Article II(2) of the Convention because the "exchange" of letters, one of which contained a written agreement to arbitrate, did not create the contract. Under Section 7(b) of this Act; however, the writing requirement has been satisfied because Buyer, by conduct, assented to the written arbitration clause in the counteroffer.[193]

In sum, Section 9(a) of this Act defines "arbitration agreement" to mean an "agreement in a record" to arbitrate and states that the arbitration agreement "may be contained in a contract or expressed in a separate agreement." Section 9(b) relaxes and clarifies when an arbitration agreement is "in a record" for purposes of the formality requirements and Section 9(c) provides that "the reference in a contract to a record containing an arbitration term is an arbitration agreement if the reference incorporates the term as part of the contract."[194]

In light of these changes, legislation implementing Article IV(b) of the Convention should be drafted to insure that if the arbitration agreement satisfies Section 9(b) of this Act, evidence of that agreement, whether signed or not, should be sufficient to satisfy the condition to obtaining recognition and enforcement of the award.[195]

6.3(4) Arbitrability: What Law Applies?

What law governs disputes over arbitrability? The answer depends upon what element of arbitrability is at issue. Assume for discussion that the

[193] A UNCITRAL Working Group has proposed to amend Model Law Article 7 by simply stating "the arbitration agreement shall be in writing."

[194] In the United States, these problems are complicated by controls placed upon form contracts by Uniform Commercial Code §2–207. For example, suppose B makes an offer that S definitely accepts in a form that contains an arbitration clause. Or suppose that S makes a counteroffer in a form that contains an arbitration clause. Suppose, further, that S ships and B uses the goods. Thereafter, S argues that B agreed to a written arbitration clause by conduct. This transaction satisfies the "written provision" requirement of FAA §2 but, under UCC 2–207(2) or (3) the arbitration clause may not be part of the agreement because B did not expressly agree to it. *See, e.g., Textile Unlimited, Inc. v. A. BMH and Co, Inc.*, 240 F.3d 781 (9th Cir. 2001) (written arbitration clause drops out under UCC 2–207(3)).

[195] *See* Section 6.5(2)(A)(3), *infra*.

dispute arises in a federal district court and there is no agreement choosing the applicable law.

Recall that Article II of the Convention both requires that the arbitration agreement be in "writing" and defines the phrase "agreement in writing." To this extent, the Convention is the source of law, even though "agreement" is not defined. The court should interpret and apply the Convention rather than resort to local law.

Disputes over the scope of the written agreement to arbitrate, however, raise somewhat different questions. In Article II(1), the Convention permits the parties to agree upon the scope of a submission but does not say how these agreements should be interpreted. Here resort to some local body of contract principles on whether there was an agreement to arbitrate,[196] and what that agreement means will be required.

Under Article II(1), if the dispute is over whether the dispute or claim concerns a "subject matter capable of settlement by arbitration," the answer depends upon the law of the forum. In the United States, that law is federal law, usually the acts of Congress creating the rights or claims at issue. If those statutes do not state clearly that the claim is to be decided by courts only, the subject matter is "capable" of settlement by arbitration and the dispute will be referred to arbitration.[197]

Finally, suppose the dispute is over whether the arbitration agreement was "null and void, inoperative, or incapable of being performed." More specifically, suppose one party contents that the arbitration agreement was "null and void" because it was unconscionable or induced by fraud. Again, Article II(3) of the Convention states the grounds for invalidation without specifying when the agreement is "null and void." In this case, the court will, unless there is an agreement to the contrary, look to local law. But should that law be state or federal law? Because federal jurisdiction is created under Section 203 of the Convention Act rather than by diversity of citizenship,[198] the court is not required to follow the law of any particular state. For example, if an arbitrability dispute under the Convention was litigated in a federal district court in Tennessee, the court would not be required to follow Tennessee law on whether the arbitration agreement was

[196] *See U.S. Titan, Inc. v. Guangzhou Zhen Hua Shipping*, 241 F.3d 135, 146–50 (2d Cir. 2001) (finding agreement to arbitrate from written communications of parties).

[197] *See* Section 6.3(2)(B), *supra*.

[198] Under Chapter 1 of the FAA, federal jurisdiction depends upon diversity of citizenship and similar questions arising under Section 2 of the FAA are answered under applicable state law. *See* Section 2.4(2)(B)(1), *supra*.

invalid because of fraud or unconscionability.[199] But what law should be followed?

Difficult thought it may be, the search should be for general principles of federal contract law infused with the pro-arbitration policies that permeate international arbitration law.[200] But are there any such general principles?

In *InterGen N.V. v. Grina*,[201] an international arbitration, the question was whether a non-signatory to an arbitration agreement could nevertheless be compelled to arbitrate because of estoppel or third-party beneficiary or agency theory. In refusing to compel arbitration, the court held that federal common law rather than divergent state law should be applied. The Convention Act was a federal statute which demanded "national uniformity" in implementing the Convention's goal to "set out uniform rules governing the recognition and enforcement of international arbitration awards." The court turned to this difficult task "mindful that federal common law incorporates general principles of contract and agency law."[202] Those general principles are set forth in legislation such as the Uniform Commercial Code and private codes, such as the Restatement, Second, of Contracts. In the absence of such codes, the court with the aid of scholars writing on the law of contracts,[203] might try to extract a working principle from the jumble of state common law precedents.

In sum, questions of arbitrability raised in United States courts turn on federal law. The source of that federal law depends on the precise question to be resolved. Thus, the question whether an arbitration agreement is in writing is determined by Article II(2) of the Convention, capability issues typically turn on restrictions in the federal statutes creating the right in dispute, and the validity of the arbitration agreement will depend upon general principles of contract law. More importantly, the legal enforceability of the agreement to arbitrate is derived from the Convention and the Convention Act, which provide, in essence, that a court "shall . . . refer the parties to arbitration" if the requirements of Article II are satisfied.[204]

[199] *See Tennessee Imports, Inc. v. P.P. Filippi & Prix Italia S.R.L.*, 745 F. Supp. 1314 (M.D. Tenn. 1990), where the court "in the absence of well-established principles of federal contract law," applied Section 2–302 of the Uniform Commercial Code.

[200] Thus, in determining the scope of an international agreement to arbitrate, the court might apply general principles of contract interpretation coupled with a presumption of arbitrability. *See Louis Dreyfus Negoce S.A. v. Bllystad Shipping*, 252 F.3d 218, 223–5 (2d Cir.), *cert. denied*, 534 U.S. 1020 (2001).

[201] 344 F.3d 134 (1st Cir. 2003).

[202] 344 F.3d at 143–4.

[203] *See, e.g.*, E. Allan Farnsworth, CONTRACTS (3d ed. 2001); Robert A. Hillman, PRINCIPLES OF CONTRACT LAW (2004).

[204] Article II(3); FAA §206. See Section 10(a) of this Act.

6.3(5) Stay of Litigation

Suppose the parties have agreed to arbitrate in London. A dispute arises and Party A sues Party B on the merits in an English court. When Party A refuses to arbitrate, Party B obtains personal jurisdiction and files a motion to compel arbitration under the Convention in a federal court in New York. Party B also petitions the court to enjoin Party A from litigating the case in London. Should the court grant the injunction? If so, how can an order compelling arbitration and staying litigation in London be enforced by a federal court in New York?

Although the Convention and the Convention Act empower the court to "refer" or "direct" the parties to arbitration,[205] nothing is said about injunctions staying litigation within the scope of the arbitration agreement. Perhaps this power is implied, but certainly, the power is given by Section 3 of the FAA that supplements and is not in conflict with the Convention or the Convention Act.[206] So if Party A refuses to arbitrate and the dispute in litigation is within the scope of the agreement to arbitrate, should the court enjoin Party A from pursuing the litigation in London?

In the *InterGen* case,[207] the court was faced with the question whether it should compel a recalcitrant party to arbitrate in London. Noting that enforcement was an "obligation" under the Convention and that courts have "regularly" compelled arbitration in countries beyond the court's jurisdiction, the court was not restrained by the fact that it could not exercise injunctive powers "beyond the reach of its jurisdiction." But this was no obstacle to the issuance of such an order because the court "has other means at hand for enforcing such an order," such as:

> [E]nter a default or an order of dismissal . . . , or adjudge a recalcitrant party in contempt. . . . We therefore hold that so long as the parties are bound to arbitrate and the district court has personal jurisdiction over them, the court is under an unflagging, nondiscretionary duty to grant a timely motion to compel arbitration and thereby enforce the New York Convention . . . even though the agreement in question requires arbitration in a distant forum.[208]

[205] Article II(1); FAA §206.

[206] *See* Van den Berg, New York Convention, *supra* Note 159 at 129 (power to stay implied). *See also Dimercurio v. Sphere Drake Ins.*, PLC, 202 F.3d 71 (1st Cir. 2000) (holding that FAA §3 supplements the Convention Act).

[207] *Supra* Note 201.

[208] 344 F.3d at 142.

The problem is a bit more complicated when a court with *in personam* jurisdiction orders a party to cease or file a motion to dismiss litigation commenced in the courts of another country. Even if the litigation is between parties to and covers issues within the scope of the arbitration agreement, courts in the Second Circuit, at least, have granted the motion "sparingly" and "only with care and great restraint."[209]

> [A] court looks to such factors, inter alia, as whether the foreign action interferes with the U.S. court's own jurisdiction, whether the foreign action is designedly vexatious or calculated to cause material and burdensome delay, and other such equitable considerations.[210]

The lines are sometimes difficult to draw. Thus, in one case an injunction was refused because the law suit in a Mexican court raised issues "arguably the province of a Mexican court rather than the arbitrators" and the defendant had not refused to arbitrate. Rather, the defendant was participating in an arbitration that was "proceeding simultaneously" with the law suit.[211] On the other hand, an injunction was issued and the defendant cited for contempt in *Paramedics Electro v. GE Medical Systems*,[212] where the district court had decided that the issues before a court in Brazil were within the scope of the agreement to arbitrate and the defendant refused both to arbitrate and to dismiss the law suit. The court of appeals concluded that: (1) the parties were the same in both matters, (2) resolution of the case before the enjoining court was dispositive of the action to be enjoined, and (3) the foreign action threatened the jurisdiction and the strong pro-arbitration policy of the enjoining forum.[213]

With this delicate balancing act in mind, Section 10(b) of this Act simply gives the court power to "stay or dismiss" a law suit brought within the scope of an enforceable arbitration agreement pending arbitration. Frequently an action to compel arbitration is combined with an action to stay litigation. In these embedded proceedings, if the controversy is arbitrable under Article 10(a) of this Act, the court can refer the parties to arbitration

[209] *China Trade & Dev. Corp. v. M.V. Choong Yong*, 837 F.2d 33, 35–6 (2d Cir. 1987).

[210] *Laif X SPRL v. Axtel, S.A. DeC.V.*, 310 F. Supp.2d 578, 581 (S.D.N.Y. 2004), *aff'd*, 390 F.3d 194 (2d Cir. 2004).

[211] *Id.*

[212] 369 F.3d 645 (2d Cir. 2004).

[213] 369 F.3d at 652. The court noted that where the "court has already reached a judgment-on the same issues, involving the same parties – considerations of comity have diminished force." *Id.* at 655.

and either issue an order staying one party from proceeding with or, if it has jurisdiction, dismiss the pending litigation.

6.3(6) Appealability

Under what circumstances are decisions by a federal district court on questions of arbitrability in international arbitration immediately appealable? This is an important question because if an immediate appeal is not available the loser must preserve the defense against a possible waiver and wait for review until after the award has been made.[214]

The complicated answer to this question is found in Section 16 of the FAA, which applies explicitly to decisions on arbitrability made under Section 206 of the Convention Act and implicitly to decisions on the stay of litigation.[215] The general principle is that an appeal may be taken from judicial orders refusing to stay any action or denying an application to compel arbitration,[216] but that an appeal may not be taken from an interlocutory order granting the stay or ordering arbitration.[217] Brooding over this is Section 16(a)(3) that provides that an "appeal may be taken from . . . a final decision with respect to an arbitration that is subject to this title."

The Supreme Court, in *Green Tree Financial Corp. v. Randolph*,[218] held that Section 16(a)(3) controls appealability even where the order grants a stay of litigation and directs arbitration to proceed. In *Green Tree*, Randolph filed a suit on the merits and Green Tree Financial responded by moving to stay or in the alternative to dismiss the litigation and to compel arbitration under the FAA. The district court denied the motion to stay, dismissed the law suit with prejudice, and entered an order compelling arbitration. On appeal, the court of appeals held that the order was appealable as a final order under Section 16(3)(a)(3) but that the arbitration agreement was not enforceable. The Supreme Court affirmed the ruling on appealability but reversed the decision on arbitrability. A decision granting a motion

[214] *See American Intern. Specialty Lines Ins. Co. v. Electronic Data Systems Corp.*, 347 F.3d 665, 667–8 (7th Cir. 2003) (arbitrability defense preserved during appeal). An award made where the dispute was not arbitrable may be denied recognition and enforcement under Article V(1) of the Convention.

[215] Section 16(a)(1)(a) and (b)(2) of the FAA applies to orders granting or denying stays under Section 3 of the FAA. We have argued that Section 3 applies in international arbitration because it is not in conflict with the Convention or the Convention Act.

[216] *See* FAA §16(a)(1). *See JLM Industries, Inc. v. Stolt-Nielsen SA*, 387 F.3d 163, 169 (2d Cir. 2004) (interlocutory appeal from denial of motion to compel arbitration).

[217] Section 16(b).

[218] 531 U.S. 79 (2000).

to compel arbitration and dismissing the law suit with prejudice is final because it "ends the litigation on the merits and leaves nothing more for the court to do but execute the judgment." This is true even though the orders favored arbitration and emerged from a so-called "embedded proceeding" that involves "both a request for arbitration and other claims for relief."[219] The Court noted, however, that if the district court had stayed rather than dismissed the litigation the order would not have been final. The Court, however, did not consider whether the district court erred in failing to take that route.[220]

In international arbitrations, it is likely that a motion to stay litigation and a request to compel arbitration will be made to the same court, even though the litigation and the place of arbitration is in another country. If one or both are denied, an appeal may be taken regardless of whether a final decision has been made. If one or both are granted, however, no appeal is permitted unless a final decision has been made, that is, that the motions are dismissed with prejudice and jurisdiction has not been retained. Thus, the strong policy favoring international arbitration is best implemented if the district court can be persuaded to direct arbitration under Section 10(a) of this Act[221] and to grant a stay of litigation, preserving jurisdiction for actions taken after the award is made.

6.3(7) Interim Relief

The question whether a court has power to grant interim relief to protect a party to an arbitration agreement is not answered by the Convention, the Convention Act, or Chapter 1 of the FAA. Although some courts have held (under Chapter 1 of the FAA) that such power is inconsistent with the agreement to arbitrate,[222] the inherent power to grant such relief has been recognized by most courts under Section 206 of the Convention Act.[223] This recognition is consistent with international norms found in Section 9 of

[219] 531 U.S. at 87.

[220] 531 U.S. at 87, n.2. All of the justices concurred in the ruling on finality.

[221] Now Section 206 of the Convention Act.

[222] *See* Alison C. Wauk, *Preliminary Injunctions in Arbitrable Disputes: The Case for Limited Court Jurisdiction*, 44 UCLA L. Rev. 2061 (1997) (reviewing cases and arguing against power unless the parties have agreed).

[223] *See Borden Inc. v. Meiji Milk Products Co., Ltd.*, 919 F.2d 822, 825–7 (2d Cir. 1990), *cert. denied*, 500 U.S. 953 (1991) (preliminary injunction in aid of arbitration is consistent with court's power to compel arbitration under §206 of the FAA). The Third Circuit disagrees. *McCreay Tire & Rubber Co. v. Ceat S.p.A.*, 501 F.2d 1032, 1038 (3d Cir. 1974).

the Model Law[224] and the international arbitration rules adopted by every modern arbitration institution.[225]

The important question is less whether the court has power to grant interim relief and more the scope of its exercise and the relationship to the power of the tribunal, once appointed, also to grant relief. For example, one well reasoned decision conceded the court's power to award interim relief in international arbitration (a writ of attachment) but held that it had no jurisdiction to act where the applicable arbitration rules (CIETAC) also gave the tribunal power to act and those arbitration procedures had not first been invoked.[226]

Section 11 of this Act, which draws on Section 9 of the Model Law and Section 8 of the Revised Uniform Arbitration Act, provides some straight forward solutions to these problems.

Paragraph (a) follows Section 9 of the Model Law. It is not incompatible with an arbitration agreement to request interim relief from a court. Nor does the request for judicial interim relief depend upon the agreement of the parties or constitute a waiver of the right to arbitrate.

Paragraph (b), which draws on Section 8 of the Revised Uniform Arbitration Act, provides for judicial interim relief before the arbitral tribunal is appointed and able to act. The purpose of interim relief is to protect and facilitate the arbitration process.

Paragraph (c) limits judicial power if the request for interim relief is made after the arbitral tribunal is appointed and able to act. At this point, the responsibility for making provisional remedies and interim awards shifts to the tribunal under Section 18 of this Act, unless the tribunal is unable or unwilling to act. The parties are free to contract out of or vary the effect of Section 18 by agreement.[227]

[224] Section 9 of the Model Law provides that it is "not incompatible with an arbitration agreement for a party to request, before or during arbitral proceedings, from a court an interim measure of protection and for a court to grant such measure." Article 17 confers similar power on the arbitral tribunal.

[225] The rules give the tribunal power to order interim relief. For an analysis of the various institutional arbitration rules on interim relief by the tribunal, *see* William Wang, *International Arbitration: The Need for Uniform Interim Measures of Relief*, 28 Brook. J. Int'l L. 1059 (2003).

[226] *See China Nat. Metal Products Import/Export Co. v. Apex Digital, Inc.*, 155 F. Supp.2d 1174 (C. D. Cal. 2001), following *Simula, Inc. v. Autoliv, Inc.*, 175 F.3d 716 (9th Cir. 1999).

[227] The power of the parties to vary the effect of institutional arbitration rules if not the enabling statute supports the primary principal of party autonomy in international arbitration. *See* Christopher R. Drahozal, *Party Autonomy and Interim Measures in International Commercial Arbitration*, Important Contemporary Questions 179 (2003) (ICCA Congress Series No. 11).

6.3(8) Non-Parties

The Convention and the Convention Act prescribe rights and duties for persons who are parties to a written agreement to arbitrate – persons who have signed or otherwise assented to the agreement.[228] The same pattern is true for the Model Law and the English Arbitration Act.[229] The rights and duties of non-parties, if any, are not covered.

Although this pattern is continued in this Act, persons who are non-signatories may have some rights and duties in and around the arbitration agreement. Thus, the transferee or a third party beneficiary of a contract containing an arbitration clause may have a right to compel arbitration. On the other hand, a non-party may be estopped by conduct to deny the duty to arbitrate or be obligated to arbitrate because of the acts of an agent.[230] These and other rarely granted exceptions are left to case law development and application.[231]

In some cases a dispute with common issues of law and fact will involve some persons who are parties to an arbitration agreement and some persons who are not. Here the arbitration agreement will be enforced "notwithstanding the presence of other persons who are parties to the underlying dispute but not to the arbitration agreement."[232] The potential inefficiency in these arbitration situations cannot be cured by joinder of parties or impleader. An arbitration award will not bind non-parties, so further litigation may be

[228] Article II(1) & (2) refers specifically to "parties" to the arbitration agreement. Section 206 of the Convention Act states that a court "may direct that arbitration be held in accordance with the agreement."

[229] Section 72 of the English Arbitration Act deals with the rights of persons "alleged to be parties" who do not participate in the proceedings.

[230] *See JLM Industries, Inc., supra* Note 216, 387 F.3d at 177–8, where the court held that "under principles of estoppel, a non-signatory to an arbitration agreement may compel a signatory to that agreement to arbitrate a dispute" where a review of the "relationship among the parties, the contracts they signed . . . , and the issues that had arisen among them discloses that the issues the non-signatory is seeking to resolve in arbitration are intertwined with the agreement that the estopped party has signed." (Internal citations and quotations omitted.)

[231] For cases recognizing but not finding exceptions of this sort, *see InterGen N.V. v. Grina*, 344 F.3d 134 (1st Cir. 2003); *E.I. Dupont de Nemours and Co. v. Rhone Poulenc Fiber & Resin Intermediaries*, 269 F.3d 187 (3d Cir. 2001) (international arbitration). *See also Bridas S.A.P.I.C. v. Government of Turkenistan*, 345 F.3d 347 (5th Cir. 2003) (FAA). *cert. denied*, 541 U.S. 937 (2004). Care should be taken to distinguish the case where a signatory "waives" its right to arbitrate, *see Menorah Insurance Co. v. INX Reinsurance Corp.*, 72 F.3d 218 (1st Cir. 1995), from the case where a non-signatory assumes a duty to arbitrate by proceeding without objection to arbitrate or incorporating a written arbitration agreement in another contract by reference.

[232] *Moses H. Cone Memorial Hosp. v. Mercury Constr. Corp.*, 460 U.S. 1, 20 (1983).

required. Similarly, if litigation involving the same dispute has been brought by the non-party and is pending, the court will order the parties to the agreement to arbitrate and cannot, under the FAA at least, compel the non-party to arbitrate or stay the litigation. According to the Supreme Court, the court must rigorously enforce the arbitration agreement even if the result is "piecemeal" litigation, absent a different rule in another federal statute.[233]

One possibility is for a party to the arbitration agreement to invoke the inherent power of the court to control the disposition of cases on its docket by moving for a stay of litigation in an action brought by a non-signatory. Such a motion might be granted if (1) there are common issues in the arbitration and the court proceeding, (2) those issues will be finally settled by the arbitration, and (3) the petitioner shows that the non-signatory "will not hinder the arbitration, that the arbitration will be resolved within a reasonable time, and that such delay that may occur will not cause undue hardship to the parties."[234] Given the complexity of this test and the discretion of the court, this strategy is not likely to succeed. Moreover, efforts to involve non-parties in arbitral proceedings collide with the private autonomy principle upon which arbitration depends.

Section 6.4 The Middle Ground between Commencement of the Arbitration and the Award

6.4(1) Introduction

It is now time to enter the tricky middle ground between commencement of the arbitration and the final award.[235] Traditionally, this is an area where the script is written by the parties and the arbitrators rather than imposed by domestic law. Moreover, it is expected that the chosen arbitral rules, whether for an ad hoc or an institutional arbitration, can be "tailored to the particular needs and expectations of the parties."[236] Although this script is consistent with de-localized arbitration, there are two persistent questions that need to be considered: (1) should domestic arbitration law provide rules

[233] *Dean Witter Reynolds, Inc. v. Byrd*, 470 U.S. 213, 221 (1985) (arbitration agreement enforced despite pending securities claims in state court).

[234] *Cosmotek Mumessillik Ve Ticaret Ltd Sirkketi v. Cosmotek USA, Inc.*, 942 F. Supp. 757, 760 (D. Conn. 1996), quoting from *American Shipping Line v. Massan Shipping Indus.*, 885 F. Supp.499, 502 (S.D.N.Y. 1995).

[235] For a brief discussion, *see* Section 2.5(3), *supra*.

[236] Hans van Houtte, *Conduct of Arbitral Proceedings*, in Petar Sarcevic, Essays on International Commercials Arbitration 113 (1989) (hereafter cited as Petar Sarcevic, Essays).

and standards for the middle ground and, if so, to what extent should they be mandatory, and (2) under what circumstances, if at all, should a court be permitted to intervene upon a petition by a party or the tribunal before the award? Because the Model Law provides answers to both questions, we will explore them in this section.

Initiation or commencement of an arbitration by a party to the arbitration agreement[237] starts a sequence of events that is intended to culminate in a final arbitration award. These events, which include the appointment of arbitrators, arranging for the hearing, conducting the hearing, and making the final award, are primarily in the hands of the parties, the arbitrators, and the arbitral institutions and are regulated in most cases by the international arbitration rules adopted by the parties. This is the essence of arbitration practice.

The nature and quality of the proceedings in this zone are difficult to document. Nevertheless, one can predict that because many arbitrations arise from complex contracts, the arbitration hearing process will also be complex and take considerable time and money to complete.[238] Moreover, one can also reasonably expect that the forces of globalization will challenge the parties and institutions to develop new procedures for arbitration in cyberspace.[239] In this new era of international commercial arbitration, it is less likely that the hearing can be completed without one or more challenges to the procedure.

Neither the Convention nor the Convention Act deal with events in the middle ground.[240] They are left for agreement by the parties. Similarly, except for the court's residual power to appoint an arbitrator and, upon request,

[237] An arbitration is usually initiated or commenced when a party gives a written notice of arbitration to the administrator and the other party that contains a statement of claim and other information. *See* Article 2 of the American Arbitration Association International Rules of 2003 (AAA). These rules can be found at the AAA Website, http://www.adr.org/ftp. *See also* Model Law Art. 21; English Arbitration Act (EAA) §14.

[238] *See* Joachim G. Frick, ARBITRATION AND COMPLEX INTERNATIONAL CONTRACTS (2001). After describing the legal characteristics of complex contracts and the law applicable to them, Dr. Frick argues that arbitrators should have greater flexibility to adjust or adapt complex contracts to changed circumstances. *Id.* at 143–227. He also suggests that arbitration of disputes arising under complex contracts needs "special tools," such as provisions for multi-party arbitration and "fast track" arbitration.

[239] Katherine Lynch, THE FORCES OF ECONOMIC GLOBALIZATION: CHALLENGES TO THE REGIME OF INTERNATIONAL COMMERICAL ARBITRATION 345–99 (2004). Exactly what those procedures will be is yet to be determined.

[240] Section 206 of the Convention Act does empower the court to "appoint arbitrators in accordance with the provisions of the agreement." *See* Section 2.5(3), *supra.*

to compel the appearance of witnesses with documents,[241] Chapter 1 of the FAA is also silent on these matters. On the other hand, both the Model Law and the English Arbitration Act of 1996 provide a rather complete set of rules for these middle ground events, the effect of which (in most cases) can be varied by agreement. The contrast with international arbitration law in the United States, therefore, is striking. In international arbitrations subject to federal law, unless the parties have adopted a comprehensive set of arbitration rules there are few legislative default rules upon which the parties, the tribunal, or the court can rely. With these legislative gaps in the middle ground, it is no wonder that several states have enacted the Model Law as state law for international arbitration.[242]

This gap in legal coverage creates another set of problems. Under what circumstances and for what purposes can a court, upon the request of a party, intervene in the arbitral proceeding before an award is made? Unless there is specific statutory authority, such as authorization to appoint an arbitrator if all else fails, most courts under Chapter 1 of the FAA refuse to remove an allegedly biased arbitrator during the arbitration on the ground that such intervention will thwart the "prime objective of arbitration law [which] is to permit a just and expeditious result with a minimum of judicial interference."[243] This statement is facially consistent with the goal of delocalized arbitration but leaves the claim of misadventures in the arbitral process to the award enforcement stage.

An arbitration, however, may be facilitated rather than thwarted if prompt judicial intervention insures that the agreement of the parties is followed or supports other values in the arbitration process. It may be better to deal now with an existing problem that the tribunal or the administrator is unable to

[241] FAA §§5, 7.

[242] The Revised Uniform Arbitration Act (RUAA), on the other hand, has several sections applicable to the middle ground. They include provisions on the initiation of arbitration [§9], consolidation of separate arbitration proceedings [§10], appointment of and disclosure and actions by arbitrators [§§11–13], immunity of arbitrators [§14], the arbitration process [§15], and discovery [§15].

[243] *Certain Underwriters at Lloyd's v. Argonaut Ins.*, 264 F. Supp.2d 926, 936 (N.D.Cal. 2003), discussing cases and quoting from *Gulf Guar. Life Ins. Co. v. Connecticut General Life Ins. Co.*, 304 F.3d 476, 492 (5th Cir. 2002). *But see In re Certain Underwriters at Lloyd's London*, 1997 WL 461035 (N.D.Ill. 1997) (court has power to remove an arbitrator for actual misconduct or to enforce contract requirements of neutrality). Courts are more willing to intervene under FAA §4 where the arbitrators have ignored or failed to follow the parties' agreement in an otherwise enforceable arbitration clause on the venue for the arbitration. *See, e.g., Sterling Financial Inv. Group, Inc. v. Hammer*, 393 F.3d 1223, 1225 (11th Cir. 2004).

resolve rather than to wait for resolution under the limited grounds to deny recognition and enforcement of a final award under the Convention.[244] Put differently, utilizing limited judicial intervention to achieve a healthy arbitration award clearly trumps the pathological exercise of attacking a suspect award under Article V of the Convention.

These realities pose the questions for this section.

First, what should the legislative rules be for the middle ground and which of them are mandatory rules, the effect of which cannot be varied by agreement? I have tried to identify the most important candidates and leave the rest to agreement by the parties.

Second, under what circumstances should a court, upon request by a party, intervene in the proceedings before the award and for what purposes? Assuming that this intervention should be limited and available only after internal procedures have failed, the likely candidates are: (1) the failure of the parties or the appointing authority to appoint an arbitrator or to replace a terminated arbitrator, (2) challenges to the jurisdiction of the arbitral tribunal, (3) challenges to the impartiality or performance of an appointed arbitrator, (4) alleged misconduct by the tribunal in conducting the hearing, (5) requests to the tribunal for interim measures of protection, and (6) requests for judicial assistance in obtaining witnesses or other evidence deemed relevant to the hearing.[245]

One might plausibly argue that any judicial intervention for any reason in the middle ground impairs private autonomy and threatens the goal of de-localized arbitration. The challenge, then, is to propose judicial intervention in a way that preserves the value of autonomy and supports de-localized arbitration. Can this be done?

6.4(2) Commencing the Arbitration

Commencing (or initiating) the arbitration is an important first step in the arbitral process. An arbitration must be commenced by one party before the

[244] For example, suppose an arbitrator challenged for bias is not removed and participates in the final award. Under Article V(1) of the Convention there is no stated ground to deny recognition and enforcement because an arbitrator was partial or evidently partial. An award involving a partial or biased arbitrator may be against public policy under Article V(2)(b), *see AAOT Foreign Economic Ass'n v. Dev. & Trade Services, Inc.*, 139 F.3d 980 (2d Cir. 1998), but this defense is rarely successful in the United States. *See* Section 6.5(2)(B)(4), *infra*.

[245] *See* Section 6 of this Act, which states that no court shall intervene upon request or sua sponte "except where so provided by this Act."

other has a duty to arbitrate.[246] In most cases, the commencement process is governed by international arbitration rules incorporated into the contract to arbitrate. For example, in an ad hoc arbitration commencement is by notice given to the other party[247] and in an institutional arbitration by notice given to the administrator.[248] The arbitration commences on the date the notice with any other required information is received.[249]

In the absence of agreed rules, Article 21 of the Model Law provides that the "arbitral proceedings in respect of a particular dispute commence on the date on which a request for that dispute to be referred to arbitration is received by the respondent."[250] But who is the respondent? Under Section 14 of the English Arbitration Act, the answer turns on whether the arbitrators are named in the agreement or are to be appointed by the parties or an appointing authority. In the case where arbitrators are named in the agreement or are to be appointed by the parties, the notice goes to the other party. In cases where there is an appointing authority (other than the parties), the notice goes to the appointing authority. In essence, the notice requires the respondent to either submit the matter to named arbitrators or to implement the arbitral selection process.[251]

Given the importance of when the arbitration commences, Section 12 of this Act contains a provision based in part on Article 21 of the Model Law. Unless otherwise agreed, the arbitration is commenced at the time when "a request for that dispute to be referred to arbitration is received by the other parties to the agreement."[252] At this point the party commencing arbitration is required only to describe "the nature of the controversy and the remedy

[246] For example, the arbitration agreement cannot be enforced unless the other party has refused or failed to arbitrate after commencement. *See* Section 10(a) of this Act.

[247] UNCITRAL Arbitration rules Art. 3(1) (hereafter cited as UAR). These rules can be found at the UN Website, at http://www.un.or.at/Uncitral. *See* Jacomijn J. Van Hof, Commentary on the UNCITRAL Arbitration Rules: The Application by the Iran-U.S. Claims Commission (1991).

[248] AAA Art. 2(1).

[249] Typically, the rules state what information the notice of arbitration must and may contain. Under the AAA Rules, the notice of arbitration also constitutes the statement of claim, to which the other party must respond with a statement or defense or a counterclaim. AAA Art. 2–4. Under the UAR, the notice of arbitration may but need not constitute a statement of claim. *See* UAR Art. 18–20. When notice in electronic form is received is stated in Section 4 of this Act.

[250] Article 3 of the Model Law states when a written communication is received. Article 23 deals with the statement of claim and defense.

[251] *See* Section 9 of the Revised Uniform Arbitration Act (RUAA), which requires notice as agreed or otherwise prescribed "to the other parties to the agreement." The notice "must describe the nature of the controversy and the remedy sought."

[252] On when notice is received, *see* Section 4 of this Act.

sought." The details of claim, defense, and counterclaim are not covered by this Act.

6.4(3) Place of Arbitration

Under Section 1(b)(1), this Act applies the if "place of the arbitration is in a state or territory of the United States." Because the exact place is a matter for agreement by the parties, this Act can be chosen if the parties agree to arbitrate in, say, New York or Chicago or Los Angeles. If the parties fail to agree and have adopted international arbitration rules, those rules stipulate who is to decide the place of arbitration and by what standards. Thus, in an ad hoc arbitration the tribunal shall decide "having regard to the circumstances of the arbitration,"[253] and in an institutional arbitration the decision will be made by the administrator.[254]

In the absence of an agreement or upon the failure of the tribunal or the institution to act, neither the Convention, the Convention Act, nor Chapter 1 of the FAA state who should select the place of arbitration. Under Section 13 of this Act, the omission is rectified by providing that, when all else fails, the decision "shall be determined by the court."

Regardless of where the arbitration takes place, it is assumed that the parties have power to choose (by agreement) the arbitration law of another country to govern the proceedings.

6.4(4) Appointment of Arbitrators and Challenges

When the arbitrator(s) are appointed the arbitration can proceed.[255] Problems arise, however, when the appointment process fails to produce an arbitrator or when a vacancy arises because an appointed arbitrator is successfully challenged or is unable or unwilling to perform his or her duties. International arbitration rules typically designate an appointing authority and state the procedures to be followed. But suppose the parties have not reached an agreement or the procedure they agreed to fails. What happens next? Does the arbitration founder?

[253] UAR Art. 16.1

[254] *See* AAA Art. 13(1). In arbitrations administered by the London Court of International Arbitration (LCIA) or the International Chamber of Commerce (ICC), the decision is made by the LCIA or the ICC "court." ICC Art. 14(1), Art. LCIA 16.1 (place of arbitration is London unless court decides that another seat is more appropriate).

[255] For a helpful overview, *see* C.C.A. Voskuil & Judith Ann Freedberg-Swartzburg, *Composition of the Arbitral Tribunal*, in SARCEVIC, ESSAYS, *supra* Note 236 at 64.

The answer, of course, should be "no," a result that is assured under Section 14 of this Act.

6.4(4)(A) Court as Appointing Authority

Solutions to these problems are facilitated under modern international arbitration rules. For example, the AAA Rules (which can be varied by agreement) provide the default number of arbitrators, procedures for appointment, standards to which prospective arbitrators must satisfy before appointment, procedures and standards for challenging arbitrators, and procedures for replacing an arbitrator.[256] In addition, Article 11 instructs the tribunal how to proceed if there is a vacancy and what to do if a vacancy is filled by an arbitrator who has not participated in prior hearings.[257]

Unlike the ICC and the LCIA rules,[258] the parties under the AAA Rules have power to mutually designate arbitrators "with or without the assistance of the administrator."[259] But if a mutual designation or an agreed or default procedure fails, it is clear that the administrator shall make the appointment and that the arbitration shall proceed. In short, under international arbitration rules neither party can avoid an otherwise valid agreement to arbitrate simply because agreed or default arbitrator appointment procedures fail. In these cases, the administrator or institutional "court" makes the appointment[260] and the parties are obligated to proceed.

It is highly unlikely that the institutional or other appointing authority will fail to act. If they do fail to act, however, Section 14(b) of this Act provides a default rule: "any party may request the court to appoint a sole arbitrator."[261] In this situation, the court's role is limited to an appointing

[256] AAA Art. 5–10.

[257] A similar pattern is found in the UNCITRAL Arbitration Rules, Art. 5–14.

[258] Under these rules, the parties may nominate potential arbitrators but the actual appointment is made by the LCIA or the ICC Court. *See* LCIA Art. 5.5 ("The LCIA alone is empowered to appoint arbitrators").

[259] AAA Art. 6(2).

[260] In an ad hoc arbitration under the UNCITRAL Rules, the same result follows either because the parties have agreed on an appointing authority or because such a person has been appointed by the Secretary General of the Permanent Court of Arbitration at the Hague. UAR Art. 6(2). *See* Jacomijn J. Van Hof, Commentary on the UNCITRAL Arbitration Rules: The Application by the Iran-U.S. Claims Commission 44–50 (1991).

[261] Section 14(a)(i) of this Act provides that unless otherwise agreed a "sole arbitrator shall be appointed." This rejects Section 10(2) of the Model Law, where the default number is three, and follows Section 15(3) of the English Arbitration Act, Section 5 of the Federal Arbitration Act, and the rules of most arbitration institutions. *See* ICC Art. 9, LCIA Art. 5.4, and AAA Art. 6(3). The reason is that the cost of three arbitrators is likely to be three times

authority and the appointment, which is final and not appealable, must be made with "due regard" to the factors stated in Section 14(c) of this Act.

6.4(4)(B) Absence of or Failure to Follow Agreed Appointment Procedures

Section 14(b) of this Act, which is consistent with Section 5 of the FAA, clarifies American law. Section 14(b) provides in part:

> The parties may agree on a procedure for appointing the arbitrator or arbitrators. If the parties fail to agree on a procedure, or one party fails to act under an agreed procedure, or an appointing authority fails to perform any function entrusted to it under such procedure, upon application the court shall appoint a sole arbitrator.

The clarification is this. Under Article V(1)(d) of the Convention, an international arbitration award may be denied recognition and enforcement if the "composition of the arbitral tribunal . . . was not in accordance with the agreement of the parties, or failing such agreement, was not in accordance with the law of the country where the arbitration took place." Under this subsection, the answer to two cases is clear. First, if the parties have adopted institutional or ad hoc arbitration rules, the award should be confirmed if those rules on appointment of the tribunal have been followed. Thus, if the parties agree to three arbitrators and three are appointed there is no problem. Second, if the parties have adopted no arbitration rules but the composition of the tribunal is in accord with the law at the seat of arbitration, the award should be confirmed. Under Section 14(1)(a) of this Act, one arbitrator should be appointed. A third case is more difficult. Suppose the parties have adopted arbitration rules that three arbitrators shall be appointed. Instead, only one arbitrator was appointed and this was in accordance with applicable law but not with the agreement. Should the award be confirmed? Or is this case within Article V(1)(d)?

Under a sensible reading of the Convention, the answer is that the award should not be confirmed. According to a leading commentator, an award may be refused under Article V(1)(d) when the composition of the arbitral

the cost of one and this burden should not be imposed on the parties unless they agree otherwise.

Section 14(a)(b) of this Act provides that "no person shall be precluded by reason of his nationality from acting as an arbitrator." This follows Article 11(1) of the Model Law, but is variable by agreement. For example, Article 6.1 of the LCIA Rules reverses the default rule for a sole arbitrator or the chair of a tribunal: they shall not have the same nationality as any party to the arbitration unless there is a contrary agreement.

tribunal "was not in accordance with the agreement of the parties, *or in the absence of an agreement* on these matters, was not in accordance with the law of the country where the arbitration took place" (emphasis added). Notice how the phrase "failing such agreement" is interpreted to mean the "absence of an agreement."[262] After discussing the complex question of applicable law, the commentator then concludes that there is no defense under Article V(I)(d) if the arbitral procedure was in accord with the agreement but not with the "mandatory provisions of the law governing these matters" but that there is a defense if the arbitral procedure "was not in accordance with the agreement of the parties although it was in accordance with the law governing these matters."[263] This interpretation, on the one hand, preserves the value of private autonomy but, on the other hand, denies enforcement to an award made under procedures that conformed to applicable law.[264]

What is applicable international arbitration law in cases like this? Again, Article V(1(d) points to the law of the "country where the arbitration took place" but does not provide an answer. Suppose the arbitration was held in New York City. Section 206 of the Convention Act provides that the court with jurisdiction to direct that arbitration be held also has power to "appoint arbitrators in accordance with the provisions of the agreement." So far so good, but suppose there was no agreement. Does this mean that the court has no power to appoint an arbitrator under the Convention? The answer is no because of Section 5 of Chapter 1 of the FAA, which authorizes a court to appoint an arbitrator where there was no agreement (as well as in cases where there was an agreement and it was not followed or availed of). This is, of course, a circuitous route to this conclusion because FAA Section 5 would not apply to an international arbitration unless that section was not in conflict with the Convention or the Convention Act – an interpretation required by Section 208 of the Convention Act.

Thus, Section 14(b–d) of this Act is a straightforward solution to the puzzle of when a court can act as an appointing authority in an international arbitration. In the interest of protecting a final arbitration award, it clarifies that if the arbitrator appointment process complied with applicable law but not the agreement the award should be confirmed.[265]

[262] Van den Berg, New York Convention, *supra* Note 159 at 322 (1981).

[263] *Id.* at 327.

[264] At least one court has confirmed an award in accord with applicable law even though the parties have failed to comply with the agreed procedure. *See Al Haddad Bros. Enterprises, Inc. v. M/S Agapi*, 635 F. Supp. 205 (D. Del. 1986), *aff'd*, 813 F.2d 396 (3d Cir. 1987) (table).

[265] An important question is why did the agreed procedure fail in the first place? One possible answer is because both parties had second thoughts and agreed by conduct or by a waiver to a different procedure. Another reason comes from the default of one party: a refusal

6.4(4)(C) Challenge to and Termination of Arbitrator Appointment

Under the Model Law the court occupies a prominent backup role in the appointment, challenge, termination, and replacement of arbitrators. As just noted, if an arbitrator is not appointed under applicable procedures, agreed or otherwise, the court shall make the appointment and that decision "shall be subject to no appeal."[266] This is the operative principle in Sections 15(b) and (c) of this Act.

(1) Disclosure and Challenge

Influenced by Articles 12 and 13 of the Model Law, all modern international arbitration rules impose a continuing duty of disclosure on potential and appointed arbitrators, state grounds to challenge an arbitrator, and provide a challenge procedure.[267] Thus, even though the Model Law has not been enacted in the country where the arbitration is held, the contract itself typically states the requirements and procedures for disclosure, challenge, and removal. These rules, however, tend to confide "sole discretion" in the administrator or appointing authority to decide the challenge.[268] Thus, if the decision denies the challenge there is no explicit authority in the contract for the challenging party to resort to court.

Under the Model Law, however, a challenge to an arbitrator is made to the arbitral tribunal rather than the appointing authority (unless otherwise agreed) which "shall decide on the challenge."[269] The unsuccessful party may make a timely request to the court to decide the challenge and "such decision shall be subject to no appeal."[270] In contrast to cases where the court acts as an appointing authority, here the court is invited to decide (not review) the challenge after the tribunal has decided against it. But should access to court also be permitted when the challenge is denied by the appointing authority

to comply. Section 14(d) insures this default will not prevent the arbitration itself from proceeding. *See* Sections 17 and 18 of the English Arbitration Act. The probable reason in this case is that the arbitrators deviated from the agreed procedure and made an award that was otherwise permitted by applicable law.

266 Model Law Art. 11(3)(a), 3(b), 4(b), 5.

267 *See, e.g.,* ICC Art. 11, AAA. Art. 8–9, LCIA Art. 5.3. Both Australia and the State of California have enacted the Model Law. In *HSMV Corp. v. ADI Ltd.*, 72 F. Supp.2d 1122 (C. D. Cal. 1999), an arbitration between an Australian and an American corporation with the arbitration held in California, the court held that Article 12 of the Model Law required arbitrator to disclose relevant information before appointment and imposed a continuing duty to disclose possible conflicts of interest after appointment.

268 AAA Art. 9 (administrator); ICC Art. 11(3) (ICC Court); LCIA Art. 10.4 (LCIA Court).

269 Model Law, Art. 13(2).

270 Model Law Art. 13(3).

rather than the arbitral tribunal? Under what circumstances does judicial intervention in that case support rather than thwart arbitration?

There are several factors to consider. First, there is no explicit ground in Article V of the Convention to deny recognition and enforcement of an award because an arbitrator was apparently (based upon what was not disclosed) partial to or dependent on one party. Thus, if the matter is not corrected before the award, the losing party will have to persuade the court that the award was "against public policy" under Article V(2)(b).[271] In the United States at least, this is virtually impossible to do.[272] Second, who decides the challenge, an appointing authority such as the AAA, or a court, or the tribunal? If the tribunal decides, one might doubt their objectivity in granting the challenge, especially if the challenged arbitrator participates in the decision. These factors tend to support judicial intervention.

Under Section 15(c) of this Act, however, the challenge is made to and decided by the "agreed appointing authority," typically an arbitration institution. Should a decision against the challenge by the appointing authority be subject to pre-award judicial review? I think that the answer is yes. Conceding that a conflict of interest is less likely in this situation, especially where a reputable institution is involved, there are arguably many appointing authorities around the world whose reputation for independence and balance in these matters is not well established. Moreover, a decision by any appointing authority against a challenge where actual bias or misconduct by an arbitrator is alleged is suspect, especially where the arbitral institution has strong cultural and legal ties to the place where the arbitration is held. Thus, Article 15(d) of this Act provides that "if a challenge is denied by an agreed appointing authority, the challenging party may make a timely motion to the court to decide the challenge, which decision shall be subject to no appeal."[273] This provision creates a right to judicial review in

[271] *See AAOT Foreign Economic Ass'n v. Dev. & Trade Services, Inc.*, 139 F.3d 980 (2d Cir. 1998) (recognizing ground but holding that the petitioner had waived its right by failing to timely object).

[272] *See* discussion at Section 6.5(2)(B)(4), *infra*. Note that an award may be vacated under FAA §10(a)(2) for "evident partiality" and that ground might not be in conflict with the Convention. *See* Convention Act §208. In other words, a court might be persuaded to use "evident partiality" as a ground to deny recognition and enforcement in an international arbitration.

[273] Section 24(1)(a) of the English Arbitration Act permits a party to apply to the court to remove an arbitrator if "circumstances exist that give rise to justifiable doubts as to his impartiality" provided that the applicant "has first exhausted any available recourse" to an "arbitral or other institution or person vested by the parties with power to remove an arbitrator." EAA §24(2).

this limited situation and, therefore, trumps institutional arbitration rules providing that such decisions by the institution are final.[274]

(2) Termination of Arbitrator Appointment

An arbitrator's appointment may be terminated for grounds other than partiality, such as the inability to perform his functions or if the arbitrator "for other reasons fails to act without undue delay."[275] Section 16 of this Act deals with these situations. If the arbitrator does not voluntarily withdraw or the parties do not agree on termination, the parties may request the appointing authority (or the court if there is no appointing authority) to decide the termination issue without a right to appeal.[276]

A nagging question when challenges are made or an appointment is terminated for other grounds is the effect on the ongoing proceedings. The general rule is that the arbitral proceedings shall continue during the challenge. Section 15(e) of this Act states that when a challenge for partiality is pending, the "arbitral tribunal, including the challenged arbitrator, may continue the arbitral proceedings and make an award." The same principle applies to terminations under Article 16. Although not specifically covered by this Act,[277] the matter is covered by applicable arbitration rules. Once the replacement arbitrator has been appointed, the institution or appointing authority typically decides "if and to what extent prior proceedings shall be repeated before the reconstituted Arbitral Tribunal."[278]

In sum, I have proposed three sections of this Act dealing with the composition of the arbitral tribunal. These sections are consistent with the Model Law and are, in the main, default rules the effect of which can be varied by agreement. In these sections the court's role is limited to appointing a sole arbitrator when all else fails and making a final decision when a challenge to an arbitrator is denied by either the tribunal or the institution. All other matters are left to the parties, the tribunal, and the arbitral institution.

[274] *See* ICC Rules Art. 7(4).

[275] Section 16(a) of this Act.

[276] Section 24 of the English Arbitration Act gives the court power to remove an arbitrator for stated grounds other than impartiality, providing that internal procedures have been exhausted.

[277] The Model Law does not cover this problem. Section 27(4) of the English Arbitration Act, however, provides that the "tribunal (when reconstituted) shall determine whether and if so to what extent the previous proceedings shall stand." Further: "This does not affect any right of a party to challenge those proceedings on any ground which had arisen before the arbitrator ceased to hold office."

[278] ICC Art. 12(4). *See* AAA Art. 11.

6.4(5) Jurisdiction of the Tribunal: Competence and Separability

6.4(5)(A) Introduction: Arbitrability Revisited

The arbitrability issues treated in Section 6.3 may arise for the first time after commencement of the arbitration in the form of a challenge by a party to the tribunal's jurisdiction.[279] Under Article II of the Convention, arbitrability involves whether there is (1) a written agreement between the parties to arbitrate something, (2) a dispute or controversy within the scope of that written arbitration agreement, (3) a dispute that is capable of being arbitrated, and (4) a written arbitration agreement that is otherwise enforceable, that is, not "null and void, inoperative or incapable of being performed."

Arbitrability questions go to the power (competence) of the tribunal to decide the merits of a dispute otherwise within the scope of the agreement to arbitrate. If a dispute is not arbitrable, the tribunal has no power to act.[280] A recurring disputed question is who, court or tribunal, has power to decide the competence question and if the tribunal has power to what degree that decision is subject to further review in the courts. For example, suppose that the power of the tribunal is challenged by one party after the tribunal was selected and the hearing is underway. Does the tribunal have power to decide its own jurisdiction? If so, should that decision be given a deferential review by the court or a de novo hearing?

The competence question is closely related to the "separability" doctrine, a doctrine that attempts to separate the arbitration clause from the written contract in which it was included. Pushed to extremes, in cases where the tribunal has no power to decide arbitrability it may have power under a broad arbitration clause to decide the enforceability of the underlying contract in which the arbitration clause is contained without deciding the validity of the arbitration clause itself. But at some point the "competence" and "separability" doctrines merge and the lines become blurred. For example, suppose one party claims that the underlying contract was void because of a forgery or the failure of mutual assent. Does the "separability" doctrine apply (meaning that the tribunal has power to decide the merits with the award entitled to deferential review), or does the question involve competence? If

[279] The issues may also arise for the first time after the award as a challenge to recognition and enforcement. *See* Convention Art. II, IV(1)(a), (b), 2(a).

[280] The "competence" and "separability" issues are treated briefly in Sections 2.4(2)(B) (5 & 6) and Section 2.5(2)(B)(4), *supra*.

the underlying contract is void, the argument goes, how can an arbitration clause contained therein be valid?

We will try (and I emphasize the word "try") to resolve these questions in this subsection.

6.4(5)(B) Competence

Under American arbitration law, the federal district court has power to decide arbitrability questions at all stages of the arbitration process. Subject to the timing of any appeal under Section 16 of the FAA, district court decisions on arbitrability are subject to a de novo review in the courts of appeal.[281] The tribunal, however, does not presumptively have power to decide arbitrability, even if the parties have agreed to a "broad" arbitration clause. In the *First Options* case, the Supreme Court held (under Chapter 1 of the FAA) that the tribunal had such power only if there was a "clear and unmistakable evidence" that the parties have agreed to arbitrate the question of arbitrability.[282] In dictum, the Court suggested that if the tribunal had such power, a decision on arbitrability might be entitled to "deferential" review in the courts. The Court, however, did not clearly say whether the decision on the merits was immune from review or, if not, what deferential standard less than a de novo review would be proper.

In international arbitration, the consensus answer is that both court and tribunal have competence to decide arbitrability issues. The court's power derives from the specific language of Articles II and V of the Convention and Sections 206 and 208 of the Convention Act. The tribunal's power, unless otherwise agreed, derives from international practice and usage, modern arbitration statutes, such as the Model Law and the English Arbitration Act, and the rules of every international arbitration institution.[283] This, however, is a concurrent power with the court and, as we shall see, is subject to some sort of judicial review.

[281] *See, e.g., JLM Industries, Inc. v. Stolt-Nielsen SA*, 387 F.3d 163, 169 (2d Cir. 2004) (reviewing district court's determination of arbitrability de novo). District court decisions on whether an award under the Convention should be confirmed are reviewed under a similar standard. *See China Minmetals Materials Import & Export Co., Ltd. v. Chi Mei Corp.*, 334 F.3d 274, 278 (3d Cir. 2003) (review district court's factual findings for clear error and its legal conclusions de novo).

[282] *First Options of Chicago v. Kaplan*, 514 U.S. 938, 944 (1995).

[283] *See, e.g.,* Tibor Varady et al., International Commercial Arbitration: A Transnational Perspective 109–35 (2d ed. 2003); Redfern & Hunter 264–76 (3d ed. 1999). *See also* Model Law, Art. 16(1); English Arbitration Act Art. 30, and the international arbitration rules of the AAA Art. 26; LCIA Art. 26.3, 26.4, and the ICC Art. 25(1).

6.4(5)(C) Separability

The "competence" question is closely allied with the separability doctrine, which gives the arbitration agreement a life independent and apart from the contract in which it is contained. In essence, "separability" means that there are two distinct contracts, the contract to arbitrate and the exchange contract in which the arbitration clause is contained.[284] In the paradigm case, suppose that the arbitration clause is otherwise valid and the parties have agreed to arbitrate all disputes "arising under or relating to" the underlying contract. Under American domestic arbitration law, the tribunal would have power to decide a claim that the underlying contract was voidable because of fraud unless there were "separate allegations" that the fraud induced the arbitration agreement rather than relating to the contract as a whole.[285] At some point however, the separability doctrine, pushed to the extreme, runs into the competence problem. Suppose, for example, that a party claims that the alleged contract in which the arbitration clause was contained was never formed because the requisite consent did not occur. If the tribunal is not competent to decide its own jurisdiction does it have power to decide an attack on the very existence of the underlying contract? Noting this dilemma, the courts have debated the point at which an attack on "very existence" of the underlying contract is an attack on the validity of the arbitration agreement, an issue which the court must decide. As one court put it:

> [W]here the very existence of an agreement is challenged, ordering arbitration could result in an arbitrator deciding that no agreement was ever formed. Such an outcome would be a statement that the arbitrator never had any authority

[284] The "separability" doctrine under Chapter 1 of the FAA was recognized in *Prima Paint Corp. v. Flood & Conklin Mfg. Co.*, 388 U.S. 395, 402–4 (1967). The Court held that the tribunal under a broad arbitration clause could decide whether the underlying contract was voidable for fraud. Because the fraud defense did not relate specifically to the arbitration agreement, the competence question did not arise. *See Primerica Life Ins. Co. v. Brown*, 304 F.3d 469 (5th Cir. 2003) (party's mental capacity to execute contract containing arbitration clause is arbitrable). Professor Ware argues for the repeal of the "separability" doctrine under Chapter 1 of the FAA, at least where the existence of the underlying contract is at issue. Section 4.2, *supra*. Whatever your view of the private autonomy principle, the separability principle is important in international arbitration law. If the default rule is that the tribunal has power to decide its own jurisdiction but that decision is subject to de novo review, the separability doctrine insures that decisions on the validity of the underlying contract, whether involving the arbitration clause or not, are on the merits of the claim (under the broad arbitration clause) and are subject to deferential review under Article V of the Convention.

[285] *See Highlands Wellmont Health v. John Deere Health Plan, Inc.*, 350 F.3d 568, 575–6 (6th Cir. 2003) (reviewing authorities).

> to decide the issues. A presumption that a signed document represents an agreement could lead to this untenable result. We therefore conclude that where a party attacks the very existence of an agreement as opposed to the its continued validity or enforcement, the court must first resolve that dispute.[286]

This interpretation of Chapter 1 of the Federal Arbitration Act conflicts with our de-localized arbitration goal and with Section 16(1) of the Model Law, which provides:

> The arbitral tribunal may rule on its own jurisdiction, including any objection with respect to the existence or validity of the arbitration agreement. For that purpose, an arbitration clause which forms part of a contract shall be treated as an agreement independent of the other terms of the contract. A decision by the arbitral tribunal that the contract is null and void shall not entail ipso jure the invalidity of the arbitration clause.[287]

6.4(5)(D) Legal Status of Tribunal Decision on Competence

Sections 17(a) and 17(b) of this Act, which follows Section 16(1) of the Model Law, are consistent with the English Arbitration Act[288] and modern international arbitration rules[289] on both the competence and separability issues. It reduces the risk that the tribunal will not have power to decide its own jurisdiction and that the separability doctrine will founder where the claim is that the underlying contract was void. Thus, under a broad international arbitration clause contained in a written contract, the tribunal has power without more to decide both disputes arising under and relating to the contract and attacks on the arbitration clause itself.

At best, however, this creates concurrent power with the courts. The fact that the tribunal has and exercises the power does not mean there is no judicial review. The questions are (1) when will that review be made, and (2) what are the standards of review?

With regard to the first question, it is possible that the court will decide the arbitrability question before the arbitration commences. If so, the decision is taken from the tribunal. But suppose the court refers the issue to the yet

[286] *Will-Drill Resources, Inc. v. Samson Resources Co.*, 352 F.3d 211, 218 (5th Cir. 2003).

[287] For a collection of cases interpreting and applying Section 16(1) *see* Henri C. Alvarez, Neil Kaplan, & David W. Rivkin, Model Law Decisions: Cases Applying the UNCITRAL Model Law on International Commercial Arbitration (1985–2001) 167–76 (2003). Australian courts have held that the tribunal has authority to determine whether the underlying contract was "void" and some Canadian courts have deferred a judicial challenge to arbitrability and sent the issue for decision to the tribunal.

[288] EAA 30.

[289] *See* AAA 26; LCIA 26.3, 26.4; ICC 25(1).

to be appointed tribunal[290] for decision or the tribunal after appointment decides it under a challenge to its jurisdiction, which is permitted under Section 17(3) of this Act. The second question now arises, what is the scope of judicial review?

Unfortunately, Section 16 of the Model Law does not answer this question. Section 16(3) provides that the tribunal may rule on its jurisdiction "either as a preliminary question or in an award on the merits."[291] Further, if the tribunal rules as a preliminary question that it "has jurisdiction," a party may file a timely petition to the court to decide the question, from which there shall be "no appeal." No standard of judicial review is stated and because the ruling is not strictly speaking an award, the limitations on review imposed by Article V of the Convention arguable do not apply. While the petition is pending the "arbitral tribunal may continue the arbitral proceedings and make an award."[292]

Suppose, however, that the tribunal rules on the question "in an award on the merits." For example, assume that the tribunal, with competence to decide, determined in an award that there was an "agreement in writing" as required by Article II(1) of the Convention and that the arbitration agreement was not "null and void." This award on arbitrability should be protected from judicial review to the extent provided by Article V of the Convention. Unfortunately, these arbitrability decisions are reviewable under Article V, even though made in a final award.[293] Article V, however, does not state how much deference if any a court should give to the award. Recent decisions by American courts have held that before granting recognition and enforcement of a foreign award, the court must at a minimum make "an independent determination of the agreement's validity and, therefore,

[290] This could happen if the arbitrability issue was raised in a motion to compel arbitration or stay judicial proceedings made before the arbitration was commenced. The issue is also raised by a motion to enjoin a pending arbitration. Courts have power to hear and grant this injunction even though it is not specifically authorized by arbitration statutes. *See Klay v. United Health Group, Inc.*, 376 F.3d 1092 (11th Cir. 2004) (recognizing power but vacating district court's issuance of injunction against arbitration as unwarranted).

[291] Model Law Art. 16(3).

[292] *See* Section 17(3) of this Act.

[293] If the tribunal decides in an award on the merits that it does have jurisdiction, the scope of review will turn on what aspect of jurisdiction has been determined. For example, an award that the arbitration agreement was valid will be denied recognition and enforcement if it was "not valid" under applicable local law. Convention Art. V(1)(a). Similarly, a decision that a dispute was within the scope of the arbitration agreement will be reviewed under Art. V(1)(c) and a decision that the dispute was "capable" of settlement by arbitration will be reviewed under the law of the country where recognition and enforcement is sought under Art. V(2)(1). No particular deference to the tribunal's award on jurisdiction is given by Article V.

the arbitrability of the dispute."[294] In short, no deference is given to the tribunal's decision.

6.4(5)(E) Some Lingering Questions

Even though Section 17 of this Act gives an international arbitration tribunal power to determine its own jurisdiction, it is a power exercised concurrently with the courts. If the tribunal decides in an award that it has jurisdiction, the court, if petitioned, will review the decision in the process of enforcing the award. Because the decision involves arbitrability rather than the merits of the dispute, American courts will give what seems to be an independent (de novo) review. On the other hand, the expanded scope of the separability doctrine reduces the risk that a "void" underlying contract, that is, where there was never mutual assent to a bargain, raises issues of arbitrability. Unless the grounds for attacking the underlying contract overlap with the grounds in Article II for attacking arbitrability, an award on the merits (that the underlying contract was not void) is entitled to deferential review under Article V of the Convention.[295] In short, there is no review of the merits.

If, in international arbitration, the tribunal has power (unless otherwise agreed) to determine its own jurisdiction and this decision is subject to de novo judicial review, does that mean the so-called "separability" doctrine has no further utility? After all, if the tribunal has power to determine its own jurisdiction and the merits of the case, what value is separability? The guarded answer is no. Despite the overlaps, if a dispute is within the scope of the separability doctrine it is entitled to deferential (no) review under Article V of the Convention. Broadly conceived, if the separability

294 China Minmetals Materials, *supra* Note 281, 334 F.3d at 289. *See also Czarina, L.L.C. v. W.F. Poe Syndicate*, 358 F.3d 1286, 1293 (11th Cir. 2004) (refusing to take at "face value" tribunal's finding that parties had agreed to arbitrate).

295 Section 7 of the English Act follows and elaborates the principle of Section 16(1) and the commentary concludes that the validity of the separate arbitration clause "must be examined as a separate issue." Bruce Harris, Rowan Planterose, & Jonothan Tecks, The Arbitration Act of 1966: A Commentary 79 (2d ed. 1999). Section 7 states that the arbitration clause "shall not be regarded as invalid, non-existent or ineffective because that other agreement is invalid, or did not come into existence or has become ineffective, and it shall for that purpose be treated as a distinct agreement." *See* Commentary at 79. Regardless of who decides the question, the standards for the validity of the arbitration agreement and the enforceability of the underlying contract differ. For a recent article that both defends the separability doctrine and proposes a revision of the FAA to clarify when the tribunal is competent to determine arbitrability issues, *see* John J. Barcelo III, *Who Decides the Arbitrator's Jurisdiction? Separability and Competence-Competence in Transnational Perspective*, 36 Vand. J. Trans'l Law 1115 (2003).

doctrine encompasses every dispute going to the validity of the underlying contract, these issues involve the merits of the dispute not questions of competence. The difficulty arises in a case where the question is whether the parties ever assented in writing to the underlying contract containing the arbitration clause. Does the separability doctrine (and deferential review) cover a case where compliance with the writing requirements of Article II of the Convention is at stake? The answer may depend upon whether the parties have power by agreement to vary the content of Article II of the Convention or any other requirement of arbitrability in the Convention. In cases of the writing requirement, capability, and validity of the arbitration agreement, the answer appears to be no. These are mandatory rules. In these cases, then, even if the tribunal has power to decide them, the award cannot escape the scrutiny of the courts.

6.4(6) Interim Measures

Section 18 of this Act deals with the power of the tribunal to order interim measures. It follows Section 11 of this Act dealing with the power of courts to order interim measures before the tribunal is appointed and limits the power of the court once the tribunal is "appointed and authorized to act."[296] But the basic principle is clear: it is not "incompatible with an arbitration agreement for a party to request, before or after the tribunal is appointed for [interim] relief and for the tribunal to grant it."[297]

The application of Section 18 is illustrated by a recent case.[298] A Chinese concern contracted with Apex, a California corporation, to export goods to the United States. The parties agreed to submit "all disputes" to arbitration in China under the CIETAC Rules. Apex found problems with the goods and suspended payments allegedly due. China National filed for a writ of attachment on Apex's assets pending the outcome of the arbitration. The magistrate granted the writ and Apex appealed, arguing that (1) the district court had no power to issue an attachment under the Convention and the Convention Act or, in the alternative, that (2) the tribunal had no authority under CIETAC Rules to order interim relief. Rather, the tribunal must submit the request for relief to a People's Court. At this time, the tribunal had

[296] Sections 11 and 18 of this Act follow Section 8 of the Revised Uniform Arbitration Act. *See* Timothy J. Heinsz, *The Revised Uniform Arbitration Act: Modernizing, Revising, and Clarifying Arbitration Law*, 2001 J. Disp. Res. 21–6. (2001).

[297] Section 16(c) of this Act.

[298] *China Nat. Metal Products Import/Export Co. v. Apex Digital, Inc.*, 155 F. Supp.2d 1174 (C. D. Cal. 2001).

not been appointed. The district court affirmed the magistrate's decision that there was power to issues a writ of attachment in aid of arbitration but vacated the writ because the CIETAC Rules, to which both parties had agreed, provided a mechanism through the tribunal to obtain interim relief.

Sections 11 and 18(a) of this Act confirm the power of a federal district court to order interim relief in arbitration subject to the Convention. The disagreement among the courts on this issue is resolved.[299] Section 18(a), however, provides that the power cannot be exercised after the "tribunal is appointed and authorized to act." Thus, in the China case under discussion, the writ of attachment should have been issued because no tribunal had yet been appointed under CIETAC Rules. Even if the tribunal had been appointed and had power to act, the Chinese party would have some protection under Section 18(b)(2). Apex's assets are in California and it is highly unlikely that the arbitrator in China or the People's Court would be able to provide an "adequate remedy."

In sum, whoever is authorized to issue an order for interim measures, court or tribunal, the order must be "necessary to protect the effectiveness of the arbitration proceeding and to promote the fair and expeditious resolution of the controversy."[300] Appropriate security may also be required. When exercised with care, these powers are consistent with the goal of delocalized arbitration.

6.4(7) Conduct of the Arbitral Proceeding

6.4(7)(A) Introduction

Neither the Convention nor the Convention Act provide any guidance on how the arbitration should be conducted. Article V of the Convention, of course, provides indirect guidance by listing the failures that justify denying recognition and enforcement to an award. Thus, recognition and enforcement "may" be denied where (1) a party was not given proper notice of the arbitration proceedings or was "otherwise unable to present his case," (2) the arbitrators decided matters beyond the "terms of the submission to arbitration," or (3) the arbitral proceeding was "not in accordance with the

[299] *See China National Metals*, *supra* Note 298, 155 F. Supp.2d at 1179–80, discussing the conflict and concluding that the "congressional desire to enforce arbitration agreements would frequently be frustrated if the courts were precluded from issuing preliminary injunctive relief to preserve the status quo pending arbitration and, ipso factor, the meaningfulness of the arbitration process."

[300] Section 18(b)(2) of this Act.

agreement of the parties."[301] Given this indirect control and the fact that most international arbitration rules state affirmative duties in the conduct of the proceedings, should this Act say anything more about the problem?

In my judgment, the answer is yes. Although the exact scope and content is open to debate, the following provisions state more clearly the mandatory rules applicable to the process, the balance between the parties' agreement and the arbitrator's discretion, and the role of the court in this process before the award is made.[302]

6.4(7)(B) Conduct of the Arbitral Proceedings

(1) Powers and Duties of the Tribunal

Section 19 of this Act deals with various aspects of the arbitral proceedings.

Subsection (a) states a mandatory due process requirement: the "parties shall be treated with equality and each party shall be given a reasonable opportunity to present his case."[303] Subsection (b) then leaves most matters of procedure to the agreement of the parties or the discretion of the arbitrators and confers broad power on the arbitrators to decide questions of evidence. Thus, under Section 19 of this Act a party is "unable to present his case" within Article V(1)(b) of the Convention when he has not been treated "with equality" or was not afforded "a reasonable opportunity to present his case."[304]

Subsection (c) gives the parties or the tribunal discretion to meet at locations other than the agreed place of arbitration and subsection (d) deals with the language in which the proceedings are to be conducted and the documentary evidence. Unless otherwise agreed, discretion in these matters is confided in the tribunal.

(2) Rights of Parties in the Hearing

Section 20 of this Act amplifies upon and expands the basic principles set out in Section 19. The rights of the parties are clearly stated. Thus, Section 20(a)(1), which amplifies the due process requirement of Section 19(a), provides that unless otherwise agreed a party has a right to an "oral hearing" and subsection (a)(2) states the extent to which a party has a right to be heard,

[301] Article V(1)(b), (c), (d).

[302] *See* RUAA §§15–17, setting out minimal rules.

[303] Section 19(a) follows Section 33(1) of the EAA. *See* Model Law Art. 16(1) (parties entitled to a "full opportunity" to present their case).

[304] *See* Section 6.5(2)(B)(2)(a), *infra*.

including cross examination of a witness. For example, if an oral hearing is held a party has the right to "cross-examine" witnesses at that hearing. At all other hearings, a party "has a right to be heard and to present evidence material to the controversy."

Other "rights" of the parties under Section 20 includes the right to (1) "sufficient advance notice" of hearings and meetings to inspect goods or documents, (2) the communication of all statements, documents, or information supplied to the tribunal by the other party and any expert report or evidentiary document upon which the tribunal may rely, and (3) when requested, the opportunity to participate in a hearing with an expert appointed by the tribunal, to "question" him, and to present its own expert testimony.

There is no express provision for judicial intervention in these matters until after the award. Given the dynamics of the process, the discretion afforded the arbitrators, and the alternative ways to present a case, it seems preferable to leave attacks based upon the alleged violations of rights under Sections 19 and 20 to review after award under Article V of the Convention.[305] At that point, the court is in the best position to determine whether the party was in fact "unable to present his case" within the meaning of Article V(1)(b) of the Convention.

(3) Consolidation

The question whether separate arbitration hearings between the same parties can be consolidated into one hearing is difficult and is not answered by the Convention, the Convention Act, or the Model Law. Section 35 of the English Arbitration Act states that the parties are "free to agree" on the consolidation of arbitral proceedings or the holding of concurrent hearings but unless the parties have agreed "the tribunal has no power to order consolidation of proceedings or concurrent hearings."[306]

The answer to the question requires a balance between the agreement of the parties, the discretion of the tribunal, and the power of the courts.

[305] This follows the Model Law pattern. The English Arbitration Act of 1996 permits judicial intervention prior to award in four different circumstances: (1) Enforcing peremptory orders of the tribunal, §42, (2) securing the attendance of witnesses, §43, (3) the taking and preservation of evidence and granting other forms of interim relief, §44, and (4) determining preliminary points of law, §44. There is no specific authority to intervene to insure that the tribunal is conducting the hearing according to due process or is following agreed procedures.

[306] EAA §35(2). Although an English court may "make an order requiring a party to comply with a peremptory order made by the tribunal", EAA §42(1), it has no independent power to order consolidation. *See* Sections 42–5, where the powers of the court are listed.

Section 21(a) of this Act follows the English Arbitration Act and takes the position that unless otherwise agreed by the parties, neither the tribunal nor the court have power to "order consolidation of separate arbitration hearings involving the parties or concurrent hearings." If the parties agree to consolidation or concurrent hearings, the tribunal is obligated to implement that agreement to the extent "feasible under the circumstances." Only if the tribunal is unwilling or unable to implement the agreement may a party petition the court for an order for consolidation or concurrent hearings. At that point, this Act limits the court's power to the conditions stated in Section 10 of the Revised Uniform Arbitration Act. In essence, the claims in the separate hearings must arise out of the same or similar transactions and involve common questions of law and fact for a consolidation to be appropriate.[307]

(4) Court Assistance in Taking Evidence

Section 22 of this Act, a model of simplicity, gives the tribunal power to request a court to assist in "taking evidence." A party to the arbitration may also request the court to assist, but only "with the approval of the arbitral tribunal." The court may then "execute the request within its competence and according to its rules on taking evidence."[308]

This section avoids the interpretive difficulties that have limited the operation of Section 7 of the FAA[309] but leaves many questions for the courts to resolve.[310] But it places the power to decide when, what, and where witnesses and documentary evidence are required in the hands of the tribunal. A petition to the court to take evidence under Section 19 should be denied unless the tribunal has approved.[311]

[307] Section 10(a) of the RUAA permits the court to order consolidation of separate arbitration proceedings unless the "agreement prohibits consolidation." Section 10(c). Although Section 21(e) of this Act limits the role of the court, the conditions for consolidation stated in RUAA §10(a) are adopted to guide the court when the tribunal "refuses or is unable to implement" the consolidation agreement. For a discussion of RUAA §10, *see* Heinz, *The Revised Uniform Arbitration Act*, *supra* Note 296 at 11–16.

[308] Section 19 follows Article 27 of the Model Law. *See* EAA §§43 & 44(2)(a) & (b) (court may take the "evidence of witnesses" and preserve evidence).

[309] *See* Section 2.5(3), *supra*.

[310] *See* RUAA §17, which is more detailed.

[311] *See In re Application of Technostroyexpert*, 853 F. Supp. 695 (S.D.N.Y. 1994), where the court, in applying 28 U.S.C. §1782(a), stated:

> It appears to be generally accepted that the rules and procedures in arbitration are intended to be radically different from the rules and procedures in courts. Arbitrators govern their own proceedings, generally without assistance or intervention by a court. Whether or not there is to be pre-hearing discovery is a matter governed by the applicable arbitration rules (as distinct from court rules) and what the arbitrators decide.

(5) Default of a Party

Section 23 of this Act states the consequences of a default by one party in the arbitration process. The most serious default is the failure of any party "to appear at a hearing or to produce documentary evidence." What should the tribunal do at this point, terminate the proceedings and leave the parties to their rights and remedies in court or continue the proceedings and make an award on the evidence before it? And if the latter course is pursued, is the award entitled to recognition and enforcement under Article V of the Convention?

Following the international consensus,[312] Section 23(c) of this Act permits the tribunal to continue the proceedings despite the default "and make the award on the evidence before it." If all other conditions are satisfied, a party in default against whom the award was made will be unable to claim (with a straight face) either that the "arbitral procedure was not in accordance with the agreement of the parties" or that the defaulting party was "unable to present his case."[313]

6.4(7)(C) Making the Award and Terminating the Proceedings

After the hearing is closed[314] and unless the case is settled,[315] the arbitrators are obligated to decide the dispute on the merits and make an award. This Act has several provisions that are relevant to the award process.

(1) Law Applicable to the Substance of the Dispute and Award

Section 24 of this Act follows the international consensus on the law applicable to the merits of the dispute.[316] The tribunal shall decide the dispute

Subsequent decisions have held that 28 USC §1782 does not apply to international arbitrations where private parties and private tribunals are involved. *See National Broadcasting Co., Inc. v. Bear Stearns & Co., Inc.*, 165 F.3d 184 (2d Cir. 1999); *Republic of Kazakhstan v. Biedermann Intern.*, 168 F.3d 880 (5th Cir. 1999).

312 *See* Model Law Art. 20; EAA §§40–1.

313 Convention Art. VI(1)(b), (e).

314 When the hearing is closed or can be reopened before the award is usually covered by applicable arbitration rules. *See* AAA Art. 24.

315 *See* Section 27 of this Act. If the case is settled before the award, the tribunal shall terminate the proceedings and if requested by the parties and not objected to by the tribunal "record the settlement in the form of an arbitral award on agreed terms." This award has the same status as any other arbitral award.

316 *See* Model Law Art. 28; EAA §46. Although the Model Law is silent on remedies, Section 48(1) of the English Arbitration Act permits the parties to agree "on the powers exercisable by the tribunal as regards remedies" and provides default remedies for the tribunal in the absence of an agreement. Section 48(5). It is also clear that the tribunal can make a separate award on remedies, Section 47, and, unless otherwise agreed, award interest. Section 49.

according the substantive law chosen by the parties or, if no law is chosen, according to the substantive law determined by "the choice of laws rules" that the tribunal "considers applicable." In all cases, the tribunal "shall decide in accordance with the terms of the contract and shall take into account the usages of the trade applicable to the transaction." But unless the parties have "expressly authorized," the tribunal shall not decide the case "ex aequo et bono or as amiable compositeur."

As will be developed in Section 5 of this chapter, courts have no authority under the Convention or the Convention Act to review an award for errors of law or fact. These decisions are insulated from judicial review.[317] As recommended in Section 32(9) of this Act, the judicially created ground to vacate an award for "manifest disregard of law" should not be available in an international arbitration, regardless of where the award was made.[318]

Suppose, however, that the parties agreed that the substantive law of Country X should govern the merits of the dispute and that the tribunal, nevertheless, applied the law of Country Y or disagreed with the law of Country X and decided the case on equitable principles. This, of course, is a "manifest disregard" of the law chosen by the parties.

But it is also a failure of the tribunal to follow the agreement of the parties. The tribunal made a decision "on matters [the choice of law] beyond the scope of the submission to arbitration." Accordingly, the award should be denied recognition and enforcement under Article V(1)(c) of the Convention.

(2) Form and Effect of the Award

Under Section 25(a) of this Act, an award by the tribunal which is in proper form and signed by the arbitrators is "final and binding on the parties" and they agree "to carry out any final award without delay." Although the proceedings and the mandate of the tribunal terminate when a final award is made,[319] the time limits within which post-award actions must be taken do not begin to run until a signed copy of the award is "delivered to each party."[320]

The award shall "be in a record and shall state the reasons upon which the award is based," unless otherwise agreed or the parties have reached a settlement under Section 27 of this Act. Unlike Section 9 of the FAA, however, the parties' agreement need not provide that a judgment of a court

[317] *See* Section 6.5(2)(B)(5), *infra*.
[318] *See* Section 32(9) of this Act.
[319] Subject to Section 28(a) & (c) of this Act.
[320] Section 25(d) of this Act.

shall be entered on the award or specify the court in which enforcement of the award is sought.[321]

(3) Confidentiality of the Award and Arbitral Proceedings

One of the preferred values for parties to international arbitration agreements is confidentiality: the hearings are held *in camera* and the record and the award cannot be made public unless the parties agree. The source and scope of the right to confidentiality, however, are not clear. Neither the Convention, the Convention Act, the Model Law, nor the English Arbitration Act of 1997 say anything about the subject. The source of the duty, therefore, appears to be express or implied terms in the contract to arbitrate, augmented by any ethical duties to which the arbitrators mat be bound.[322]

Section 26 of this Act states a broad duty of confidentiality which is imposed on the parties and on the arbitrators and any administrator.[323] It extends to the award and "all matters relating to the arbitration and award, including the deliberations of the tribunal and all materials and documents created or produced for the arbitration." The duty may be lifted in whole or in part by the consent of both parties or "as required by law." The exact scope of what is "required by law"[324] and the available remedies if the duty of confidentiality is breached are left to development by the courts. Presumably, the remedies include damages and injunctive relief where appropriate.

(4) Termination of the Proceedings and Post-Award Correction and Interpretation

The consensus view is that when the arbitration proceedings are terminated the mandate of the arbitrators also terminates. They are *functus officio*. The question not answered by the Convention or the Convention Act is when do the proceedings terminate. Article 28 of this Act deals with this question. Another question imperfectly answered is whether there are any exceptions

[321] Section 30(b) of this Act. *See Phoenix Aktiengsellschaft v. Ecoplas, Inc.*, 391 F.3d 433 (2d Cir. 2004) (consent requirement in FAA §9 conflicts with award enforcement provisions of Convention and Convention Act).

[322] Varady et al., International Commercial Arbitration, *supra* Note 283 at 495–512 (reviewing cases and ethical standards).

[323] This is an exception to any immunity conferred on the arbitrators or the administrator under Section 8 of this Act.

[324] The circumstances justifying disclosure include "where the information is in the public domain; where disclosure is required by law or a regulatory body; where there is a reasonable necessity for the protection of a party's legitimate interests; and, where it is in the interests of justice or in the public interest." UNCITRAL, Note by the Secretariat on Possible Future Work I in the Area of International Commercial Arbitration A/CN.9/460, at par. 67 (Apr. 6, 1999).

to the termination of the tribunal's mandate. Can they be called back into duty and, if so, for what purposes? Under this Act, they can be called back for the limited purpose of correcting or interpreting an award under Section 29 of this Act or upon remand by a court for the purpose of avoiding possible grounds for the denial of recognition and enforcement under Section 31(c) of this Act.

(a) Termination of proceedings. Under Section 28(a) of this Act,[325] the arbitral proceedings and the mandate of the tribunal are terminated when the final award is made. The proceedings can also be terminated by order of the tribunal when any one of three other conditions are satisfied.[326] One condition is where the parties agree to terminate. Another is where the tribunal finds that the "continuation of the proceedings has for any reason become unnecessary or impossible."[327]

The third condition is where the claimant "withdraws his claim." This conduct should be distinguished from the situation where the claimant "fails to communicate his statement of defense in accordance with the agreement or applicable law."[328] The failure to communicate is not a default but, nevertheless, the tribunal "shall terminate the proceedings." If the claimant, however, withdraws his claim Section 28(b)(1) of this Act, the game is not over. The other party may object. If so, the proceedings are not terminated if the "tribunal recognizes a legitimate interest on his part in obtaining a final settlement of the dispute." If the tribunal so finds, presumably the claim withdrawal is treated as if it were a default and the tribunal "may continue the proceedings and make an award on the evidence before it."[329]

(b) Correction or interpretation of the award: Additional awards. How final is final? Section 29 of this Act[330] provides three exceptions to finality, all of which can be implemented by the tribunal rather than the court. The court, however, may, upon request, "suspend" any proceedings to confirm or set aside an award "to give the tribunal an opportunity to

[325] Section 28 follows Section 32 of the Model Law.

[326] *See* Section 28(b).

[327] Section 28(b)(3). For example, suppose that the parties settled the dispute but did not request that the settlement be reduced to an award. Or suppose that the place of arbitration is in a country that is in a state of war.

[328] *See* Section 23(a) of this Act.

[329] Section 23(c) of this Act.

[330] Section 29 follows Article 33 of the Model Act. *See* EAA §57. Under Section 28(c) of this Act, the termination of the mandate of the tribunal is subject to "Section 26 on correction and interpretation of award."

resume the arbitral proceedings or to take such other action as in the tribunal's opinion will eliminate the grounds for setting aside.[331] This includes a remand by the court to the tribunal for action authorized under Section 29(c) of this Act.[332]

The first exception involves correcting the award to remove "any errors in computation, any clerical or typographical errors of any errors of a similar nature." Corrections if justified can be made by the tribunal upon request of one party or sua sponte and should comply with the requirements for an award imposed by Article 25 of this Act.[333]

The second involves the tribunal giving an "interpretation of a specific point or part of the award." The parties, however, must agree to interpretation and the tribunal must consider the request to be justified.[334]

The third permits the tribunal if justified to "make an additional award as to claims presented in the arbitral proceedings but omitted from the award."[335] The parties, however, may agree otherwise. All of these matters must be resolved in a timely manner and be reflected in a corrected or modified award. Unlike Section 57(3) of the English Arbitration Act, there is no requirement of a hearing before the correction or modification is made.

In all of this, care must be taken to insure that interpretation and modifications deal with claims that are within the scope of the agreement to arbitrate.

6.4(8) Conclusion: De-Localization and the Middle Ground

At present, neither the Convention nor the Convention Act provide legislative rules for the middle ground. In this gap, parties and the tribunal must rely on the contract to arbitrate. Courts are reluctant to intervene at this stage of the arbitration process. Thus, when things go wrong the

[331] Section 31(c) of this Act.

[332] *See M & C Corp., D/B/A Connelly v. Erwin Behr GMBH & Co.*, KG, 326 F.3d 772, 781–5 (6th Cir. 2003), holding that a federal district court had power to remand for clarification of an ambiguity under Chapter 1 of the FAA and the Convention.

[333] Section 29(a)(1), (b).

[334] Section 29(a)(2). Under Section 57(3)(a) of the English Arbitration Act, the tribunal may upon application of a party or sua sponte "clarify or remove any ambiguity in the award." The relief of interpretation is not authorized under Section 11 of the FAA.

[335] Section 29(c). *See* EAA §57(2)(b). Compare Section 11(b) of the FAA, which gives the court power to modify or correct an award where the arbitrators "have awarded on a matter not submitted to them" unless the merits of the dispute are not involved.

parties must proceed with the arbitration and hope that the situation can be remedied in the award process.

This section proposes that the gap be filled with a set of default rules. The effect of some default rules can be varied by agreement. Others are mandatory rules that structure the process. In addition, this Act clarifies when it is proper for a court, upon a petition by one of the parties or the tribunal, to intervene in the arbitration process before the award. Although mandatory rules and judicial intervention limit private autonomy, the goal of de-localization is not impaired because the default rules and the grounds for judicial intervention are consistent with international norms, derived from the Model Law, modern international arbitration rules, and the English Arbitration Act. They are not dependent upon domestic arbitration law.

I recognize that these proposals are controversial. Nevertheless, as international arbitration becomes more prevalent and complex, proposals such as these are necessary to protect the integrity of the process and to give guidance to the parties and the courts. Put differently, they establish a clearer relationship between what should happen in arbitration and the grounds for denying recognition and enforcement under Article V of the Convention.

For example, the proposed mandatory rules for this Act include requirements for arbitrator disclosure, the arbitrator's duty to treat the parties with equality, the right of a party to a reasonable opportunity to present his case and to an "oral hearing," and the right of the parties to notice, documents and information supplied to the tribunal and to confront an expert appointed by the tribunal. These rules are consistent with the values of arbitrator neutrality and the right to a fundamentally fair hearing – values important to both domestic and international arbitration.

The approach to judicial intervention follows the Model Law pattern rather than the more intrusive system established by the English Arbitration Act. In essence, under this Act no court shall intervene "except where so provided in this Act" and the court authorized to act is the federal district court. In the middle ground, the court may intervene to (1) grant an interim measure of protection, either before or after the tribunal is appointed, (2) determine the place of arbitration if the tribunal or institution fails to determine the place, (3) appoint a sole arbitrator if the appointment procedures fail, (4) decide a challenge to an arbitrator if the challenge is denied by the appointing authority, (5) decide the jurisdiction of the tribunal when the tribunal has ruled in favor of jurisdiction as a preliminary question, and (6) assist the tribunal in the taking of evidence. In these limited cases, the court intervenes to support the arbitration process in the absence of agreement or when agreed procedures have failed.

Section 6.5 Enforcing International (Non-Domestic) Arbitration Awards

6.5(1) Introduction

6.5(1)(A) Effect of the Final Award

Let us assume that the tribunal has made a final award[336] in an international arbitration. It is final and binding between and among the parties. What is the effect of the award and how is that award enforced in the United States?[337] More importantly, how consistent is the answer to this question with the objective of de-localized arbitration?[338]

The question, of course, is moot if the losing party voluntary complies with or pays the award, including allocated fees and costs. This is the goal of any arbitration.

Even if there is no voluntary compliance, the arbitration award, under the doctrine of *res judicata*, has the same preclusive effect as a state court judgment. As one court put it:

> [A]n arbitration award, unless and until invalidated creates or authoritatively declares rights even as a judgment does and further litigation of a claim submitted to an arbitrator is precluded by the entry of an award thereon.... Furthermore, the preclusive effect of the award also extends to those claims that should have been but were not submitted to the arbitrator... In other words, a confirmed arbitration award will render some claims that should have been raised at the arbitration res judicata, regardless of whether or not they in fact were raised.[339]

[336] Neither the Convention nor Section 207 of the Convention Act define "arbitral award" or say when it was made. This has caused some confusion in the courts because an action to confirm must be made "within three years after an arbitral award falling under the Convention is made." *See* Susan L. Karamanian, *The Road to the Tribunal and Beyond: International Commercial Arbitration in United States Courts*, 34 G.W. Int'l L. Rev. 17, 93–96 (2002) (hereinafter cited as Karamanian, *Road to the Tribunal*). Under this Act, an award is final (and thus made) when the requirements of Section 25 have been satisfied.

[337] Section 207 of the Convention Act says simply that "an award falling under the Convention" may be confirmed. Neither this section nor the Convention state when an award is final. The assumption is that the parties intend the award to be final when it is made. Thus, Section 58(1) of the English Arbitration Act states that "unless otherwise agreed by the parties, an award made by the tribunal pursuant to an arbitration agreement is final and binding both on the parties and on any persons claiming through them." *See also* Model Law Art. 31–2; AAA International Arbitration Rules Art. 27(7).

[338] Recall that under de-localization theory, a foreign award should be enforced by the courts of the forum without regard to local arbitration law anywhere in the country where the defendant has assets.

[339] *Brody v. Hankin*, 299 F. Supp.2d 454, 459 (E.D. Pa. 2004) (reviewing cases under domestic arbitration law).

Neither international nor domestic arbitration law, however, deals explicitly with the scope and effect of *res judicata*.[340] This matter is left to the courts.

6.5(1)(B) Enforcement of the Final Award: Foreign and Non-Domestic Awards

In many cases, however, the winning party will petition a federal district court to have the award recognized and enforced (confirmed) against the losing party under Article V of the Convention and Section 207 of the Convention Act. The hope is that under this "carefully structured framework for the review and enforcement of international arbitration awards"[341] a court with jurisdiction will enter a judgment on the award and enforce it (under local non-arbitration procedure) as if it were a judgment entered on a judicial decision. This hope is strongly supported by the Convention and the Convention Act. Thus, Article III states that "each contracting State shall recognize arbitral awards as binding and enforce them" and Section 207 states that the "court shall confirm the award unless it finds one of the grounds for refusal or deferral of recognition or enforcement of the awards specified in [Article V] the said Convention." So far so good.

At this point the distinction between a "foreign" arbitration award and a non-domestic award should again be noted. Although both types of awards are international for purposes of the Convention, the former is an award made in another country and enforced in the United States and the latter is an award made and enforced in the United States. The distinction is important because the enforcement of a non-domestic award may encounter defenses available under both the Convention and domestic arbitration law, that is, Chapter 1 of the FAA in the United States.

Suppose that an award in a dispute between an American and an English corporation is made in London and recognition and enforcement is sought in the United States. In this paradigm case of a foreign award, the standards for review and enforcement are contained exclusively in the Convention and the Convention Act. Chapter 1 of the FAA, in theory, does not apply.

[340] *See* Sabrina M. Sudol (student author), *The United Nations Convention on the Recognition and Enforcement of Foreign Arbitral Awards and Issue Preclusion: A Traditional Collateral Estoppel Determination*, 65 U. Pitt. L. Rev. 931, 946 (2004) (arguing that while a future legal action based upon the same claim is precluded if decided by the arbitrator, collateral estoppel is not necessarily mandated: an issue decided in the arbitration could be relitigated in a new action based upon a "different claim").

[341] *See Karaha Bodas Co., L.L.C. v. Perusahaan Pertambangan Minyak*, 364 F.3d 274, 287 (5th Cir.), *cert. denied*, 125 S. Ct. 59 (2004).

If, however, the award between the same parties was made in New York, it would be a non-domestic award[342] which could be confirmed and enforced in the United States under the Convention by the winner. But whether or not confirmation is sought, the non-domestic award can be vacated under Section 10 of the FAA by the loser. The reason is that Article V(1)(e) provides a defense to recognition and enforcement when an award has been "set aside or suspended by a competent authority of the country in which, or under the law of which, that award was made." According to the courts, Article V(1)(e) creates "concurrent jurisdiction"[343] between the Convention and Chapter 1 of the FAA, with the result that even though the award is non-domestic, local and somewhat different standards for the vacatur of awards may be applied to deny recognition and enforcement of the award.[344] Because this outcome is inconsistent with de-localization theory, we will discuss it in more detail and propose a solution in Section 6.5(3).

[342] Article I(1) of the Convention provides that the Convention applies to "arbitral awards not considered as domestic awards in the State where their recognition and enforcement is sought." Section 202 of the Convention Act provides that an "award arising out of . . . a relationship which is entirely between Citizens of the United States shall be deemed not to fall under the Convention unless that relationship involves property located abroad, envisages performance or enforcement abroad, or has some other reasonable relation with one or more foreign states." A persuasive interpretation is that if the award is made in a country that has ratified the Convention and decides a dispute between entities incorporated in different countries, the award is not domestic. *See Industrial Risk Insurers v. M.A.N. Gutehoffnungs Shutte GmbH*, 141 F.3d 1434 (11th Cir. 1998), *cert. denied*, 525 U.S. 1068 (1999). Conversely, if the award is made in a country that has ratified the Convention and the dispute is between entities both of which are incorporated in that country, the award is domestic unless the performance of the contract in another country. *Lander Co. v. MMP Investments, Inc.*, 107 F.3d 476 (7th Cir.), *cert. denied*, 522 U.S. 811 (1997) (goods under contract to be distributed in Poland). *See* Section 1(c) of this Act (defining international).

[343] The court in *Karaha Bodas Co., supra* Note 341, explained the matter in terms of "primary" and "secondary" jurisdiction. In case of a "foreign" award, a court in the United States has "secondary" jurisdiction and is limited by Article V of the Convention in deciding whether to confirm the award. In case of a non-domestic award, the court where the award was made has "primary" jurisdiction and can vacate the award under domestic arbitration law because such a result is permitted by Article V(1)(e) of the Convention. 364 F.3d at 287.

[344] A leading case adopting this view is *Yusuf Ahmed Alghanim & Sons v. Toys "R" Us, Inc.*, 126 F.3d 15 (2d Cir. 1997), *cert. denied*, 522 U.S. 1111 (1998) (grounds to vacate include those in FAA §10 and "manifest disregard" of law). Professor Park criticizes the analysis in *Toys "R" Us* and concludes that the issue should be governed by standards consistent with Article V of the Convention rather than current Section 10 of the FAA. *See* William W. Park, *The Specificity of International Arbitration: The Case for Reform*, 36 VAND J. TRANSN'L L. 1241, 1245–8, 1269–75, 1307–8 (2003) (hereafter cited as Park, *Specificity*). Although I quibble with his analysis, *infra* at Section 6.5(3), I agree with his conclusion that a statutory revision is required.

As you read the balance of this chapter, please consult Part Four of Appendix B, where the recommended statutory revisions and interpretive polices in the important area of award enforcement are contained.

6.5(2) The Paradigm Case: Enforcing a "Foreign" Award in a Country Other Than Where the Award was Made

Assume first that an arbitration between an English buyer and an American seller is held in London and an award in favor of the English buyer is made. Because the "seat" of the arbitration is in England, the English Arbitration Act of 1996 will normally apply.[345] There is no requirement in English law or under the Convention that the award be registered or deposited before it can be enforced in another country.[346] Although the winner may obtain a judgment on the award in an English court,[347] it is the arbitration award rather than the English judgment on it is that is enforced in another country.[348] The loser, of course, may challenge the award in an English court under the English Arbitration Act – an action that will complicate the winner's motion for recognition and enforcement in another country.[349]

6.5(2)(A) Pre-Conditions to Recognition and Enforcement

Assume then that the British buyer files a motion against the American seller to obtain recognition and enforcement of the "foreign" award in the federal district court in New York. What are the pre-conditions to recognition and enforcement?

[345] EAA §2(1), 3. Although the EAA does not distinguish between domestic and international arbitrations when the seat of the arbitration is in England, the essence of the Convention is preserved. *See* EAA §9(4) and §§100–4 (dealing with foreign awards). The situation is slightly complicated by the Geneva Convention on International Commercial Arbitration of 1961, which might apply in cases where a signatory to the Geneva Convention has not subsequently ratified the New York Convention. *See* EAA §99.

[346] *See* Redfern & Hunter, 8–64 (3d ed (1999). Registration for purposes of enforcement, however, is optional in England and may be done for strategic reasons.

[347] EAA §66. The award can then be enforced as a judgment in England.

[348] This preferred view is that the arbitration award is not merged with the English judgment for purposes of enforcing the award in another country. This view is prompted in large part by the absence of an international treaty on the enforcement of foreign judgments. *See Oriental Commercial & Shipping Co. (U.K.) v. Rosseel, N.V.*, 769 F. Supp. 514 (S.D.N.Y. 1991).

[349] *See* Convention Art. V(1)(e), discussed *infra* at Section 6.5(3). An example of these complications is *Four Seasons Hotel and Resorts, B.V. v. Consorcio Barr SA*, 377 F.3d 1164 (11th Cir. 2004), where after protracted litigation the case was remanded for the district court to determine whether a foreign award had been annulled in the country where it was made.

Because the Convention applies,[350] the answer turns on Articles III and IV of the Convention and Section 207 of the Convention Act.

Article III of the Convention provides:

> Each Contracting State shall recognize arbitral awards as binding and enforce them in accordance with the rules of procedure of the territory where the award is relied upon, under the conditions laid down in the following articles. There shall not be imposed substantially more onerous conditions or higher fees or charges on the recognition or enforcement of arbitral awards to which this Convention applies than are imposed on the recognition and enforcement of domestic arbitral awards.

Article III, then, states that the motion for recognition and enforcement will be processed under local procedural rules, such as the Federal Rules of Civil Procedure, and announces a principle of equal and non-discriminatory treatment of foreign awards that is essential for the goal of de-localized arbitration.[351] On the face of it, this is consistent with de-localization theory.

Article IV(1) then requires, as a condition to recognition and enforcement, that the moving party supply "at the time of the application . . . (a) the duly authenticated original award or a duly certified copy thereof; (b) the original agreement referred to in Article II or a duly certified copy thereof." This Article, which is somewhat archaic in an age of cyberspace arbitration, requires proof at the award stage that the formal requirements at the arbitrability stage have been satisfied.

Finally, Section 207 of the Convention Act provides:

> Within three years after an arbitral award falling under the Convention is made, any party to the arbitration may apply to any court having jurisdiction under this chapter . . . for an order confirming the award against any other party to the arbitration.[352] The court shall confirm the award unless it finds one of the grounds for refusal or deferral of recognition or enforcement of the award specified in the said Convention.

350 The Convention applies to this award because it is made in the "territory of a State other than the State where recognition and enforcement is sought." Article I(1). Further, the dispute between these corporations arises from a commercial relationship, the award is not considered to be a domestic award under United States law, and both countries, England and the United States, have ratified the Convention. *See* Convention Act §202; Model Law Art. I(3).

351 *See* Redfern & Hunter, *supra* Note 346 at 10–28.

352 A non-party against whom the award cannot be enforced includes persons who have not signed the written arbitration agreement or do not fall into any of the categories of exception to the signature requirement, such as "incorporation by reference, assumption, agency, veil-piercing/alter ego, and estoppel." *Compagnie Noga D'Importation S.A. v. Russian Federation*, 361 F.3d 676, 683 (2d Cir. 2004). *See Arbitration between Monegasque S.A.M. v. Nak Naftogaz of Ukraine*, 311 F.3d 488, 493–94 (2d Cir. 2002).

As previously noted, in the case of a foreign award (made in England) the enforcement provisions of Chapter 1 of the FAA do not apply[353] and the loser cannot file a motion in a United States court to vacate the award under Section 10 of the FAA.[354]

(1) Jurisdiction

Section 207 of the Convention Act provides that "any party to the arbitration may apply to any court having jurisdiction under this chapter ... for an order confirming the award as against any other party to the arbitration and Section 203 of the Convention Act states that an "action or proceeding falling under the Convention shall be deemed to arise under the laws and treaties of the United States" and that the district courts "shall have original jurisdiction over such an action or proceeding, regardless of the amount in controversy." Thus, it would appear that "any" federal court would have "subject matter" jurisdiction over an action seeking recognition and enforcement of an arbitral award subject to the Convention.

Must the court also have personal jurisdiction over the defendant? Suppose, for example, that the action is brought in a district where the defendant owns property but does not do business. No personal service can be obtained. Should the action be dismissed?

Neither the Convention nor the Convention Act clearly answers this question. Article III directs the court to enforce arbitral awards in "accordance with the rules of procedure of the territory where the award is relied upon" and Section 207 of the Convention Act states that a party "may apply to a court having jurisdiction under this chapter ... for an order confirming the award." One can argue that these provisions coupled with strong policy

[353] FAA §10 is in conflict with Article V of the Convention. Convention Act §208. *See M & C Corp. v. Erwin Behr*, 87 F.3d 844 (6th Cir. 1996), holding that FAA §10 was not available as grounds to deny confirmation of an award made in London. The plaintiff had filed a motion to confirm the London award and the court noted that the only grounds to deny recognition and enforcement were contained in Article V of the Convention. In cases where the award was made in another country, FAA §10 is simply not available to vacate the award, whether or not a motion to confirm has been made.

[354] American courts have concluded (quite properly) that Article V of the Convention states the exclusive grounds for denying recognition and enforcement of an award subject to the convention. One ground, stated in Article V(1)(e) is that recognition and enforcement may be denied where the award has been "set aside or suspended by a competent authority of the country in which, or under the law of which, that award was made." If the award has not been set aside in the country where made, there is no ground to deny recognition and enforcement under Article V, which preempts Section 10 of the FAA. *See M & C Corp. v. Erwin Behr GmbH &Co*, KG, 87 F.3d 844 (6th Cir. 1996); *Coutinho Caro & Co. v. Marcus Trading, Inc.*, 2000 WL 435566 (D. Conn. 2000).

favoring international arbitration either dispense with the need for personal jurisdiction or reduce the minimal contacts normally required to satisfy procedural due process. This argument, of course, would be consistent with de-localization theory, which posits that an international award should be enforced in any country where the defendant has assets.

To date, the courts have rejected the argument that personal jurisdiction is not required when the court has subject matter jurisdiction and have held that the mere presence of the defendant's property in the district does not by itself satisfy the minimal contacts required by due process. For example, in *Glencore Grain RotterdamB. V. v. Shivnath Rae Harnarian Co.*,[355] the plaintiff, invoking the pro-enforcement bias underlying the Convention, argued that there was no personal jurisdiction requirement because it was not expressly required by the Convention and the Convention Act and was not listed as one of the seven defenses to recognition and enforcement in Article V of the Convention.[356] The court rejected this argument, holding that "in suits to confirm a foreign arbitral award under the Convention, due process requires that the district court have jurisdiction over the defendant over whom enforcement is sought or his property."[357] The court also held that personal jurisdiction was not conferred simply because the defendant had property in the forum.[358] The court stressed that the due process requirements underlying personal jurisdiction were rooted in the Constitution of the United States.

A potential ground for personal jurisdiction, however, may be found in Rule 4(k)(2) of the Federal Rules of Civil Procedure, which provides:

> If the exercise of jurisdiction is consistent with the Constitution and laws of the United States, serving a summons or filing a waiver of service is also effective, with respect to claims arising under federal law, to establish personal jurisdiction over the person of any defendant who is not subject to the jurisdiction of the courts of general jurisdiction of any state.

[355] 284 F.3d 1114 (9th Cir. 2002).

[356] 284 F.3d at 1120–21.

[357] 284 F.3d at 1122.

[358] *Accord: Base Metal Trading v. OJSC* "Novokuznetsky Aluminum Factor," 283 F.3d 208 (4th Cir.), *cert. denied*, 537 U.S. 822 (2002). The court in *Dardana Ltd v. Yuganskneftegaz*, 317 F.3d 202, 206 (2d Cir. 2003), ducked the "difficult" question whether personal jurisdiction was required by remanding the case to the district court to determine whether, in fact, personal jurisdiction had been obtained. Possible grounds included an alleged consent by the defendant to jurisdiction and FRCP Rule 4(k)(2). The plaintiff's argument that the award should be treated as a money judgment under which enforcement is proper "anywhere [the creditor] reasonably believes that the debtor has assets" was also to be considered on remand. 317 F.3d at 207–8.

Thus, if the defendant was not otherwise subject to personal service of process in any state but had property in the district which when combined with assets or property in other districts satisfied the "minimum contacts" requirement of due process, personal jurisdiction would exist.[359]

On balance, it is difficult to conclude that personal jurisdiction is not required in actions to confirm an international award. Moreover, an even handed application of the personal jurisdiction requirement appears to be consistent with Article III of the Convention. The obstacle to enforcement in most cases will be minor, especially where the defendant does business and owns property in the United States. Where defendants own property but do not do business in the United States, Rule 4(k)(2) exists for the pooling of assets owned in different districts to satisfy minimum contacts. A final award, however, is not a judgment until it is confirmed. The defendant, who has defenses that can be invoked under Article V, should be entitled to the minimum protections typically required by due process.[360]

(2) Venue

If the court has jurisdiction, to what extent can a petition for recognition and enforcement be dismissed because the forum chosen for enforcement is not convenient? For example, suppose the place of arbitration and award was London and the dispute arose from a contract between an English corporation and a German corporation to be performed in Europe. The winner, the English corporation, seeks recognition and enforcement of the award in the United States because the defendant has assets there.[361]

The apparent answer is found in Section 204 of the Convention Act:

> An action of proceeding over which the district courts have jurisdiction [under 9 U.S.C. §203] may be brought in any such court in which save for the arbitration agreement an action or proceeding with respect to the controversy between the parties could be brought. . . .

[359] This argument was raised but rejected on the facts in *Base Metal Trading, supra* Note 358, 283 F.3d at 215–16. The issue was remanded to the district court for determination in *Dardana, Ltd, supra* Note 358, 317 F.3d at 207.

[360] Despite this, the courts should strive to avoid setting aside international arbitration awards on procedural grounds not provided for or endorsed by Article III of the Convention. *See* Pelagia Ivanova (student author), *Forum Non Conveniens and Personal Jurisdiction: Procedural Limitations on the Enforcement of Foreign Arbitral Awards under the New York Convention,* 83 B. U. L. Rev. 899 (2003).

[361] In fact, the winner could seek confirmation of the award in any country where the defendant has assets.

A broad reading supports the conclusion that unless the parties have otherwise agreed, an action to confirm a foreign or non-domestic award can be brought in any federal district court with subject and personal jurisdiction over the defendant.

Despite this, the Second Circuit has concluded that the doctrine of *forum non conveniens* is available under Article III of the Convention as a procedural defense, provided that it is not applied in a substantially more onerous way than in the case of domestic arbitration.[362] Under this interpretation, the defenses in Article V of the Convention are "substantive" and the conditions imposed in Article III are "procedural." As stated by the Second Circuit:

> The signatory nations simply are free to apply differing procedural rules consistent with the requirement that the rules in Convention cases not be more burdensome than those in domestic cases. . . . Although the Convention establishes jurisdiction in the United States as a signatory state through a venue statute appended to the Federal Arbitration Act, see 9 U.S.C. §§203, 204, there remains the authority to reject that jurisdiction for reasons of convenience, judicial economy and justice.[363]

Unless otherwise agreed, it is understandable that the winner may seek to confirm the award in more than one country. Given this, the procedural requirements of personal jurisdiction and convenience help to control excesses in forum shopping. But they also give courts discretion to dismiss on convenience grounds – a discretion that is inconsistent with de-localization theory and a broad reading of Section 203. Accordingly, the *forum non conveniens* defense should not be available to dismiss motions to confirm international awards where the court has both subject matter and personal jurisdiction.

But what about petitions to vacate or annul an award? In these cases, the arbitration law of the place of arbitration determines the merits of the case. Does this mean that the only convenient forum for vacatur is a court where the award was made? The answer should be yes if the parties have so agreed. In the absence of agreement, the answer is (probably) no. Suppose, for example, that the award was made in London and the motion to vacate was made in a federal court in the United States. If the court has jurisdiction, it could decide that the forum was convenient for deciding (under English arbitration law) whether the award should be vacated. The

[362] The leading case is *In re Arbitration between Monegasque*, *supra* Note 352, 311 F.3d at 495–7.

[363] 311 F.3d at 496, 497. In this case, the place of arbitration and award was Moscow and the dispute was between a Russian company and a Ukranian company.

difference between vacating and enforcing the award, however, is that the *forum non conveniens* decision is not controlled by Article III of the Convention. Because neither the Convention nor the Convention Act apply to a motion to vacate the award, the domestic law of *forum non conveniens* applies.[364]

(3) Article IV: Formal Requirements

To obtain recognition and enforcement, a party petitioning a court with jurisdiction and proper venue must also satisfy the documentary requirements of Article IV of the Convention. The party "shall at the time of the application, supply (a) the duly authenticated original award or a duly certified copy thereof; (b) the original agreement referred to in article II or a duly certified copy thereof."[365] If the "award or agreement is not made in an official language of the country in which the award is relied upon," the party "shall" also produce a certified translation.[366] These are the "only conditions with which the party seeking enforcement has to comply": there is no requirement that the award first be registered or a judgment entered on it in the country where the award was made.[367]

There is a trap here for the unwary. Can you satisfy the conditions of Article IV if the contention is that there was no "original agreement" that met the requirement of an "agreement in writing" in Article II(1)? In *Czarina, L.L.C. v. W.F. Poe Syndicate,*[368] the parties agreed to submit the question to the tribunal which found that there was an agreement in writing. Despite this, the defendant argued that the award could not be enforced. It attacked the tribunal's decision on the merits and asserted that the requirements of Article IV had not been satisfied.

If the court had deferred to the tribunal's award, the matter would have been resolved and the award confirmed. This was not to be. The court first concluded that the requirements of Article IV(1)(b) were jurisdictional: unless there was an "original agreement referred to in Article II," the court had no subject matter jurisdiction. The court next held that despite the

[364] *See* Park, *Specificity, supra* Note 344 at 1285–7. Professor Park contends that motions to vacate should be decided by courts at the place of arbitration and is concerned lest the permissive approach to venue under the Federal Arbitration Act, i.e., that a motion to vacate can be properly made in a district other than where the award was made, will be applied to international arbitration with "dramatically disagreeable results."

[365] Art. IV(1).

[366] Art. IV(2).

[367] *See* Van den Berg, New York Convention, *supra* Note 159 at 262 (1981).

[368] 358 F.3d 1286 (11th Cir. 2004).

apparent agreement giving the tribunal power to decide, no power had been conferred unless there was an "original agreement" that satisfied Article II. The court, following a decision in the Third Circuit,[369] concluded that the district court had authority to "second guess" the decision of the tribunal on its competence by a de novo review and that the decision of the district court that there was no such agreement in writing was correct.

This is a highly formalistic interpretation of the relationship between Article II(1)'s requirement of an "agreement in writing" and Article IV's conditions to the confirmation of an award. It both limits the methods by which the agreement to arbitrate can be satisfied and ignores argument that Article IV(1) is not jurisdictional: it simply requires prima facie evidence of the agreement at the time of submission.[370] More importantly, the emphasis upon jurisdiction obviates the possibility that federal courts should give a deferential review to decisions of the tribunal on its own jurisdiction in cases where the parties have agreed to confer that power. This court will review that issue de novo regardless of what the parties intended.

It is hard to imagine an interpretation of Article IV that is less consistent with de-localization theory and more infused with the so-called "American" approach to separability and competence. Consequently, Section 32(2) of this Act provides that the requirements of Article IV(1)(b) of the Convention are satisfied if the alleged agreement to arbitrate satisfies the relaxed formality requirements of Section 9 of this Act.

(4) Time

Section 207 of the Convention Act, as opposed to the one year limitation of Section 9 of the FAA, gives a party "three years" after an award falling under the Convention, to "apply to any court having jurisdiction under this chapter . . . for an order confirming the award." Moreover, unlike Section 9 of the FAA, there is no requirement that the parties "have agreed that a

[369] *China Minmetals Materials Import and Export Co. v. Chi Mei Corp.*, 334 F.3d 274 (3d Cir. 2003).

[370] *See* Van den Berg, New York Convention, *supra* Note 159 at 250–8. Van den Berg argues that the requirement of submission at the "time of the application" can be satisfied by proof later in the proceedings. This approach was followed in *Al Haddad Bros. Enterprises, Inc. v. M/S Agapi*, 635 F. Supp. 205, 207 (Del. 1986) *aff'd*, 813 F.2d 396 (3d Cir. 1987) (table), where the court said that the "purpose for requiring submission of the original agreement or a certified copy is to prove the existence of an agreement to arbitrate" and the requirement is satisfied if proof exists from other sources, i.e., prior judicial decisions finding that an written agreement to arbitrate existed.

judgment of the court shall be entered on the award"[371] and unless the parties have agreed otherwise, no explicit limitation on the court in which the motion may be filed. Nevertheless, the doctrine of *forum non conveniens* is applicable to motions under Section 207 provided that the application of this doctrine would not constitute "substantially more onerous" procedures proscribed by Article III(1) of the Convention.[372]

6.5(2)(B) Article V Grounds for Denying Recognition and Enforcement

Under Section 207 of the Convention Act, if a timely motion to confirm "the award" is made, the court "shall confirm the award unless it finds one of the grounds for refusal or deferral or recognition or enforcement of the award specified in the said Convention." There are two types of grounds specified in Article V, those under Article V(1) that must be raised by the party against whom recognition and enforcement is sought and those under Article V(2) that may be raised by a party or *sua sponte* by the court. Thus, the defendant must raise the defense that it was "unable to present its case" under Article V(1)(b) but the court on its own motion may refuse to enforce an award that is "contrary to public policy" under Article V(2)(b).

Although Article V provides the exclusive grounds for denying recognition and enforcement of an arbitral award made in another country, those grounds are permissive. Both Article V(1) and V(2) state that recognition and enforcement "may be refused" if a ground is established. The judicial discretion to deny a defense is bolstered by a policy in United States courts to "construed narrowly" defenses that are raised[373] Thus, a "pro-enforcement bias"[374] has been built into Article V by the courts. As a result, very few foreign arbitration awards have been denied recognition and enforcement in the United States under Article V of the Convention.

Undeterred by these results, losers in big cases continue to resist recognition and enforcement under Article V. The result of this litigation is a series of analytical problems in the application of Article V and the Convention's

[371] The absence of such a requirement in Section 207 creates a conflict with Section 9 of the FAA. *See McDermott Intern. v. Lloyds Underwriters of London*, 120 F.3d 583, 588–9 (5th Cir. 1997). *See* Section 30(a) of this Act.

[372] *In re Arbitration between Monegasque*, *supra* Note 352, 311 F.3d at 495–7.

[373] *See generally Parsons & Whittemore Overseas Co. v. Societe Generale De L'Industrie Du Papier (RAKTA)*, 508 F.2d 969, 973 (2d Cir. 1974). *See also* Redfern & Hunter, *supra* Note 346 at 10–30, 10–31.

[374] *Karaha Bodas Co.*, *supra* Note 341, 364 F.3d at 296.

relationship to domestic arbitration law. It is these problems rather than a careful review of each ground for denial upon which we will focus.

(1) Arbitrability Issues Raised at the Award Stage

(a) Validity of the agreement to arbitrate. Article V(1)(a) permits a post-award review of issues that could have and perhaps should have been raised at the arbitrability stage, namely whether the parties were "under some capacity" or whether the arbitration agreement was "valid" under applicable law.[375] Note that if the issue was timely raised and decided in favor of arbitration, either by the court of a tribunal with power to decide its own jurisdiction, and an appeal could not be taken at that time, the issue may now be ripe for review.[376] On the other hand, if the issue could have be raised and was not, the opportunity to raise it after the award may have been waived. Thus, to avoid the waiver trap, there must be evidence that the party raising "validity" issues after the award protested early and often that the tribunal did not have jurisdiction.[377]

It should be said that these questions are further complicated by the fact that "validity" issues include the Convention's requirement in Article II(1) that the agreement to arbitrate be in writing and that the issue of validity may have been already decided by the tribunal. For example, suppose that the tribunal under an alleged agreement giving it power decides that there

[375] "Validity" questions arise at the arbitrability stage when one party claims that the arbitration agreement is "null and void, inoperative or incapable of being performed." Art. II(3).

[376] *See* FAA §16(b), which provides that an appeal may "not be taken from an interlocutory order... compelling arbitration under section 206 of this title" [the Convention Act]. At the appropriate time, decisions by federal district courts on questions of arbitrability are given a de novo review by the circuit courts of appeal.

[377] A perfect example is *Four Seasons Hotels and Resorts, B.V. v. Consorcio Barr S.A.*, 377 F.3d 1164 (11th Cir. 2004). The defendant argued that the agreement to arbitrate had been invalidated by a court in Venezuela. The tribunal, claiming power to decide, determined that the agreement was valid. The defendant participated in the hearings and after the award challenged the tribunal's power to decide. The court held that the defendant, merely by participating in the hearings, had not waived its right to challenge. Rather, the defendant "did virtually everything in its power to prevent the arbitration from going forward." Otherwise, the defendant would be compelled to make a choice, not required by the Convention, to either refuse to participate in the hearing or participate and waive the defense. 377 F.3d at 1171. The court distinguished the case of *Slaney v. Intern. Amateur Athletic Fed'n*, 244 F.3d 580, 591 (7th Cir.), *cert. denied*, 534 U.S. 828 (2001) where the plaintiff "willingly and without reservation" allowed the arbitration to proceed without raising the validity question.

was an agreement in writing as required by Article II(1) of the Convention. Should a court review this decision and, if so, by what standard?

These questions were raised and decided in *China Minmetals Materials Import and Export Co., Ltd v. Chi Mei Corp.*,[378] a long and somewhat complex opinion in which the competence and separability issues also raised their ugly heads. In essence, disputes arising under contracts between an American and a Chinese corporation were arbitrated in China under the CIETAC Rules. The American party claimed that because of forgery and other defects a valid contract was never formed between the parties and as a result, the arbitration clause in that writing was invalid because there was not a signed agreement in writing to arbitrate. Article 4 of the CIETAC Rules, however, authorized the tribunal to decide on "the existence and validity of an arbitration agreement" and Article 5, in adopting the "separability" rule, stated that the "validity of an arbitration clause or an arbitration agreement shall not be affected by any . . . invalidity, or non-existence of the contract."[379] The tribunal decided that the underlying contract was enforceable and made an award for the Chinese corporation (Minmetals). Minmetals motion to confirm the award under the Convention was granted by the district court and Chi Mei appealed. The court of appeals vacated the confirmation and remanded the case.

The first question was whether the Convention's requirement of an "agreement in writing" was incorporated into the validity defense under Article V(1)(a). Not surprisingly, the court held that it was. Reading the Convention as a whole, the court concluded that a court "should enforce only valid agreements to arbitrate and only awards based on those agreements." This was especially true, because the "agreement in writing" requirement was imposed by Article II(1) of the Convention rather than some other law.[380]

The second and more important question was if the tribunal had power under the CIETAC arbitration rules to decide whether the contract was void and decided that it was not, what should the court do about it? Arguably there were three possible choices: (1) review the decision de novo; (2) treat the decision as one on the merits of the dispute (i.e., the validity of the underlying contract) which, under the Separability Doctrine, is not subject to review on the merits; or (3) develop a standard of deferential review somewhere between the extremes.

[378] 334 F.3d 274 (3d Cir. 2003).

[379] The CIETAC Rules are consistent with Article 16(1) of the Model Law. *See also* Sections 7, 30–2 of the English Arbitration Act.

[380] 334 F.3d at 286. The court distinguished several cases and held also that there was no waiver of the right to raise the validity question.

The court, working under the shadow of *First Options*,[381] seemed to duck the issue by rephrasing the question: the question in this case was whether the parties "actually agreed" to incorporate the CIETAC Rules, not the effect of a tribunal decision if there was actual agreement. Given this restatement, the court was able to embrace the accepted international norms favoring the tribunal's power to decide its own jurisdiction yet conclude that the norms themselves say "nothing about the role of judicial review." The court then concluded that it "seems clear that international law overwhelmingly favors some form of judicial review of an arbitral tribunals's decision that is has jurisdiction over a dispute, at least where the challenging party claims that the contract on which the tribunal rested its jurisdiction was invalid." Having said this, the court, rather than distinguishing *First Options* as precedent for domestic arbitration law alone, concluded:

> For these reasons, we hold that, under the rule of *First Options*, a party that opposes enforcement of a foreign arbitration award under the Convention on the grounds that the alleged agreement containing the arbitration clause on which the arbitral panel rested its jurisdiction was void *ab initio* is entitled to present evidence of such invalidity to the district court, which must make an independent determination of the agreement's validity and therefore of the arbitrability of the dispute, at least in the absence of a waiver precluding the defense.[382]

In sum, *China Metals* seems to elevate the requirement of a writing in Articles II(1) and IV(1) of the Convention to the status of mandatory rules over which the courts have primary jurisdiction. Even if the parties clearly confer power on the tribunal to decide those questions, the decision is still subject to de novo review. This, of course, is the antithesis of de-localized arbitration. Conceding that some judicial review is expected when a tribunal with power decides the validity of the agreement to arbitrate, the preferred approach is to develop a deferential scope of review that is consistent with the allocation of power adopted by Section 17 of this Act,

[381] *First Options of Chicago, Inc. v. Kaplan*, 514 U.S. 938 (1995). *First Options*, a case under Chapter 1 of the FAA, held that the arbitrator's decision on arbitrability was, in effect, reviewable de novo because the parties had not clearly and unmistakably agreed to confer that power on the arbitrators. If the parties had clearly and unmistakably given the arbitrators that power the Court suggested that review should be under the "more deferential standard applied to arbitrator's decisions on the merits" or set aside the decision "only in certain narrow circumstances," citing FAA §10. In short, the Court did not decide that a de novo review of the arbitrator's decision on arbitrability, here the validity of the agreement to arbitrate, was proper in every case.

[382] 334 F.3d at 288–90. *Accord: Czarina, L.L.C. v. W.F. Poe Syndicate*, 358 F.3d 1286, 1293–4 (11th Cir. 2004).

the Model Law and the arbitration rules of every major international arbitration institution.[383]

(b) The capability question. The overlap between arbitrability issues and the award stage is also evident on the "capability" question. Article II(1) of the Convention requires that a written agreement to arbitrate concern a "subject matter capable of settlement by arbitration" and Article V(2)(a) gives a court discretion on its own motion to deny recognition and enforcement of an award if the "subject matter of the difference is not capable of settlement by arbitration" under the law of the country where enforcement is sought. Thus, what disputes or claims are not capable of arbitration at either stage depends upon the law of the forum.

There are no cases in the United States denying recognition and enforcement of an award under Article V(2)(a), presumably because it is difficult to find a claim or dispute that is not capable of settlement by international arbitration. The test, whether at the arbitrability or the enforcement stage, is whether Congress has clearly stated that a particular controversy or statutory claim is reserved solely for judicial determination.[384] If the parties have agreed to arbitrate the claim and Congress has not "evinced an intention to preclude a waiver of judicial remedies for the statutory rights at issue," then arbitration will be ordered "so long as the prospective litigant effectively may vindicate [his or her] statutory cause of action in the arbitral forum."[385]

[383] Assume that the parties have apparently assented to and signed a contract for sale and then signed a separate writing agreeing to arbitrate "all disputes arising out of or relating" to the contract for sale. In addition, the separate writing incorporated arbitration rules that gave the tribunal power to decide whether the arbitration agreement was valid. If one party later claims that the contract for sale was void because its signature was forged, this dispute would clearly be arbitrable under the separate agreement to arbitrate and an award on the merits would not be subject to review. If, however, the written arbitration agreement was contained in the allegedly void contract for sale the dispute, on the face of it, is still arbitrable. It goes to the merits of the claim. But now the validity of the arbitration clause is indirectly at stake – if the underlying contract is void because of forgery how can the arbitration clause be valid? The answer is that it may not be valid, but the parties, nevertheless, have tried to confer power on the tribunal to decide the issue. The tribunal has apparent power to decide its own jurisdiction even though they may decide that they do not have it.

[384] The leading international case on "capability" is *Mitsubishi Motors Corp. v. Solar Chrysler-Plymouth, Inc.*, 473 U.S. 614, 639, Note 21 (1985), where the Court compelled arbitration of antitrust claims under a "broad" arbitration clause and declined to "subvert the spirit of the United States' accession to the Convention by recognizing subject-matter exceptions where Congress has not expressly directed to do so."

[385] *Green Tree Financial Corp. v. Randolph*, 531 U.S. 79, 80 (2000).

Some potential problems lurk on the fringes.[386] Capability issues usually involve statutory claims of some social significance. The claims, although arbitrable, may be mandatory in that their legal effect cannot be varied by private agreement. The public policies behind the claim transcend the interests of the private disputants. Under a regime of limited judicial scrutiny, how can we be sure that the parties have a fair opportunity to vindicate their rights and that the final award is correct? Because a court at the arbitrability stage cannot predict how well the tribunal will perform and a court at the review stage cannot review the merits of the award, a challenging problem (which we will discuss infra) is posed – the problem of the "elusive second look."[387]

(2) Defenses Arising from the Conduct of the Arbitration Hearing

(a) Fraud and partiality. Most domestic arbitration law directs that an award shall not be enforced if there is fraud in the arbitration process or the arbitrators were partial. For example, Section 68(1) of the English Arbitration Act of 1996 permits a party to challenge an award in court "on the ground of serious irregularity affecting the tribunal, the proceedings, or the award." Subsection (2) defines "serious irregularity" to mean an "irregularity of one or more of . . . the kinds [stated in subsection (3)] which the court considers has caused or will cause substantial injustice to the applicant." Included in the nine "kinds" listed in subsection (3) are several dealing with the conduct of the proceedings and the award, including an "award procured by fraud" and "any irregularity in the conduct of the proceedings or in the award which is admitted by the tribunal or by any arbitral or other institution or person vested by the parties with powers in relation to the proceedings or the award." Similarly, Section 10 of the FAA permits vacatur where the award was "procured by corruption, fraud, or undue means" or where there was "evident partiality or corruption in the arbitrators," or where the arbitrators were "guilty of misconduct" in conducting the hearing.

Article V(1) of the Convention is more limited in scope and says nothing about what sort of irregularity must exist be before recognition and enforcement may be denied. For example, Article V does not list fraud in

[386] For example, suppose a claim in an international agreement to arbitrate in London is not capable of arbitration under English law but an action to enforce the agreement or award is brought in the United States where the claim is capable of arbitration. Whose law governs arbitrability under Article II(1) of the Convention? Most commentators conclude that it is the law of the forum and thus, the agreement or award should be enforced. *See* Van den Berg, New York Convention, *supra* Note 159 at 367.

[387] *See* Karamanian, *Road to the Tribunal, supra* Note 336 at 52–4. *See also* Section 6.5(2)(B)(5), *infra.*

the procurement of the award or partiality by the arbitrators as grounds for denial of recognition and enforcement. Does this mean that international awards infected by fraud or partiality should be enforced? Probably not, because it is well understood that an award procured by fraud or made by a biased or partial arbitrator will not be enforced under Article V(2) as "contrary to the public policy" of the country where enforcement is sought.[388] To this extent, Section 10 of the FAA can be regarded as a statement of public policy on these issues even though that section cannot be directly applied to the problem.[389]

(b) Denial of due process. Section 18 of the UNCITRAL Model Law imposes a duty on the arbitrators to treat the parties "with equality" and to give "each party . . . a full opportunity of presenting his case."[390] Neither the Convention, the Convention Act, nor the FAA impose such an affirmative duty,[391] but Article V(1)(b) of the Convention states that recognition and enforcement may be denied if a party "was otherwise unable to present his case."[392] As one commentator observed in 1981, this is a popular defense

[388] *See generally* Abdulhat Sayed, Corruption in International Trade and Arbitration 391–423 (Kluwer 2004) (corrupt award against public policy).

[389] As usual there is room for interpretation. Section 207 of the Convention Act directs that the award shall be confirmed unless the court finds "one of the grounds for refusal or deferral or recognition and enforcement of the award specified in the said Convention." On the other hand, Section 208 states that Chapter 1 of the FAA applies to "actions and proceedings" brought under Chapter 2 of the FAA "to the extent that chapter 'is not in conflict' with this Chapter or the Convention . . . " Suppose in a foreign award there is evidence that the so-called neutral arbitrator was partial to one of the parties, a ground for vacatur under FAA §10(a)(2). Does Article V preempt Section 10(a)(2) or should that subsection be treated as supplementary to and not in conflict with the Convention? And if Article V is preemptory, does the public policy exception in Article V(2)(b) offer protection?

[390] *See* Section 33 of the English Arbitration Act, a mandatory rule, which requires the tribunal to act "fairly and impartially between the parties," to give "each party a reasonable opportunity of putting his case and dealing with that of his opponent," and to "adopt procedures" that avoid unnecessary delay or expense "so as to provide a fair means for the resolution of matters" to be determined.

[391] Such as duty, however, will be imposed by the international arbitration rules adopted by the parties. *See, e.g.,* AAA International Arbitration Rules 16(1).

[392] Other grounds relevant to conduct of the hearing for denying recognition and enforcement include (1) failure to give a party against whom the award was made "proper notice of the appointment of the arbitrator or of the arbitration proceedings," V(1)(b), (2) an award dealing with differences or matters beyond the scope of the submission to arbitration, V(1)(c), and (3) the composition of the arbitral tribunal or the arbitral procedure was not in accordance with the agreement of the parties or "failing such agreement, was not in accordance with the law of the country where the arbitration took place." V(1)(d) *See*

that has "rarely been successful."[393] Nothing has changed in the last twenty-five years to challenge this observation. Thus, American courts will state that the parties are entitled to a "fundamentally fair hearing" – one that meets the "minimal requirements of fairness" – but because of the nature and objectives of arbitration, Article V(1)(b) should be "narrowly construed."[394]

An illustration of this narrow construction comes from the case of Olympic distance runner, Mary Decker Slaney, who was sanctioned by the International Amateur Athletic Federation after a random urine test showed a high ratio of testosterone in her body.[395] Slaney, claiming that the testosterone was due to pathological or physiological factors rather than ingestion, went to arbitration. The arbitrator, however, concluded that under the IAAF Rules if the testosterone level exceeded a stated ratio (it did), there was presumption that the testosterone was ingested (exogenous) and the burden shifted to Slaney to prove that the condition was pathological. This she was unable to do, so the award went to the IAAF. The district court, inter alia, denied that she was "unable to present her case" and she appealed.

The court, in holding that Slaney received a "fundamentally fair" hearing, noted that parties "who have chosen arbitration rather than litigation should not expect the same procedures that they would find in the judicial arena" and that arbitrators are "not bound by the rules of evidence." The arbitrator must provide an "adequate opportunity" to present evidence and arguments and that the exclusion of relevant evidence must "actually deprive a party of a fair hearing" before the defense would be granted. On the facts, the court concluded:

> This defense to enforcement of a foreign arbitration need not apply when a panel employs a burden-shifting test in a fair manner. Slaney was not denied an opportunity to present her evidence. Rather, the arbitrator's decision merely maintained the same standard of proof the IAAF has always been guided by. As such, Slaney's complaint does not truly attack the procedure implemented by the arbitration panel, but rather an underlying evidentiary decision of the

First State Insurance Co. v. Banco de Seguros, 254 F.3d 354 (1st Cir. 2001) (rejecting the claim that the notice was not proper).

[393] Van den Berg, New York Convention, *supra* Note 159 at 297.

[394] *See, e.g., Consorcio Rive, S.A. De C.V. v. Briggs of Cancun*, 134 F. Supp.2d 789, 796 (E.D. La. 2001) (rejecting defense). *See also Karaha Bodas Co. v. Perusahaan Pertambangan Minyak*, 364 F.3d 274, 298–9 (5th Cir. 2004), citing authorities and stating that the "right to due process does not include the complete set of procedural rights guaranteed by the Federal Rules of Civil Procedure."

[395] *Slaney v. Intern. Amateur Athletic Fed'n*, 244 F.3d 580 (7th Cir. 2001), *cert. denied*, 534 U.S. 828 (2001).

panel. Unfortunately for Slaney . . . arbitrators are not bound by the rules of evidence."[396]

Nevertheless, under Section 19(a) of this Act, arbitrators shall give the parties a "reasonable opportunity" to present their case. The ultimate test, I believe, is stated in Section 32(4) of this Act: A party is "unable to present his case" if an "act or omission by the tribunal in conducting the arbitration results in substantial prejudice."

(c) Deviation from agreed or required procedures. Under Article V(1)(d), there is a defense to recognition and enforcement when the "composition of the arbitral authority or the arbitral procedure was not in accordance with the agreement of the parties or, failing such agreement, was not in accordance with the law of the country where the arbitration took place."

In most international arbitrations there will be agreement, often detailed, on composition of the tribunal and the procedures to be followed in the arbitration. In the rare case where the agreement is not followed, the question remains how serious the deviation must be before the defense can be established. No answer is provided in the Convention, the Convention Act, or the few cases where Article V(1)(d) was raised.[397]

In the absence of an agreement,[398] the court where recognition and enforcement is sought must determine whether the composition or procedure was in accordance with the law of the "country where the arbitration took place." In England or a country enacting the Model Law, that law

[396] 244 F.3d at 592–3. The panel's adoption of the IAAF's rebuttable presumption test was reasonable (according to the court) because there is no reliable method of proving the presence of exogenous testosterone in the body. Unfortunately, Slaney was unable to rebut the presumption by proving that the substance was pathological.

[397] In *Karaha Bodas Co., supra* Note 394, 364 F.3d at 294–8, the court rejected claims that the agreement was not followed in consolidating claims under two contracts into one arbitration proceeding and selecting an arbitrator by interpreting the contract to permit them. The court noted that the Convention "embodies a pro-enforcement bias" and that, in any event, there was "no prejudice arising from the consolidation that would justify a refusal to enforce the award." 364 F.3d at 296.

[398] *See* Van den Berg, New York Convention, *supra* Note 159 at 322 ("failing such agreement" means the "absence" of any agreement). But in *Al Haddad Bros. Enterprises, Inc. v. M/S Agapi*, 635 F. Supp. 205 (D. Del. 1986), *aff'd*, 813 F.2d 396 (3d Cir. 1987) (table) when the agreed composition of the tribunal failed because one party refused to cooperate in the appointment process, a sole arbitrator was appointed as was permitted by English law. The court denied the defense and confirmed the award because the composition procedure, although not in accord with the agreement, was in accord with English arbitration law. *See* Section 32(5) of this Act.

will be readily available. In the United States, however, there are no default rules on these issues and it is an open question what a court should do.[399] Accordingly, a solution is proposed in Section 32(5) of this Act.

(3) Award Set Aside or Suspended in the Country Where Made

Article V(1)(e) states that a court in a country where recognition and enforcement is sought "may" refuse upon proof that the "award was not yet become binding on the parties, or has been set aside or suspended by a competent authority of the country in which, or under the law of which, that award was made." Article VI provides that if an application to set aside or suspend the award has been made under Article V(1)(e), the court where recognition and enforcement is sought "may" adjourn the proceedings and, upon application of the party claiming enforcement, may order the other party to give suitable security. Article VII(1) then states that the provisions of the Convention "shall not . . . deprive any interested party of any right he may have to avail himself of an arbitral award in the manner and to the extent allowed by the law or treaties of the country where such an award is sought to be relied upon." How do these sections work together?

Assume that the arbitration was held and the award made in Country X. The tribunal awarded Party A, an American corporation, $1M in damages against Party B, a corporation doing business in Country X. Party B promptly moved to vacate the award under the arbitration law of Country X and the motion was granted. The grounds were that the arbitrators made material mistakes of law and fact. Nevertheless, Party A sought recognition and enforcement of the award against Party B in the United States. Party B then moved to deny recognition and enforcement under Article V(1)(e).

Although the Convention does not state when an award becomes "binding," Section 31(1) of the Model Law implicitly suggests that an award is "final" when it is "made in writing and . . . signed by the arbitrator or arbitrators,"[400] and this is made more explicit in most arbitration rules.[401] Thus, it should be fairly easy for a court to determine whether the award had "become binding on the parties." Similarly, if a motion by Party B to set aside or suspend the award has been made in Country X but not decided,

[399] *But see* RUAA §§11(a) & 15(a).

[400] *See* EAA §52 (in accord).

[401] For example, Article 27(1) of the AAA International Arbitration Rules states that awards "shall be made in writing, promptly by the tribunal, and shall be final and binding on the parties."

it should be relatively easy for the court to decide whether to adjourn the enforcement motion and demand security under Article VI.[402]

If the award is binding and has been set aside or suspended by a court in the country where made or "under the law of which the award was made,"[403] however, the grounds for the defense have apparently been established. But in our case, we have an American citizen whose award has been set aside in another country on grounds not available in the United States. Should the award be enforced? Conceding that there is some discretion under Article VII(1), there is persuasive authority that the defense should be granted especially if the parties had agreed that the arbitration law of Country X should be applied and that law was followed in vacating the award.[404] This result honors the primary jurisdiction given by Article V(1)(e) to the arbitration law at the place of award and refuses to invoke Article VII(1), which would lead to a different result.

In the infamous *Chromalloy* decision,[405] however, the United States District Court for the District of Columbia held that Article V(1)(e), which is permissive, was subject to Article VII(1), which provides that the provisions of the Convention "shall not deprive any interested party of any right he may

[402] *See Europcar Italia, SPA v. Maiellano Tours, Inc.*, 156 F.3d 310 (2d Cir. 1998) (exercising discretion to stay action pending decision on motion to vacate where award made).

[403] The courts recognize that if recognition and enforcement of an award made in China is sought in the United States, the defense in Article V(1)(e) applies only if the award is set aside or suspended in China or under the arbitration law chosen by the parties. For a particularly lucid analysis, *see Coutihno Caro & Co. U.S.A. v. Marcus Trading, Inc.*, 2000 WL 435566 (D. Conn. 2000). *See also Karaha Bodas Co., supra* Note 394, 364 F.3d at 287–93. The court reasoned that under Article V(1)(e), only a court with "primary jurisdiction" over the arbitration proceedings could set aside or suspend the award under its domestic arbitration law. The court in the country of enforcement had "secondary jurisdiction" and could deny recognition and enforcement only under the Convention. In an elaborate analysis, the court concluded that Switzerland where the award was made had primary jurisdiction and, therefore, the decision by an Indonesian court to set aside the award was not a defense under Article V(1)(e). At an earlier stage of this complex and extended litigation, the court, after balancing the various interests, had refused to enjoin the defendant from seeking to annul the Swiss award in Indonesia. *Karaha Bodas v. Perusahaan Pertambangan Minyak Dan Gas Bumi Negara*, 335 F.3d 357 (5th Cir. 2003).

[404] A leading case is *Baker Marine (Nig) Ltd v. Chevron (Nig) Ltd*, 191 F.3d 194 (2d Cir. 1999), where the court refused to confirm an international award (parties doing business in different countries) made in Nigeria and set aside by a court in that country. Even though the grounds for set aside in Nigeria were different from those in the United States, the parties had chosen Nigerian arbitration law by agreement and there was no evidence that the law had been misapplied. Given this and the risk that a "mechanical application" of Article VII(1) would undermine finality, the court found no reason under Article V or VII(1) to ignore the action by the Nigerian court.

[405] *Chromalloy Aeroservices v. The Arab Republic of Egypt*, 939 F. Supp. 907 (D. D. C. 1996). To date the case stands alone.

have to avail himself of an arbitral award in the manner and to the extent allowed by the law . . . of the country where such award is sought to be relied upon." In *Chromalloy*, the place of arbitration was in Egypt and the award was in favor of Chromalloy. The defendant obtained a nullification of the award in an Egyptian court on the ground that the award was not properly grounded in applicable substantive law. The district court concluded (1) that the Egyptian court had, in effect, reviewed the award for errors in law, a ground not available under Section 10 of the FAA, and (2) that the award would have been enforced under Chapter 1 of the FAA. Noting that the grounds for defense under Article V were permissive and that the rights protected under Article VII(1) were mandatory, the court held that there was no conflict between them and that it was required to protect any rights that Chromalloy had "under the domestic laws of the United States."[406]

Does this mean that every time an American corporation has an award set aside in the country where made it can still obtain recognition and enforcement in the United States if that award would have been confirmed under Chapter 1 of the FAA? This result has been resisted by the commentators on the grounds that Article V(1)(e) gives primary jurisdiction of the award to the courts of the country where made and recognizes that other and even lesser grounds under the law of that country may be invoked to vacate the award. If it is clear that the arbitration law of the place where the award was made applied and that the decision appears to follow that law, there is at least a presumption that the award should be denied recognition and enforcement in the United States. It is not enough to rebut the presumption simply by showing that the party seeking recognition and enforcement would have greater rights under the arbitration law of the place of enforcement. Arguably, the presumption is rebutted if there was a flagrant denial of due process or a failure of integrity by the court with primary jurisdiction. Unfortunately, until every country has enacted modern legislation such as the Model Law, there will be differences in the grounds for vacatur with which courts in this country must deal.[407]

(4) The Public Policy Defense

Suppose that a final and binding award is made in England, recognition and enforcement is sought in the United States, and none of the defenses stated in Article V(1) have been satisfied. Article V(2)(b) provides that

[406] 939 F. Supp. at 914.

[407] For a discussion, *see* Karamanian, *The Road to the Tribunal*, *supra* Note 336 at 96–9; Ray A. Chan, *The Enforceability of Annulled Foreign Arbitral Awards in the United States: A Critique of Chromalloy*, 17 B.U. Int'l L. J. 141 (1999).

recognition and enforcement "may also be refused" if the "court finds" that "the recognition or enforcement of the award would be contrary to the public policy of that country." The argument is that even if the dispute is arbitrable and there are no defenses under Article V(1), recognition and enforcement may be denied if the impact or effect of enforcing the award is against public policy.

Despite its obvious allure, it is difficult to find a case where recognition and enforcement in the United States has been denied on that ground.[408] The tone was set in an early, influential decision where the court concluded that the "Convention's public policy defense should be construed narrowly" and that enforcement should be denied "only where enforcement would violate the forum state's most basic notions of morality and injustice."[409] Since then, the defense has been frequently raised and regularly denied.[410]

The tension between the policy of limited judicial review under Article V(1) and the "public policy" defense in Article V(2)(b) is strikingly illustrated by the *Baxter International* case.[411] In deciding an antitrust claim the arbitrators seemingly interpreted a licensing agreement in such a way that enforcement would violate antitrust laws in the United States. The court still confirmed the award on the ground that it could not review the award for mistakes of law. To do so would, in the court's words, "throw the result in the waste basket and litigate the antitrust issues anew,"[412] a result not sanctioned in the *Mitsubishi* case.[413] In dissent, Judge Cudahy took the position that even if deference was given to the arbitrator's decision on the antitrust

[408] One possibility is where an international award has been obtained by fraud or made by a partial arbitrator. Unlike Section 10 of the FAA, Article V(1) does not specifically list fraud or partiality as grounds to deny recognition and enforcement. A Convention award, however, might be against public policy if the arbitrators were corrupt or partial. *See AAOT Foreign Economic Ass'n v. Intern. Dev. & Trade*, 139 F.3d 980 (2d Cir. 1998) (recognizing defense but finding waiver for failure to timely challenge).

[409] *Parsons and Whittemore Overseas Co. v. Societe Generale de L'Industrie Du Papier (RAKTA)*, 508 F.2d 969, 973 (2d Cir. 1974).

[410] *See* cases discussed in *Baxter International*, cited *infra* at Note 411. *See also Karaha Bodas Co., supra* Note 394, 364 F.3d at 306; *Europcar Italia, S.p.a.V. v. Maillellano Tours, Inc.*, 156 F.3d 310, 315 (2d Cir. 1998).

[411] *See Baxter Intern., Inc. v. Abbott Laboratories*, 315 F.3d 829, 831 (7th Cir. 2003), r'hg denied, 325 F.3d 954 (7th Cir.), *cert. denied*, 540 U.S. 963 (2003). Although not discussed by the court, the arbitration was held and the award was made in Chicago, Illinois. It was a non-domestic award, however, because the parties were incorporated and did business in different countries. In this case, recognition and enforcement was sought under the Convention and the primary defense in the district court was Article V(2)(b). Section 10 of the FAA was not involved. The district court confirmed the award, 2002 WL 467147 (N.D. Ill. 2002), and this was affirmed on appeal.

[412] 315 F.3d at 832.

[413] *Mitsubishi Motors Corp. v. Soler Chrysler-Plymouth, Inc.*, 473 U.S. 614 (1985), to be discussed in Section 6.5(2)(B)(5), *infra*.

claim, the court should not enforce an award that commanded illegal conduct under the antitrust laws. The court should examine the "effect of the outcome commanded by the arbitral award" and if the effect is illegal the award should not be enforced on grounds of public policy.[414]

The majority opinion by Judge Easterbrook in *Baxter* clearly supports the objectives of de-localized arbitration and pushes the "public policy" defense even further into the background. But was the court correct in refusing the review the merits of the tribunal's decision on the antitrust claim?

(5) Direct and Indirect Review of the Merits: The Ghost of *Mitsubishi Motors*

(a) The ground rules. To what extent can or should a court in the United States review the merits of an international award made in another country? Put differently, should recognition and enforcement be given to an award where there are clear errors of fact or law?[415] This troublesome question was noted twenty years ago by the Supreme Court in the *Mitsubishi Motors* case and still broods over the Convention's enforcement process.

Under Article 28 of the Model Law and the modern rules of international arbitration, the arbitrators shall decide the dispute in accordance with the rules of substantive law chosen by the parties or, in the absence of agreement, shall apply the law "determined by the conflict of laws rules which it considers appropriate." Moreover, they are expected to give reasons for the decision. Thus, judicial review of the merits, if permitted, is easier in international arbitration because a court can decide what body of law the arbitrator should have applied and whether it was properly applied to decide the dispute.

Nevertheless, Article V of the Convention, implemented by Section 207 of the Convention Act, does not authorize such a review. Thus, American courts refuse to review the award for mistakes of law and fact[416] or to hold that enforcing an award with such mistakes is contrary to public policy under Article V(2)(b).[417] More importantly, in cases where confirmation of a foreign award is sought in a court of the United States, the judicially

[414] 315 F.3d at 833–9.

[415] Section 69 of the EAA still preserves limited right of a party to appeal a question of law arising out of an award.

[416] *See Baxter Intern., Inc., supra* Note 411, 315 F.3d at 831, where the court said:

> [A] mistake of law is not a ground on which to set aside an award. . . . [quoting Section 207 of the Convention Act] Legal errors are not among the grounds that the Convention gives for refusing to enforce international awards. Under domestic law, as well as under the Convention, arbitrators have 'completely free reign to decide the law as well as the facts and are not subject to appellate review.'

[417] *See Karaha Bodas Co., supra* Note 403, 364 F.3d at 306 (erroneous legal reasoning or misapplication of law generally not a violation of public policy within meaning of Convention).

created defense of "manifest disregard of the law," available to supplement the statutory grounds to vacate in Section 10 of the FAA, is arguably not available under Article V of the Convention.[418] This defense, by expanding the grounds to deny recognition and enforcement, is in "conflict" with the provisions of the Convention and the Convention Act.[419] It is also inconsistent with de-localization theory. Following the implications of this, it is unlikely that the parties have power by contract to vary the effect of a treaty with preemptive effect, either by expanding or contracting the grounds to deny recognition and enforcement.[420] This appears to be the result under FAA Section 10, but there is disagreement among the courts.[421]

To put the matter somewhat differently, even though certain statutory claims are "mandatory" in that their legal effect cannot be varied by private agreement, they are capable of being arbitrated and the merits of the tribunal's award are insulated from judicial review. Furthermore, the enforcement of an award infected with errors of fact or law is not against public policy. Finally, the defenses in Article V are mandatory in that their effect cannot by varied by private agreement. A stronger support for de-localized arbitration cannot be imagined.

(b) The ghost of **Mitsubishi Motors.** *Mitsubishi Motors*[422] involved an international arbitration where the agreed place of arbitration was Japan.

[418] This was the holding in *Brandeis Intsel Ltd v. Calabrian Chemicals Corp.*, 656 F. Supp. 160 (S.D.N.Y. 1987) ("manifest disregard" defense not permitted by Art. V(1) of Convention and award in manifest disregard of the law is not "contrary to public policy" under Art. V(2)(b). *But see Duferco Intern. Steel Trading Co. v. T. Klaveness Shipping AS*, 333 F.3d 383 (2d Cir. 2003) (suggesting but not squarely holding that "manifest disregard" defense is available to London award); *M & C Corp. v. Erwin Behr GmbH & Co.*, 326 F.3d 772 (6th Cir. 2003) (remand of motion to confirm foreign award to clarify grounds, "manifest disregard" defense available).

[419] In the Second Circuit, at least, the standard for "manifest disregard" of law is stringent:

> The error must have been obvious and capable of being readily and instantly perceived by the average person qualified to serve as an arbitrator. Moroever, the term 'disregard' implies that the arbitrator appreciates the existence of a clearly governing legal principle but decides to ignore or pay no attention to it.... Factual findings and conclusions of law are not reviewable.

Shanghai Foodstuffs Import & Export Corp. v. Intern'l Chemical, Inc., 2004 WL 213019 (S.D.N.Y. 2004) (discussing cases).

[420] This is the outcome under the UN Model Law and the English Arbitration Act of 1996. *See* Section 6.2(2), *supra.*

[421] *See Kyocera Corp. v. Prudential-Bache*, 341 F.3d 987 (9th Cir. 2003), *cert. dismissed*, 540 U.S. 1098 (2004) (*en banc* holding that parties have no power to expand grounds to vacate award under FAA 10 to include errors of law). The Fifth Circuit disagrees: *Harris v. Parker College of Chiropractic*, 286 F.3d 796 (5th Cir. 2002). The issue is discussed in Sections 3.5, 4.4(2), and 6.2(2), *supra.*

[422] *Supra* Note 384.

The dispute arose when Mitsubishi, part of a joint-venture, sought to enforce a distributorship agreement against Soler, who claimed that restrictions in the agreement constituted violations of the Sherman Antitrust Act. Mitsubishi sought an order compelling arbitration in Japan and Soler defended on two grounds, (1) the "broad" arbitration agreement should not be interpreted to include antitrust claims, and (2) the antitrust claims were not capable of being arbitrated. The Court decided both defenses against Soler and remanded the case for further proceedings.

As posed, this was not a garden-variety commercial dispute. Antitrust and other statutory claims were, at that time, thought to be not capable of arbitration. Even assuming that arbitrators have the capacity to handle such complex matters, an antitrust claim is not just a private matter. Broader interests and policies are involved. So even if the claims were sent to arbitration (a result the Court endorsed), the Court was nervous about what might happen next. Eschewing any intention of pre-judging the agreed arbitration process in Japan, the Court stressed that, at a minimum, that Soler must have an opportunity to "vindicate its statutory cause of action in the arbitral forum" and if the combination of a choice of forum (arbitration) and a choice of law clause amounted to a "prospective waiver" of the right to "pursue statutory remedies for antitrust violations, we would have little hesitation in condemning the agreement as against public policy."[423]

What about the award-enforcement stage under the Convention? Here the Court was more elusive. Having concluded that the antitrust claim was "capable of settlement by arbitration" under Article II(1) of the Convention it was highly unlikely that the Court would permit a second look at that issue under Article V(1)(a). Once capable always capable. But what about the "public policy" defense under Article V(1)(b), which the Court specifically mentioned? Suppose, for example, that the arbitral tribunal in Japan made an award against Soler that contained any one of the three following defects: (1) the tribunal applied the wrong body of antitrust law, (2) the tribunal applied the correct law but made clear errors of fact or law, or (3) the award, if enforced in the United States, would be illegal under domestic antitrust law.

The Court's response to problems like these was to say:

> Having permitted the arbitration to go forward, the national courts of the United States will have the opportunity at the award-enforcement stage to ensure that the legitimate interest in the enforcement of the antitrust laws has been addressed. [The Court then quoted Article V(2)(b) of the Convention.] While the efficacy of the arbitral process requires that substantive review at the award-enforcement stage remain minimal, it would not require intrusive

[423] 473 U.S. at 637.

inquiry to ascertain that the tribunal took cognizance of the antitrust claims and actually decided them.[424]

This response, of course, was *dictum*, and the Court has not had an opportunity to revisit these issues in a case where the recognition and enforcement of a foreign award was sought. As noted previously, the "manifest disregard" of law defense probably is not available when enforcement of an award made in another country is sought under the Convention. Because the merits are, in all probability, insulated from direct judicial review and it is not against public policy per se to enforce an award based upon an error in law, the best option seems to be to test the impact of enforcement of the award under domestic law. If the award is wrong as a matter of law and enforcement would be illegal in the country where recognition and enforcement is sought, the award is arguably against public policy. According to the Seventh Circuit, however, the public policy defense cannot be invoked to second guess an award that is insulated from judicial review.[425]

(c) A possible solution? Should anything be done about this situation? One approached, supported by Professors Brunet and Ware, is to permit the parties to expand the scope of judicial review by agreement to include errors of fact and law.[426] Unfortunately, it is not clear that the defenses in Article V of the Convention could (or even should) be expanded by agreement. How can the effect of a Treaty with preemptive force within the United States be varied by private agreement? Accepting this limitation (and some will not) and the current reality that Congress is unlikely by legislation to withdraw certain claims from arbitration and that the courts are unlikely to expand the narrow scope of the public policy defense, what is left? One plausible answer is suggested by Professor Ware: if the effect of the claim involved cannot be varied by agreement (a mandatory claim), then a decision by an arbitrator on that claim should be reviewable on the merits.[427] This answer, which is adopted in Section 32(9) of this Act, is consistent with the principle of private autonomy without trumping the broader public interests that are at stake.[428]

[424] 473 U.S. at 638.

[425] *See Baxter, supra* Note 411. The court refused to subvert the promises made in the Convention and the dictum in *Mitsubishi Motors* by reviewing the merits of the award for errors in law. 315 F.3d at 832.

[426] *See* Sections 3.4 and 4.4(4), *supra.*

[427] *See* Section 4.4(2), *supra.*

[428] *See* Philip J. McConnaughay, *The Risks and Virtues of Lawlessness: A "Second Look" at International Commercial Arbitration*, 93 Nw. U. L. Rev. 453, 514–15 (1999) (award on mandatory law claim should be denied recognition and enforcement unless "demonstrably correct").

6.5(3) Enforcement of an International (Non-Domestic) Award in the Country Where the Award was Made

Suppose that in a case like *Mitsubishi Motors* the place of arbitration was New York rather than Tokyo and the award was against Soler. Mitsubishi then filed a motion to recognize and enforce the award under the Convention and Soler filed a motion to dismiss, arguing that Chapter 1 of the FAA rather than the Convention applied because the award was not "made in the territory of a State other than the State where the recognition and enforcement of such awards are sought."[429] In other words it was a "domestic" award to which the Convention does not apply.

This argument was rejected in *Sigval Bergesen v. Muller Corporation*,[430] where the court, after a careful review of the legislative history of the Convention and the Convention Act, held that the Convention applied to an arbitration between two foreign parties held in New York. The Convention applied to a non-domestic award not because it was made abroad but because is was made "within the legal framework of another country, e.g., pronounced in accordance with foreign law or involving parties domiciled or having their principal place of business outside the enforcing jurisdiction." Through an interpretation of Section 202 of the Convention Act, this principle has been extended to cover arbitrations in the United States where just one party is a foreign corporation[431] or where both parties are American corporations but performance of the contract is to take place abroad.[432]

The *Sigval Bergesen* court also concluded that where the non-domestic award was made in the United States there was "overlapping coverage" between the Convention and Chapter 1 of the FAA and that Bergesen could have chosen the regime that was most advantageous to enforce the award. Here some care must be given to the analysis. If a party chooses to enforce a non-domestic award only under Chapter 1 of the FAA, the Convention does not apply and the plaintiff must contend with the FAA with all of its strengths and weaknesses. If the plaintiff seeks recognition and enforcement

[429] Convention Art. I(1). This issue would not arise under the English Arbitration Act of 1996, which treats all arbitrations, whether domestic or international, under the same rules if the "seat" of the arbitration is in England.

[430] 710 F.2d 928 (2d Cir. 1983).

[431] *See Industrial Risk Insurers v. M.A.N. Gutehoffnungshutte*, 141 F.3d 1434, 1440–1 (11th Cir. 1998), *cert. denied*, 525 U.S. 1068 (1999).

[432] *Lander Co. v. MMP Invs., Inc., supra* Note 342. The expansive interpretation of "non-domestic" awards has been lauded for giving the "broadest possible recognition and enforcement of awards with foreign elements." Hans Smit, *A-National Arbitration*, 63 Tul. L. Rev. 629, 644 (1989).

under the Convention, however, the FAA would apply only to the extent that it is "not in conflict" with the Convention Act.[433] Thus, the scope of the overlapping coverage in this situation depends upon an analysis of what is and what is not in conflict with the Convention Act.

This question was squarely raised in the *Toys "R" Us* case,[434] where the plaintiff sought recognition and enforcement of a non-domestic award under the Convention and the defendant moved to vacate the award under Section 10 of the FAA. The key question was to what extent, if at all, does Section 10 apply in a case where the plaintiff chooses to enforce the non-domestic award under the Convention? The court's answer emerged in two parts. First, the court affirmed that Article V states the exclusive grounds for denying recognition and enforcement to a non-domestic award and that without more the judicially created "manifest disregard of law" defense impliedly engrafted onto Section 10 was in conflict with the Convention and the Convention Act.[435] Second, the court noted that Article V(1)(e) of the Convention provided that recognition and enforcement may be denied when the award "has been set aside or suspended by a competent authority of the country in which, or under the law of which, that award was made." After due consideration, the court concluded that "Article V(1)(e) of the Convention . . . allow[s] a court in the country under whose law the arbitration was conducted to apply domestic arbitral law, in this case the FAA, to a motion to set aside or vacate that arbitral award." Thus, the losing party can either resist a motion for recognition or enforcement under Article V of the Convention or file an independent motion to vacate under Section 10.[436]

> In sum, we conclude that the Convention mandates very different regimes for the review of arbitral awards (1) in the state in which, or under the law of which the award was made, and (2) in other states where recognition and enforcement are sought. The Convention specifically contemplates that the state in which, or under the law of which, the award is made, will be free to set aside or modify an award in accordance with its domestic arbitral law and its full panoply of express and implied grounds for relief . . . However, the Convention is equally clear that when an action for enforcement is brought in

[433] Convention Act §208.

[434] *Yusuf Ahmed Alghanim & Sons v. Toys "R" Us, Inc.*, 126 F.3d 15 (2d Cir. 1997), *cert. denied*, 522 U.S. 1111 (1998).

[435] 126 F.3d at 20.

[436] For example, if the winner sought recognition and enforcement of the award in England rather than the United States, the loser could move to vacate the award in the United States under FAA §10 and, if successful, raise the vacatur as a defense in England under Article V. *See* EAA §103(2)(f).

a foreign state, the state may refuse to enforce the award only on the grounds explicitly set forth in Article V of the Convention.[437]

The result of this exercise of concurrent jurisdiction in the Second Circuit is that the "manifest disregard" defense – a defense frequently raised but almost never granted–sneaks in through the back door of Article V(1)(e).[438]

Despite critical comments[439] and an apparent disagreement in the Eleventh Circuit,[440] the *Toys "R" Us* decision is a proper reading of the Convention. The problem is that interstate arbitration law, represented by Section 10 of the FAA, is out of sync with Article V of the Convention. This exacerbates the tension in the arena of concurrent jurisdiction, especially when losers constantly claim that an award was in "manifest disregard" of the law. This problem would be solved if Congress were to enact Article 34 of the Model Law. Article 34 permits recourse against the non-domestic award whether or not a motion for recognition and enforcement has been filed under the same standards provided in Article V. Thus, the domestic law of the United States for purposes of Article V(1)(e), whether here or abroad, would be consistent with Article V and the "manifest disregard" exception would be relegated to the international trash can.[441]

[437] 126 F.3d at 23. *Accord: Coutinho Caro & Co. U.S.A., Inc. v. Marcus Trading, Inc.*, 2000 WL 435566 (D. Conn. 2000) (Section 10 of FAA not available to vacate award made in China where recognition and enforcement sought in U.S.).

[438] *See Shanghai Foodstuffs Import & Export Corp. v. International Chemical, Inc.*, 2004 WL 2130019 (S.D.N.Y 2004) (following *Toys "R" Us* but finding no manifest disregard); *Certain Underwiters at Lloyd's London v. BCS Ins.*, 239 F. Supp.2d 812, 815 (N.D. Ill. 2003) (following *Toys "R" Us*).

[439] Professor Park is highly critical of *Toys "R" Us* and proposes a new statute to resolve the problem. *See* Park, *Specificity*, *supra* Note 344 at 1245–9, 1307–8. Although I agree with the thrust of his ultimate solution, Professor Park does not give sufficient weight to Article V(1)(e) in his analysis. Dean Karamanian, on the other hand, does not disagree with the analysis in *Toys "R" Us*, but does worry about the inconsistent treatment of Article V(1)(e) in United States courts when a party seeks recognition and enforcement of a foreign award. Karamanian, *Road to the Tribunal*, *supra* Note 336 at 96–9.

[440] *Industrial Risk Insurers v. M.A.N. Guterhoffnungshutte*, 141 F.3d 1434 (11th Cir. 1998), *cert. denied*, 525 U.S. 1068 (1999). In response to a non-domestic award in an arbitration between a German and a United States corporation, the U.S. party filed a motion to vacate under FAA Section 10. Apparently the German party filed a motion to confirm the award under the Convention, although this is never specifically stated by the court. The court reviewed the award under the seven defenses provided in Article V and rejected the argument that the non-domestic award could be vacated because it was "arbitrary and capricious." This was an implied ground for vacatur available under the FAA in the Eleventh Circuit but not under the Convention. 141 F.3d at 1446. The court, however, did not discuss the effect of Article V(1)(e).

[441] States that have enacted the Model Law as state law usually omit Articles 34 and 35, deferring to Article V of the Convention and the FAA. California is one of those states. *See HSMV Corp. v. ADI Ltd.*, 72 F. Supp.2d 1122 (C. D. Cal. 1999) (vacating international award made in California for "evident partiality" under FAA Section 10).

6.5(4) Summary and Conclusion

On the one hand, American courts have consistently enforced foreign and non-domestic awards under the Convention and the Convention Act. The term "non-domestic" award has been given a broad interpretation and the various defenses under Article V have been strictly construed and rarely granted. Despite the confusion generated by the "concurrent jurisdiction" doctrine, it is Article V(1)(e) of the Convention, not the courts, that creates the problem. Section 31(a) of this Act minimizes the problem by providing that a motion to vacate a non-domestic award shall be governed by Article V of the Convention rather than Section 10 of the FAA.

On the other hand, the trend toward de-localization is hindered somewhat by recent decisions interpreting and applying Articles III and IV(1) of the Convention. There is a risk that an international award otherwise entitled to recognition and enforcement will become ensnared in the varying requirements of personal jurisdiction and venue. Moreover, the requirements of Article IV(1) have been labeled jurisdictional and the controversial reading of Articles V(1)(e) and VII(1) of the Convention in[442] the *Chromalloy* decision remains.

Finally, the question whether awards deciding statutory and other claims which are capable of arbitration but are mandatory (in that the rights created cannot be varied by private agreement) can or should be reviewed on the merits is still partially open.

From a legislative standpoint, there are three possible solutions.

First, Congress could review the legislation creating various regulatory rights and remedies and state clearly what rights are not capable of arbitration. This solution is contemplated by Article V(2)(a), although it would reduce the arbitrability of some claims arising out or related to the contract. This, of course, is not likely to happen.

Second, Congress or the courts could state that under Article V(2)(b) of the Convention the enforcement in the United States of an award deciding a "mandatory" right or claim that contained errors of fact or law is against public policy. This approach, which was rejected by the Seventh Circuit but agrees with the recommendation made by Professor Ware in Section 4.4(2) of this book, is an indirect route to a result now foreclosed under Article V(1). It permits a court to review the merits of an award on mandatory law.

Third, Congress could provide that written agreements by the parties permitting the courts to review awards on mandatory claims for errors of

[442] I propose a solution to this problem in Section 32(6) of this Act.

fact and law are enforceable. This, of course, supports private autonomy at a cost to international uniformity and without any guarantee that the parties would pick the best (if any) claims for judicial review. Moreover, it is, arguably, not permitted by Article V of the Convention.

My conclusion is stated in Section 32(9) of this Act:

> In an arbitration subject to the Convention, a court may deny recognition and enforcement of an award only if the defenses stated in Article V are satisfied. The court may not review an award to determine whether the tribunal's decision was in manifest disregard of the law. The court may, however, deny recognition and enforcement on grounds of public policy if the award decides issues of mandatory law in the United States and that award contains clear errors of law or fact.

CHAPTER SEVEN

Tension Points: Where the Authors Disagree

This chapter is written in a point-counterpoint format to provide a candid exchange of individual views among the four authors. Disagreement and tensions dominate this chapter.

Section 7.1 Comments of Professor Richard Speidel

7.1(1) Speidel's Opening Thoughts

Speidel: I have constructed [in Chapter 6 and Appendix B] a legal regime for international commercial arbitration that is distanced from the regimes of interstate and intrastate arbitration law in the United States. This was intentional. The objective was to test the extent to which international commercial arbitration in the United States could be de-localized from interstate arbitration and national public policy even though the place of arbitration was in the United State and judicial proceedings were conducted in federal district courts. The conclusion was that, under the Convention, de-localized theory is alive and well in the courts, but its scope and consistent implementation requires a revised Chapter 2 of the FAA. In short, I have drafted a new Convention Act.

The distance is, of course, somewhat artificial. There are commonalities in both the concept of arbitration and the legal issues that arise in any arbitration.[1] One wonders why a basic arbitration statute can't be drafted that covers international, interstate, and intrastate arbitration. Why perpetuate three legal regimes? Apart from the politics of federalism, what can possibly justify the cost and confusion of (at least) three different sets of arbitration law?[2] When a modern national arbitration law arbitration is

[1] *See* Chapter 2, *supra*.

[2] Other than the cost and confusion of drafting and enacting such an act.

combined with arbitration procedures agreed to by the parties and administration by competent arbitral institutions, shouldn't all be well?

Perhaps in a perfect world. But reality must creep into the drafting of any legislation of such scope and preemptive effect. Reality suggests (to me at least) that there are values in the international arbitration community that are not in common with interstate arbitration under Chapter 1 of the FAA (i.e., the "separability, competence" issue) and could not easily be accommodated on the more local level. The strength and weaknesses of our federal system of government continue to confound us. One could draft a comprehensive statute for Congress to enact, such as the English Arbitration Act of 1996, without the remote possibility that it would be enacted.[3]

So, if international commercial arbitration is consigned to its own legal regime, what about interstate and intrastate arbitration? What should be done about that?

7.1(2) What About Chapter 1 of the FAA and State Arbitration Law?

My colleagues, **Ed**, **Steve**, and **Jean**, have expressed their views on this question. In essence, two of them, Steve and Jean, have staked out positions at opposite ends of the proposed revision of Chapter 1 and Ed seeks a better balance between interstate and intrastate arbitration law.

Steve proposes a minimalist revision of an eighty-year-old, Chapter 1 of the FAA.[4] He argues that if the parties have the power to contract for it, Chapter 1 should support the enforcement, by specific performance, of agreements in a record to arbitrate and the confirmation of final awards that emerge from the process. He is in love with the value of private autonomy. Along the way, Steve recommends several revisions with which I tend to agree: (1) enforce electronic agreements, see Section 4.3(1);[5] (2) delete the

[3] The same fate could easily befall my proposed Revised Chapter 2.

[4] He proposes no clarifications to or revisions of sections that have prompted continuing disagreement and litigation. *See, e.g.*, FAA §9, first sentence, discussed briefly in Section 2.4(4) at Note 57. He also reduces rather than expands sections dealing with problems arising in the "middle ground." Put differently, except for Section 5 dealing with the judicial appointment of arbitrators, all other questions concerning middle ground issues are left to the contract between the parties – a contract that is assumed but never mentioned or discussed. This omission from the middle ground is at odds with the numerous "middle ground" provisions in the Revised Uniform Arbitration Act. *See* Section 2.6(3), *supra*. The failure of Chapter 1 of the FAA to deal with the middle ground is a glaring omission that has caused confusion in the courts. *See* Section 2.4(3), *supra*.

[5] *See also* Section 6.2(4), *supra*.

transportation exception in Section 1, see Section 4.3(1);[6] (3) clarify that Chapter 1 should apply to agreements in a record to arbitrate "any existing or subsequent controversy" not just those "arising out of . . . a contract, transaction, or refusal"; and (4) actions involving Sections 1 and 2 of the FAA may be brought in either state or federal courts, but "all other sections of this act shall apply only in courts of the United States."[7]

I have more difficulty with some of Steve's other proposed revisions.

First, he abolishes the "separability doctrine" by providing in Section 4 that a case shall be referred to arbitration if the court is satisfied that the "contract containing the agreement for arbitration" has been made. The arbitrators apparently have no power to decide whether the contract containing the arbitration clause is enforceable even though this is a dispute on the merits and would be within the scope of a broad arbitration clause. This recommendation is inconsistent with common understanding in international commercial arbitration.[8] Why there should be such a disconnect between international and interstate arbitration law is not clear. Moreover, the proposal does not consider the effect of an explicit agreement by the parties to confer competence on the tribunal to decide this and other questions involving the validity of the arbitration agreement or the deference that should be given an award on competence under such an agreement. In a regime that rests upon private autonomy backed by a pro-arbitration policy, the failure to deal with the effect of such an agreement is puzzling.[9]

Second, Steve would delete Section 7 of Chapter 1, which deals with the power of the courts to enforce a summons from the arbitrators to compel the attendance of witnesses with documents at the hearing, because the parties do not have the power by agreement to authorize such actions.[10] Private autonomy aside, why shouldn't a modern arbitration act give the courts discretion to intervene at the request of the arbitrators to assist in the conduct of a hearing? Another core value of arbitration is fairness: the parties should have an opportunity for a fair hearing.[11] In some cases, this value

[6] *See also* Section 6.2(1)(B)(3), *supra*.

[7] This is a sensible clarification, but why retain diversity jurisdiction for actions under FAA Chapter 1?

[8] *See* Section 6.4(5), *supra*.

[9] The solution in international arbitration is that the tribunal has power to determine its own jurisdiction unless otherwise agreed and, also, has power to determine whether the contract containing the arbitration is "void" under the separability doctrine. Awards made within the separability doctrine are subject to deferential review under Article V of the Convention.

[10] *See* Section 4.4(1), *supra*.

[11] *See* Section 1.7, *supra*. In fact, enforcement of an award will be denied if one party is unable to present his case. *See* FAA §10(a)(3).

modifies if not trumps the private autonomy value, especially where external assistance is needed by the arbitrators in conducting the hearing. In my view, this deletion is anachronistic. It is inconsistent with the RUAA, the English Arbitration Act, and the Model Law, and leaves the tribunal in interstate arbitration without any access to recalcitrant witnesses and needed evidence through the courts.[12] Put differently, the deletion of Section 7 and the failure to provide for any judicial assistance in the middle ground neglects other core arbitration values that are important to the process. At best it leaves such matters to the discretion of the courts and at worst leaves failures in the arbitration process that might have been corrected through judicial action to the limited review process after the award.

Finally, I find myself more sympathetic to Steve's proposals on the scope of judicial review of the award but wishing for a bit more elaboration. Both Steve and Ed conclude that the parties should be able by agreement to expand the scope of judicial review under FAA Section 10 to include errors of law or fact in deciding the merits of the claim.[13] This conclusion claims that FAA Section 10 is, in part at least, a default rule the effect of which can be varied by agreement. But what about other sections of Chapter 1? Which of them impose mandatory arbitration rules and which can be varied by agreement? Answers for this question are provided by the English Arbitration Act and the RUAA but they are left hanging for Chapter 1.[14] Can the parties, for example, reduce the grounds for vacating an award under FAA Section 10? At what point is tinkering with FAA Section 10 so inconsistent with award finality that the process is really not arbitration at all?

The proposal for judicial review of awards deciding mandatory claims, that is, claims created by statute or otherwise the effect of which cannot be varied by agreement, is more intriguing. Suppose, for example, that the parties have agreed to arbitrate a statutory claim that Congress has not clearly reserved exclusively for judicial determination. Under current law, an award on that claim is not reviewable on the merits and will be enforced

[12] *See* Section 22 of Revised Chapter 2 of the FAA, Appendix B. *See also* Section 6.4(7)(B)(4), *supra*. Moreover, Section 5, the only remaining section in the Chapter 1 middle ground, is limited to court appointment of an arbitrator (when all else fails). There are no other default rules dealing with the court's role in such things as selection the place of arbitration, dealing with challenges to an arbitrator or the failure of the tribunal to follow agreed procedures, or interim relief. Provisions on these matters are found in the Model Law, the English Arbitration Act, and the Revised Uniform Arbitration Act. There should be a comparable provision in revised Chapter 1 of the FAA.

[13] *See* Section 3.5 and Section 4.4(2), *supra*. I have concluded that such agreements should not be enforced under the Convention. *See* Section 6.2(2), *supra*.

[14] *See* discussion at Section 6.2(2), *supra*.

(at least in the Seventh Circuit) even though the result is illegal in the United States. This is consistent with the dicta in *Mitsubishi Motors* that the court's power to review is limited to determining whether the claim was actually decided by the tribunal.[15] Steve's proposal, with which I agree,[16] permits the court to review the merits of a claim that the parties had no power to vary or contract out of by agreement. It helps to ensure that important federal policies are preserved without getting into the messy question of whether an award not subject to review on the merits is somehow against public policy.

Jean proposes a federal preemptive statute that invalidates consumer arbitration agreements "arising out of interstate commerce" before the dispute arises but permits arbitration after the dispute has materialized. She rejects the notion that better information or choice at the time of contracting will suffice. I have reservations about this, preferring an approach that gives the consumer maximum information at the time of contracting and provides that the consumer may agree to arbitration or not without losing the underlying contract that is offered.[17] I am also concerned that individuals in employment contracts (who encounter the same problems) are not included in this regulatory measure. Nevertheless, Jean's firmly stated and well supported position reverses the usual presumptions in contract matters of this nature[18] and, as a practical matter, shifts the burden to the organizations that insist on pre-dispute arbitration as a condition to contracting to explain why a position more consistent with private autonomy should be sustained.

Ed is concerned about the extent to which state arbitration law should figure in disputes seemingly involving interstate arbitration. Suppose, for example, that Steve's revisions of Chapter 1 of the FAA are adopted and the Revised Uniform Arbitration Act is enacted in every state. Suppose, also, that some states have laws that regulate the enforceability of arbitration agreements (like requiring 10-point type) or stating that some claims arising under state law are not capable of arbitration. We know the story of how these limitations on the federal contract to arbitrate have been treated by the Supreme Court. How does Ed deal with them?

[15] *See* Section 6.5(2)(B)(5), *supra*.

[16] *See* Section 32(9) of Revised Chapter 2 of the FAA, Appendix B.

[17] *See* Richard E. Speidel, *Consumer Arbitration of Statutory Claims: Has Pre-Dispute (Mandatory) Arbitration Outlived its Welcome*? 40 Ariz. L. Rev. 1069, 1093–4 (1998) (proposing statute that regulates all consumer arbitration agreements).

[18] I.e., that anything objectively assented to is presumptively valid until the assenting party proves that it is not.

The solution is subtle and undercuts the current force of Chapter 1 of the FAA. First, Ed recommends that the scope of Chapter 1 be limited to transactions or conduct that "affect" interstate commerce. This is more restrictive than the current language, which includes transactions "evidencing a transaction involving commerce." Thus, fewer agreements to arbitrate will be within the scope of Chapter 1. Second, even if the arbitration is within the scope of Chapter 1, Ed reduces the situations where state arbitration law is preempted: state arbitration law must not stand as an "obstacle" to enforcing an agreement to arbitrate. Thus, a state law prescribing the conditions for consent to arbitration might survive federal preemption but a law precluding arbitration of a state created claim otherwise within the scope of the agreement to arbitrate would not. If you are an advocate for intrastate arbitration law, a grin should appear on your face. Third, Ed supports, as does the Supreme Court, a choice by the parties to adopt state arbitration law even though the transaction is otherwise within the scope of Chapter 1. Presumably, this choice would be enforced unless the state law chosen was in conflict with (an "obstacle" to) the federal contract to arbitrate. Thus, the parties could choose the Revised Uniform Arbitration Act as the applicable arbitration law for most cases. Even if they did not, the RUAA might offer a persuasive body of law for analogical extension in the middle ground where revised Chapter 1 is silent. In short, even though Steve leaves the middle ground wide open in his revision of Chapter 1, the middle ground provisions in the RUAA (whether we like them or not) are fair game for choice by the parties and, perhaps, a court.

7.1(3) Final Thoughts

Perhaps Professor Coase's famous theorem makes great sense (in economic efficiency terms) in the regime of arbitration: The theory posits that it makes no difference which law initially applies if the parties can by agreement (and with no transaction costs) negotiate to a different, more efficient (for them) position.[19] What difference could it possibly make whether federal or state arbitration law initially applies to the routine issues that arise in commercial arbitration? For that matter, why should international arbitration be afforded special treatment? If the mandatory arbitration rules are clearly spelled out (and consumers are appropriately protected), commercial parties, at least, should be free to contract for a more efficient arbitration regime.

[19] R. H. Coase, *The Problem of Social Costs*, 3 J. Law. & Econ. 1 (1960).

But, again, the matter comes down to the difference between property rules (mandatory) and liability rules (variable). **Jean** is clear what the mandatory rules should be in consumer arbitration. **Ed** argues for greater choice between interstate and intrastate arbitration law. **Steve**, although espousing a broad theory of private autonomy, doesn't speak clearly to the issue. If the parties are free to expand the grounds for judicial review under Section 10 are they also free to vary the effect of other sections that confer power on the courts? Surely not. But if not, what sections should be variable?[20] Until that question is answered for Chapter 1 of the FAA, the scope of private autonomy in interstate arbitration cannot be clearly established.

7.1(4) Brunet's Response to Speidel

Brunet: I wish to address **Dick Speidel's** assertion that by my recommendation for an "affecting commerce" test I will narrow the scope of the FAA. I did not intend to decrease the scope of federal arbitration law by substituting the words "affecting commerce" for "involving commerce." In the *Terminix* decision, Justice Breyer treats these two concepts as interchangeable. *Terminix* stands for the proposition that the federal arbitration legislation should be co-extensive with the scope of the commerce power. Other federal statutes reach this result with the more familiar "affecting commerce" jargon. I am merely urging a clarification of a housekeeping nature by making this recommended change.

Dick wants more elaboration on whether the parties to an arbitration agreement could reduce or even eliminate grounds for review set forth in **Steve Ware's** model statute. Like Steve, I plead guilty to a love affair with party autonomy. I have urged that the parties should be free to expand the scope of judicial review.[21] However, this does not mean that parties necessarily possess the authority to enter into a binding agreement to reduce the minimal standards for vacatur set forth in the existing FAA or Professor Ware's suggested amendment of the FAA. The rules for vacating awards need to set a mandatory floor of minimal grounds for review. They are default rules that can be added to or expanded but cannot be diminished. This interpretation is consistent with the important arbitration value of fundamental fairness, which is acknowledged and emphasized by Speidel.

[20] This question has confounded and perplexed the commentators. *See, e.g.*, Richard R. W. Brooks, *The Relative Burden of Determining Property Rules and Liability Rules: Broken Elevators in the Cathedral*, 97 Nw. U. L. Rev. 267 (2002).

[21] *See* Section 3.5, *supra*.

Section 7.2 Comments of Professor Edward Brunet

7.2(1) Brunet's Thoughts on Employment Arbitration

Brunet: The first six chapters of this book say very little about employment arbitration, a topic of growing significance. In Chapter Four's treatment of domestic American arbitration, **Professor Steve Ware** sets out a version of the FAA that would broadly permit employers to readily create binding arbitration systems with their non-unionized employees. I disagree.

I am very concerned about the direction taken by courts in upholding agreements to arbitrate employment disputes entered into near or at the time of a job offer. My point of concern is not with arbitration systems negotiated in collective bargaining contexts. Employment grievance arbitration between unionized employees and their employers has had a long and distinguished history. Labor law scholars have correctly explained that these successes are due largely to the self-governance that is achieved when systems of grievance arbitration become institutionalized and routine. These are relational contracts between collective groups of employees and their employers that need a private system of dispute resolution to achieve optimal mutual gains. Labor grievance arbitration in the unionized setting is not the focus of my criticisms.

In contrast, today's typical employment arbitration contract is far from the unionized grievance arbitration and achieves little in the way of self-governance virtues. We are living in the era of the fungible, non-union workforce characterized by employees and employers who lack a long-term relationship. In the modern non-union alleged agreement to arbitrate there is seldom a relational contract. Two all too common hypothetical illustrations that recur daily need to be addressed.

> *Example #1:* A newly minted, recently graduated engineer is offered a job by a high technology employer. She is handed an employment contract on this day of her marriage to her employer. The multiple page, boilerplate employment contract contains an arbitration clause near the end of the agreement. Thrilled to be offered a job, the prospective employee signs the contract without seriously reviewing it with legal counsel.

> *Example #2:* A restaurant chain offers a job to a potential waiter, a part-time twenty-three-year-old student who needs to work to support himself and pay tuition. The interviewer offers a job on the spot and hands the applicant a contract that does not contain an arbitration clause but does

contain a sentence specifying that the "employee agrees to follow the procedures set out in the Employee Handbook." The student, thrilled to be offered a job, signs. The interviewer concludes by giving a copy of an eighty-seven-page handbook to the new employee. On Page 59, the handbook sets forth a company dispute resolution policy that includes a mandatory arbitration clause.

The traditional analysis of Example #1 supported by Steve is straightforward. The employee signed the agreement to arbitrate and the signature is all it takes to trigger mandatory arbitration. Arbitration case law creates a duty to read the contract and rejects the contention that a failure to assent particularly to the arbitration feature can avoid the operation of the arbitration clause.[22] In the words of Learned Hand, "[A] man must indeed read what he signs and he is charged, if he does not."[23] As explained by Stephen Ware, a contract notion of consent is all it takes to trigger mandatory arbitration.[24] The context of the example is irrelevant. The emotion of the job offer must yield to the formal signing of the agreement.

I find the traditional analysis troublesome. For most employees the offer of a job is a celebratory moment that prevents rational analysis of any written terms regarding potential subsequent conflict. Empirical research demonstrates that individual employees systematically overestimate their bargaining positions and concludes that workers lack basic information needed to engage in rational bargains.[25] The employee in Example #1 will not be able to understand the impact of signing the employment contract. The newly hired employee lacks the ability to understand the results of a later possible termination of employment.[26] In contrast, the employer seems very

[22] *See, e.g., Avila Group, Inc. v. Norma J.*, 426 F. Supp. 537, 540 (S.D.N.Y. 1977) (mandating arbitration and rejecting argument that a failure to point out arbitration feature prevented enforcement of agreement to arbitrate); *Southern Tile v. Commercial Const. Co.*, 548 So. 2d 2047 (La. Ct. App. 1989) (upholding signed arbitration clause because of a duty to read a signed contract).

[23] *Gaunt v. John Hancock Mut. Life Ins. Co.*, 160 F.2d 599, 602(2d Cir.), *cert. denied*, 331 U.S. 849 (1947).

[24] See generally Stephen J. Ware, *The Effects of Gilmer: Empirical and Other Approaches to the Study of Employment Arbitration*, 16 Ohio St. J. Disp. Res. 735 (2001).

[25] *See* Pauline T. Kim, *Bargaining With Imperfect Information: A Study of Worker Perceptions of Legal Protection in an At-Will World*, 83 Cornell L. Rev. 105, 111 (1997) (study of 330 workers "raises serious doubts about whether workers have the most basic information necessary for understanding the terms on which they have contracted").

[26] *See* Samuel Issacharoff, *Contracting for Employment: The Limited Return of the Common Law*, 74 Tex. L. Rev. 1783, 1795 (1996) (comparing the process of hiring to a first date between a polygamist who has had many prior dates and a monogamist who is faithful).

likely to be fully informed of the proposed terms, including the arbitration clause.[27]

To be sure, there are highly skilled employees offered executive level jobs who are capable of evaluating exit strategy within the context of a negotiated job offer. I recently studied written employment contracts between CEOs and their companies and found that a healthy percentage of such contracts contained arbitration clauses.[28] There is every reason to uphold such arms-length bargains between two sophisticated parties capable of understanding the need for an exit strategy and able to enlist the aid of an attorney to evaluate whether an arbitration clause would be optimal.

Informed consent is essential to a reformed theory of arbitration and may be one possible answer to the problem of mandatory employment arbitration. In example #1, the employer has done nothing to inform the potential employee of the arbitration option. A huge and inefficient information imbalance exists. Because informed consent has not been achieved, we should be unwilling to uphold such a bargain based on asymmetric information. My position closely approximates the one taken by **Professor Jean Sternlight** in her discussion of consumer arbitration,[29] an arbitration subject matter in which the standard of consent is used appears to me to be inadequate.

Example #2 is even easier for me. The traditional analysis would conclude that the employee's signature on the bare-bones contract bootstraps the entire employee handbook into the agreement, including the arbitration option. Never mind that nothing was said to the employee about arbitration and its meaning, either orally or in the contract. The employee signed up for a relationship that included every feature of a detailed handbook and there is no reason to look beyond the formal signatures on the short contract.

Example #2 also lacks informed consent to arbitrate. The arbitration option has been imposed upon the unsuspecting potential employee in a stealth fashion. The lack of informed consent caused the Ninth Circuit to refuse to compel arbitration in *Kummetz v. Tech Mold, Inc.*[30] There the employer was presented with the handbook and a form "acknowledgment"

[27] *See, e.g., id.*; Richard Epstein, *In Defense of the Contract at Will*, 51 U. Chi. L. Rev. 947, 953–5 (1984) (noting that parties to employment contracts bargain with full information and advance their own interests).

[28] *See* Edward Brunet, *Seeking Optimal Dispute Resolution Clauses in High Stakes Employment Contracts*, 23 Berk. J. Employ. & Lab. L. 107, 108 (2002) (noting that 33 firms in study of 93 publicly traded corporations that submitted their CEO contracts to Corporate Library database included arbitration features and concluding that a CEO appeared to be the drafting party of some agreements).

[29] *See* Chapter 5, *supra*.

[30] 152 F.3d 1153 (9th Cir. 1998).

that he had read the accompanying handbook. Despite proof that the employee had signed the form, the court of appeals was troubled by the consent issue. Stressing that the form acknowledgment was silent regarding any mention of arbitration, *Kummetz* mandates a duty upon the employer to inform that employee of its arbitration program as a condition of effectively bootstrapping the handbook into the employment contract.

Although *Kummetz* is a step in the right direction, I question whether it goes far enough in mandating the informed selection of an arbitration option.[31] It appears that the employer need only reference the inclusion of the arbitration clause in the form acknowledgment in order to pass the minimal test demanded to compel arbitration. An informed arbitration participant needs to know that arbitration means a process characterized by no jury, minimal discovery, and without a requirement that legal rules apply. No such warning requirements were mandated by the Ninth Circuit.

Informed consent to arbitrate, although preferable to the present situation, may not be the answer. There is reason to question whether a court should uphold employment arbitrations based upon mere satisfaction of informed employee consent. The problem of asymmetric information and stakes abounds. To the employee, there is minimal need for carefully analyzing a distant dispute resolution mechanism such as arbitration. The optimism created by a job offer can cause the employee to risk what is perceived as an improbable future arbitration process that may seem to merit little preparatory analysis. In contrast, the repeat player employer knows that a percentage of employees will eventually file claims against it and, on advice of counsel, can analyze future dispute resolution risk in a careful neutral manner. The stakes are comparatively higher for a repeat player employer, thereby causing a habitual power imbalance in both Example #1 and 2.[32] The factual context here is similar to the asymmetric stakes set out by Jean in her discussion of consumer aribtration.[33]

The solution to the pervasive problem of mandatory, take-it-or-leave-it employment arbitration is not necessarily complex. We could simply

[31] *See generally* Clyde W. Summers, *Mandatory Arbitration: Privatizing Public Rights, Compelling the Unwilling to Arbitrate*, 6 U. PA. J. LAB. & EMP. L. 685, 733–4 (2004) (criticizing the "small and unsure baby steps" taken by courts to limit "the potential abuses of mandatory arbitration, particularly in the nonunionized employment setting" and describing the "emptiness of the [Due Process] Protocol").

[32] *See* Paul H. Haagen, *New Wineskins for New Wine? The Need to Encourage Fairness in Mandatory Arbitration*, 40 ARIZ. L. REV. 1039, 1059–60 (1998) (arguing that "there is a good public policy reason to supervise contracts to substitute private dispute resolution mechanisms for public ones" and reasoning that "lowest cost avoider, presumably the party seeking to impose a mandatory arbitration agreement, . . . [should] provide reliable information to the party being asked to give up the right to go to court").

[33] *See* Chapter 5, *supra*.

revise the Federal Arbitration Act to expressly forbid individual, non-union employment arbitration agreements entered into at the time of a job offer, well before a dispute arises.[34] This would not amount to having legislation overrule *Circuit City Stores, Inc. v. Adams*.[35] Although the latter idea holds some appeal, it would permit states to legislate allowing employment arbitration. Some kind of "executive exemption," allowing highly skilled employees to contract to arbitrate, should be included. This solution, while blunt, is sorely needed to protect the set of legal rights that need to govern the employment relationship.

Inconsistent case law policing of employment arbitration contracts has not worked successfully. Although some decisions use common law weapons to refuse to enforce allegedly one-sided employment arbitration agreements,[36] the judicial urge to compel arbitration is necessarily strong. Judicial approval of potentially unfair employment arbitration arrangements is common. In *Great Western Mortgage Corp v. Peacock*,[37] the Third Circuit affirmed a trial court order to compel arbitration in a "stacked deck" situation where the arbitration clause shorted the limitations period for filing a claim against the employer and limited the remedies available to the arbitrator.[38] In *Metro East Center for Conditioning and Health v. Quest Communications International, Inc.*,[39] Judge Easterbrook of the Seventh Circuit asserted that trial courts should enforce employment agreements limiting remedies that prevent the arbitrators from awarding attorneys fees.

Such cases illustrate the limitation of case by case policing of employment arbitration. A clear legislative solution works far more efficiently, casting a bright line and encouraging employers to be guided by substantive employment law. The present situation, relying on sporadic case law regulation through common law attacks on arbitration, discourages employers to

[34] *See id.* at 731–2.

[35] 532 U.S. 105 (2001) (construing Section 1 of the Federal Arbitration Act exemption to exempt transportation workers and not employees generally).

[36] *See, e.g., Floss v. Ryan's Family Steak Houses, Inc.*, 211 F.3d 306 (6th Cir. 2000)(concluding that employer role in determining arbitrator pool is fundamentally unfair); *Hooters of America, Inc. v. Phillips*, 173 F.3d 933 (4th Cir. 1999) (finding one-sided agreement to arbitrate a breach of the covenant of good faith and fair dealing); *Campbell v. Gen. Dynamics Gov. Sys. Corp.*, 321 F. Supp. 2d 142 (D. Mass. 2004) (refusing to compel employment arbitration where employer notified employee of arbitration policy in an email).

[37] 110 F.3d 222 (3d Cir. 1997).

[38] *See* Martin H. Malin, *Ethical Concerns in Drafting Employment Arbitration Agreements After Circuit City and Green Tree*, 41 U. Louisville L. J. 779, 788 (2003). Professor Malin also points out that JAMS, selected to administer the employment dispute in the agreement, refused to process the case because of the limitation on remedies and the limitations period reduction.

[39] 294 F.3d 924 (7th Cir. 2002).

follow positive law and lacks the clarity essential to effective law enforcement through individual adherence to legal norms.

7.2(2) Federal Subject Matter Jurisdiction and Arbitration

Brunet: Should a revised FAA include a provision creating federal subject matter jurisdiction for claims brought under it? **Steve's** discussion of domestic arbitration takes the position that the present law, which requires a separate basis for independent subject matter jurisdiction, ought not to be amended.[40]

Strangely, the filing of a claim to compel arbitration under the FAA creates no basis for federal subject matter jurisdiction.[41] It seems paradoxical, but the FAA, found somehow to be substantive under the reasoning of *Southland v. Keating*,[42] fails to state a federal claim arising under federal law under 28 U.S.C. §1331.[43] There would unquestionably be federal subject jurisdiction under this statute if courts used the typical inquiry: subject matter jurisdiction exists because the basis of federal jurisdiction is predicated upon a federal statutory claim, the FAA's provision for orders compelling arbitration. As conceded by the Court in the *Moses H. Cone Mem'l Hosp.* decision, the lack of federal jurisdiction for a federal substantive right under the FAA creates "something of an anomaly in the field of federal court jurisdiction."[44]

When manufacturer X sues buyer Y to compel arbitration in federal court, the claim is based upon the policies inherent in the FAA, which opens the doors of courts to force parties to honor agreements to arbitrate. Federal subject matter jurisdiction is seemingly created because the claim seeking enforcement of an agreement to arbitrate is based under Section 2 of the FAA, which makes arbitration agreements "valid, irrevocable, and enforceable."[45] Under the straightforward analysis of Justice Holmes in *American Well Works Co. v. Layne & Bowler Co.*,[46] the litigation "arises under the law that creates

[40] *See* Section 4.5(2)(C), *supra*.

[41] *See, e.g., Moses H. Cone Mem'l Hosp. v. Mercury Const. Corp.*, 460 U.S. 1, 25 (1983).

[42] 465 U.S. 1(1984).

[43] *See Southland*, 465 U.S. 1, 16 n.9 (noting that the FAA "creates federal substantive law" but "does not create any independent federal-question jurisdiction"); David S. Schwartz, *Correcting Federalism Mistakes in Statutory Interpretation: the Supreme Court and the Federal Arbitration Act*, 67 Law & Contemp. Prob. 5, 9 (2004) (asserting that lack of federal court subject matter jurisdiction for FAA enforcement is hard to explain).

[44] 460 U.S. at 25.

[45] 9 U.S.C. §2.

[46] 241 U.S. 257 (1916).

the cause of action." Because Section 2 creates the action to enforce the arbitration clause, federal jurisdiction would appear to be available.

Of course, this is not the present status of the law under the current FAA. Congress has made apparent its distaste of broad FAA federal subject jurisdiction by inserting language into the FAA requiring a federal action to have an independent basis of federal jurisdiction.[47] Accordingly, the present doctrinal bar to easy federal jurisdiction is textually premised upon clear legislation.

Should the revised FAA we are seeking create federal subject matter jurisdiction for arbitration claims predicated under federal arbitration law? Such an amendment would cure the so-called anomaly and normalize the construction of the FAA to that of a typical federal substantive statute. In that sense, an amendment to create federal subject matter jurisdiction potentially seems a positive development.

The impact upon forum shopping of this possible change merits analysis. At present a suit to compel arbitration can be filed in state court, assuming the parties are not diverse, free of any chance of removal. However, removal would be readily available if this change were made to confer federal subject matter jurisdiction upon claims made under the FAA, because the suit to compel arbitration filed in state court could have been filed in the original jurisdiction of the federal court.

Whether the enhanced availability of removal of arbitration actions to federal court increases forum shopping is an interesting question. Surely some suits to compel arbitration are filed in state court for forum shopping reasons. At present these actions remain in state court unless there is an independent ground for removal. The FAA confers no such right to remove. If the FAA were amended to present a federal question – a result seemingly unnecessary because a federal question *is presented* by the FAA – removal by defendants would be far more available.

Enhanced removal of state court cases based on the FAA would create a new right of the defendant to forum shop by increasing the likelihood of removal. This right, however, may not necessarily be viewed as a negative development, because it is a countervailing way to neutralize the original choice of the state forum by the plaintiff. Because many of these state court arbitration suits will seek to enforce or compel arbitration clauses, many of the plaintiffs will be corporations and likely defendants will be former employees, who allege violations of employment laws, or product buyers.

[47] *See* 9 U.S.C. §4 (party aggrieved by failure to arbitrate may petition a United States court "which, *save for such agreement, would have jurisdiction under Title 28*) (emphasis added).

In other words, I speculate that such enhanced removal would increase forum shopping options via removal for the weaker parties in arbitration litigation.

The precise rationale for limiting federal subject matter jurisdiction may be based upon a possible federalism rationale. After all, the precise meaning of "arising under . . . has resisted all attempts to frame a single, precise definition"[48] and every legal theory bottomed on federal law will not arise under federal law within the meaning of §1331.[49] For example, in *Shoshone Mining Co. v. Rutter*,[50] the Supreme Court construed a federal statute that provided for the issuance and adjudication of mining patents located on federal land. Under this legislation suits would decide the party entitled to possession. Although the lawsuit might involve issues of federal law, the Court refused to find a basis of federal subject matter jurisdiction, reasoning that the basis of decision would turn on issues of local and state law. The litigation lacked a substantial federal policy interest that would necessitate a federal forum and that might be able to justify an additional workload for the federal courts.[51] In other words, attention to structural federalism values yielded the lack of a good policy reason to trigger federal jurisdiction in this case.

The *Shoshone Mining Co.* analysis may explain why there should not be federal jurisdiction over any claim based on the revised FAA. Under this case, there must be a principled policy justification for federal subject matter jurisdiction before a claim is found to arise under federal law. Such a justification might be lacking in this context. The forum shopping concerns, while possible, are not so substantial to form a coherent basis for jurisdiction. Uniform interpretations of the FAA are not essential in a system of concurrent jurisdiction for arbitration enforcement. There is no reason state court judges cannot process the typical suit to compel arbitration or the motion to stay litigation pending arbitration. Such matters can often turn on issues of state contract doctrine, triggered by the savings clause of the FAA, and fully within the expertise and competence of state court judges.

48 *Franchise Tax Board of California v. Construction Laborers Vacation Trust for Southern California*, 463 U.S. 1, 8 (1983).

49 Peter W. Low & John C. Jeffries, Jr., Federal Courts and the Law of Federal-State Relations 484 (Thomson 2004) (noting that "while *American Well Works* states a reliable rule of thumb, it does not follow that *every* cause of action created by federal law presents a case arising under federal law") (emphasis in original).

50 177 U.S. 505 (1900).

51 *See* William Cohen, *The Broken Compass: The Requirement that a Case Arise "Directly" Under Federal Law*, 115 U. Pa. L. Rev. 890, 903 (1967) (noting that the Supreme Court "has refused to extend federal jurisdiction to a large class of cases which would, in most instances, involve no clearly defined federal interest and no issue of federal law").

In short, while an anomaly, the lack of federal court subject matter jurisdiction for actions brought under the FAA is not enough of a problem to justify amendment. As ably reasoned by Professor Steve Ware, the lack of federal subject matter jurisdiction has not created perceptible harm that would warrant revision.[52]

Section 7.3 Comments of Professor Jean Sternlight

7.3(1) Employment Arbitration

Sternlight: Although I agree with the concerns set out by **Ed Brunet** with respect to employment arbitration, I write to add some additional perspectives. After outlining our points of agreement I will go on to consider some additional issues not raised by Ed. In many ways my concerns about employment arbitration overlap with the concerns I have raised in Chapter 5 with respect to consumer arbitration. However, employment discrimination claims also give rise to some unique issues.

First, I completely agree with Ed that there is a world of difference between arbitration imposed unknowingly on lower level employees, and that which is agreed to knowingly and voluntarily by high level executives. In my view, no matter the font size and no matter the disclosure routine, it is virtually impossible for a lower level employee to knowingly consent to arbitration that is imposed pre-dispute. In the real world, when a lower level employee is provided with a large pile of documents or sent an employee handbook that contains an arbitration provision, the employee is almost never aware of the existence of that clause, much less its meaning.

Moreover, even if the employee were to read and even understand the clause, psychologists explain that most employees would inappropriately discount any costs imposed by such a clause. Instead, such employees would over-optimistically assume that they would have no future disputes with the employer, and they would be most reluctant to lose a job over such a seemingly petty issue.[53] Also, they would presume that other employers would impose a similar condition. Nor, in my view, can an employer solve

[52] *See* Ware, Section 4.5(2)(C), *supra* (stating that "[A] Revised FAA should continue to create no federal jurisdiction because experience has not shown a significant or widespread problem with state court application of the FAA").

[53] *But see Lagatree v. Luce, Forward, Hamilton, & Scripps*, 88 Cal. Rptr. 2d 664 (Cal. App. 1999) (upholding termination of legal secretary discharged for failing to sign pre-dispute arbitration agreement imposed by employer).

this problem by offering employees the chance to opt out of arbitration within a short period such as thirty days. Although such a provision may look quite attractive to courts,[54] in reality only the rarest of employees would be aware of that option or dare to exercise it without the fear of retaliation. I worry that to the extent a lower level employee contracts to resolve future disputes in arbitration rather than litigation, that contract will almost never be knowing and voluntary. As has been discussed in Chapter 1, I do believe that voluntariness is a core value of arbitration.

Second, I also agree with Ed that there are important differences between grievance arbitration, in which employees have the opportunity to be assisted by knowledgeable union representatives or attorneys, and non-unionized mandatory arbitration. Whereas the union has both the knowledge and the leverage to ensure that grievances are typically handled in a fair manner, individual employees lack this kind of knowledge or clout. That is, whereas unions and management are both "repeat players"[55] individual employees are not. Thus, like Ed, I worry most about mandatory employment arbitration when it is imposed upon lower level non-unionized employees. This is the group that is least likely to have agreed to arbitration knowingly and voluntarily, and it is also the group that is least able to take steps, after the fact, to ensure that the arbitration is fairly handled.

Third, I share Ed's perspective that "case law policing" of employment arbitration is not sufficient to ensure that employment arbitration is fair and just. Apart from issues of consistency, already addressed by Ed, case law is not sufficient to protect lower level employees from unfair arbitration because most employees will not have the knowledge or resources necessary to challenge an arbitration clause as unfair. As I have discussed in Chapter 5, the employee or consumer has been held to bear the burden of proof to show that an arbitration clause is invalid, and this task can be extremely expensive and time consuming. Given these costs, it is evident that we cannot rely on courts to strike down all the unfair clauses that might be imposed by employers. Rather, many clauses will go unchallenged, and even those that are challenged may often be upheld due to the employee's inability to muster the resources necessary to defeat an arbitration provision.

[54] *See, e.g., Circuit City Stores, Inc. v. Ahmed*, 283 F.3d 1198 (9th Cir. 2002) (holding that employer's provision of a thirty day opt-out opportunity from arbitration clause prevented court from holding clause unconscionable, regardless of its substantive terms).

[55] *See* Marc Galanter, *Why the "Haves" Come out Ahead: Speculations on the Limits of Legal Change*, 9 Law & Soc'y Rev. 95 (1974) (discussing multiple advantages of "repeat players" over "one shotters" in our legal system).

I also have some additional thoughts about employment arbitration that were not addressed by Ed. In my view, a critically important difference exists between employment discrimination claims and other types of employment claims (typically breach of contract). Employment discrimination claims often raise issues of public interest, whereas breach of contract claims may well not. Specifically, as I have explained in detail elsewhere,[56] not only individuals but also society as a whole often has an interest in how discrimination claims are resolved. "As societies work to eliminate employment discrimination, they are attempting to reshape core values and behavior."[57] That is, not only the current set of disputants but also future employers and future employees have interests in how employment discrimination disputes are resolved. We use public interpretations of employment discrimination statutes to deter improper conduct and to shape future behavior. Given this societal interest, we ought to endeavor to set up a dispute resolution process that would ensure that discrimination statutes are fairly and accurately applied and that those applications are publicized. Clear well-reasoned decisions are important, and substantial sanctions against wrongful conduct may also be needed. These public interests seem to call out for the use of litigation to resolve employment discrimination disputes.[58]

At the same time, there obviously are downsides to relying exclusively on litigation to resolve employment discrimination disputes. To the extent court processes are designed to ensure that facts are widely explored and the law is fully developed, it is virtually inevitable that the litigation process will be both slow and expensive. Moreover, litigation processes do not tend to focus on non-legal emotional or other interests. Thus, serving the public interests can sometimes be in tension if not conflict with private interests of both employees and employers. My research has shown that some countries respond to this tension by predictably cycling between formal and informal dispute resolution processes.[59]

Given society's interest in the public resolution of employment discrimination disputes, what are the implications for regulation of mandatory

[56] Jean R. Sternlight, *In Search of the Best Procedure for Enforcing Employment Discrimination Laws: A Comparative Analysis*, 78 Tul. L. Rev. 1401, 1483–5 (2004).

[57] *Id.* at 1483.

[58] *See also* Geraldine Szott Moohr, *Arbitration and the Goals of Employment Discrimination Law*, 56 Wash. & Lee L. Rev. 395, 396 (1999) (arguing that permitting employers to mandate that employees resolve employment discrimination claims through binding arbitration rather than through litigation is inconsistent with the public policies served by employment discrimination laws).

[59] Sternlight, *In Search of the Best Procedure For Enforcing Employment Discrimination Laws*, *supra* Note 56 at 1465–6, 1488.

arbitration in the employment area? My own conclusion is that private mandatory imposition of arbitration with respect to employment discrimination disputes is unjust not only for the reasons outlined by Ed Brunet, but also because private proceedings and private awards offer no opportunity for non-disputants to learn from what happened. Nor is there an incentive for arbitrators to follow precedent and develop a body of decisions consistent with the rule of law.[60]

I also fear that providing private employers with control over the nature of the dispute resolution process gives them undue power to choose the neutrals who will decide discrimination claims. In my view, it is far more desirable that a government entity, rather than a private disputant, select the neutral to decide such highly contested claims.

To my knowledge the United States is the only country in the world that permits private companies to require employment discrimination disputes to be resolved in private arbitration, rather than in court. In many jurisdictions, private companies would clearly be prohibited from depriving their employees of access to court for their discrimination disputes. For example, the European Union has laws in place that would prevent companies from insisting on private arbitration.[61] I believe that other countries would prohibit companies from privatizing the resolution of employment discrimination because they recognize that such forced arbitration would not serve public interests in justice.

In sum, for all of the reasons set out above I believe that the U.S. ought to revise the FAA to prohibit companies from requiring their employees to arbitrate employment discrimination claims. Although I am open to allowing upper level employees to knowingly and voluntarily agree to arbitrate non-discrimination claims, I urge the U.S. Congress to protect non-unionized lower level employees from mandatory arbitration of any types of claims.

Yet, my rejection of mandatory private arbitration for employment discrimination claims should not be taken as an endorsement of our current litigation system as the exclusive means to resolve employment disputes. Critics of our current litigation system make many good points, such as that many employees lack the resources, whether financial or emotional, to resolve their disputes in court. We need to explore voluntary mediation and negotiation as well as reforms to our litigation system in order to improve employees' access to justice.

[60] For further exploration of these issues see Jean R. Sternlight, *Creeping Mandatory Arbitration: Is It Just?* 57 STAN. L. REV. 1631 (2005).

[61] Jean R. Sternlight, *Is the U.S. Out on a Limb?: Comparing the U.S. Approach to Mandatory Consumer and Employment Arbitration to that of the Rest of the World*, 56 U. MIAMI L. REV. 831, 848–50 (2002).

Section 7.4 Comments of Professor Stephen Ware

7.4(1) Introduction

Ware: My primary disagreement with my co-authors is that I view contractual freedom more favorably than they do. I support freedom of contract generally, and am especially supportive when the contract in question is an agreement to arbitrate.[62] Thus, I support the contractual approach to arbitration law, discussed in Chapter 4. As I note there, the FAA very much embodies this contractual approach, as do most of the Supreme Court's arbitration decisions over the last twenty years or so.[63] Although my Chapter 4 suggests changes to the FAA and criticizes some of what the Supreme Court has done, I acknowledge that the perfect is sometimes the enemy of the good. The current FAA and attendant body of case law *is* good. From my perspective, it may be better, on balance, than the aggregate of what my co-authors have proposed in this book.

Certainly, I prefer current arbitration law to what **Jean Sternlight** proposes in Chapter 5. I am ambivalent about whether I prefer current arbitration law to what **Ed Brunet** proposes in Chapter 3 because I favor some of his proposals and oppose others. And, although I have a few disagreements with him, I believe that what **Richard Speidel** proposes in Chapter 6 would generally improve upon current law.

7.4(2) Replies to Professor Sternlight

It will come as no surprise to **Jean Sternlight** that I prefer current law to what she proposes in Chapter 5. She and I have debated consumer arbitration at length.[64] As always, I consider her a "worthy adversary," because she thoroughly marshals the evidence supporting her position and she argues that position well.

[62] Arbitration moves disputing parties from government courts to private courts. This privatization appeals to me for its own sake and because I am broadly and deeply dissatisfied with the procedural and substantive law government courts apply in adjudicating cases. I am confident that the procedural and substantive law produced by a market process (arbitration) is, and will be, an improvement over the law produced by a political process. *See supra* Chapter 4, Note 89, citing Stephen J. Ware, *Default Rules from Mandatory Rules: Privatizing Law through Arbitration*, 83 Minn. L. Rev. 703, 744–54 (1999).

[63] Accordingly, I disagree with some of this book's introduction. I do not agree with its statements that the FAA is "completely outmoded" or that it "has been consistently disregarded by the Supreme Court."

[64] *See* Stephen J. Ware, *Contractual Arbitration, Mandatory Arbitration and State Constitutional Jury-Trial Rights*, 38 U.S.F. L. Rev. 39, 43 n.18 (2003) (citing eleven articles in which I engaged Professor Sternlight in debate on the enforcement of arbitration agreements).

Professor Sternlight and I disagree both about what is and what ought to be, the descriptive and the normative. The normative disagreement is simple. She would prohibit courts from enforcing consumers' pre-dispute arbitration agreements. In contrast, I believe that some, but not all, such agreements should be enforced and that courts should apply ordinary contract law in deciding which ones to enforce.

I do not have much hope of persuading Professor Sternlight to change her mind about this normative question. I recognize that the degree of one's support for contractual freedom tends to be determined by one's political philosophy and that such philosophical views tend not to change dramatically after a certain age. So I cannot realistically hope for a big increase in Professor Sternlight's support for contractual freedom any more than she can realistically hope for a big decrease in mine.

What I do hope for, however, is a convergence of views on the descriptive. I hope to persuade Professor Sternlight of a few descriptive points. The first descriptive point is economic:

> Whatever lowers costs to businesses tends over time to lower prices to consumers. *All* the cost-savings is passed on to consumers under conditions of perfect competition.[65] *Some* of the cost-savings is passed on to consumers under non-competitive conditions, even monopoly.[66] Therefore, "[a]ssuming that consumer arbitration agreements lower the dispute-resolution costs of

[65] *See, e.g.*, Richard A. Posner, Economic Analysis of Law 8 (5th ed. 1998) ("The forces of competition tend to make opportunity cost the maximum as well as minimum price."); Stephen J. Ware, *Paying the Price of Process: Judicial Regulation of Consumer Arbitration Agreements*, 2001 J. Disp. Resol. 89, 91–3.

[66] *See, e.g.*, Posner, *supra* Note 65 at 299–300 & Figure 9.4 (5th ed. 1998) ("If costs fall (unless these are fixed costs), the optimum monopoly price will fall and output will rise.") And "virtually all costs are variable in the long run." *Id.* at 136. The extent to which cost savings are passed on to consumers is determined by the elasticity of supply and demand in the relevant markets. *See, e.g.*, Richard Craswell, *Passing on the Costs of Legal Rules: Efficiency and Distribution in Buyer-Seller Relationships*, 43 Stan L Rev 361, 367 (1991).

That there is a difference in degree (but not in kind) between the pass-on effects in perfectly competitive markets and non-competitive markets applies to cost increases just as it applies to cost decreases. I have made this point with respect to higher labor costs. Stephen J. Ware, *The Effects of Gilmer: Empirical and Other Approaches to the Study of Employment Arbitration*, 16 Ohio St. J. on Disp. Resol. 735(2001).

> higher production costs are, in competitive product markets, completely passed along to consumers. In non-competitive product markets, i.e., those in which firms (employers) are earning economic profits, only some of the higher production costs are passed along to consumers, with the rest absorbed by employers in the form of lower profits.

Id. at 742 (citing Randall K. Filer et al., The Economics of Work and Pay 226–8 (6th ed. 1996) and Daniel S. Hamermesh & Albert Rees, The Economics of Work and Pay 110 (3d ed. 1984)).

> businesses that use them, competition will (over time) force these businesses to pass their cost-savings to consumers."[67]

Professor Sternlight addresses this point in the following passage:

> Some defenders [of consumer arbitration] also urge that to the extent companies reduce their own dispute resolution costs, market forces will ensure that they pass on such savings to their customers in the form of lower prices. To the extent that sufficient competition exists, any company that did not pass on these savings would be driven out of the market by the lower-priced competitors who did pass on the savings. Of course, critics of mandatory arbitration dispute that the conditions of perfect competition exist in many markets, and therefore dispute the proposition that all profits will be passed on to the consumers. Defenders, responding to this point, may urge that at least *some* of companies' savings will be passed on to consumers, even absent all the features of perfect competition. In response the debate will then turn to the question of whether such savings are zero, minuscule, or large, and whether any such savings justify any costs in terms of fairness or justice that are imposed by mandatory arbitration.

In this passage, Professor Sternlight rejects the economic point above with her conclusion that the "debate will then turn to the question of whether such savings are zero, minuscule, or large." That is not where the debate should be. The debate should be whether such savings are minuscule or large. The possibility that they are zero is inconsistent with economic theory so long as consumer arbitration agreements lower the dispute-resolution costs of businesses that use them.[68] And why else would such businesses use them?

Professor Sternlight can defer to economic theory by conceding that the enforcement of consumer arbitration agreements lowers prices and still move on to her argument that such arbitration should be prohibited even though this prohibition will raise prices. As Professor Sternlight has written, "[m]any government regulations clearly increase companies' costs, and these

[67] Stephen J. Ware, *Paying the Price of Process: Judicial Regulation of Consumer Arbitration Agreements*, 2001 J. Disp. Resol. 89, 91.

[68] Professor Sternlight may object that this conclusion is based merely on theory and that "no published studies show that the imposition of mandatory arbitration leads to lower prices." Jean R. Sternlight & Elizabeth J. Jensen, *Using Arbitration to Eliminate Consumer Class Actions: Efficient Business Practice or Unconscionable Abuse?* 67 Law & Contemp. Probs. 75, 95 (2004). Conversely, no published studies show that it does not lead to lower prices. In the absence of empirical study should we go with the predictions of economic theory or the opposite?

Consistent with economic theory, there is anecdotal evidence that some businesses are willing to lower prices for consumers who accept arbitration. *See, e.g., Stiles v. Home Cable Concepts, Inc.*, 994 F. Supp. 1410, (M.D. Ala.1998) (consumer had choice between arbitration and 16.96% interest rate and no arbitration and a 18.96% rate).

regulations may even increase prices, but policymakers have determined that these regulations make sense nonetheless. For example, we require manufacturers of tires, drugs, and cars to meet minimum standards to protect public health and safety."[69] If Professor Sternlight would just change "may even increase prices" to "probably will increase prices" then, I venture to say, she would be stating the consensus position of mainstream public policy analysts. This consensus takes as a given that prices are generally raised by "consumer protection" regulation (including regulation by the judiciary), but concludes that, for consumers, the benefits of such regulation outweigh the costs of higher prices and reduced consumer choice.[70]

This cost-benefit analysis is complicated in the case of arbitration, however, by uncertainty about the source(s) of arbitration's cost-savings to business.[71] One possible source is that comparable cases brought by consumers generally lead to lower awards in arbitration than in litigation. If this is true then enforcement of consumer arbitration agreements has costs to consumers (lower awards and, therefore, lower settlements and deterrence effect) as well as benefits (lower prices).

By contrast, a different possible source of arbitration's cost-savings to business defendants is that arbitration reduces the business defendant's process costs – the time and legal fees spent on pleadings, discovery, motions, trial or hearing, and appeal. It is possible that the amount of awards is identical in arbitration and litigation but the business defendant's cost of getting to the award is lower in arbitration. If this is true – if all arbitration's benefits to the business defendant come from lower process costs – and some of those benefits are passed onto consumers through lower prices

[69] Jean R. Sternlight & Elizabeth J. Jensen, *Using Arbitration to Eliminate Consumer Class Actions: Efficient Business Practice or Unconscionable Abuse?* 67 Law & Contemp. Probs. 75, 95 (2004).

[70] Reduced consumer choice follows from the fact that the regulation raises prices. For example, a safety regulation eliminates some less-safe/lower-price options and leaves only more-safe/higher-price options. Similarly, Sternlight

> does not want individual consumers to be free to choose between the high-price/no-arbitration option and the low-price/arbitration option. She wants the law to prohibit the second option, forcing consumers to take the first option. That is mandatory. Freedom of contract is voluntary, while consumer "protection" laws, whatever their merits, are mandatory.

Stephen J. Ware, *Contractual Arbitration, Mandatory Arbitration and State Constitutional Jury-Trial Rights*, 38 U.S.F. L. Rev. 39, 48(2003).

[71] The following analysis, with respect to consumer arbitration, is an adaptation of the analysis with respect to employment arbitration in Stephen J. Ware, *The Effects of Gilmer: Empirical and Other Approaches to the Study of Employment Arbitration*, 16 Ohio St. J. on Disp. Resol. 735, 747–51(2001).

then arbitration benefits some or all parties (including consumers) while harming no one, except those (like lawyers) who sell process.

Thus the source of consumer arbitration's benefit to the business defendant matters in assessing the costs and benefits to consumers of enforcing consumer arbitration agreements. Of course, the analysis is more complicated if arbitration results in both lower process costs for the business defendant and generally lower awards for consumers. And the analysis is still more complicated if (as I suspect) arbitration tends to result in lower awards for some types of cases but higher awards in other types of cases. Empirical studies of employment arbitration, which must be taken with a huge grain of salt,[72] indicate that employees win a higher percentage of their claims in arbitration than in litigation but employees who win in litigation win more money than employees who win arbitration.[73] The anecdotes I have heard from practicing lawyers suggest similar results in consumer arbitration: (1) claims that would result in big-dollar jury awards or class action litigation tend to see lower awards in arbitration, but (2) smaller-yet-meritorious claims, some of which might not be cost-effective to pursue at all in litigation, tend to see higher awards in arbitration.

If this empirical/anecdotal picture is accurate then a cost-benefit analysis of arbitration for consumers must weigh: (1) the costs of lower awards on claims that could lead to a big-dollar jury award or class action against the benefits of (2) higher awards on smaller-yet-meritorious claims, and (3) the price reduction. Although I have no doubt that, for the vast majority of consumers, the benefits of 2 and 3 outweigh the costs of 1, Professor Sternlight may disagree. This disagreement may reflect differences about the amount of good for consumers done by claims that could lead to a big-dollar

[72] Stephen J. Ware, *The Effects of Gilmer: Empirical and Other Approaches to the Study of Employment Arbitration*, 16 Ohio St. J. on Disp. Resol. 735, 755–8(2001).

[73] *Id.* at 753–5. These studies also indicate that arbitration does have lower process costs.

There is also a more recent study comparing employment arbitration and litigation. Theodore Eisenberg & Elizabeth T. Hill, "Employment Arbitration and Litigation: An Empirical Comparison" (Mar. 5, 2003) (unpublished draft), available at http://ssrn.com/abstract=389780. It shows higher employee-win rates in arbitration when comparing the litigation of claims by all employees with only the arbitration of claims by higher-income employees, i.e., employees whose agreement was negotiated, rather than promulgated. *Id.* at 13–14. The study makes this comparison between all litigation and only the arbitration of higher-income employees based on the assumption that "the economics of obtaining counsel effectively exclude most lower pay employees from litigation." *Id.* This study finds an "absence of evidence of significantly different award amounts between higher pay employee arbitrations and tried cases," *id.* at 19, although it shows higher mean awards in litigation than in arbitration. *Id.* at 18. For a closely related paper, see Elizabeth Hill, *Due Process at Low Cost: An Empirical Study of Employment Arbitration Under the Auspices of the American Arbitration Association*, 18 Ohio St. J. on Disp. Resol. 777 (2003).

jury award or class action. It may also reflect differences about the amount of good for consumers done by price reductions and providing access to justice for smaller-yet-meritorious claims. It may even reflect differences about how to tradeoff the interests of some consumers against other consumers. I suspect that Jean Sternlight is generally more sympathetic than I am to the consumers who bring claims that could lead to a big-dollar jury award or class action. Conversely, I may be more sympathetic than she is to consumers who care about the price reduction or access to justice for smaller-yet-meritorious claims.

Professor Sternlight may reply that there is no need to tradeoff the interests of some consumers against other consumers because both sorts of consumers would benefit from a legal rule making only consumers' *post-dispute* arbitration agreements enforceable.[74] Consumers who, after consulting their lawyers, conclude that their claims would do better in arbitration can agree to arbitration while consumers who, again after consulting their lawyers, conclude that their claims would do better in litigation can refrain from agreeing to arbitration.

It is not realistic, however, to think that business defendants would often agree, post-dispute, to arbitrate claims in which arbitration is more favorable to the consumer than litigation. Conversely, it is unrealistic to think that consumers, after consulting their lawyers, would often agree, post-dispute, to arbitrate claims in which arbitration is more favorable to the business than litigation. Thus post-dispute arbitration agreements are unlikely to occur even if both parties believe that the process costs (for both sides) are lower in arbitration than litigation.[75]

By contrast, pre-dispute agreements are formed at a time when both parties have an incentive to choose the forum that reduces process costs.[76] Both sides are uncertain about whether there will be a dispute and, if so,

[74] Professor Sternlight asks "Why not just let consumers and companies agree to take disputes to arbitration rather than litigation after the dispute has arisen?"

[75] *See* Stephen J. Ware, "Arbitration under Assault: Trial Lawyers Lead the Charge, CATO Institute Policy Analysis," no. 433, April 18, 2002, at 9. http://www.cato.org/pubs/pas/pa–433es.html.

Note that this argument distinguishes between claims in which arbitration is more favorable to the consumer than litigation and claims in which litigation is more favorable to the consumer. It does not distinguish between strong and weak claims. *See* Sternlight, Section 5.3(3), *supra* (responding to an argument that does distinguish between strong and weak claims).

[76] The business, through its management and lawyers, consciously responds to this incentive by putting an arbitration clause in the form contract with the belief that this will lower process costs. The consumer (usually unconsciously) responds to the incentive (to choose the forum that reduces process costs) by shopping on price.

what sort of dispute it will be. This explains why enforcement of pre-dispute arbitration agreements benefits consumers as a whole even though it would be against some particular consumers' interests to agree to arbitration once a dispute has arisen.

Here it is important to see how the interests of consumers' lawyers differ from the interests of consumers as a class. Professor Sternlight rightly points out that "If the arbitration is fair and cheap and quick plaintiffs' lawyers operating on a contingent fee will flock to that process." Notice, however, the post-dispute perspective inherent in this point. If, and this is a big "if," the consumer already has a dispute and – another big "if" – the consumer has already found a lawyer who has taken the case, then the consumer's lawyers interests are well aligned with the interests of that particular consumer.

But if the empirical/anecdotal picture discussed above is accurate then arbitration's benefits to consumers go to consumers who do not have a dispute (the price reduction) and to consumers with disputes that may not attract a lawyer (smaller-yet-meritorious claims). Consumers' lawyers have no reason to take these pro-consumer features of arbitration into account.

In fact, from a pre-dispute perspective, the interests of consumers' lawyers as a whole are opposed to the interests of consumers as a whole. As stated previously, I have no doubt that, for the vast majority of consumers, arbitration's benefits of the price reduction and greater leverage on smaller-yet-meritorious claims outweigh arbitration's costs – reduced leverage on claims that could lead to a big-dollar jury award or class action. Yet consumers' lawyers make a living on the claims that could lead to a big-dollar jury award or class action so they lobby for arbitration law that increases consumers' leverage on such claims, while disregarding the harm this does to consumers with small-yet-meritorious claims and, most importantly, to consumers who never have a claim but pay the price increase caused by those who do.

> Regrettably, the pro-consumer benefits of arbitration (lower prices and increased access to justice for small-but-meritorious claims) have a lower profile than the large-liability claims so dear to trial lawyers. Well-organized and well-funded trial lawyers eagerly draw media attention to the drama of the large-liability claim. By comparison, price reductions and wage increases from arbitration's lower costs occur through Adam Smith's "invisible hand" so they cannot be easily dramatized by the media. Furthermore, benefits spread over so many consumers and employees are individually are too small to justify political action. So too with access to justice for small-but-meritorious claims. The many who would benefit from increasing access do not have a political

organization as focused and effective as the trial lawyers who seek to restrict access.[77]

In sum, there is no reason to believe that lawyers who primarily represent consumers speak for the interests of consumers as a whole when it comes to arbitration. Consumers' lawyers, as they should, speak for the interests of the particular consumers who are these lawyers' clients. But these particular consumers' interests are, with respect to arbitration, opposed to the interests of consumers as a whole.[78]

Finally, in reply to the point that businesses are not likely to form post-dispute agreements to arbitrate claims in which litigation is more favorable to them, Professor Sternlight says "perhaps it would be fairer to require companies to arbitrate certain cases than it would be to permit companies to require consumers to arbitrate all cases." In essence, Professor Sternlight seems to be proposing that arbitration be the consumer's post-dispute option. Consumers who, after consulting their lawyers, conclude that their claims would do better in litigation get their claims heard in litigation while consumers who, again after consulting their lawyers, conclude that their claims would do better in arbitration get their claims heard in arbitration. Leaving aside whether this "heads I win, tails you lose" system would be fair to business defendants, it is patently unconstitutional because it deprives the business defendant of its right to a jury trial. By contrast, current arbitration law – which is "contractual" rather than "mandatory" – relegates parties (including consumers) to arbitration only when the parties have waived their jury-trial right through contractual consent.[79]

7.4(3) Replies to Professor Brunet

To some extent, my disagreements with **Jean Sternlight** are also disagreements with **Ed Brunet**. When it comes to consumer (and other "adhesive") arbitration agreements, I envision a continuum with Sternlight and Ware on opposite ends and Brunet somewhere in the middle. So when comparing my disagreement with Brunet to my disagreement with Sternlight, I see a difference of degree rather than of kind.

[77] Stephen J. Ware, "Arbitration under Assault: Trial Lawyers Lead the Charge, CATO Institute Policy Analysis," no. 433, April 18, 2002, at 10. http://www.cato.org/pubs/pas/pa-433es.html.

[78] This point can also be made with respect to many other issues related to civil justice reform.

[79] Stephen J. Ware, Alternative Dispute Resolution §§2.2 & 2.55 (2001). *See also* Stephen J. Ware, *Arbitration Clauses, Jury-Waiver Clauses and Other Contractual Waivers of Constitutional Rights*, 67 Law & Contemp. Probs. 167 (2004).

Thus, the crux of my disagreement with Professor Brunet is contractual freedom, or more generally, autonomy. Brunet's view is that "The policy of self-determination inherent in party autonomy must incorporate a broad notion of actual consent to arbitrate."[80] Brunet's insistence on "actual" consent is an insistence on "knowing" consent.[81] He implies that respect for the value of autonomy requires that people be held to their agreements only when they knew or understood, in some meaningful way, what they were agreeing to.

I disagree. I contend that the value of autonomy requires that people be bound by agreements they formed even when they did not know or understand, in any meaningful way, what they were agreeing to.

> All decisions are made with "incomplete" information because no one is omniscient. Thus, when making any choice – whether to buy a certain car, or marry a certain person – one must first choose what information to acquire before making the choice. Sometimes one regrets making a choice on "too little" information. Conversely, it is also possible to overinvest in the acquisition of information. More information is not always better because it comes at a cost of time or money and the additional information may not turn out to be worth that additional cost. Who is to say what information a consumer should acquire before making a decision? Contract law leaves that up to the consumer who can decide how much time and money to invest in the acquisition of information. Mandatory disclosure laws take that discretion away from the consumer. Far from fostering autonomy, mandatory disclosure laws are "parentalist" restrictions on autonomy.[82]

For these reasons, I believe it is entirely appropriate that arbitration law, like contract law generally, does not inquire into whether an agreement was "knowing." I favor contract law's prevailing objective standards of consent over the subjective knowing-consent standards proposed by Professor Brunet and other critics of the FAA.[83]

[80] *See* Section 1.1, *supra*.

[81] He says: "A consumer who is forced to arbitrate a dispute without having knowledgeably consented to arbitration loses both the freedom to use the court system and the freedom to contract in a knowing fashion." *Id.*

[82] Stephen J. Ware, *Consumer Arbitration as Exceptional Consumer Law*, 29 McGeorge L. Rev. 195, 214 n.97 (1998).

[83] *See id.* at 204–5

> Contract law does not call for inquiry into whether assent is "genuine," "true," or "comprehending." Courts cannot peer into consumers' heads to determine whether these tests are met. They can, however, ask whether a reasonable person in the drafting party's position would perceive the consumer's conduct to be a manifestation of assent to particular terms.

Id. at 204–5.

With respect to arbitration law doctrine, this difference between Brunet and me is reflected in Brunet's criticism of a case I support, *Doctor's Associates, Inc. v. Casarotto*.[84] The case involved the following Montana statute: "Notice that a contract is subject to arbitration . . . shall be typed in underlined capital letters on the first page of the contract; and unless such notice is displayed thereon, the contract may not be subject to arbitration."[85] The Supreme Court held that the Montana statute is preempted by the FAA because the Montana statute "conditions the enforceability of arbitration agreements on compliance with a special notice requirement not applicable to contracts generally."[86] The FAA "precludes States from singling out arbitration provisions for suspect status, requiring instead that such provisions be placed 'upon the same footing as other contracts.'"[87]

Brunet acknowledges that there are different standards of consent and that the contract-law standards of consent in the FAA are lower than the standards of consent in the Montana statute.[88] But he says:

> Simply because the standards of consent are more demanding under state law does not mean state law is preempted; the appropriate test for preemption does not look for differences between state and federal law. Federalism concerns should not permit the Supremacy Clause to condemn mere differences between state and federal arbitration law. Because application of the Montana statute created no substantial obstacle to arbitration – compliance would have been readily accomplished by revising the boilerplate Subway franchise contract – there is still no reason to think that *Casarotto* reached the correct result.

Although Professor Brunet characterizes the contract-law standards of consent in the FAA and the higher standards of consent in the Montana statute as "*Mere differences* between state and federal arbitration law," they are, in my view, differences about something important. They are differences, as the previous paragraphs showed, about what is required by the value of autonomy. The Montana statute reflects the view of Professor Brunet

[84] *Doctor's Assocs., Inc. v. Casarotto*, 517 U.S. 681 (1996).

[85] Mont.Code Ann. §27-5-114(4) (1995). This language was deleted from the statute in 1997.

[86] *Id.* at 687.

[87] Id.

[88] *See* Section 3.3, *supra*. For a discussion of consent needed to enforce agreements to arbitrate, *see generally* Stephen J. Ware, *Arbitration Clauses, Jury-Waiver Clauses, and Other Contractual Waivers of Constitutional Rights*, 67 Law & Contemp. Probs. 167, 170–5 (2004)(explaining that "[A]rbitration-law standards of consent are contract-law standards of consent" and noting that critics of existing federal arbitration consent argue for a "more exacting" standard).

(and other advocates of a knowing-consent standard) that the value of autonomy requires that people be held to their agreements only when they knew or understood, in some meaningful way, what they were agreeing to. By contrast, the FAA's endorsement of contract-law standards of consent reflects the view of **Professor Ware** (and others who support the objective theory of contract) that the value of autonomy requires that people be bound by agreements they formed even when they did not know or understand, in any meaningful way, what they were agreeing to.

Professor Brunet can join Professor Sternlight and other critics of the FAA in arguing that the FAA's contract-law standards of consent should be jettisoned in favor of knowing-consent standards like those Montana enacted. But it is hard for him to argue that a state's adoption of knowing-consent standards is consistent with, and stands as no obstacle to, the FAA. The core purpose of the FAA was to place arbitration agreements "upon the same footing as other contracts."[89] The FAA's adoption of contract-law standards of consent is crucial to that.[90] Allowing states to impose higher standards of consent (and how much higher?)[91] would gut the core purpose of the FAA.

My other disagreement with Professor Brunet's Chapter 3 is with a portion of its treatment of *Volt Info. Sciences, Inc. v. Board of Trustees*.[92] I agree with Professor Brunet and *Volt* that, under the FAA, party autonomy trumps federal preemption so courts should enforce clauses that choose state arbitration law over the FAA.[93] On the other hand, I think such clauses are extremely rare.[94] For example, I think the contract in *Volt* should have been interpreted as a choice of California over other states' laws rather than over federal law. It is the rare choice of law clause that manifests an intent to opt

[89] H.R.Rep.No. 68–96, at 2 (1924).

[90] I have several times contrasted the FAA's contract-law standards of consent with the (higher) knowing-consent standard advocated by many critics of current arbitration law. *See* Stephen J. Ware, *Arbitration Clauses, Jury-Waiver Clauses and Other Contractual Waivers of Constitutional Rights*, 67 Law & Contemp. Probs. 167, 170–6 (2004); Stephen J. Ware, *Contractual Arbitration, Mandatory Arbitration and State Constitutional Jury-Trial Rights*, 38 U.S.F. L. Rev. 39, 44–8 (2003); Stephen J. Ware, *Consumer Arbitration as Exceptional Consumer Law*, 29 McGeorge L. Rev. 195, 216–21 (1998).

[91] Examples are discussed at Stephen J. Ware, *Arbitration Clauses, Jury-Waiver Clauses and Other Contractual Waivers of Constitutional Rights*, 67 Law & Contemp. Probs. 167, 174–6 (2004).

[92] 489 U.S. 468 (1989).

[93] Stephen J. Ware, *Punitive Damages in Arbitration: Contracting Out of Government's Role in Punishment and Federal Preemption of State Law*, 63 Fordham L. Rev. 529, 551–8 (1994).

[94] *Id.*

out of federal preemption. Thus I disagree with Professor Brunet and agree with the lower courts he criticizes in the following passage:

> Lower court decisions have interpreted *Mastrobuono* to mandate application of the Federal Arbitration Act unless a party choice of state law is clear. These cases effectively limit the application of the *Volt* decision by mandating a choice of law clause that explicitly refers to state arbitration law rather than the far more common generic choice of a particular state's law. . . .
>
> This broad reading of the decision in *Mastrobuono* and narrow reading of the party autonomy trade-off reached in *Volt* ignores the overriding importance of self-determination in arbitration theory. When a contract calls for the application of state law, the contract must be construed as desiring all state law and not just a part of it. Any other result displays a weak vision of federalism principles inherent in party selection and represents a mistaken construction of the contract by rewriting the custom-forged wishes of the contracting parties. Such a result is also inconsistent with the fundamental premise of the FAA, to interpret arbitration agreements in the same manner as other contracts. Contracts are interpreted as a single, integrated unit and are typically read to make sense as a whole.[95]

I disagree with the premise that "when a contract calls for the application of state law, the contract must be construed as desiring all state law and not just a part of it." To the contrary, "[c]hoice-of-law clauses (in all sorts of agreements) are virtually always interpreted as giving the parties' answer to the question 'Which state's law governs?', not 'Does federal or state law govern?'"[96] As Justice Brennan's dissent in *Volt* stated:

> It seems to me beyond dispute that the normal purpose of such choice-of-law clauses is to determine that the law of one State rather than that of another State will be applicable; they simply do not speak to any interaction between state and federal law. A cursory glance at standard conflicts texts confirms this observation: they contain no reference at all to the relation between federal and state law in their discussions of contractual choice-of-law clauses.[97]

[95] *See* Section 3.4, *supra*.

[96] Ware, *Punitive Damages in Arbitration*, 63 Fordham L. Rev. at 553.

[97] Volt, 489 U.S. at 488–9 (Brennan, J., dissenting) (citing R. Weintraub, Commentary of the Conflict of Laws 7.3C (2d ed. 1980); Eugene F. Scoles & Peter Hay, Conflict of Laws 632–52 (1982); Robert A. Leflar et al., American Conflicts Laws 147 (4th ed. 1986)). Justice Brennan concluded,

> The same is true of standard codifications. See Uniform Commercial Codes 1–105(1) (1978); Restatement (Second) of Conflict of Laws §187 (1971). Indeed, the Restatement of Conflicts notes expressly that it does not deal with "the ever-present problem of determining the respective spheres of authority of the law and courts of the nation and of the member States." Id., §2, Comment c.

Id. at 489 (Brennan, J., dissenting). "Choice-of-law clauses simply have never been used for the purpose of dealing with the relationship between state and federal law." *Id.* at

To reiterate, Brunet and I agree that courts should enforce clauses that choose state arbitration law over the FAA. We just disagree about whether a typical choice-of-law clause is best interpreted as doing this.

Although I generally agree with the rest of Professor Brunet's Chapter 3 and his Chapter 1, both which insightfully draw on Brunet's broad and eclectic research, I do have one quibble with Chapter 1 on the core values of arbitration. Unlike Professor Brunet, I do not see secrecy, arbitrator expertise, adjudication efficiency or finality as *necessary* values of arbitration. I see autonomy as the value that transcends these other values. Because arbitration law gives the parties autonomy, they can choose to have their arbitration be secret or not. Because arbitration law gives the parties autonomy, they can choose to have their arbitrator be an expert or not. Because arbitration law gives the parties autonomy, they can choose to have their arbitration use quick and efficient procedures or not. Because arbitration law gives the parties autonomy, they can choose to make their arbitration final or – by having an appellate arbitration panel or expanding the grounds for vacatur – not.

It is certainly true that most parties to arbitration agreements choose to use their autonomy to advance the values of secrecy, arbitrator expertise, adjudication efficiency, and finality. But, in my view, that does not show that these are core values of arbitration; it shows that these are core values of most of the parties who agree to arbitrate. If the values of those people changed, arbitration would change accordingly; but it would do so because of its core value, autonomy, not because it was abandoning other core values.

7.4(4) Replies to Professor Speidel

My disagreements with **Professor Speidel** are few. His Chapter 2 is the only one of my co-authors' chapters with which I have no significant disagreements. His Chapter 6 is a thorough and well-written survey of international arbitration. Its reform proposals are well-reasoned and seem to me generally to reach the best conclusions.

To the limited extent Professor Speidel and I do disagree, it is on the predictable ground that he does not consistently place autonomy, freedom of contract, above all other values in arbitration law, as I do. This explains, for example, his objection to my proposal to eliminate court enforcement

490 (Brennan, J., dissenting). *See also* Robert Coulson, *AAA President Says Volt Decision Creates Setback for Arbitration*, 3 ADR Report (BNA), Apr. 13, 1989, at 136 ("Choice-of-law clauses are commonly used in domestic contracts to determine which state law will apply, not to dilute the preemptive effect of federal statutes.").

of arbitration subpoenas. In making this objection, Speidel says, "Private autonomy aside, why shouldn't a modern arbitration act give the courts discretion to intervene at the request of the arbitrators to assist in the conduct of a hearing?" I agree completely. He and I do not disagree about the approach one would take after putting autonomy aside. We disagree about whether to put autonomy aside.

The knottier issues on which Professor Speidel and I disagree are separability and competence, the "who decides" issues. Although Speidel disagrees with my proposal to abolish the separability doctrine, I cannot tell where he thinks my argument goes astray. Perhaps it is nothing more complicated than he, again, valuing autonomy less than I do so he would say my argument goes astray at the start, with its premise of autonomy.[98]

Also on separability, Speidel says "Why there should be such a disconnect between international and interstate arbitration law is not clear." I thought the scope of my Chapter 4 precluded me from saying much about how I would like to reform international arbitration law but I did feel compelled to include footnote 28, which at least begins to explore whether separability should also be abolished in the international context or if that context is different enough to warrant a different legal rule.

On competence, Professor Speidel says

> The [arbitral] tribunal, however, does not presumptively have power to decide arbitrability, even if the parties have agreed to a 'broad' arbitration clause. In the *First Options* case, the Supreme Court held (under Chapter 1 of the FAA) that the tribunal had such power only if there was a 'clear and unmistakable evidence' that the parties have agreed to arbitrate the question of arbitrability.[99]

That is not quite how I would describe *First Options*. I would not say the arbitral tribunal "does not presumptively have power to decide arbitrability." I cannot imagine anyone having a problem with the arbitral tribunal ruling on its own jurisdiction. The only controversy I see there is over the deference, if any, a court will give to the tribunal's ruling. And I think *First Options*' answer to that is no deference, unless the parties formed an enforceable

[98] In Section 7.5, Speidel suggests that the separability doctrine serves autonomy but does not address the arguments of Section 4.2(3), especially regarding duress and misrepresentation. There may also be miscommunication contributing to the differences between Speidel and me on separability and competence. For example, Speidel says my "proposal does not consider the effect of an explicit agreement by the parties to confer competence on the tribunal to decide this and other questions involving the validity of the arbitration agreement," although I thought I had addressed this in my Note 43 and, less directly, in my Note 7 discussing the *First Options* case.

[99] Section 6.4(5)B, *supra*.

contract submitting to the tribunal the power the decide the tribunal's jurisdiction, in which case the court should give great deference. If this is what *First Options* says, then I agree with it, although Professor Speidel may not.

A distinct question from whether the arbitral tribunal has the "power" to rule on its own jurisdiction is whether a court will rule on that question before giving the tribunal a chance to do so. Of course, a court should not do this unless a party asks it to do so. But if a party does ask a court to rule that the arbitral tribunal lacks jurisdiction (because the party never agreed to submit its disputes to this tribunal), then the court should do so. Refusing to do so would violate the same principle that the separability doctrine violates, the principle that a court should not send a dispute to arbitration unless the parties have formed an enforceable contract requiring arbitration of that dispute.[100]

Finally, I agree with Professor Speidel's point that there should be clarity about which legal rules are mandatory and which are default. I intended to accomplish this (in the reforms proposed in Chapter 4) with respect to FAA section 10. I am open to Speidel's suggestion that, with respect to other sections of FAA Chapter 1, current law is also unclear about what is mandatory and what is default, but I am not aware of any such sections. Professor Speidel wants the text of the FAA itself to state explicitly which portions of it are mandatory and which are default, while I prefer to leave the statutory language alone unless and until a lack of clarity in that language produces a circuit split, as occurred with respect to FAA Section 10.

Section 7.5 A Last (for this book at least) Response from Speidel to Ware

Speidel: For perspective, consider the "separability" issue in the international context. The origin of the doctrine was not through an interpretation of existing legislation, like Section 4 of the FAA. Rather, the doctrine emerged over time from judicial decisions, contract provisions, and arbitral practice.[101] In that evolution, the logical proposition that if the container contract was invalid so must be the arbitration clause was trumped by the principle of private autonomy (manifested by a broad arbitration clause) and a policy preferring arbitral rather than judicial decision on all matters

[100] *See* Section 4.2, *supra*, especially Note 7.

[101] *See* Tibor Varady, John J. Barcelo III, & Arthur T. Von Mehren, International Commercical Arbitration: A Transnational Perspective 118–35 (2d ed. 2003) (discussing cases and practice).

involving the container contract.[102] The end point (for now at least) of the evolution is Section 16(1) of the Model Law:

> The arbitral tribunal may rule on its own jurisdiction, including any objections with respect to the existence or validity of the arbitration agreement. For that purpose, an arbitration clause which forms part of a contract shall be treated as an agreement independent of the other terms of the contract. A decision by the arbitral tribunal that the contract is null and void shall not entail ipso jure the invalidity of the arbitration clause.

This "end point" has been incorporated into the leading international arbitration rules and adopted by the English Arbitration Act as domestic and international arbitration law in England.[103] The consequences of this victory of experience over logic are clear for international arbitration: the scope of the decisions by the tribunal that are subject to deferential review (under Article V of the Convention) is increased. The remaining issues of competence, complex though they may be, must be given a different treatment.[104]

In light of this transnational approach to separability, I am puzzled by **Professor Ware's** conclusion that in a hearing under Section 4 of the FAA the court must determine the validity of the "contract containing the agreement for arbitration." This is, in my judgment, a step backwards for commercial arbitration in the United States, especially at a time when the lines between domestic and international arbitration are difficult to draw. Although the conclusion is ostensibly based upon the private autonomy principle, that principle invoked here depends upon "the logical proposition that if the container contract is invalid, everything in it must also be invalid."[105] But

[102] As Dean Karamanian put it, the separability doctrine is "another arrow in the quiver of those favoring arbitration." Susan L. Karamanian, *The Road to the Tribunal and Beyond: International Commercial Arbitration and United States Courts*, 34 G. W. INT'L L. J. 17, 58 (2002) (discussing *Prima Paint*).

[103] *See* my discussion at Section 6.4(5), *supra*. The "separability" principle adopted in England is even stronger than that in the Model Law. *See* EAA §7. As one commentator put it, under Section 7 "a decision by the arbitral tribunal that a main agreement is null and void . . . will not itself entail a similar consequence for the arbitration clause. The validity of the latter, regarded as a separate, collateral agreement, must be examined as a separate issue." *See* Bruce Harris, Rowan Planterose & Jonathan Tecks, THE ARBITRATION ACT OF 1996: A COMMENTARY 79 (2d ed. 2000).

[104] I find myself in agreement with the conclusions reached in John J. Barcelo, *Who Decides the Arbitrators' Jurisdiction? Separability and Competence-Competence in Transnational Perspective*, 26 VAND J. TRANSNAT'L L. 1115 (2003) (arguing for a more nuanced and balanced approach). *See* Section 6.4(5), *supra*.

[105] *See* Barcelo, *supra* Note 104 at 1120. Professor Barcelo might describe Professor Ware as a "separability discontent." *Id.*

why hunker down behind a somewhat circular argument when there are realistic alternatives that support private autonomy and give the tribunal greater power to decide the merits of any dispute involving the container contract? If both the separability and the competence principles are default rather than mandatory rules, isn't private autonomy (and commercial arbitration) served when a broad arbitration clause – any dispute "arising out of or relating to this contract" – is interpreted to include any dispute over the validity of the container contract? I think so and, in this, I am not alone.[106]

In sum, I believe that Chapter 1 of the FAA should be revised to follow the English Arbitration Act on both the separability and the competence issues, at least in commercial cases. That Act embraces the separability doctrine as a statutory default rule (which can be varied by agreement) and gives to the tribunal any dispute involving the validity of the container contract. Similarly, the Act provides as a default rule (which can be varied by agreement) that the tribunal "may rule on its own substantive jurisdiction."[107] By creating legislative default rules that support separability and competence unless otherwise agreed, a revised FAA would, in my judgment, better support private autonomy and the arbitration process.[108]

[106] *See* Alan Scott Rau, *The Arbitrability Question Itself* (1999). AM. REV. INT'L ARB. 287.

[107] EAA §30(1).

[108] Under these default rules, tribunal decisions on "separability" would be given deferential review. Tribunal decisions on competence, however, could be reviewed by a less deferential standard on the merits, either during the arbitration proceeding or after the award. *See* Section 6.4(5)(D), *supra*.

APPENDIX A

Ware's Revised Chapter 1 of the Federal Arbitration Act: 9 U.S.C. §§1–17

Chapter 1. General Provisions

§1. "Maritime Transactions," "Commerce" and "Record" Defined

"Maritime transactions," as herein defined, means charter parties, bills of lading of water carriers, agreements relating to wharfage, supplies furnished vessels or repairs to vessels, collisions, or any other matters in foreign commerce which, if the subject of controversy, would be embraced within admiralty jurisdiction; "commerce," as herein defined, means commerce among the several States or with foreign nations, or in any Territory of the United States or in the District of Columbia, or between any such Territory and another, or between any such Territory and any State or foreign nation, or between the District of Columbia and any State or Territory or foreign nation; "Record," as herein defined, means information that is inscribed on a tangible medium or that is stored in an electronic or other medium and is retrievable in perceivable form.

§2. Validity, Irrevocability, and Enforcement of Agreements to Arbitrate

In any maritime transaction or a contract evidencing a transaction involving commerce, an agreement contained in a record to submit to arbitration any existing or subsequent controversy is valid, irrevocable, and enforceable, save upon such grounds as exist at law or in equity for the revocation of any contract. In the absence of such a ground, the arbitration agreement is enforceable by the remedy of specific performance.

§3. Stay of Proceedings Where Issue Therein Referable to Arbitration

If any suit or proceeding be brought in any of the courts of the United States upon any issue referable to arbitration under an agreement in writing for such arbitration, the court in which such suit is pending, upon being satisfied that the issue involved in such suit or proceeding is referable to arbitration under such an agreement, shall on application of one of the parties stay the trial of the action until such arbitration has been had in accordance with the terms of the agreement, providing the applicant for the stay is not in default in proceeding with such arbitration.

§4. Failure to Arbitrate under Agreement; Petition to United States Court Having Jurisdiction for Order to Compel Arbitration; Notice and Service Thereof; Hearing and Determination

A party aggrieved by the alleged failure, neglect, or refusal of another to arbitrate under a written agreement for arbitration may petition any United States district court which, save for such agreement, would have jurisdiction under Title 28, in a civil action or in admiralty of the subject matter of a suit arising out of the controversy between the parties, for an order directing that such arbitration proceed in the manner provided for in such agreement. Five days' notice in writing of such application shall be served upon the party in default. Service thereof shall be made in the manner provided by the Federal Rules of Civil Procedure. The court shall hear the parties, and upon being satisfied that the making of the contract containing the agreement for arbitration or the failure to comply with the agreement for arbitration is not in issue, the court shall make an order directing the parties to proceed to arbitration in accordance with the terms of the agreement. The hearing and proceedings, under such agreement, shall be within the district in which the petition for an order directing such arbitration is filed. If the making of the contract containing the arbitration agreement or the failure, neglect, or refusal to perform the arbitration agreement be in issue, the court shall proceed summarily to the trial thereof. If no jury trial be demanded by the party alleged to be in default, or if the matter in dispute is within admiralty jurisdiction, the court shall hear and determine such issue. Where such an issue is raised, the party alleged to be in default may, except in cases of admiralty, on or before the return day of the notice of application, demand a jury trial of such issue, and upon such demand the court shall make an order referring the issue or issues to a jury in the manner provided by the Federal Rules of Civil Procedure, or may specially call a jury for that purpose. If the jury find that no contract containing an agreement in a record for arbitration was made or that there is no default in proceeding under the agreement for arbitration, the proceeding shall be dismissed. If the jury find that a contract containing an agreement for arbitration was made in a record and that there is a default in proceeding under the agreement for arbitration, the court shall make an order summarily directing the parties to proceed with the arbitration in accordance with the terms thereof.

§5. Appointment of Arbitrators or Umpire

If in the agreement provision be made for a method of naming or appointing an arbitrator or arbitrators or an umpire, such method shall be followed; but if no method be provided therein, or if a method be provided and any party thereto shall fail to avail himself of such method, or if for any other reason there shall be a lapse in the naming of an arbitrator or arbitrators or umpire, or in filling a vacancy, then upon the application of either party to the controversy the court shall designate and appoint an arbitrator or arbitrators or umpire, as the case may require, who shall act under the said agreement with the same force and effect as if he or they had been specifically named therein; and unless otherwise provided in the agreement the arbitration shall be by a single arbitrator.

§6. Application Heard as Motion

Any application to the court hereunder shall be made and heard in the manner provided by law for the making and hearing of motions, except as otherwise herein expressly provided.

§7. Witnesses before Arbitrators; Fees; Compelling Attendance

[repealed]

§8. Proceedings Begun by Libel in Admiralty and Seizure of Vessel or Property

If the basis of jurisdiction be a cause of action otherwise justiciable in admiralty, then, notwithstanding anything herein to the contrary, the party claiming to be aggrieved may begin his proceeding hereunder by libel and seizure of the vessel or other property of the other party according to the usual course of admiralty proceedings, and the court shall then have jurisdiction to direct the parties to proceed with the arbitration and shall retain jurisdiction to enter its decree upon the award.

§9. Award of Arbitrators; Confirmation; Jurisdiction; Procedure

If the parties in their agreement have agreed that a judgment of the court shall be entered upon the award made pursuant to the arbitration, and shall specify the court, then at any time within one year after the award is made any party to the arbitration may apply to the court so specified for an order confirming the award, and thereupon the court must grant such an order unless the award is vacated, modified, or corrected as prescribed in sections 10 and 11 of this title. If no court is specified in the agreement of the parties, then such application may be made to the United States court in and for the district within which such award was made. Notice of the application shall be served upon the adverse party, and thereupon the court shall have jurisdiction of such party as though he had appeared generally in the proceeding. If the adverse party is a resident of the district within which the award was made, such service shall be made upon the adverse party or his attorney as prescribed by law for service of notice of motion in an action in the same court. If the adverse party shall be a nonresident, then the notice of the application shall be served by the marshal of any district within which the adverse party may be found in like manner as other process of the court.

§10. Same; Vacation; Grounds; Rehearing

(a) In any of the following cases the United States court in and for the district wherein the award was made shall make an order vacating the award upon the application of any party to the arbitration –
   (1) Where the award was procured by corruption, fraud, or undue means.
   (2) Where there was evident partiality or corruption in the arbitrators, or either of them.
   (3) Where the arbitrators were guilty of misconduct in refusing to postpone the hearing, upon sufficient cause shown, or in refusing to hear evidence pertinent and material to the controversy; or of any other misbehavior by which the rights of any party have been prejudiced.

(4) Where the arbitrators exceeded their powers, or so imperfectly executed them that a mutual, final, and definite award upon the subject matter submitted was not made.
(5) Where the award was based on the arbitrators' error of law and, at the time of their most recent agreement submitting the controversy to arbitration, the parties could not have formed an enforceable contract to avoid such law.
(6) Where vacating the award would enforce the agreement submitting the controversy to arbitration.

(b) Where an award is vacated and the time within which the agreement required the award to be made has not expired the court may, in its discretion, direct a rehearing by the arbitrators.
(c) The United States district court for the district wherein an award was made that was issued pursuant to section 580 of title 5 may make an order vacating the award upon the application of a person, other than a party to the arbitration, who is adversely affected or aggrieved by the award, if the use of arbitration or the award is clearly inconsistent with the factors set forth in section 572 of title 5.

§11. Same; Modification or Correction; Grounds; Order

In either of the following cases the United States court in and for the district wherein the award was made may make an order modifying or correcting the award upon the application of any party to the arbitration –

(a) Where there was an evident material miscalculation of figures or an evident material mistake in the description of any person, thing, or property referred to in the award.
(b) Where the arbitrators have awarded upon a matter not submitted to them, unless it is a matter not affecting the merits of the decision upon the matter submitted.
(c) Where the award is imperfect in matter of form not affecting the merits of the controversy.

The order may modify and correct the award, so as to effect the intent thereof and promote justice between the parties.

§12. Notice of Motions to Vacate or Modify; Service; Stay of Proceedings

Notice of a motion to vacate, modify, or correct an award must be served upon the adverse party or his attorney within three months after the award is filed or delivered. If the adverse party is a resident of the district within which the award was made, such service shall be made upon the adverse party or his attorney as prescribed by law for service of notice of motion in an action in the same court. If the adverse party shall be a nonresident then the notice of the application shall be served by the marshal of any district within which the adverse party may be found in like manner as other process of the court. For the purposes of the motion any judge who might make an order to stay the proceedings in an action brought in the same court may make an order, to be served with the notice of motion, staying the proceedings of the adverse party to enforce the award.

§13. Papers Filed with Order on Motions; Judgment; Docketing; Force and Effect; Enforcement

The party moving for an order confirming, modifying, or correcting an award shall, at the time such order is filed with the clerk for the entry of judgment thereon, also file the following papers with the clerk:

(a) The agreement; the selection or appointment, if any, of an additional arbitrator or umpire; and each written extension of the time, if any, within which to make the award.
(b) The award.
(c) Each notice, affidavit, or other paper used upon an application to confirm, modify, or correct the award, and a copy of each order of the court upon such an application.

The judgment shall be docketed as if it was rendered in an action.

The judgment so entered shall have the same force and effect, in all respects, as, and be subject to all the provisions of law relating to, a judgment in an action; and it may be enforced as if it had been rendered in an action in the court in which it is entered.

§14. Contracts Not Affected

This title shall not apply to contracts made prior to January 1, 1926.

§15. Inapplicability of the Act of State Doctrine

Enforcement of arbitral agreements, confirmation of arbitral awards, and execution upon judgments based on orders confirming such awards shall not be refused on the basis of the Act of State doctrine.

§16. Appeals

(a) An appeal may be taken from –
  (1) an order –
    (A) refusing a stay of any action under section 3 of this title,
    (B) denying a petition under section 4 of this title to order arbitration to proceed,
    (C) denying an application under section 206 of this title to compel arbitration,
    (D) confirming or denying confirmation of an award or partial award, or
    (E) modifying, correcting, or vacating an award;
  (2) an interlocutory order granting, continuing, or modifying an injunction against an arbitration that is subject to this title; or
  (3) a final decision with respect to an arbitration that is subject to this title.

(b) Except as otherwise provided in section 1292(b) of title 28, an appeal may not be taken from an interlocutory order –
  (1) granting a stay of any action under section 3 of this title;
  (2) directing arbitration to proceed under section 4 of this title;
  (3) compelling arbitration under section 206 of this title; or
  (4) refusing to enjoin an arbitration that is subject to this title.

§17. Constitutional Authority

This Act is enacted pursuant to United States Constitution Article I, Section 8, Clause 3, and Article III, Section 1. Sections 1 and 2 of this Act apply in courts of the United States and in courts of any State or Territory of the United States and of the District of Columbia. All other sections of this Act apply only in courts of the United States.

APPENDIX B

Speidel's Revised Chapter 2 of the Federal Arbitration Act

Part One: General Provisions

Section 1: Scope of Application

(a) The Convention on the Recognition and Enforcement of Foreign Arbitral Awards of June 10, 1958, shall be enforced in United States Courts in accordance with this Act [9 U.S.C. §§1–32].

In hearing motions under this Act, the court shall be guided by a policy favoring arbitration as a method of international dispute settlement and, when appropriate, use expedited procedures to make a decision without unnecessary delay or expense.

(b) (1) Subject to any agreement [treaty] in force between the United States and any other country or countries, this Act, except Sections 10, 30, and 31, applies to international commercial arbitration if the place of arbitration is in a state or territory of the United States.

(2) This Act repeals former Section 2 of the Federal Arbitration Act (FAA) and, unless otherwise specifically stated, displaces:

(i) Chapter 1 of the FAA; and

(ii) the law of any state or territory dealing with arbitrations within the scope of this Act.

(3) This Act shall not affect any other law of the United States, including judicial decisions, under which certain disputes or claims are not capable of submission to arbitration or may be submitted to arbitration only according to provisions other than those of this Act.

(4) This Act does not apply to labor arbitration, consumer arbitration, or employment arbitration as those terms are defined in subsection (c).

(c) (1) An arbitration is international if:

(i) the parties to an arbitration agreement have, at the time of the conclusion of that agreement, their places of business in different States; or

(ii) one of the following places is situated outside the State in which the parties have their places of business:

the place of arbitration if determined in, or pursuant to, the arbitration agreement;

Any place where a substantial part of the obligations of the commercial relationship is to be performed or the place with which the subject matter of the dispute is most closely connected; or

(iii) the parties have expressly agreed that the subject matter of the arbitration agreement relates to more than one country; and

(iv) the places stated in (b)(1) or the place where the award was made are in a State that has ratified the New York Convention.

(2) For purposes of paragraph (b)(1) of this Article:

(i) if a party has more than one place of business, the place of business is that which has the closest relationship to the arbitration agreement;

(ii) if a party does not have a place of business, reference is to be made to his habitual residence.

(d) An international arbitration is commercial if [*insert* Model Law, Footnote 2.]

(e) Exclusionary definitions:

(i) "Consumer arbitration" means an arbitration agreement, whether or not contained in a contract, where one party is a purchaser for personal, family, or household purposes;

(ii) "Employment arbitration" means an arbitration agreement contained in an employment contract, including contracts of employment of seamen, railroad employees, or any other class of workers engaged in foreign or interstate commerce;

(iii) "Labor arbitration" means an arbitration agreement covering employees contained in contracts between an employer and a labor organization [collective bargaining agreements].

Sources

1. This section implements Article I of the New York Convention and displaces 9 U.S.C. §§201, 202 (the Convention Act). The section follows Article 1 of the UNCITRAL Model Law and is influenced by Sections 1, 2, and 3 of the English Arbitration Act of 1996 (EAA).
2. For discussion, see Sections 2.5 and 6.2(1) of this text.

Section 2. Definitions and Rules of Interpretation

For purposes of this Act:

(1) "arbitration" means an agreement in a record between two or more parties to submit an existing or a future dispute or controversy to an arbitral tribunal for a decision intended by them to be final. It includes any arbitration whether or not administered by an arbitral institution.
(2) "arbitral institution" or "institution" means an association, agency, tribunal, commission, or appointing authority, whether permanent or not, that is neutral and initiates, sponsors, or administers an arbitration proceeding or is involved in the appointment of an arbitrator.
(3) "arbitral tribunal" or "tribunal" means a sole arbitrator or a panel of arbitrators.
(4) where a provision of this Act refers to an agreement of the parties, such an agreement includes any arbitration rules referred to in that agreement.
(5) where a provision of this Act refers to a claim, it also applies to a counter-claim, and where it refers to a defense, it also applies to a defense to such counter-claim.
(6) "record" means information that is inscribed on a tangible medium or that is stored in an electronic or other medium and is retrievable in perceivable form.
(7) "signature" includes an "electronic signature," which means an electronic sound, symbol, or process attached to or logically associated with a record and executed or adopted by a person with the intent to sign the record.

Sources

This section is new. See Section 4 of the English Arbitration Act. For discussion of electronic commerce, see Section 6.2(4) of this text.

Section 3. Power of Parties to Derogate from or Vary the Effect of this Act

(a) The parties may not derogate from or vary the effect of provisions of this Act unless otherwise provided in a particular section by the phrase "unless otherwise agreed," the word "may," or other permissive language. In cases of doubt, this Act should be interpreted to permit derogation or variance by agreement.
(b) If the parties have power to determine a certain issue by agreement, that power includes the right to authorize a third party, including an arbitral tribunal, to make that determination.

Sources

This section is new. See EAA §4. See also Section 6.(2)(2) of the text.

Section 4. Receipt of Communications in a Record

(a) A non-electronic record is deemed to have been received if it is delivered to the addressee personally or if it is delivered at his or her place of business, habitual residence or mailing address; if none of these can be found after making a reasonable inquiry, a non-electronic record is deemed to have been received if it is sent to the addressee's last-known place of business, habitual residence or mailing address by registered letter or any other means that provides a record of the attempt to deliver it.
(b) An electronic record is received when [as defined by Section 15(b) of the Uniform Electronic Transactions Act].
(c) A non-electronic record is received on the day delivered and an electronic record is received on the day when the recipient is able to retrieve it.
(d) This section does not apply to communications in court proceedings.

Sources

This section, which is new, is based upon Article 3 of the Model Law and Section 15 of the Uniform Electronic Transaction Act.

Section 5. Waiver of Right to Object

A party who knows that a provision of this Act from which the parties may derogate from or vary the effect of by agreement or any term of the arbitration agreement that has not been complied with and yet proceeds with the arbitration without stating an objection to the non-compliance without undue delay or, if a time limit is provided for in the Act or the agreement, within such time period, shall be deemed to have waived the right to object during the arbitral proceedings and in any related legal proceedings.

Sources

This section, which is new, is based on Article 4 of the Model Law and is not subject to derogation or variance. See EAA §73. The question when a party has waived its right to arbitrate is not covered by this Act.

Section 6. Extent of Court Intervention

In matters governed by this Act, no court shall intervene, either sua sponte or upon motion, except where so provided in this Act. The functions to be performed by a court under this Act shall be performed by a federal district court of the United States.

Sources

This section, which is new, is based upon Articles 5 and 6 of the Model Law. See also EAA §1(c). For discussion, see Section 6.2(3) of the text.

Section 7. Jurisdiction of Court; Venue; Removal; Act of State Doctrine

(a) *Subject Matter Jurisdiction.* Any action or proceeding authorized by or falling under the Convention or this Act shall be deemed to arise under the laws and treaties of the United States. The district courts of the United States shall have original jurisdiction over such action or proceeding, regardless of the amount in controversy.

(b) *Venue.* Subject to Article III of the Convention, any action or proceeding over which the courts have jurisdiction under Section 7(a) may be brought in the district, which embraces the place of arbitration designated in the arbitration agreement, if such place is within the United States. In the absence of agreement, an action or proceeding may be brought in any court in which an action or proceeding with respect to the controversy between the parties could be brought.

(c) *Removal.* State courts have no subject matter jurisdiction over actions or proceedings authorized by or falling under the Convention or this

Act. Such actions or proceedings may be removed at any time by any party to the arbitration agreement to a district court with venue under Section 7(c) of this Act. For purposes of this Act, any action or proceeding removed under this subsection shall be deemed to have been brought in the district court to which it is removed.

(d) *Act of State Doctrine Inapplicable.* Enforcement of arbitral agreements, recognition and enforcement of arbitral awards, and execution upon judgments based on orders confirming such awards shall not be refused on the basis of the Act of State doctrine.

(e) *Motions.* Any application to a court under this Act shall be made and heard in the manner provided by law for the making and hearing of motions, except as otherwise herein expressly provided.

Sources

1. Section 7(a) is based upon Section 203 of the Convention Act. See Sections 6.2(5) and 6.5(2)(A) of the text.
2. Section 7(b) is based on Section 204 of the Convention Act.
3. Section 7(c) is based on Section 205 of the Convention Act.
4. Section 7(d) is based on Section 15 of the Federal Arbitration Act. See Section 6.2(6)(B) of the text.
5. Section 7(e) is based on Section 6 of the FAA.

Section 8. Immunity of Arbitrator and Arbitral Institution

(a) An arbitrator is not liable for anything done or omitted in the discharge or purported discharge of his or her functions as an arbitrator unless the act or omission is shown to have been in bad faith.

(b) An arbitral institution is not liable for anything done or omitted in the nomination or appointment of an arbitrator or for anything done or omitted by an arbitrator appointed by the institution in the discharge or purported discharge of the arbitrator's functions unless acts or omissions in the discharge or purported discharge of the nomination or appointment function by the institution were in bad faith.

Sources

1. Subsection (a) is based upon Section 29(C) of the English Arbitration Act.

2. Subsection (b) is based upon Section 74 of the English Arbitration Act. See Section 14 of the Revised Uniform Arbitration Act.

Part Two: Arbitration Agreement

Section 9. Definition and Form of Arbitration Agreement

(a) "Arbitration agreement" means an agreement in a record between two or more parties to submit an existing or future dispute or controversy in respect to a defined legal relationship, whether contractual or not, to an arbitral tribunal for a decision intended by them to be final. An arbitration agreement may be contained in a contract or expressed in a separate agreement.

(b) An arbitration agreement is in a record if it is contained in (i) a record that is signed by the parties, (ii) an exchange of letters, telex, telegrams or other means of communication which provide evidence of the agreement, (iii) in a record to which the parties have otherwise assented, or (iv) an exchange of statements of claim and defense in which the existence of an arbitration agreement is alleged by one party and not denied by the other.

(c) The reference in a contract to a record containing an arbitration term is an arbitration agreement if the reference incorporates the term as part of the contract.

Sources

Section 9 is new and implements Article II of the Convention.

1. Section 9(a) is derived from Article 7(1) of the Model Law. See EAA §6. See also Section 6.3(3)(A) of this text.
2. Section 9(b) supplements Article II(2) of the Convention and is based on Article 7(2) of the Model Law and Section 5 of the English Arbitration Act. See Section 6.3(3)(B) of this text.
3. Section 9(c) is based on Section 6(2) of the English Arbitration Act.

Section 10. Enforcement of Arbitration Agreement; Arbitrability; Stays

(a) Upon the failure or refusal of a party to arbitrate under an alleged arbitration agreement, any party may petition the court for an order referring the parties to arbitration at the place agreed upon or, if no place is agreed, at a place determined by the court, whether within or outside of the United States. The court shall grant the motion if:

- (i) There was an arbitration agreement in a record;
- (ii) The dispute or controversy was within the scope of the arbitration agreement;
- (iii) The dispute or controversy concerns a subject matter that is capable of settlement by arbitration; and
- (iv) The arbitration agreement was not null and void, inoperative, or incapable of being performed.

(b) A party to an arbitration agreement against whom proceedings are brought in court with respect to a dispute or controversy within the scope of an arbitration agreement may petition the court to stay or dismiss the action pending arbitration. The party may also petition the court to refer the dispute or controversy to arbitration under Section 10(a). The court shall grant the petition if the requirements of paragraph (a) are satisfied but may, within its discretion, either dismiss the judicial action with prejudice or stay the judicial action until the arbitration has been had in accordance with the terms of the arbitration agreement.

(c) When proceedings have been brought under paragraph (b), the arbitration may nevertheless be commenced or continued and an award made while the action is pending before the court.

(d) Whether an appeal can be taken from a order by the court under this section shall be determined by Section 16 of the FAA.

(e) Nothing in this section shall preclude:

- (i) the court from issuing an order for interim protection under Section 11 of this Act; or
- (ii) the arbitral tribunal from determining its own jurisdiction under Section 17 of this Act.

Sources

1. Section 10(a) implements Article II(1) and (3) of the Convention and replaces Section 206 of the Convention Act. See Article 8(1) of the Model Law. For discussion, see Section 6.3(3) of the text.
2. Section 10(b) is new. See Section 9 of the English Arbitration Act. For discussion, see Chapter 6.3(4) of the text.
3. Section 10(c) is based on Article 8(2) of the Model Law.
4. Section 10(d) incorporates Section 16 of the FAA. For discussion, see Chapter 6.3(5) of the text.

Section 11. Interim Measures by Court

(a) It is consistent with an arbitration agreement under this Act for a party to request from a court, either before or after the arbitration commences, an interim measure of protection and for a court to grant such measure.
(b) If a request for interim relief is made before the arbitral tribunal is appointed and able to act, the court may issue orders for interim relief which it finds necessary to protect the effectiveness of the arbitration proceeding and to promote the fair and expeditious resolution of the controversy, to the same extent and under the same conditions as if the controversy were the subject of a civil action.
(c) After the tribunal is appointed and able to act, a party to an arbitration agreement may move the court for an interim measure only if the matter is urgent and the arbitrator is unable to act in a timely manner or the arbitrator cannot provide an adequate remedy under Section 18 of this Act.
(d) The court may require any party to provide appropriate security in connection with any interim measure of protection granted.

Sources

1. This section is new. Paragraph (a) follows Section 9 of the Model Law and paragraphs (b) and (c) follow Section 8 of the Revised Uniform Arbitration Act. Section 18 of this Act deals with the power of the tribunal to order interim relief.

For discussion, see 6.3(6) of the text.

Part Three: The Middle Ground between Commencement of the Arbitration and Final Award

A. COMMENCEMENT OF ARBITRATION; THE TRIBUNAL

Section 12. Commencement of Arbitral Proceedings

Unless otherwise agreed, the arbitral proceedings with respect to a particular dispute commence on the date on which a request in a record for that dispute to be referred by arbitration is received by the other parties to the agreement. The request must describe the nature of the controversy and the remedy sought.

Sources

1. This section, which is new, is based on Article 21 of the Model Law. See EAA §14; RUAA §9(a). For discussion, see Section 6.4(2) of the text.

Section 13. Place of Arbitration

(a) Unless otherwise agreed, the place of arbitration shall be determined by the arbitral tribunal having regard to the circumstances of the case, including the convenience of the parties. If the tribunal or any designated arbitral institution or appointing authority fails to make the determination, the place of arbitration shall be determined by the court.
(b) Unless otherwise agreed, the tribunal may select a location other than the place of arbitration for consultation among members, hearing witnesses, experts or the parties or for inspection of goods, other property or documents.

Sources

1. This section, which is new, is based on Article 20 of the Model Law. For discussion, see Section 6.4(3) of the text.

Section 14. Appointment of Arbitrators

(a) Unless otherwise agreed:
   (i) a sole arbitrator shall be appointed;
   (ii) no person shall be precluded by reason of his nationality from acting as an arbitrator.
(b) The parties may agree on a procedure for appointing the arbitrator or arbitrators. If the parties fail to agree on a procedure, or one party fails to act under an agreed procedure, or an arbitral institution or other appointing authority fails to perform any function entrusted to it under such procedure, the court on motion shall appoint a sole arbitrator. An arbitrator appointed by the court has all of the powers of an arbitrator designated in or appointed pursuant to the agreed procedure.
(c) In appointing an arbitrator, the court shall have due regard to any qualifications required of the arbitrator by the agreement and to such considerations as are likely to secure the appointment of an independent and impartial arbitrator. In the case of a sole or third

arbitrator, the court shall consider the advisability of appointing an arbitrator of a nationality other than those of the parties.

(d) The appointment of an arbitrator by an arbitral institution under agreed procedures or the court acting as the appointing authority is final and not appealable.

Sources

1. Subsection 14(a) is based upon Section 15 of the English Arbitration Act.
2. Subsections 14(b)–(d) are based upon Article 11 of the Model Law.

For discussion, see Section 6.4(4)(A) of the text.

Section 15. Disclosure and Challenge

(a) A person approached in connection with the possible appointment as an arbitrator shall disclose any circumstances likely to give rise to justifiable doubts as to his impartiality or independence. An arbitrator, from the time of his appointment and throughout the arbitral proceedings, shall without delay disclose any such circumstances to the parties unless they have already been informed of them by him.

(b) An arbitrator may be challenged by a party but only under circumstances that give rise to justifiable doubts as to his impartiality or independence, or whether he possesses qualifications agreed to by the parties. A party may challenge an arbitrator appointed by him, or in whose appointment he has participated, only for reasons of which he becomes aware after the appointment has been made.

(c) The parties may agree on a procedure for challenging an arbitrator. If the parties fail to agree on a procedure, a timely challenge may be made to the agreed appointing authority or, if there is none, to the court. In either case, the challenge shall be decided under the standards set forth in Section 15(b) of this Act.

(d) If a challenge is denied by an agreed appointing authority, the challenging party may make a timely motion to the court to decide the challenge, which decision shall be subject to no appeal.

(e) While a challenge under this subsection is pending, the arbitral tribunal, including the challenged arbitrator, may continue the arbitral proceedings and make an award.

Sources

1. Section 15 is based upon Articles 12 and 13 of the Model Law. See EAA §24.
2. For discussion, see Section 6.4(4)(B) of the text.

Section 16. Failure or Impossibility to Act; Appointment of Substitute Arbitrator

(a) If an arbitrator becomes unable to perform his functions or for other reasons fails to act without undue delay, his mandate terminates if he withdraws from his office or if the parties agree on the termination. Otherwise, if a controversy remains concerning any of these grounds, any party may request the appointing authority or, if none is agreed, the court to decide on the termination of the mandate. The decision of the appointing authority or the court shall be subject to no appeal.

(b) The withdrawal of an arbitrator from his office for any reason or the agreement of a party to the termination of the mandate of an arbitrator does not imply acceptance of the validity of any ground referred to in this Article or Article 16(a).

(c) Where the mandate of an arbitrator terminates for any reason a substitute arbitrator shall be appointed according to the rules that were applicable to the appointment of the arbitrator being replaced.

Sources

1. Section 16 is based upon Articles 14 and 15 of the Model Law. See EAA §§24–28. See Section 6.4(4)(C)(2) of this text.

B. COMPETENCE OF TRIBUNAL; SEPARABILITY; INTERIM MEASURES

Section 17. Competence of Arbitral Tribunal to Rule on Its Own Jurisdiction; Separability

(a) Unless otherwise agreed, the arbitral tribunal may rule on its own jurisdiction, including any objections to the existence, validity or scope of the arbitration agreement.

(b) In ruling on its own jurisdiction, an arbitration clause that forms part of a contract shall be treated as an agreement independent of the other terms of the contract. A decision by the tribunal that the contract is null and void goes to the merits of the dispute and does not entail ipso jure the invalidity of the arbitration clause.

(c) A challenge by any party to the jurisdiction of the tribunal shall be made to the tribunal. The tribunal may rule on a timely challenge to its jurisdiction either as a preliminary question or in an award on the merits of the challenge. If the tribunal rules as a preliminary question that it has jurisdiction, any party may make a timely request that the court decide the matter, which decision when made shall be final. While such a request is pending, the tribunal may continue the arbitral proceedings and make an award.

Sources

1. Subsection (a) is based on Section 16(1) of the Model Law. See EAA §30(1).
2. Subsection (b) is based on Section 16(1) of the Model Law. See EAA §7.
3. Subsection (c) is based on Section 16(3) of the Model Law. See EAA §30(2).
4. Section 16(2) of the Model Law, on the timing of pleas to the arbitral tribunal, is omitted from this Act. See EAA §31.

For discussion, see Section 6.4(5) of this text.

Section 18. Power of Tribunal to Order Interim Measures

(a) Before the arbitral tribunal is appointed and is authorized and able to act, the court, upon motion of a party and for good cause shown, may enter an order for interim measures of relief as provided in Section 11 of this Act.
(b) After the tribunal is appointed and authorized to act:
   (1) the tribunal may issue such orders for interim measures, including interim awards, as the tribunal finds necessary to protect the effectiveness of the arbitration proceeding and to promote the fair and expeditious resolution of the controversy; and
   (2) a party to an arbitration proceeding may move the court for an interim measure only if the matter is urgent and the tribunal is not able to act timely or the tribunal cannot provide an adequate remedy.
(c) It is not incompatible with an arbitration agreement for a party to request, before or after the tribunal is appointed, relief under this section and for the tribunal to grant it.

(d) The tribunal may require any party to provide appropriate security in connection with any interim measure of protection granted.

Sources

1. Sections 11 and 18 of this Act are based upon Section 9 of the Model Law and Section 8 of the Revised Uniform Arbitration Act. See EAA §§38, 39, 44.
2. For discussion, see Section 6.4(6) of this text.

C. CONDUCT OF ARBITRAL PROCEEDINGS

SECTION 19. CONDUCT OF ARBITRAL PROCEEDINGS

(a) The parties shall be treated with equality and each party shall be given a reasonable opportunity to present his case.
(b) Subject to subsection (a), the parties are free to agree on the procedure to be followed by the arbitral tribunal in conducting the proceedings. Failing such agreement, the tribunal may conduct the arbitration in such a manner as it considers appropriate. The power conferred upon the tribunal includes the power to determine the admissibility, relevance, materiality and weight of any evidence.
(c) Unless otherwise agreed:
    (1) The tribunal shall determine the language or languages to be used in the proceedings. This agreement or determination, unless otherwise specified, shall apply to any statement in a record by a party, any hearing and any award, decision or other communication by the tribunal.
    (2) The tribunal may order that any documentary evidence shall be accompanied by a translation into the language or languages agreed upon by the parties or determined by the tribunal.

Sources

1. Subsection (a) is based upon Article 18 of the Model Law. See EAA §33.
2. Subsection (b) is based upon Article 19(1) and (2) of the Model Law. See EAA §§34, 38(1); RUAA §15(a).

3. Subsection (c) is based on Article 22 of the Model Law.
4. For discussion, see Section 6.4(7)(B)(1) of this text.

SECTION 20. HEARINGS; DOCUMENTS; EXPERTS

(a) (1) Unless otherwise agreed, the tribunal shall decide whether to hold oral hearings for the presentation of evidence and argument, or whether the proceedings shall be conducted on the basis of documents and other materials. However, unless the parties have agreed that no oral hearings shall be held, the tribunal shall hold such hearings at an appropriate stage of the proceedings, if so requested by a party.

(2) At any hearing under this subsection, a party has a right to be heard and to present evidence material to the controversy, and, in an oral hearing, to cross-examine witnesses appearing at the hearing.

(b) The parties shall be given sufficient advance notice of any hearing and of any meeting of the tribunal for the purposes of inspection of goods, other property or documents.

(c) All statements, documents or other information supplied to the tribunal by one party shall be communicated to the other party. Any other expert report or evidentiary document on which the tribunal may rely in making its decision shall also be communicated to the parties.

(d) Unless otherwise agreed:

(1) The tribunal may appoint one or more experts to report to it on specific issues to be determined by the tribunal and may require a party to give the expert any relevant information or to produce, or to provide access to, any relevant documents, goods or other property for his inspection.

(2) If a party so requests or the tribunal considers it necessary, the expert shall, after delivery of his report, participate in a hearing where the parties have the opportunity to put questions to him and to present expert witnesses in order to testify on the points at issue.

Sources

1. Section 20 is based upon Articles 24 and 26 of the Model Law. See also RUAA §§15, 17, & 18.
2. For discussion, see Section 6.4(7)(B)(2) of this text.

SECTION 21. CONSOLIDATION

(a) Unless otherwise agreed, the arbitral tribunal has no power to order consolidation of separate arbitration hearings involving the parties or concurrent hearings.
(b) The parties may agree that the arbitral proceedings shall be consolidated with other arbitral proceedings between them or that concurrent hearings shall be held on such terms as may be agreed.
(c) The tribunal shall implement the parties' agreement under subsection (b) to the extent feasible under the circumstances. If the tribunal refuses or is unable to implement the agreement of the parties, a party to the agreement to arbitrate or the arbitration proceedings may petition the court for an order consolidating separate arbitration proceedings or directing concurrent hearings. The court shall grant the petition if satisfied that the conditions stated in Section 10 of the Revised Uniform Arbitration Act have been met.

Sources

1. This section, which is new, is based on Section 10 of the Revised Uniform Arbitration Act. See EAA §35. For discussion, see Section 6.4(7)(B)(3) of this text.

SECTION 22. COURT ASSISTANCE IN TAKING EVIDENCE

The arbitral tribunal or a party with the approval of the tribunal may request from a competent court assistance in taking evidence. The court may execute the request within its competence and according to its rules on taking evidence.

Sources

1. This section is based on Article 27 of the Model Law. See also EAA §§43–44; RUAA §17(a), (g).
2. For discussion, see Section 6.4(7)(B)(4) of this text.

SECTION 23. DEFAULT OF A PARTY

Unless otherwise agreed by the parties and without a showing sufficient cause,

(1) if the claimant fails to communicate his statement of claim in accordance with the agreement or applicable law, the tribunal shall terminate the proceedings;

(2) if the respondent fails to communicate his statement of defense in accordance with the agreement or applicable law, the tribunal shall continue the proceedings without treating such failure in itself as an admission of the claimant's allegations;

(3) if any party fails to appear at a hearing or to produce documentary evidence, the arbitral tribunal may continue the proceedings and make the award on the evidence before it.

Sources

1. This section is based on Article 25 of the Model Law. For discussion, see Section 6.4(7)(B)(5) of this text.

D. MAKING OF AWARD AND TERMINATION OF PROCEEDINGS

Section 24. Rules Applicable to Substance of Dispute and Award

(a) After the hearing is closed, the arbitral tribunal shall decide the dispute under such rules of law as are chosen by the parties as applicable to the substance of the dispute. Any choice by the parties of the law or legal system of a given State shall be construed, unless other expressed, as directly referring to the substantive law of that State and not to its conflict of laws rules. In the absence of a choice of law by the parties, the tribunal shall apply the law determined by the conflict of laws rules that it considers applicable.

(b) The tribunal shall not decide *ex aequo et bono or as amiable compositeur* unless the parties have expressly authorized it to do so.

(c) In all cases, the tribunal shall decide the dispute in accordance with the terms of the contract and shall take into account the usages of the trade applicable to the transaction.

(d) Unless otherwise agreed, where there is more than one arbitrator, any decision of the tribunal shall be made by a majority of all its members. However, questions of procedure may be decided by the presiding arbitrator, if so authorized by the parties or all members of the tribunal.

Sources

1. Subsections (a)-(c) are based on Article 28 of the Model Law. See EAA §46.

2. Subsection is based on Article 29 of the Model Law.
3. For discussion, see Section 6.4(7)(C)(1) of this text.

Section 25. Form, Content, and Effect of the Award

(a) Unless otherwise agreed, the tribunal's award is final and binding on the parties. The tribunal shall also have authority to make interim, interlocutory, or partial awards. The prevailing party in any pre-award ruling may request the tribunal to incorporate the ruling into the final award under this subsection. The parties agree to carry out any final award without delay.
(b) The award shall be in a record and shall state the reasons upon which the award is based, unless the parties have agreed that no reasons are to be given or the award is an award on agreed terms under Section 27.
(c) An award shall be signed by the arbitrators and shall contain the date on which and the place where the award was made. Where there are three arbitrators and one of them fails to sign, the award shall state the reason for the absence of the signature.
(d) After the award is made, a copy signed by the arbitrators in accordance with subsection (a) of this section shall be delivered to each party.

Sources

1. Subsection (a) is based on Section 58(1) of the English Arbitration Act.
2. Subsections (b)-(d) are based on Article 31 of the Model Law. See EAA §§54, 54–57.
3. For discussion, see Section 6.4(7)(C)(2) of this text.

Section 26. Confidentiality of Award

Unless otherwise agreed, the award may be made public only with the consent of both parties or as required by law. In addition, the arbitrators and any arbitral institution shall keep confidential all matters relating to the arbitration and award, including the deliberations of the tribunal and all materials and documents created or produced for the arbitration.

Sources

1. Section 26 is based on Article 30 of the London Court of International Arbitration Rules. For discussion, see Section 6.4(7)(C)(3) of this text.

Section 27. Settlement

(a) If the parties settle the dispute during arbitral proceedings, the tribunal shall terminate the proceedings and, if requested by the parties and not objected to by the tribunal, record the settlement in the form of an arbitral award on agreed terms.
(b) An award on agreed terms shall be made in accordance with Section 25 of this Act and shall state that it is an award. Such an award has the same status and effect as any other award on the merits of the case.

Sources

1. Section 27 is based on Article 30 of the Model Law. See EAA §51.

Section 28. Termination of Proceedings

(a) The arbitral proceedings are terminated by the final award or by an order of the arbitral tribunal in accordance with subsection (b) of this Section.
(b) The tribunal shall issue an order for the termination of arbitral proceedings when:
  (1) The claimant withdraws his claim, unless the respondent objects thereto and the tribunal recognizes a legitimate interest on his part in obtaining a final settlement of the dispute;
  (2) the parties agree on the termination of the proceedings;
  (3) the tribunal finds that the continuation of the proceedings has for any reason become unnecessary or impossible.
(c) The mandate of the tribunal terminates with the termination of the arbitral proceedings, subject to Sections 29(e) and 31(c) of this Act.

Sources

1. Section 28 is based on Article 30 of the Model Law. See Section 6.4(7)(C)(4) of this text.

Section 29. Correction and Interpretation of Awards; Additional Award

(a) Within thirty days of receipt of the award, unless another period of time has been agreed by the parties:
  (1) A party, with notice to the other party, may request the arbitral tribunal to correct in the award any errors in computation, any clerical or typographical errors or errors of a similar nature;

(2) If so agreed by the parties, a party, with notice to the other party, may request the tribunal to give an interpretation of a specific point or part of the award.
If the tribunal considers the request to be justified, it shall make the correction or give the interpretation within thirty days of receipt of the request. The interpretation shall form part of the award.

(b) The tribunal may correct any error of the type referred to in subsection (a) on its own initiative within thirty days of the date of the award.

(c) Unless otherwise agreed by the parties, a party, with notice to the other parties, may request within thirty days of receipt of the award, the tribunal to make an additional award as to claims presented in the arbitral proceedings but omitted from the award. If the tribunal considers the request to be justified, it shall make the additional award within sixty days.

(d) The tribunal may extend, if necessary, the period of time within which it shall make a correction, interpretation, or an additional award under subsections (a) and (b) of this Section. The provisions of Section 25 of this Act shall apply to a correction or interpretation of the award or to an additional award.

(e) If, in an action under Sections 30 or 31 of this Act, a party moves for a correction or interpretation of the award or an additional award, the court shall, if feasible, remand the case to the Tribunal for appropriate action. If the remand is not feasible or the Tribunal is unable to act within a reasonable time, the court shall decide the motion under Section 29.

Sources

1. Section 29 is based upon Article 33 of the Model Law. See EAA §57; RUAA §§20, 24; FAA §11. For discussion, see Section 6.4(7)(C)(4)(b) of this act.

Part Four: Enforcing the Arbitral Award

Section 30. Enforcing the Arbitral Award

(a) Within three years after an arbitral award falling under the Convention is made in conformance with Section 25 of this Act, any party to the arbitration may apply to the court for an order confirming the award as against any other party to the arbitration. The court shall confirm the award unless it finds one of the grounds for refusal or deferral of recognition or enforcement of the award specified in Article V of the Convention.

(b) Sections 9–13 of Chapter 1 of the FAA shall not apply to a motion to confirm made or any defense to confirmation raised under this Act. In particular, it is not necessary for confirmation of the award that the parties have agreed that a judgment shall be entered by a court on the award or have specified the court.

Sources

1. Subsection (a) is based on Section 207 of the Convention Act.
2. Subsection (b) is new. See FAA §9. For discussion, see Section 6.5(1) and 6.5(2) of this text.

Section 31. Recourse Against the Arbitral Award

(a) The grounds stated in Article V of the Convention for denying recognition and enforcement to a non-domestic award shall also apply to any motion to vacate or obtain recourse against the award, regardless of whether a motion to confirm the award has been made.

(b) To vacate or obtain recourse against an award made in the United States or its territories, the award must be a non-domestic award subject to the Convention and this Act. An application to vacate or obtain recourse against the award must be made within three months from the date which the party making the application received the award or if a request has been made for action under Section 29 of this Act, the date when any correction, interpretation, or additional award were made.

(c) If a timely motion to confirm an arbitral award is made after a timely motion to vacate or obtain recourse against the award has been made, the court shall proceed as if the motion to confirm had been made first. In any case where defenses permitted under Article V are raised, the court may, where appropriate and so requested by a party, suspend the proceedings for an appropriate period of time to give the tribunal an opportunity to resume the arbitral proceedings or to take such other action as in the tribunal's opinion will eliminate the grounds for setting the award aside.

Sources

For discussion, see Section 6.5(3) of this text.

Section 32. Recognition and Enforcement: Interpretive Policies

In interpreting and applying Articles III-VII of the Convention and this Act, the court shall be guided by the following policies:

(1) In actions arising under the Convention and this Act, the court has in personam jurisdiction when it has personal jurisdiction over any party or the party has contacts within the United States as a whole that are sufficient to satisfy consitutional requirements.
(2) The requirements of Article IV(1)(b) of the Convention are met if the agreement to arbitrate satisfies the requirements of Section 9 of this Act.
(3) If defenses to recognition and enforcement of an award are raised under Article V that were available under Article II of the Convention to deny enforcement to the agreement to arbitrate, the defense shall be considered by the court to the extent permitted under Article V unless the defense was:
   (i) waived by the party raising it by participating in the arbitral process with reason to know of the defense and without timely objection or otherwise;
   (ii) granted by the trial court but reversed upon appeal by a court that made a final order to arbitrate.
(4) A party is "unable to present his case" under Article V(1)(b) if an act or omission by the tribunal in conducting the arbitration results in substantial prejudice.
(5) In Article VI(1)(d), the phrase "or failing such agreement" shall be interpreted to include both the absence of an agreed procedure and the failure of the parties or the appointing authority to follow an agreed procedure.
(6) Recognition and enforcement of an award which was suspended or set aside in the country where the award was made shall be denied under Article V(1)(e) unless:
   (i) the parties have agreed to the arbitration law of a country other than that of the place where the award was made and the award was binding on the parties and has not been set aside or suspended by competent authority of the law chosen;
   (ii) the provisions of Convention Article VI apply and have been invoked by the court;
   (iii) an award otherwise entitled to confirmation under Article VII(1) in the United States was set aside under procedures and principles

that deviated substantially from those of the country where confirmation was sought.

(7) In interpreting Article V(2)(a) and Article II(1), the subject matter of a difference is "capable of settlement by arbitration" under United States law unless Congress or the federal courts have clearly stated that the difference is to be resolved only by the courts and not by arbitration.

(8) In interpreting Article V(2)(b), an award "contrary to public policy" includes both an award that is obtained by corruption or made by arbitrators who are partial or evidently partial and an award where the enforcement is inconsistent with fundamental public policy in the United States.

(9) In an arbitration subject to the Convention, a court may deny recognition and enforcement of an award only if the defenses stated in Article V are satisfied. The court may not review an award to determine whether the tribunal's decision was in manifest disregard of the law. The court may, however, deny recognition and enforcement on grounds of public policy if the award decides issues of mandatory law in the United States and that award contains clear errors of law or fact.

Sources

1. For discussion of Section 32(1) of this Act, see Section 6.5(2)(A)(1) of the text.
2. For discussion of Section 32(2) of this Act, see Sections 6.3(2)(B) and 6.5(2)(A)(3) of the text.
3. For discussion of Section 32(3) of this Act, see Section 6.5(2)(B)(1) of the text.
4. For discussion of Section 32(4) of this Act, see Section 6.5(2)(B)(2)(b) of the text.
5. For discussion of Section 32(5) of this Act, see Section 6.5(2)(B)(2)(c) of the text.
6. For discussion of Section 32(6) of this Act, see Section 6.5(2)(B)(3) of the text.
7. For discussion of Section 32(7) of this Act, see Section 6.5(2)(B)(1)(b) of the text.
8. For discussion of Section 32(8) of this Act, see Section 6.5(2)(B)(4) of the text.
9. For discussion of Section 32(9) of this Act, see Section 6.5(2)(B)(5) of the text.

APPENDIX C

Sternlight's Proposed Amendments to the Consumer Arbitration Statute

An Act Protecting Consumers' Access to Court

Section 1: Short Title of Act

This Act shall be known as the Act Protecting Consumers' Access to Court of 2006.

Section 2: Definitions

For the purposes of this Act,

(a) commerce includes all transactions arising out of interstate or international commerce;
(b) a consumer is any person who uses, purchases, acquires, attempts to purchase or acquire, or is offered or furnished any real or personal property, tangible or intangible goods, services, or credit for personal, family or household purposes, and includes passengers and shippers of goods on common carriers in commerce.

Section 3: Prohibition of Consumer Arbitration

Subject to the provisions of Section 4 of this Act, a contract between a consumer and a provider of goods or services is invalid to the extent that it purports to use binding arbitration to deny the consumer access to courts that would otherwise be available to the consumer to enforce legal claims.

Section 4: Exception

Notwithstanding the provisions of the foregoing Section 3 of this Act, this law shall not preclude enforcement of an arbitration agreement made knowingly and voluntarily with respect to a dispute existing between the parties at the time the agreement is made, so long as such dispute is specifically described in the arbitration agreement and so long as such arbitration agreement is signed.

APPENDIX D

Brunet's Federal Arbitration Act

(Note: This proposed legislation consists of several recommended changes to federal arbitration legislation)

[Insert at start of §2]

Scope of Federal Legislation: This legislation applies to transactions or conduct that affects interstate commerce. [Alternative: strike word "involving" before word "commerce" in existing section two of the FAA and substitute word "affecting."].

[insert as the new last sentence of §2]

State Law to Govern Savings Clause: The rule of decision to be applied when deciding the validity of an arbitration agreement should be state law.

[insert as new §10(a)(7)]

Party Authority to Enhance Review: The parties may contract for judicial review of the arbitration award for reasons beyond the grounds set forth in this act.

[insert as new §10(a)(8)]

Awards Contrary to Public Policy: Courts may vacate awards that are plainly inconsistent with public policies expressly set out in legislation or legal precedents.

[insert as new §18]

Preemption. No intent to preempt the field: States may regulate arbitration, provided that state law does not stand as an obstacle to enforcing consensual agreements to arbitrate.

INDEX